the Vegan Baking Bible

KAROLINA TEGELAAR

Over 300 Recipes for Bakes,
Cakes, Treats and Sweets

To Judit & Edgar

PAVILION

Pavilion
An imprint of HarperCollins*Publishers* Ltd
1 London Bridge Street
London SE1 9GF

www.harpercollins.co.uk

HarperCollins*Publishers*
Macken House
39/40 Mayor Street Upper
Dublin 1
D01 C9W8
Ireland

10 9 8 7 6 5 4 3 2

First published in Great Britain by Pavilion
An imprint of HarperCollins*Publishers* 2022

ISBN 978-1-911682-49-3

Reproduction by Rival Colour Ltd., UK
Printed and bound by GPS Group in Bosnia and Herzegovina

A 15-cm cake covered in white chocolate buttercream, yellow ganache and piped white-chocolate buttercream coloured with pink and purple. Inspired by *Alice's Adventures in Wonderland* by Lewis Carroll.

FOREWORD

I hate the low standards that are so common in vegan baking. I have hated them ever since I became a vegan over a decade ago, when I realized what people would accept and what was served as vegan. The whole point of baking is that it should be luxurious and decadent. My feeling is that anything you bake that doesn't taste really good is pointless. Therefore, this book is not just one baking book among many. It is not just about feel-good baking, it is packed with information. It does not just want you to bake cakes, it wants you to learn a new way of baking and make the world a better place at the same time. You will learn how to eliminate the dark-coloured base from the bottom of a sponge cake, and how to fix a cake that has risen too much, is too dense or too sticky. These are things that are not necessary in a normal baking book but are needed here. Together we need to veganize all our old favourites until they are perfect. No cake should be left unveganized and no one should have to compromise on taste. You might need to test bake a recipe over 100 times or develop it over ten years, but if we do it together it will be much easier. I think the picture comparisons in the introduction are particularly important. You can see that just because a cake *looks* good, it does not mean that it *tastes* good, which I think is something that is often missed when talking about vegan baking. If a cake looks like every other cake people assume it has a good flavour and texture, which is often far from the truth.

With this book I want to show that traditional recipes can be veganized, or modernized, without lowering our expectations. There has never been a basic book about vegan baking, but one like this couldn't have been written before as the methods needed to succeed did not exist until now. I have tried to explain all my findings so that you can use them in your own baking. This is so you can better understand the composition of my recipes, but also for you to create your own bakes with the best possible results. This book brings together my experiences from over ten years of developing recipes. Since I started in 2010, I have written 15 books, and here I have included the recipes I like the most. Sometimes they are the same as when they were first published, but I have worked on almost all of them and each time I learned something new, so only a few of them are completely unchanged. Many other recipes are completely new and have not appeared in any of my previous books.

The recipes I am most proud of are the sponge cakes, the kladdkaka, the madeleines, the simple muffins, the brownies and my pancakes. If you don't know where to start in the book I think that one of those is a good start. These are all recipes that I have worked with for many years, many of them for over a decade, before I felt that they were absolutely right. Traditional recipes using eggs and cow's milk have often been developed over several hundred years and by thousands of people. The development of vegan baking has only just started but we can learn from what bakers and home bakers have done in traditional baking.

After over a decade as a vegan recipe developer, I have now stopped writing about the 'replacements' or vegan 'alternatives' I use in my recipes. 'Ordinary' milk to me is vegan and since other bakers don't say 'cow's milk' or 'dairy cream cheese' in their recipes I am not going to do that either. I have simply used the words 'milk' and 'cream' in my recipes, because this is a vegan cookery book.

I have developed and test baked all the recipes in this book many times so that you can succeed when using them. However, as I also discovered and developed many of the methods used, it is important that you read the instructions at the beginning of the book so that you understand how they work. Particularly important is the section on the different stages of whisking aquafaba, as otherwise it is easy to overwhip the aquafaba and the sugar, which produces poor results.

CONTENTS

INTRODUCTION 10

VEGAN BAKING 12
EGG REPLACEMENTS 18
AQUAFABA 22
LIGHT SPONGE CAKES 28
MOIST SPONGE CAKES 30
REVERSE CREAMING 32
DAIRY PRODUCTS & FAT 34
FLOUR 38
SUGAR 40
RAISING AGENTS 44
INGREDIENTS 50
GLUTEN FREE 52
FLOUR MIXES 53
COLOUR 54
BEFORE YOU START 56
WHY IS THE CAKE … 58
MEASUREMENTS 59
TINS 60

MUFFINS & OTHER BAKES 67

SIMPLE MUFFINS 68
FLAT-TOPPED CUPCAKES 70
VANILLA CUPCAKES 70
REVERSE CUPCAKES 71
CHOCOLATE MUFFINS 72
NEW CHOCOLATE MUFFINS 74
BANANA MUFFINS 76
CARROT MUFFINS 78
PUMPKIN MUFFINS 80
CORN MUFFINS 82
MADELEINES 84
SWISS ROLL 86
CHOCOLATE SWISS ROLL 88

SPONGE CAKES 91

BASIC SPONGE CAKES 92
CLASSIC SPONGE CAKE 94
GENOISE CAKE 96
AMERICAN BUNDT CAKE 98
LEMON & YOGHURT CAKE 100
POPPY SEED CAKE 102
GOLDEN LEMON CAKE 104
BOLO DE FUBÁ 106
OLIVE OIL CAKE 108
MARBLE CAKE 110
CHOCOLATE CAKES 112
CHOCOLATE CAKE 114
AMBROSIA & SILVIA CAKE 116
TOSCA CAKE 118
ALMOND CAKES 120
NUT SPONGE CAKES 122
PASSION FRUIT & LEMON CAKE 124
CLEMENTINE CAKE 126
CITRUS CAKE 128
CLASSIC APPLE CAKES 130
MORE APPLE CAKES 132
SUNKEN APPLE CAKE 134
CAKES WITH GRATED APPLE 136
FRUIT CRUMBLE CAKE 138
STRAWBERRY CAKE 140
CHERRY CAKE 141
CLASSIC BANANA BREADS 142
CARAMEL BANANA BREAD 144
MORE BANANA BREADS 146
BANANA SPONGE CAKES 148
UPSIDE-DOWN BANANA CAKE 150
GINGER CAKES 152
CHRISTMAS CAKE 154

CLASSIC CARROT CAKE	156
CARROT CAKE WITH PURÉE	158
CARROT CAKE	160
BANANA CARROT CAKE	162
GINGERBREAD CAKE	164
SAFFRON CAKES	166

TRAYBAKES — 169

CRUMBLE CAKE	170
BERRY SQUARES	172
RHUBARB SQUARES	174
AUTUMN SQUARES	176
LOVE TREATS	178
CHOCOLATE SQUARES	180
BANANA SQUARES	182
CARROT SQUARES	184
COURGETTE CAKES	186
APPLE SQUARES	188
AMERICAN APPLE SQUARES	189

LAYER CAKES — 191

CLASSIC LAYER CAKE	193
PRINCESS CAKE	194
MINI CAKES	196
AMERICAN LAYER CAKE	198
DARK CHOCOLATE LAYER CAKE	200
CHOCOLATE LAYER CAKES	202
FUDGE LAYER CAKE	204
CARROT LAYER CAKE	206
HUMMINGBIRD CAKE	208
LEMON LAYER CAKE	210
PUMPKIN LAYER CAKE	212
MOUSSE & CURD FILLING	214
FILLED & COVERED CAKES	216
USING SUGAR PASTE	218

FROSTING & FILLINGS — 221

PIPING TIPS	222
PIPING NOZZLES	224
VANILLA FROSTING	226
FLAVOURED FROSTING	228
CHOCOLATE FROSTING	230
MERINGUE BUTTERCREAM	232
MOUSSE	234
CARAMEL	236
GANACHE	238

BRUNCH — 241

SWEDISH PANCAKES	242
PANCAKES	244
BANANA PANCAKES	246
CRISPY & SOFT WAFFLES	248
BELGIAN WAFFLES	250
LIÈGE WAFFLES	252
FRENCH TOAST	254
PIKELETS	255
BAGHRIR	256
SCONES	258
CHOCOLATE SPREADS	260
CURD	262

CHOCOLATE — 265

KLADDKAKA	266
FRUIT KLADDKAKA	268
FRENCH CHOCOLATE CAKE	270
BROWNIES	272
COCOA BROWNIES	274
CHOCOLATE SOUFFLÉ	276
CHOCOLATE FONDANT	278

COOKIES	281
COOKIES	282
PIPED COOKIES	284
MERINGUES	286
MACARONS	288
NUT TARTLETS	290
MAZARINS	292
BISKVI BASES	294
BISKVI FILLING	296
ITALIAN ALMOND COOKIES	298
COCONUT MACAROONS	300
FORTUNE COOKIES	302
SLICED CHOCOLATE COOKIES	304
THIN FRENCH CLASSICS	306
AMARETTI	308
BISCOTTI	309
CHOCOLATE CHIP COOKIES	310
CLASSIC CHOCOLATE CHIP COOKIES	312
BROWNIE COOKIES	314
SNICKERDOODLES	316
SUGAR COOKIES	318
GINGERBREAD	320
GINGERBREAD HOUSE	322
ROYAL ICING	324
CHOCOLATE BALLS & PUNSCH ROLLS	326
CAKE POPS	328

RAISED DOUGHS	331
CINNAMON BUNS	332
SEMLA	334
SUGAR KNOTS & CUSTARD BUNS	336
TWO WINNING SAFFRON BUNS	338
DANISH PASTRY DOUGH	340
PAIN AU CHOCOLAT	342
DANISH PASTRIES	344
DOUGHNUTS	346
GLAZING SCHOOL	348
BRIOCHE	350
CONCHAS	352
JAPANESE MILK BREAD	354
BAGELS	356
CHOCOLATE BREAD	358
OVERNIGHT RAISED ROLLS	360

ICE CREAM	363
ICE CREAM MAKING	364
VANILLA ICE CREAM	366
FRUIT ICE CREAM	368
CHERRY ICE CREAM	370
CHOCOLATE ICE CREAM	372
CARAMEL ICE CREAM	374
COFFEE ICE CREAM	376
RUM & RAISIN ICE CREAM	378
NUT ICE CREAM	380
GINGER ICE CREAM	382
COCONUT ICE CREAM	382
LEMON ICE CREAM	384

PIES   **387**

CRUMBLES   388
SWEDISH APPLE CAKE   390
COBBLER   392
AMERICAN APPLE PIE   394
SOUR CHERRY PIE   396
PEAR PIE   398
PEACH FILLING   400
BLUEBERRY PIE   401
FRANGIPANE PIE   402
APPLE BUTTER PIE   404
LEMON MERINGUE PIE   406
LIME PIE   408
PASSION FRUIT PIE   410
STRAWBERRY PIE   412
MOUSSE CAKES   414
CHEESECAKE   416
PUFF PASTRY TARTS   418
TARTE TATIN   420

CREAMS & SAUCES   **423**

PASTRY CREAMS   424
PETIT POTS DE CRÈME   426
CRÈME BRÛLÉE   428
PANNA COTTA & JELLY   430
SAUCES   432

SWEETS   **435**

SOFT CARAMEL   436
FUDGE   438
DARK CHOCOLATE FUDGE   440
LUXURY FUDGE   440

ACKNOWLEDGEMENTS   **442**
INDEX   **444**

WHY VEGAN?

Many people think that baking books for vegans are about bakes that are healthy, dry and boring, but the recipes in this book are made with exactly the same amount of sugar and fat as their predecessors. Being vegan does not mean that you are counting calories but that you exclude animal products from your diet. This includes all kinds of ingredients that come from animals in one form or another. I think it should be possible to bake without lowering our expectations or using products derived from animals. No creature should have to die or live cooped up in a small cage for us to be able to bake. That is absurd.

Sometimes I am asked why I am a vegan. I think I am asked this because I grew up on a farm and have a degree in ethology, which is the science of animal behaviour. People assume that I would eat meat because I know what animal care looks like and I have seen how we treat our animals. I say that my knowledge has encouraged the opposite view: even though I grew up on a farm and have a degree in ethology, I have become a vegan because I think that is the only reasonable choice.

Because I am a scientist and teach natural sciences, I know how important good sources are – refer to the United Nations (UN) and the World Wide Fund for Nature (WWF) as reliable sources for climate change and health.

In general, you can say that it takes about ten times more energy to produce animal products compared to vegetable products. That is because every step in the food chain means that 90 per cent of the energy is taken up with life-sustaining functions such as breathing and maintaining body temperature. That means that 10kg of soya beans gives close to 10kg of plant-based food, but if you feed that to a pig or a cow, you will get less than 1kg of meat. This is known as trophic levels and forms part of the Swedish biology curriculum in secondary schools. On top of this, animals need to drink water during their lifetime and their faeces affect water quality.

According to the UN, livestock accounts for 14.5 per cent of greenhouse gas emissions. Eating more vegetarian food therefore does make a difference. The UN's Food and Agricultural Organization (FAO) says we need to shift to a more sustainable diet and food production system, even though that might be challenging at the moment, and that a shift towards plant-based food focussing on local and seasonal produce will be the way to success. You can read more about it on the FAO website, www.fao.org. There are a number of reports about food production and its effects on the environment. For information from the UN about animal products and their production costs and effects on the environment, you can read the Intergovernmental Panel on Climate Change's report 'Assessing the environmental impacts of consumption and production – priority products and materials' and the FAO report 'Livestock's long shadow: environmental issues and options'.

According to a report from the WWF, a total of 96 per cent of mammal biomass is comprised of humans (36 per cent) and livestock (60 per cent). The challenge of feeding such a large number of animals is affecting our planet and its ecosystem, and it takes up vast amounts of resources. WWF has found that the human impact on climate for a diet based on meat can be up to 50 times higher than a plant-based diet. Because of this, vegetarian sources of protein are a more efficient way of feeding the population than using cereals and leguminous plants to feed animals before they become food themselves. Less land is required, which reduces the pressure on land being turned over to farming, and biological diversity is maintained in areas where valuable land is often used to grow soya to feed the animals. You can read more about this on the WWF website, www. wwf.org.uk.

SOME E NUMBERS
CONTAINING
ANIMAL PRODUCTS

E 120 = Derived from insect scales
E 441 = Gelatine
E 901 = Beeswax
E 904 = Shellac

People often ask me what I'm allowed to eat as a vegan. I usually say that I'm allowed to eat everything, just like whoever it is who is asking me, but that I don't want my food to contribute either to the suffering of animals or to climate change. It is a choice I make every day, not something you decide on a whim and then have to follow for the rest of your life. I want to be vegan every day and now it feels both natural and easy. Besides, now you can bake and enjoy vegan *fika* – a Swedish idea that you should take a moment to slow down and appreciate the good things in life, like coffee and sweet treats with friends.

VEGAN BAKING

Baking is chemistry and it helps to understand the function of each ingredient to achieve a similar result when developing vegan recipes. For example, when developing recipes without eggs you need to understand what it is that an egg does in baking, and how to replace it with a plant-based ingredient in different recipes. I have test baked loads of ideas and failed thousands of times as I have tried to understand how different ingredients work. I have also read all the books about baking and cakes that I have been able to get my hands on during the past 10 years. The most important thing is to try to recreate the original recipes using the same amount of fat and sugar, as these are the ingredients that give our bakes the right texture and taste.

Eggs coagulate when they are heated, the proteins denaturate (perish) and remain stable after baking. Air and sugar are bound together in the process, which means that when these are included in the mixture, what we bake sets when heated. Eggs can bind double their own amount of liquid, and one egg yolk can make an emulsion with twice the amount of oil. One egg can bind and stabilize around 100ml of liquid, which is what makes eggs hard to replace. Few foods have that function. In recipes including eggs that are not baked in the oven, such as vanilla pastry cream, it is much easier to replace them, as starch has the same function. This idea is developed further on page 14.

According to the Swedish National Food Agency, raw eggs should not be eaten because of the risks of bacteria. If you follow their advice, you should not eat icing, batter, dough or candied leaves made using traditional methods. It can be dangerous for children, elderly people and pregnant women.

In some recipes, eggs are actually **unnecessary** and they will work perfectly well without them. Sweet, wheat-based doughs used for pastries are usually equally good without eggs. This doesn't, however, apply for doughnuts, which need an extra rise and have to react with the heat of the deep frying oil. In that case, you need baking powder and cornstarch or aquafaba, so that the doughnuts don't become dense blobs of dough that will not expand in the oil.

When I replace eggs, I calculate the volume of the liquid provided by the egg in the traditional recipe. I think it is important to maintain the same proportion of each ingredient in a recipe and change it to something similar when replacing the egg to get the best results possible. Then I consider how important the stabilizing or the rising effect of the eggs is in that recipe and calculate what combination of egg replacement will work best for that particular recipe. I try to use egg replacements that you can find in any supermarket so that the recipes are easy to make. The ingredients I use as egg replacements completely depend on what I am baking and which part of the egg I am replacing. If you look at my recipes, you can see that I often use many different tricks that are included here. In this book, there are various solutions for almost every recipe as it is hard to find one egg replacement that can perform all the functions of an egg. You need to know about the ingredient's characteristics and how they affect what you bake in different quantities in order to be successful, and I have tried to explain that thoroughly here. Usually, a number of ingredients are being combined and you might, for example, need to replace some of the sugar with icing sugar, replace some of the flour with starch, and add acid or introduce heat that will react with the raising agent. As we now have aquafaba, we finally have an egg replacement that works in a plain form and can also be whipped; this can be used in most pastries as a direct egg replacement. The way this works is thoroughly explained on page 22 and elsewhere in the book.

The only way to learn how to develop recipes is to fail and learn from your mistakes. If you forget to add sugar, you will see how that affects what you are baking; you may add an extra teaspoon of baking powder or forget the vinegar in a cake using bicarbonate of soda. It has taken hundreds of baking mistakes to finish this book and I recommend that you change just one detail at a time when developing recipes. If you adjust a number of things at the same time in a recipe, you will never learn from these changes as you will not know what has caused what. With one change at a time, you can draw better conclusions from your test baking. Make sure you write down the recipes you are working on and what the result was in the same place. I have a big board in my kitchen but a notebook or a file on your computer may be enough. It can be hard to remember what you changed for next time you are test baking, which means that the work you have done and what you learned is lost.

A general tip is that when sponge cakes come out with a dome on top, you either need some more sugar in the batter, or less liquid. However, if the cake sinks in the middle, you should reduce the amount of sugar or fat in the recipe. I usually adjust the amounts of sugar, fat or liquid when I work on sponge cakes. If the cake gets extremely dry you can, of course, also adjust the amount of

> Spiced sponge cakes = fruit purée/yoghurt
> Chocolate cakes = bicarbonate of soda + vinegar
> Cookies = aquafaba
> Small cookies = aquafaba, cream, syrup
> Creams = cornstarch, cream and oil
> Egg yolk = cornstarch and oil
> Brushing = cream

plain flour. In cookies, however, the amount of plain flour is often an important factor, and that is explained in more detail on page 38.

When is it simple?
Dairy products are easy to replace if you make sure that you have the right percentage of fat in the vegan replacements, which you can read about on page 34. Usually, it is the eggs that are more difficult to leave out, but in some recipes it is simpler.

In sponge cakes, particularly ones that contain fruit or vegetables, like carrot cakes, banana cakes or soft gingerbread, you can replace the egg with fruit purée or yoghurt combined with bicarbonate of soda that help the cake to rise. The fruit or the yoghurt will activate the bicarbonate of soda, but you can also use vinegar. In spiced cakes, any aftertaste or colour changes from the vinegar or bicarbonate of soda is lost completely. Together with some liquid, such as yoghurt, you can then replace the egg. The quantities

for replacing one or several eggs are thoroughly explained on page 23, but one egg corresponds to 50ml liquid. In cookies and small biscuits, eggs can be easily replaced with aquafaba, while in a custard that uses egg yolks, you can mimic their function by adding starch, such as cornstarch or potato starch. The fat in the yolk also needs to be replaced, which is why I add oil. For brushing our bakes, cream works best according to my tests. I have given a few options on page 330. If you want to replace egg wash, you can read more about that on page 331.

When is it extra difficult?
In light-coloured bakes like muffins, sponge cakes and layer cakes, eggs were hard to replace before we had aquafaba, and it was not until I realized that whipped aquafaba could replace whipped eggs that these recipes became easier to veganize. However, traditional recipes where no fat is added, apart from the fat in the egg, are very hard to nail as the egg can create an emulsion from its own fat, but the aquafaba is more sensitive. Read more about this on page 22. In my recipes for similar bakes, I have replaced the fat from the egg with a little added oil. Without it the sponge has a dry, chewy texture. This goes for Swiss roll and genoise, for example.

In recipes with a higher quantity of sugar than sponge cakes, it is extra difficult to bind all of the fat and sugar. This applies to bakes such as madeleines, kladdkaka and brownies. The function of the egg here is to keep the rise in the oven when the air that has been whipped into the batter expands. Also, the egg helps bind the sugar and the fat so that they don't separate and burn in the oven. Many people think that a brownie is thin and gooey because there is no baking powder in the recipe, but this means that they do not understand the function of the sugar in a cake. Sugar is what provides moisture, and even if you did add baking powder to a kladdkaka you would get the same result, because the sugar prevents the baking powder from providing a raising effect as the cake collapses and becomes flat. If you reduce the amount of sugar or fat in a brownie to stop these ingredients from separating, you lose the sticky texture and end up with a dry cake that doesn't melt in the mouth. Here, aquafaba is the key to success, even though you can make these recipes without it if you use a combination of tricks. Aquafaba can bind together fat and sugar, both in its plain form and when whipped;

if you bind the fat as described on pages 24 and 30, you can use the same amount of fat and sugar as in traditional recipes. If you don't want to use aquafaba, you can replace caster sugar with icing sugar and use yoghurt, for example, to replace the liquid from the egg. A little cornstarch can also help to stabilize the mixture. My kladdkaka with yoghurt on page 266 uses that kind of technique. On page 40, you can read about what I have discovered about replacing sugar with icing sugar and how this affects the bake.

Fruit and fruit purée

Some of the functions of an egg can be replaced with grated vegetables, mashed banana and other fruit, jam or purées, such as carrot purée, lingonberry jam or apple sauce. It is the fibres in the fruit that bind the ingredients and maintain the rise. Mashed fruit can both keep the mixture together and give a nice rise, but it also adds flavour and colour. Combined with bicarbonate of soda and vinegar, the bake will take on a darker colour or dark patches, but fruit cakes are usually not light in colour, so this doesn't matter that much. Baking powder keeps the batter light coloured when baking with fruit. If you use yoghurt instead of vinegar, you can also make light-coloured bakes where the egg is replaced by fruit mash. If you replace eggs with fruit purée or jam, you will have to consider that these contain a lot of sugar, which means that you might need to adjust the amount of sugar in the recipe to prevent the cake from sinking in the middle. Fruit mash and cocoa together can make the texture chewy with large bubbles, which is why I don't recommend that combination. In recipes that contain fruit purée, you can also find alternative ways to give the cake extra rise and stability – like yoghurt, bicarbonate of soda and icing sugar. Read more on page 49 about how fruit purée colours the cakes together with bicarbonate of soda. Apple sauce with a high percentage of fruit, preferably up to 90 per cent apples, gives the best results.

It is a common myth that eggs can be replaced with mashed banana, but it is true that mashed banana has a stabilizing effect in baking. However, it will always be a banana cake, so can only really be used when you want to bake a terrific vegan banana cake. If you look at my recipes that include banana, you will notice that I usually include other tricks like aquafaba, bicarbonate of soda (the fruit activates the bicarbonate of soda and no vinegar is needed), yoghurt or icing sugar, as mashed banana is not a complete egg replacement.

Some examples of where I have used fruit, fruit purée or jam in the book are the classic carrot cake, biscotti, the pumpkin recipes, banana cake, banana muffins, courgette cake, banana pancakes and lingonberry cake.

Starch and thickening

In pies, cookies or custards made using egg yolks, you can replace the egg with oil, cream, yoghurt or aquafaba combined with a little starch: about 1 tablespoon of starch per egg yolk. For custards, curds and ice cream, I often use cream, oil and starch to replace all the functions of the egg yolks in the best way possible. Usually, I calculate the amount of fat there would be in the yolks that are being replaced to get the smooth texture from the fat. You need around 1–3 teaspoons of fat per egg yolk or egg. When making custards for creams, curds or ice cream, it is good not to work with eggs, since they are easily ruined if you accidentally heat the mixture over 60–80°C/140–176°C, depending on if you have included the whole or just parts of the egg. In similar recipes, replacing the egg with starch and a little fat works better than the egg you would traditionally use. The only thing you lose is the yellow colour. Cornstarch is often included in many pastry creams and custards, even in traditional recipes, but it is used in smaller amounts as you also include egg yolks or whole eggs. One example where using cornstarch is common is as a thickener for ice cream. After having tested all sorts of different starch, I chose cornstarch as the stabilizer and the French/ Sicilian method as the base for my ice cream recipes. You can read more about how it affects the ice cream on page 363.

Cornstarch is a starch extract that comes from sweetcorn. Just like other starch, cornstarch is a good thickener and it is my favourite replacement for egg yolk in custards. Corn is a common allergen and cornstarch can be replaced with other types of starch, such as potato starch, tapioca starch or arrowroot. I use starch as an egg replacement in frangipane, mazarines, doughnuts and in my first apple cake, which is made with cream.

In pies, starch is used to stop the fruit juice from

Here I used the dough for snickerdoodles on page 316 flavoured with 2 teaspoons of vanilla extract. Some have been decorated with sprinkles, either inside the dough or sprinkled on top. The bottom row without sprinkles using sugar on the surface affects the result. On the left they have been made without being rolled in sugar and on the right they have been rolled in sugar. You can also roll the cookies in icing sugar after rolling them in caster sugar. This gives them a lovely cracked surface.

becoming watery; you can read more about that on page 387 and about how different variations are used in different pies.

Plain flour can also be used as a thickener in both traditional cooking and baking, and the flour partly replaces the stabilizing function of the egg in many recipes that I have developed. Some examples from this book include the mazarin filling, frangipane filling, lemon meringue pie and Helena pastry. Read more about this on page 38.

Both starch and plain flour can be used in the traditional version of frosting, which is also called American custard frosting, and I have included both a vanilla frosting with plain flour or cornstarch, and a chocolate frosting with cornstarch that is wonderfully soft and airy thanks to the thickening. It is common for egg replacements to consist of starch as it can replace some of the characteristics of eggs when baking. The product NoEgg contains mostly starch from tapioca and potato. It appears in my comparison of egg replacements and gives a good result. However, this is not as easy to use in larger sponge cakes and layer cakes in particular. If you are using pure starch you will get roughly the same result.

Yoghurt

In light-coloured bakes that include a little bicarbonate of soda, I often use yoghurt as the acid to activate the bicarbonate of soda. I do that to disguise the taste and colour changes. Yoghurt has a stabilizing effect that remains after baking, and before aquafaba was discovered I often used 50g yoghurt to replace the amount of liquid provided by an egg. Together with some starch this worked in many recipes as an egg replacement and gave good results. Examples using yoghurt in this book are kladdkaka with yoghurt, the carrot cakes, pancakes, soft gingerbread and the chocolate sponge cake.

Salt

A pinch of salt should be added to all recipes for taste. Salt affects the batter of bread and cakes, and a small amount of salt not only improves the taste, but also helps the rise in a sponge cake. A quarter of a teaspoon is enough; more salt makes the texture chewy as the salt affects the ability of the gluten strands to bind together. In bread this is desirable, but sponge cakes you should not add too much salt.

Gelling agent

Jelly is used in cooking and baking all over the world. In large parts of Asia, the gelling agent is made of algae and long complex chains of carbohydrates, also known as polysaccharides. In much of Europe and North America, jelly comes from gelatine, which is made from protein derived from pigs and cows. The skin and bones of the animals are boiled and the gelatine is then extracted from the hot water. The protein that is used is called collagen and the food additive number is E441. Gelatine takes longer to set than the algae equivalent, which sets at room temperature and does not need to be cooled in a fridge. The jelly from gelatine is permanently damaged when heated too much as the proteins denaturate and are destroyed. Algae-based jellies can cope with high temperatures, and can be melted again if they set before they have been used. They will then set again when they cool. Sheets of gelatine are often used as windows in gingerbread houses, but you can substitute sheets of rice paper that are used for spring rolls. You can also melt coloured sweets in the gingerbread windows during the last minutes as the sections of the house are being baked in the oven.

The most common algae jellys are agar and carrageenan, which are both extracted from red algae. Carrageenan is the gelling agent in Vege-Gel, gelling sugar and Vegeset. Agar is often sold as pure flakes and as powder: 1 teaspoon of powder equals about 1 tablespoon of flakes. The powder dissolves easily in liquid and is the easiest one to use. Agar will not dissolve in cold water and needs to boil for about 5 minutes for all the jelly to be activated, the jelly will set between 32 and 45°C. Carrageenan only needs to be quickly boiled together with the liquid. Carrageenan gives a slightly softer jelly than the agar and is therefore more similiar to gelatine. Agar gives a firmer jelly that does not wobble like classic gelatine-based jellies. Today, there are also many other gelling agents on the market, and these are used in the recipes for panna cotta on page 430. Carrageenan IOTA, Carrageenan KAPPA and Low Acyl Gellan Gum are used for softer jellies, and these are the ones I have used in this book.

BROWNIES

Aquafaba was used to replace eggs. The plain flour was folded in first to bind the right amount of fat together. Icing sugar was used instead of caster sugar to get the right amount of sugar without the cake collapsing. A little salt was added to replace the salt in the butter. I have also added crushed Oreos.

EGG REPLACEMENTS

JUST WATER

BAKING POWDER

BICARBONATE OF SODA

EGG REPLACEMENT

YOGHURT

CREAM

AQUAFABA

WHIPPED AQUAFABA

TOFU

BANANA

APPLE SAUCE

AVOCADO

SOAKED PSYLLIUM HUSK

PSYLLIUM HUSK

CHIA SEEDS

LINSEEDS

The egg replacement also affects the appearance of the cake. Here, you can see the baked surface using different egg replacements.

If you think that an eggless cake is never going to rise, you may well be surprised when you replace the egg with tofu, avocado or linseeds, and the result actually looks like a normal cake. However, you should not be fooled into thinking this is a magic egg replacement. You might not realize that you would have got the same result if you had just used water. This does not mean that eggs can be replaced by water. The cake might look okay, but it needs to be baked for longer, it will taste of plain flour, the texture will be watery, it will not melt in the mouth and you will not be able to cut it into thin slices.

There is a lot of information out there about how you can easily replace eggs with seeds, banana, tofu or baking powder, for instance. I don't use any of these ingredients as I don't think they give a good enough result. Therefore, I have produced a guide to try to explain how many of the most recommended egg replacements actually work in sponge cakes. For comparison, I have taken a picture using plain aquafaba in the normal replacement quantity. You can read more about this on page 22. Some replacements don't work as well in light-coloured cakes but are really good in a chocolate cake (bicarbonate of soda), fruit cakes or spiced cakes (bicarbonate of soda, apple sauce and yoghurt) or in banana cakes (banana). Of all the examples, apple sauce, yoghurt and aquafaba are the only egg replacements I use in many of the recipes in the book. Read about how I use fruit purée on page 14 and yoghurt on page 16. Banana is only used in banana cakes. Bicarbonate of soda is only used in chocolate cakes and spiced cakes.

Aquafaba and egg replacement are the only egg substitutes here that don't give an aftertaste to the finished cake, or that don't produce a compact texture that gives you a ball of dough in the mouth. Aquafaba is the only ingredient that gives cake layers that can be thinly sliced.

People seem to think that if you just stabilize the batter, the cake will be stable after baking in the oven, with the sugar and the fat that is added. This is why they think that seeds, tofu and cream are good as egg replacements. However, it is not the batter that should be stabilized, but the rise from the oven, and none of these substitutes achieve that. If you take a look at a slice of one of these cakes you can see large bubbles that indicate that the batter was too dense and could not rise when baked in the oven. None of these have produced a lighter or taller cake than those made just using water. This is why I don't think these ingredients should be used as egg replacements in sponge cakes. There will also be dark seeds in the batter if you don't separate the seeds from the jelly, and I think this is just too much work as it neither stabilizes the cake nor gives it a good rise, but instead stabilizes the batter a bit too much. Psyllium husk does not contain any visible seeds, but it does come from psyllium seeds and they are no better when baking than the psyllium husk that I used here. Usually about 1 tablespoon of psyllium husk or psyllium seeds is recommended to replace the eggs, but this makes the cake chewy and unpleasant. That is why I have reduced it to 1 teaspoon but the texture is still too chewy. In one of the cakes, the psyllium husk has been left to expand for a few minutes, which is normally recommended, but it makes the cake completely dense. In the other cake, the psyllium husk is mixed straight into the batter which gives a better result. However, both are dense at the bottom and have a chewy texture. For this reason, I don't even use it in gluten-free cakes. Instead, I have used xanthan gum, which I have found to be the best gluten replacement. Read more on page 52.

Tofu almost always gives a tofu aftertaste when used in baking and is therefore not something I use myself or recommend in vegan baking. Cream together with cornstarch can be a good egg substitute in pastry creams or custards. Cream is also my favourite for brushing buns and pies to give a golden crust.

An egg's volume increases when whipped compared to all other egg replacements and would have given a slightly higher cake than the ones you can see in my comparisons. Eggs also give a softer and more pliable cake that can be cut into thin slices, which is very difficult when using most of these egg replacements. Aquafaba is the egg replacement that gives the softest interior and that gives the thinnest slices. However, it is important that a cake has a pleasant texture and that the egg replacement doesn't give it an aftertaste. It is only for layer cakes with cream and marzipan cakes that you need to slice the layers thinly. For other sponge cakes, texture and taste are the most important things.

As you may have realized I think most guides to egg substitutes are misleading and rarely give good results: the recipes are more complicated, results are disappointing, and people will lower their expectations if they think this is the best they can achieve without eggs.

WATER

The egg has been replaced with 50ml water. This is a cake for comparison. The cake is watery and a bit doughy instead of the sense of it melting in the mouth.

BAKING POWDER

The egg has been replaced with 50ml water mixed with 1 teaspoon of baking powder. The cake tastes of flour and does not melt in the mouth. It is better than only replacing it with water, but the cake cannot maintain the height from the raising agent so it sinks after being baked in the oven and the bottom of the cake is dense. Read more about baking powder on page 44.

BICARBONATE OF SODA

The egg has been replaced with 50ml water and ½ teaspoon bicarbonate of soda has replaced ½ teaspoon baking powder. The cake is raised evenly but tastes distinctly of bicarbonate of soda and is slightly yellow in colour. It is moist but it also melts in the mouth. Read about bicarbonate of soda on page 44.

EGG REPLACEMENT

2 tablespoons of water and 2 teaspoons of NoEgg, which is one of many commercial egg replacements. Read more on page 16. The egg has been replaced according to the instructions on the box for one egg. The texture is a bit dry compared to other egg replacements, which have a more watery texture and it melts in the mouth. No aftertaste. No big rise.

YOGHURT

The egg has been replaced with 50ml natural yoghurt. The cake has a good texture and melts in the mouth. It tastes good, but with a hint of yoghurt. The cake is baked without cracks and has a nice golden colour on the top.

CREAM

The egg has been replaced with 50ml cream. The texture is okay. The cake tastes of the cream. Note that it has a lower rise than the cake that uses just water instead of the egg.

UNWHISKED AQUAFABA

The egg has been replaced with 50ml unwhisked aquafaba. The cake tastes good. The texture is spongy and a bit dry compared to the other egg replacements, but it melts in the mouth. It has a nice surface and about the same rise as the cake with only water instead of eggs.

In these cakes, one egg, equivalent to 50ml of liquid, has been replaced by the most common tips in vegan guides for egg replacements. In the cakes the recipes and procedure are the same apart from the egg replacements, which are different. This shows how the most common tips for egg replacements affect the cakes. Note that this applies to smaller cakes of 15cm diameter. If the cakes had been bigger the disadvantages of the egg replacements would have been even clearer as bigger cakes are harder to bake. They burn easily on the sides, they become drier and they crumble. I think that this comparison shows the differences clearly enough.

BANANA
The egg has been replaced with 50g mashed banana. The cake has a slightly dry texture but has a nice taste of banana. However, it needs a little bit more banana to be a perfect banana cake since it is a bit too dense and slightly doughy in the mouth. It has a nice colour on the surface.

TOFU
The egg has been replaced with 50ml of silken tofu mixed with the liquid. The cake is somewhat dense. It has a strange taste. Note that it has about the same rise as the cake with only water in place of egg.

AVOCADO
The egg has been replaced with 50g well-mashed avocado. The cake has a good texture and melts in the mouth. It has a distinct taste of avocado. The cake has a nice golden colour on the surface. A very expensive egg replacement.

APPLE SAUCE
The egg has been replaced with 50g of apple sauce. The cake has quite a good texture and melts relatively quickly. It has a good but sweet taste and has a golden colour on the surface. Good and even rise.

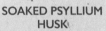

SOAKED PSYLLIUM HUSK
The egg has been replaced with 50ml water mixed with 1 teaspoon of psyllium husk, which has soaked for a few minutes, which is usually recommended. The cake is dense. It is doughy in the mouth and the texture is almost like rubber. The bottom of the cake is dense. Note that it has a lower rise than the cake that just uses water instead of egg.

PSYLLIUM HUSK
The egg has been replaced with 50ml water mixed with 1 teaspoon of psyllium husk directly mixed into the batter. The cake is still dense with large bubbles, which indicates that the batter was too firm. It is doughy in the mouth. The bottom of the cake is dense. Note that it has a lower rise than the cake that just uses water instead of egg.

CHIA
The egg has been replaced with 50ml water mixed with 1 tablespoon of chia seeds. The cake tastes of flour and does not melt in the mouth. It is quite dense. It contains visible seeds that you can feel when taking a bite. Note that it has a lower rise than the cake that just uses water instead of egg.

LINSEED
The egg has been replaced with 50ml water which has been mixed with 1 tablespoon of ground linseed. The cake has a nice taste, but does not melt in the mouth. It has risen a bit but has visible seeds that you can feel when taking a bite.

AQUAFABA

Aquafaba is the liquid that is created when you boil peas and beans. It was first tested in autumn 2014 in France by Joël Roessel and has been used to make light sorbets for a long time. However, it was not until August 'Goose' Wohlt used aquafaba to make meringues that internet forums for vegans exploded. Since then, vegan baking has never been the same. On 8 March 2015, I saw a post about water derived from beans, or 'légg' as it was called in my English translations, created from the words 'egg' and 'legumes'. Myself and a group of others who were developing recipes, together with Goose in the original group Vegan Meringue Hits and Misses, talked about what we should call the liquid and we chose Goose's suggestion 'aquafaba'. The name means 'bean water' in Latin. That is the name I have used in my recipes.

Lecithins, saponins and starch from peas or beans are absorbed by the liquid that it has been boiled in, which gives aquafaba its ability to form a foam. You can easily use the aquafaba from a tin or carton of peas or beans, but you can also boil your own beans and save the liquid. All my recipes have been developed using the liquid from tinned chickpeas, although other beans also give good results. Studies of whipped aquafaba done in laboratories show that the quality of the liquid varies between different brands, so if one recipe doesn't work it might be worth trying again with chickpeas from another brand. One 400g tin of chickpeas usually gives 100–150ml of aquafaba. You can put the aquafaba in the freezer, and it will keep in the fridge for 3–6 days in a sealed jar. When it has gone off it will smell, which is why you should smell it if you think it is too old. Shake the tin before pouring out the liquid so you don't waste the thick liquid at the bottom.

At first many recipes did not include a specific quantity of aquafaba, and instead would say 'liquid from a tin of chickpeas'; but as this can vary from between 50–200ml this would rarely give a good result. You need to measure the aquafaba and recipes should give a particular amount as this affects the result. I started developing recipes with quantities for meringues and went on to develop a light-coloured sponge cake and a layer cake with aquafaba. It took me over 100 test bakes to make the world's first vegan 'genoise', a French cake using only plain flour, sugar and eggs, and in my case, plain flour, caster sugar, aquafaba and a little oil to replace the fat in the egg yolk. Since then, I have managed to develop more complex recipes, such as brownies, kladdkaka, cookies, sponge cakes, madeleines, muffins and many more. These were recipes that before aquafaba came along, were a real challenge as it was hard to leave out the eggs and still keep the usual amount of fat and sugar in the mixture. That goal, I believe, is the key to uncompromising vegan baking. If you reduce the amount of fat and sugar, you are using less of the things that give the best taste and texture. Without the right amount of sugar and fat you will get a drier, less tasty cake that often forms a big lump of dough in the mouth, instead of melting. Another advantage is that aquafaba cannot be overworked like egg whites, for example when making meringues.

Aquafaba can be used in almost all recipes, but not in custards as it does not have the same characteristics as egg yolks. The biggest difference is that aquafaba cannot bind fat in the same way that eggs do, and the amount of fat it can hold depends on how the aquafaba is whipped, and how you fold in the flour. When whipped firmly it binds in air just as well as egg whites, but the amount of fat in this kind of batter needs to be reduced to prevent the cake from collapsing. Macaroons, for instance, contain almond flour that contains fat, which means you need to be careful when folding in the almond flour and not overwork the batter. Meringues can't include colours that contain fat or oil-based essences, such as peppermint oil or citrus oil. Basically, you should have no fat at all in firmly whipped aquafaba before stirring in the plain flour. When baking without eggs you sometimes need to calculate the amount of fat from the egg yolk to give your cake a good texture. Moreover, you cannot make the aquafaba frothy or whip it until stiff to a meringue with the zest from citrus fruit as this contains fat. In addition, some sugars, such as coconut sugar, cannot be mixed with aquafaba due to fat residue.

AQUAFABA SUMMARY PAGE

WORKS

- Whipping aquafaba, or aquafaba and sugar, and trapping air in various, stable stages – just like eggs.
- Emulsifying and stabilizing sugar, fat and liquid.
- Air that is whipped into the batter is retained and the cake rises in the oven as the air expands.
- Brushing aquafaba on cookies so toppings will stick.
- Freezing aquafaba and using once thawed.

DOESN'T WORK

- Whisking aquafaba to a foam with any fat in the mixture, for example oil, lemon peel, colour, cocoa or nuts.
- Replacing egg yolk with aquafaba in custards like pastry cream or ice cream (starch works as a great replacement).
- Whisking together fat, sugar and aquafaba in a cake batter and keeping the rise in the cake. This does work for cookies. This is called the creaming method. Reverse creaming is used for thick batters. For lighter batters, beating aquafaba to frothy stage works.
- Replacing eggs with aquafaba in choux pastry.

GUIDELINES WHEN REPLACING EGGS

One egg is most often replaced with 2–3 tbsp (30–50ml) of aquafaba. In recipes with a low ratio of egg, a higher quantity of aquafaba can be used (50ml per egg), compared to recipes with higher egg ratio (25–30ml per egg). The richer the recipe is in fat and sugar, the less aquafaba can be used successfully. Emulsified with the fat, a larger amount of aquafaba can be used. One can of chickpeas contains on average 150ml of aquafaba.

EGG FACTS: 1 egg = 3 tbsp, 50ml | 1 egg white = 2 tbsp, 30ml | 1 egg yolk = 1 tbsp, 15ml

AQUAFABA AMOUNTS USED FOR EGG REPLACEMENTS

 1 EGG = 40–50ml 2 EGGS = 75–100ml 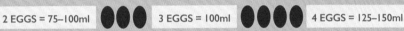 3 EGGS = 100ml | 4 EGGS = 125–150ml

DIFFERENT WAYS TO USE AQUAFABA SUCCESSFULLY

PLAIN AQUAFABA

Aquafaba is stirred into the batter unwhipped, just like raw eggs. In these recipes we can use the largest amount of aquafaba per egg, up to 50ml. Works in recipes with a large amount of fat, such as cookies, shortcrust pastry, muffins, cupcakes and even traybakes. In sponge cakes, large amounts of unwhipped aquafaba will most often result in a texture that is too dense.

PALE & FROTHY

If you whisk aquafaba with sugar until frothy, you can bind more fat into the cake batter than if it is whipped firmer or used unwhipped. The air you trap in the batter expands in the oven just like recipes that use beaten eggs in the batter. It is important to note that aquafaba can not be whipped with any fat, not even lemon peel. This method replaces the creaming method for light-textured cakes together with reversed creaming. Make sure you don't whip to ribbon stage (see page 26), as this will cause the cake to collapse. Used in sponge cakes and pancakes.

FROTHY + FLOUR FIRST

When the aquafaba is whipped pale, thick and frothy (see page 26) you can increase the amount of fat it is possible to use in the recipe by adding the flour first (see page 31). If you incorporate the plain flour before the liquid and the fat in the whipped aquafaba, you can add more fat than when you just whip the mixture until frothy. Here you can generally use 2 tablespoons of aquafaba per egg. Used in rich cakes, moist sponge cakes, brownies and madeleines.

MERINGUE

Aquafaba and sugar beaten until firm. See page 25 for different stages. Acids like cream of tartar make the batter firmer. NOTE! Does not tolerate fat like beaten egg whites. Used in meringues, macarons, meringue buttercream and Italian meringue.

REVERSE CREAMING

Mix, whisk or rub together the flour and fat first. The fat is then incorporated and cakes turn out incredibly light, even if you cannot whip the aquafaba until frothy. These recipes are simple as everything is made in one bowl. Replaces the creaming method where the batter needs to be thick and stable, for example traybakes with crumbles, cakes with heavy toppings and rich sponge cakes.

RIBBON STAGE

When the sugar and aquafaba is whipped until pale and really thick (see page 26). This is whipped for longer than frothy aquafaba. More air is trapped in the batter and it is firmer. When you lift the mixer attachment or whisk from the mixture, the batter falls back in thick trails. The lines of mixture will remain on top of the mixture, and will be clearly visible on the surface for a few moments before slowly disappearing. The batter is able to bind significantly smaller amounts of fat than frothy aquafaba, but more than meringue. This method is rarely used, but you need to know about it so it can be avoided. Aquafaba whipped with sugar reaches this stage if overwhipped, a high sugar ratio increases the risk and shortens the time it takes to reach ribbon stage. Used in Swiss rolls and genoise. Will give sunken, dense cakes if used in other sponge cakes (see page 27).

EMULSION

If oil and aquafaba form an emulsion, this stabilizes the fat and allows you to create extra moist cakes, such as classic olive oil cakes or carrot cakes. In the USA, chocolate cakes are sometimes baked using mayonnaise, and this type of cake can be recreated with emulsions of aquafaba and oil. In very fat-rich chocolate bakes, such as chocolate fondant and rich chocolate cakes, it is the key to success. Used in moist cakes, carrot cakes, chocolate cakes and chocolate fondant.

When aquafaba was discovered, meringue-whipped aquafaba was tested in every recipe and every sponge cake collapsed (page 27). Even in sponge cakes that didn't contain fat (apart from the egg yolks) the cakes did not work. If the fat is omitted, sponge cakes made with aquafaba will be chewy as you have not replaced the fat from the egg yolk. A small amount of fat will often be enough to achieve the right texture. You can see that in my Swiss roll, biscotti and genoise. In many other recipes the fat replacing the egg can be folded into a sponge cake with firmly whipped aquafaba if the batter contains plain flour, but if you want to fold in more fat you need to beat the aquafaba no more than frothy.

Aquafaba is a unique egg replacement that results in the same baking time as cakes with eggs and gives sponge cakes a beautiful colour all over so they look like cakes made with eggs. No other egg replacement has achieved this.

Plain aquafaba can bind together bakes containing a high amount of fat, which includes cookies, for instance. Plain aquafaba in sponge cakes usually results in a sponge that is slightly less light than the whipped version, but for reverse creaming, traybakes, muffins or thin sponge cakes it works perfectly. In bakes where the aquafaba is frothy, you replace the egg with 3 tablespoons of aquafaba, one egg white is replaced by 2 tablespoons, and in bakes with a high quantity of fat and sugar, the egg is replaced with 2–2½ tablespoons of aquafaba. Egg yolks are replaced with 1 tablespoon of aquafaba, but not in custards or in creams, as aquafaba does not thicken when heated. Read more about custards on page 14. To increase aquafaba's ability to bind the fat and increase the volume of batter when baking, you can whip the aquafaba until frothy with the sugar, just as you do in egg-based recipes, something I realized in 2017. It can then cope with a higher quantity of fat, and the air you whipped into bubbles expands when heated and gives the cake a rise just like a frothy egg would do. If you whip the batter a little more than frothy this is known as 'ribbon stage', see pages 25–26. If you drip the batter into the bowl it should not sink in straight away, but remain on the surface: it should create 'ribbons' of batter from the whisk. This batter will not bind as much fat as frothy aquafaba, and if you accidentally whip it too much you will need to carefully fold a little flour into the batter before you mix in the fat. During 2018, I developed two more methods where you can increase the amount of fat. If you whip the aquafaba until frothy and then fold in the plain flour before the fat, you can bind as much fat as you can using frothy eggs in traditional baking. This means you can make successful brownies, classic pound cakes and rich fruit cakes. In a similar way, you can combine the plain flour and fat before mixing them into the aquafaba. The plain flour will then combine with the fat and the aquafaba will not collapse because of the larger amount of fat. You can rub them together, whip them or mix the flour and the fat together first (reverse creaming), which allows you to bind more fat into the mixture. This technique is old, but is now frequently replaced with recipes where you whip the butter and sugar first (creaming). Creaming does not work easily with aquafaba, but to veganize these recipes you can use frothy aquafaba or reverse creaming, which gives the same effect and is a stable batter. On pages 25–33 there is a guide to versions with whipped or reverse creaming using aquafaba that I have developed for sponge cake batter.

You can also make an emulsion out of oil and aquafaba for baking. There is a big difference in the end result: it will be lighter, it will rise more in the oven and it will keep the rise when cool. It will not be soggy underneath like a sponge cake with too much fat. This method is used for chocolate fudge cake, banana and carrot cakes, and in the olive oil cake. Page 37 shows the difference between cakes made using mixed and emulsified oil. Aquafaba can also be reduced on a low heat to make it more concentrated and increase stability; this is used in my Italian meringue, meringue buttercream and macarons.

Short summary for aquafaba

Plain aquafaba	=	Cookies, biscuits, muffins, traybakes
Frothy aquafaba	=	Sponge cakes, muffins, pancakes
Frothy aquafaba, flour folded in first	=	Pound cakes, traditional sponge cakes, brownies
Ribbon stage	=	Genoise, Swiss rolls
Meringue	=	Meringues, macarons
Aquafaba emulsion with oil	=	Extra rich sponge cakes and chocolate cakes
Reduced aquafaba	=	Extra firm meringue and macarons

SOFT PEAKS

SOFT PEAKS
At the soft peak stage, the aquafaba and sugar have been whipped to a soft meringue. The peaks in the meringue on the whisk are not yet stiff. The meringue is not stable, and even if you can already turn the bowl upside down and pipe meringues, these will not keep their shape when baked.

STIFF PEAKS

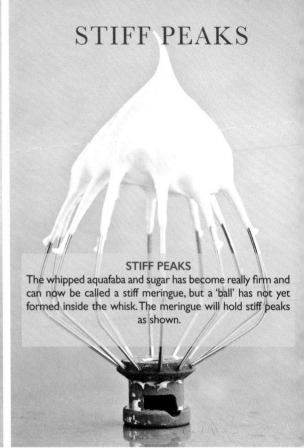

STIFF PEAKS
The whipped aquafaba and sugar has become really firm and can now be called a stiff meringue, but a 'ball' has not yet formed inside the whisk. The meringue will hold stiff peaks as shown.

STIFFER PEAKS

STIFF PEAKS + BALL
The whipped meringue has now formed a 'ball' in the whisk and has become really stiff and stable. It is now perfect for meringues that keep their shape and decoration on pies.

DRIED AQUAFABA
Today dried aquafaba powder is also available for baking. To use this in my recipes, mix the quantity of aquafaba indicated in the recipe using the same amount of water and the corresponding quantity of aquafaba powder required. Approximate quantities are given below, but this might vary for different brands.

Aquafaba powder gives a better result if it is allowed to sit for a while in the water before using.

2 tablespoons of water mixed with ¼ teaspoon aquafaba powder.
3 tablespoons/50ml of water mixed with ½ teaspoon of aquafaba powder.
75ml of water mixed with ¾ teaspoon of aquafaba powder.
100ml of water mixed with 1 teaspoon of aquafaba powder.
150ml of water mixed with 1 ½ teaspoons of aquafaba powder.

PLAIN

PLAIN AQUAFABA AND SUGAR
Clean utensils are important here because it is not possible to whip aquafaba with the slightest trace of fat in the bowl. Glass or metal are best as they are easiest to get properly clean; plastic is the most difficult.

FROTHY

FROTHY AQUAFABA
The whipped aquafaba should be pale, thick and frothy. You w the mixture to start to show marks made by the whisk, these should disappear immediately when you stop whisk and not remain in the mixture as for ribbon stage.

RIBBON STAGE

RIBBON STAGE
The whipped aquafaba should be white, thick and frothy. The whisk should leave marks in the mixture, which should not disappear straight away when you stop whisking, but remain visible in the mixture for a short time.

MERINGUE

MERINGUE
The aquafaba and sugar has been whipped to soft mering stage and now holds its shape. See the different stages whipped meringue on page 25.

In the cakes below, the recipes and the method used are the same, apart from how much I have whipped the aquafaba. This is to show you how the different stages of whipping in the sugar will affect the batter. You can use both ribbon and meringue stage in bakes containing fat if you adjust the batter to cope with that, but here, I have used a classic cake batter to show how aquafaba works in general. If you omit or reduce the amount of baking powder or reduce the fat, you can even get pointed sponge cakes using frothy aquafaba. If you reduce the amount of baking powder and fat, the ribbon stage works in sponge cakes – take a look at Swiss rolls and genoise. Aquafaba at meringue stage is used, for example in macarons and meringue buttercream.

PLAIN AQUAFABA

The cake has a nice flavour with no aftertaste. The texture is spongy and the cake melts in the mouth. The cake has an even rise and is less crumbly when using aquafaba and is baked more quickly compared to other egg replacements. The surface baked to a nice colour, which is difficult without using aquafaba.

FROTHY AQUAFABA

The cake has a nice flavour with no aftertaste. The texture is spongy and the cake melts quickly in the mouth. The cake has an even rise and a lovely crust.

RIBBON STAGE

If aquafaba and sugar are whipped to ribbon stage, normal cake recipes do not work. You need to adjust the recipe and reduce the fat. The cake will collapse in the middle and will not have a good texture. Bubbles appear in the cake and it will be dense at the bottom as the cake cannot retain the rise from the air that was whipped in.

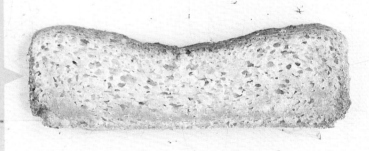

MERINGUE

If aquafaba and sugar are whipped to meringue stage, normal cake recipes do not work. The cake will collapse and the texture will not be light and spongy. Large bubbles are created and the whole cake will be dense as it is unable to retain the big rise from the air that has been whipped in.

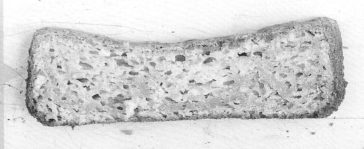

LIGHT SPONGE CAKES

Recipes with less fat produce cakes with a light texture, and they are easier to mix as you do not have to be as careful when adding the fat. In recipes with frothy aquafaba, you should whip the aquafaba and the sugar until frothy, but not to ribbon or meringue stage. Read more about this on page 24. If you accidentally whip the mixture too much, fold in the flour before you add the fat. This will reduce the risk of the cake collapsing.

This batter is not always ideal for cakes containing fruit or other ingredients that are added to the batter as it is loose and they will sink to the bottom. Light sponge cakes will, however, work when you add flavour with a liquid as you can replace the milk with the liquid. This recipe has the highest quantity of liquid out of the three versions I have developed. In the book this method of mixing the batter with frothy aquafaba is also used for other recipes like muffins, kladdkaka and pancakes.

1. Grease the tin and add breadcrumbs, semolina or plain flour to the greased surface. The tin in picture 1 is 1 litre and has been dusted with semolina. See page 62 for more about different ways to prepare tins.

2. Pour the aquafaba and caster sugar into a bowl.

3. Whip the aquafaba and the sugar until pale and frothy with an electric mixer or a stand mixer.

4. Add the flour (mixed with baking powder and salt), the liquid and the melted margarine.

5. Use a spatula to mix until the batter is smooth.

6. Pour the batter into the tin. Be careful not to get anything on the sides, as that will ruin your careful preparation.

7. Bake until a skewer comes out clean from the middle of the cake.

8. Leave to cool on a wire rack before turning it out of the tin.

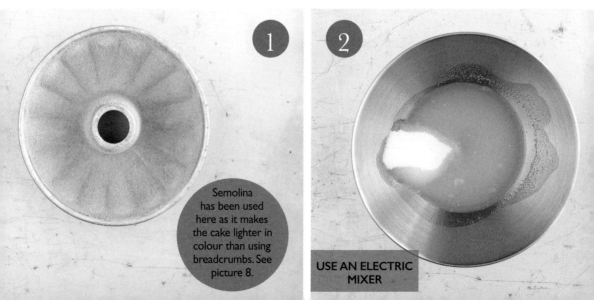

Semolina has been used here as it makes the cake lighter in colour than using breadcrumbs. See picture 8.

USE AN ELECTRIC MIXER

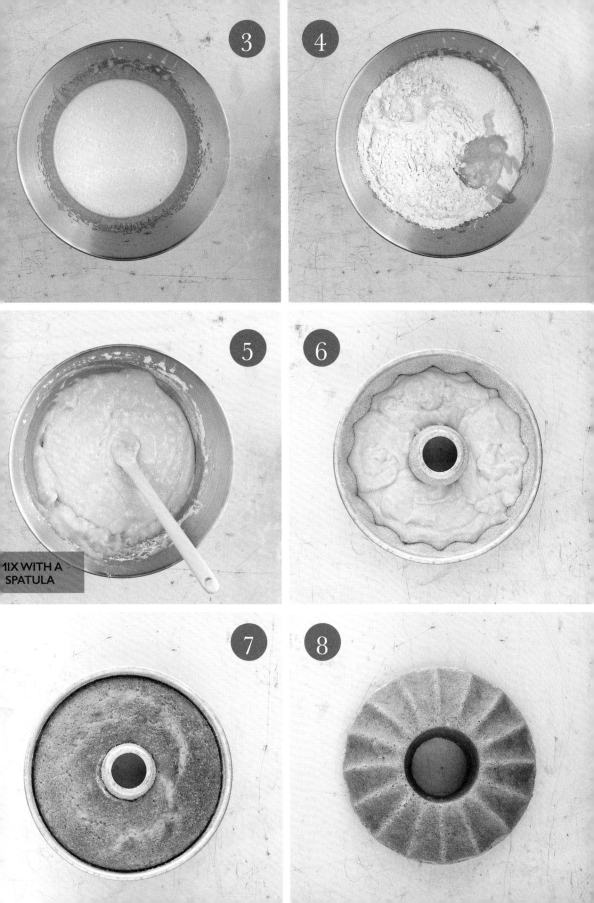

MIX WITH A
SPATULA

MOIST SPONGE CAKES

Recipes with a higher quantity of fat produce moist cakes. These are a little more difficult to mix than the light sponge cakes. You need to be careful about when you add the fat as the aquafaba will gradually collapse each time you stir the batter after adding the fat. This kind of recipe makes a firm batter that is good for cakes to which you want to add nuts, fruit or berries. They will not sink to the bottom of the cake like they would in a looser batter. This recipe can also cope with a topping, but for those cakes, such as crumbles or coffee cakes, reverse creaming works best.

For recipes with frothy aquafaba, you should whip aquafaba and sugar until frothy but not to ribbon or meringue stage. See page 26.

1. Grease the tin and add breadcrumbs, semolina or plain flour to the greased surface. In picture 1, the tin is 1.2 litres and has been dusted with plain flour. Read more on page 62 about different ways to prepare tins.

2. Whip the aquafaba and sugar until pale and frothy with an electric mixer or a stand mixer.

3. Add the flour that has already been mixed with salt and baking powder in a separate bowl.

4. Carefully fold in the flour without overworking it. You do not need to mix it perfectly, as you may overwork the batter and lose the air that has been whipped into the aquafaba. Picture 4 shows how much the flour needs to be folded in.

5. Fold in the margarine and the liquid you want to add in two or three batches, depending on the quantity. Fold in carefully and as little as possible to minimize the amount of air lost.

6. Use a spatula to make the batter smooth.

7. Pour the batter into the tin. Be careful not to get anything on the sides, as that will ruin your careful preparation.

8. Bake until a skewer comes out clean from the middle of the cake.

9. Leave to cool on a wire rack before turning it out of the tin.

1

Plain flour has been used to prepare the tin and the cake comes out darker than when using breadcrumbs, but not as golden. See page 33 for a cake made with breadcrumbs.

2

USE AN ELECTRIC MIXER

3

USE A SPATULA

4

5

6

7

8

REVERSE CREAMING

This type of batter is firmer and more stable than the other versions of the sponge cake and will rise a lot in the oven. It is used in many traditional recipes, such as coffee cake. This is a good technique to replace recipes where you whip fat and sugar together first, which is called creaming. I have not yet managed to make that kind of sponge cake work perfectly, but this method is just as good. This type of recipe makes a firm batter that is good for cakes to which you want to add nuts, fruits or berries, as they do not sink to the bottom of the cake. This batter is also good for cakes with heavy toppings, such as crumbles and coffee cakes. In some of the recipes in this book, I mix the sugar with the flour straight away, which also works. For sponge cakes with reverse creaming it is important not to fill the tin to more than two thirds as it will rise a lot when baked.

This batter can also be made in a food processor instead of a stand mixer, or with an electric hand mixer. Follow the same steps, but instead of using a bowl for whipping, as shown in the pictures, you do everything in the mixing bowl. This kind of batter will be smoother than the batter made with an electric hand mixer.

1. Grease the tin and add breadcrumbs, semolina or flour to the greased surface. In picture 1, the tin is 1.2 litres and has been dusted with breadcrumbs. Read more on page 62 about different ways to prepare tins.

2. Add the flour and baking powder to the bowl.

3. Mix everything together thoroughly.

4. Dice the margarine.

5. Whip or mix the flour and the margarine together until the margarine is the size of peas.

6. Add the sugar and salt.

7. Mix the margarine into the dry mixture until fine. If you are using a stand mixer or an electric hand mixer you might need to make sure that everything is evenly distributed in the bowl and break up any bigger lumps.

8. Add the aquafaba and liquid.

9. Whip or mix until the batter is well combined.

10. Pour the batter into the tin. Be careful not to pour anything on the sides, as that will ruin your carefully prepared tin and the cake might stick to the sides.

11. Bake until a skewer comes out clean from the middle of the cake.

12. Leave to cool on a wire rack before turning it out of the tin.

1 Breadcrumbs have been used to dust the tin to give the cake a golden colour. See picture 12.

8 USE AN ELECTRIC MIXER

DAIRY PRODUCTS
& FAT

Plant milks

Rice milk, soya milk, nut milk, coconut milk, hemp milk and oat milk can all be used when a recipe says milk. The milk in the recipes can also be replaced with water or any other vegetable milk. However, rice milk will burn more easily than other milks and should not be used for cakes that need to be baked in the oven for a long time, as it can make the cake taste burned and sometimes gives dark patches to light-coloured bakes. Sweetened condensed milk is available from many manufacturers but the quality varies. I like to use a light, runny version based on coconut milk from the brand Nature's Charm. You can find it in vegan or health food shops if you search for it online.

Cream

Single cream is now available in the form of rice cream, oat cream, almond cream and soy cream. Most are available in well-stocked grocery shops and in other speciality shops. Dairy double cream has around 40 per cent fat, which means that in some recipes it is important to compensate for the lost fat when replacing it with a cream with a lower proportion of fat. The plant-based double cream used in this book contains around 25–30 per cent fat. If you want a really firmly whipped plant-based cream, add a few drops of lemon juice or vinegar after whipping it for some time, and then whip it again thoroughly for a few more minutes. See page 409.

Yoghurt and cream cheese

Plant-based yoghurt made from soya beans, coconut or oats, for example, is easy to find in grocery shops. I always use natural yoghurt in my recipes adn the fat content should be 2–5%. You can find plant-based cream cheese made with rice, cashew nuts and soya beans, but I think it is hard to work with vegan cream cheese in both frosting and cheesecakes as they are all different and react in different ways when mixed with sugar and when baked in the oven. This is why I do not have a brand I can recommend and you will have to be aware that the cheese you buy will

not behave the same as the cheese I used when developing the recipes in this book, as they may have completely different characteristics.

Baking margarine

On page 19 of the 1965 edition of the classic Swedish baking book *Sju sorters kakor* ('Seven Kinds of Cakes') (ICA Provkök), it says 'after tests we have seen that cakes baked with butter have a special smell when newly baked. However, cakes baked with margarine will stay fresh for a considerably longer period of time.' These test bakers knew what they were talking about and they were not influenced by the norm – they just evaluated the results. I can live with a slight loss of smell and the cakes still taste good enough when newly baked. Today you can find dairy-free margarine from many different producers that work just like the butter, apart from in frosting where margarine will not give the same flavour or have the same melting point as butter. However, you can easily use vegan spread, instead.

Margarine has had a bad reputation for a long time because it used to contain trans fats, and some types contain unhealthy additives. That is not the case today and in Sweden, the National Food Agency advises people to use margarine without the fear of additives as it contains a good balance between saturated and unsaturated fatty acids. They write: 'Nowadays margarine basically contains no industrial trans fat. Butter and cooking fat blends containing butter can contain up to 2–3g of trans fat per 100g.'

Margarine can handle high temperatures better than butter, and in pastry just a pinch of salt is enough to lift the pastry to the same level as pastry made with butter. It is especially good for incorporating into doughs, which is why vegan puff pastry is common. In America and the UK, there are many alternatives to margarine for use in baking, and I hope that in Sweden too we will soon have a baking margarine that gives a good texture and has a better melting point.

LIQUIDS

HALF THE AMOUNT OF LIQUID
e cake is flat and the surface has large cracks.

HALF THE AMOUNT OF LIQUID
The firm batter has not risen fully. There are chewy bubbles and the cake has a dense texture and is doughy in the mouth.

CORRECT AMOUNT OF LIQUID
A slightly domed surface with no large cks. The batter was losing enough to rise fully in the oven.

CORRECT AMOUNT OF LIQUID
The cake melts in the mouth.

DOUBLE THE AMOUNT OF LIQUID.
ives a pointed shape and bread-like surface with large cracks.

DOUBLE THE AMOUNT OF LIQUID
Gives a very tall cake. The batter is looser and contains neither too much sugar nor fat to weigh down the batter; the rise is maintained even after being baked. The bottom of the cake is light but soggy and has a doughy texture rather than melting in the mouth.

In these three cakes, everything was the same apart from the amount of liquid used. The cakes are photographed from above and as a cross-section. You can see here how too little or too much liquid affects the end result for both look and taste.

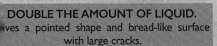

A good baking margarine contains at least 80 per cent fat and does not include added Vitamin D3 from sheep's wool, although this is no longer as common. If you are unsure, choose a margarine that is labelled vegan. Margarine can be replaced with the same amount of oil for most recipes in this book that use melted margarine. You can usually replace 100g of margarine with 100ml oil, even though margarine practically consists of around 80g of fat and 20g of liquid.

Vegan spread

What is currently lacking is a vegan baking margarine that has both a great texture and a lower melting point. Baking margarine usually has a higher melting point (40–60°C/104–140°F) than butter and spreads (30–35°C/86–95°F). Vegan spread can replace firmer baking margarine in recipes for frosting and pastry creams as it melts more pleasantly in the mouth. This can't be used for cakes cooked in the oven as vegan spread does not contain enough fat, but vegan spread is an important ingredient for recipes that do not require baking. This means that recipes I never thought could be veganized, like simple frosting, can be made in the same way as traditional recipes. In my previous books, I often used coconut oil and similar ingredients to make them softer, but they usually become too hard when chilled. Now you can just replace the butter with vegan spread. On page 258, there is a tip for whipping margarine to make it extra light and soft for your morning toast, or to make scones extra special. In recipes where vegan spread is required, it is stated clearly in the ingredients list.

In the USA and the UK there are several high quality vegan butter alternatives to margarine. These can be used as replacements for both margarine and vegan spread.

Oil

Oils such as rapeseed oil, sunflower oil and other hot pressed oils used in cooking have a more neutral flavour and are better for baking than cold pressed oils. One exception is the olive oil cake on page 108, which is baked using an oil rich in flavour to achieve the best results. I usually use hot pressed rapeseed oil if I want to bake soft, light-coloured sponge. Coconut oil can also be used in baking as it has a low melting point and is solid at room temperature, which is why it melts on your tongue and works well for frosting and glazes. Do remember that coconut oil will harden up in the fridge. If you keep bakes with coconut oil in the frosting or the glaze in the fridge, it will be too solid to serve. It will need to be kept at room temperature for some time to become soft again. That is why I only use coconut oil in frosting if the cakes are being served soon after decoration and do not need to be chilled. This is what has helped me succeed with fruit mousses, where the coconut oil is used to make the mousse sufficiently firm. Always use coconut oil that does not smell or taste of coconut. The coconut oil should be weighed out or measured as a liquid. Make sure that you use room temperate ingredients and do not mix products that are cold from the fridge into the batter as they will harden the coconut oil. Never throw away coconut fat, coconut oil or deep frying oil down the sink as it will clog the pipes when it cools and becomes hard. Coconut oil is not used because it is more healthy than other oils, but because of its characteristics.

Fat

When baking, fat does not just make the cake moist, it also holds the flavours and it is important to use the right amount of fat to succeed with uncompromising bakes. When you leave out the egg you remove the emulsion, and it is important to incorporate the oil properly into the batter, otherwise the fat will sink to the bottom and make it darker and stickier than the rest of the cake. You can, for instance, mix the oil with mashed fruit, yoghurt or aquafaba so that it emulsifies for long enough to bake evenly. The fat in margarine is already emulsified. In recipes with a lot of oil and aquafaba, the emulsification of the fat makes a big difference (see the picture below). I do this in recipes where more fat needs to bind together, such as in my olive oil cake or the fudge layer cake.

Here, the aquafaba has been stirred into the mixture in a recipe that contains a lot of oil. The cake has not risen as much and it is soggier at the bottom. There is a higher chance of a dense base.

This is the same recipe, but the oil has been mixed with the aquafaba before being mixed into the batter.

A CAKE WITH NO FAT

e cake has risen to a dome, like the recipe with too much
on page 35. The texture is firm and is doughy in the mouth.

5% liquid and 25% oil. Slightly dense and feels a little doughy
instead of melting in the mouth. A little more oil is needed.

% oil and 50% liquid. Melts in the mouth. There is almost too
ch oil. Sunk in the middle and is almost dense at the bottom.

25% liquid and 75% oil.
The batter is a lot firmer.

Just fat and no liquid. The batter is very
firm and the consistency is like a brownie.
Melts in the mouth.

The same recipe has been used for all five sponge cakes
above and the total quantity of liquid/oil remains the same
for each. However, the amount of fat varies and you can see
how the amount of fat affects the result.

FAT

In the three cakes below, everything is the same except for
the amount of fat. They contain either not enough, the right
amount or too much. The total amount of added fat/liquid
varies here, as opposed to those on the left where only the
amount of fat has changed.

HALF THE OIL
Creates more bubbles in a drier batter but
also gives a more bread-like consistency.
The cake feels doughy instead of melting
in the mouth.

CORRECT AMOUNT OF OIL
A slightly domed surface with no large cracks.
Melts in the mouth and has a good flavour.

DOUBLE THE AMOUNT OF OIL
The cake is darker and denser at the bottom. The cake is
flatter than the cake with the correct amount of oil. If the
recipe contained even more oil, there would have been a
dense line at the base. If you find this type of line at the
bottom of a cake, you can either reduce the amount of
sugar or oil, or both. The cake will have a dark, grainy surface
with white spots.

FLOUR

When I develop recipes for sponge cakes I don't usually adjust the amount of flour in the recipes. Instead, I usually focus on the amount of sugar or fat in the batter. However, for small biscuits and cookies it is often the amount of flour that is adjusted. I always recommend you test bake one before putting the whole tray in the oven.

Different recipes require very different ratios of baking powder depending on the amount of sugar and fat included, and this is why I use plain flour instead of self-raising flour. With plain flour you can add the perfect amount of baking powder for each recipe. It is important to use ordinary plain flour, and not strong bread flour, as these contain extra gluten that makes cakes dense. Strong bread flour contains extra gluten, which is perfect for wheat bread; in the book it is used for bread recipes and my croissant dough. Never add all the flour at once in raised doughs. Add it in batches to prevent a dry dough. Strong flour should never be used in sponge cakes, cookies or pastry cases as for these you want to avoid activating the gluten strands; the more gluten the plain flour contains the greater the risk. See page 16 for information on how plain flour can replace the thickening function of egg.

There is a risk of overworking the batter in sponge cakes if you mix it too much, or use an electric hand mixer after the flour has been added. This is because the gluten strands are activated and bind together when kneaded. They will also bind together more easily in a dough that contains a lot of acid, which is why you always should mix the batter as quickly as possible. Otherwise, there is a risk that the gluten strands will make the sponge chewy and the dough will not rise as much. I often mix dry ingredients with a spatula; if I use an electric hand mixer it is to mix the wet ingredients. In cookies and pastry cases you also need to make sure the gluten strands are not developed. If you rub or mix together the fat and the plain flour before adding any liquid, you stop the flour from absorbing the liquid. You will get a dough that does not shrink and shortcrust pastry that melts in the mouth. In pastry cases, where it is important that the dough does not shrink, the fat, liquid and sometimes the flour are cold.

A traditional sponge cake using eggs contains a smaller proportion of plain flour than traditional pre-aquafaba egg-free recipes, as the egg absorbs a large amount of the batter and is being replaced by something that cannot bind in air and increase the volume in the same way as eggs. If you leave out the egg and use the same amount of flour, this changes the flavour and gives a stronger taste of flour. To limit the effect of the loss of binding ability in the egg, you can replace some of the flour with starch, up to 100g in a recipe originally containing 180–240g of flour. You can, for instance, use cornstarch, potato starch or tapioca starch, depending on what you prefer or might be allergic to. This will reduce the taste of wheat, and the starch will help to keep the mixture together and stabilize it. This is no problem in cakes using aquafaba as the egg replacement as it replaces approximately the same amount as the egg and also expands in the oven like egg recipes where more fat needs to bind together, such as in my olive oil cake or the fudge layer cake.

60g of plain flour

30g plain flour missing

Perfect according to me

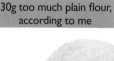

30g too much plain flour, according to me

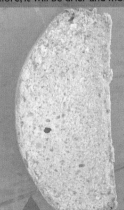

MIX TOGETHER
The batter has just been lightly mixed until smooth.

The batter has just been lightly mixed together with a spatula until it is smooth with no lumps.

SLIGHTLY OVERWORKED
The batter has been mixed for a few minutes after adding the plain flour.

OVERWORKED
A lovely surface with no cracks. However, we are concerned about the inside, not the outside.

Here, the batter has been mixed for about 2 minutes and you can see a clear difference in the rise from the oven. The batter is firmer and the cake cannot rise in the ideal way. Therefore, it will be drier and more dense.

In these three cakes, everything is the same except for the amount of time the batter has been mixed for. The same cakes can be seen here both from above and as a cross-section. The cake at the top has just been lightly mixed together. The one in the middle has been mixed for about 2 minutes. The one at the bottom has been mixed for about 4 minutes. The most important difference is in the rise.

Here, the batter has been mixed for about 4 minutes. The cake is denser than the other two but still has an acceptable texture, although slightly drier than is ideal. However, it has considerably less rise than the cake where the batter was only mixed. The batter thickens the more it is mixed when the gluten strands start to activate.

SUGAR

Even though it sounds contradictory, sugar acts as a liquid in a batter, and it is important not just for the flavour but also for the consistency and how moist the bake will be. When you increase the amount of sugar, you will get a looser batter; and if you reduce the amount of sugar, the batter will be firmer. Using the wrong amount of sugar can also produce sponge that forms lumps in the mouth instead of melting pleasantly on the tongue. It is important to use the exact amount of sugar given in the recipe to get the right flavour and consistency, even in eggless sponge. The egg's proteins denaturate, stabilize and bind together the sugar in the mixture. It can be difficult to use the same amount of sugar in eggless baking without the cake collapsing in the middle. Something I discovered early on when developing recipes and that I have continued to work on is that icing sugar does not behave like caster sugar, even though it is exactly the same product. Icing sugar gives the same flavour and the right consistency in eggless sponge but does not give a loose batter in the same way, which helps the cake keep its rise when baking in the oven. The icing sugar absorbs more liquid. This is why I often replace some of the caster sugar with icing sugar when developing recipes. This helps the cake maintain the same amount of sugar without collapsing, becoming sugary or burnt when the sugar separates from the batter. Soft brown sugar has the same baking characteristics as caster sugar.

To succeed with a recipe, it is important to use the original amount of sugar and fat. In recipes that use a lot of sugar and fat this can be very difficult, but replacing granulated with icing sugar can make a big difference. I use this method mainly in recipes using chocolate that contains a lot of fat. It gives me a perfect texture as icing sugar in a light-coloured cake will give a drier result. In recipes that include fruit or vegetables, the fruit gives enough liquid to prevent the cake from becoming dry. Icing sugar is used, for instance, in light-coloured banana squares, carrot squares and the courgette cakes. Even recipes that use a lot of yoghurt or cream can be baked with icing sugar, for example, my basic apple cake and baked cheesecake.

A few guides on egg replacements say that you can replace eggs with syrup, but that only applies to cookies, as it neither binds the sugar together nor gives rise to a sponge cake. However, syrup does give a smooth shortcrust pastry to which you can add more flour if it is too loose. One example of this is the sliced chocolate cookies on page 304. I also use syrup in my simple gingerbread frosting as it can replace the smoothness the egg gives the frosting. In brownies and chocolate-rich cakes, which is extra fatty and sweet, the syrup is a poor egg replacement as the extra sugar increases the risk of the sugar and the fat separating from the cake and gathering around the edges or leaking out of the tin. This increases the risk of hard edges in a brownie or kladdkaka.

People often ask me if it is possible to reduce the amount of sugar to make a cake healthier. But I say that my recipes are adjusted to get the perfect texture and flavour. If you reduce the sugar to get an less tasty but 'healthier' cake then the whole purpose of the cake has been lost. White caster sugar is produced from sugar beet and is not more refined than other sugar that is sold as naturally produced from vegetables. However, different plants produce different sugars that can taste more or less sweet. Raw cane sugar can be used instead of caster sugar in all recipes. Coconut sugar cannot be whipped together with aquafaba as it contains a small amount of fat from the coconut. Read more about this on page 22. This means that it is not possible in all recipes but the reverse creaming technique will work. Some sugar-free sweeteners do not behave like liquids in a batter but are dry products, which makes it difficult for them to succeed. You will have to adjust the amount of liquid to get the batter loose enough. If you take a look at page 35 you can see that liquids do not give the same kind of consistency as the moisture from sugar. It will give a wetter consistency and a watery taste. Altering the ingredients always increases the chance of failure, but if you are lucky you will become wiser and learn what is needed to use your favourites.

Read about how I replaced the combination of caster sugar, cream and butter in sweets on page 435. Margarine does not caramelize in the same way as butter, which is why I use sugar that provides the same type of caramelization and compensates for the flavour in that way.

SPRINKLE

In a recipe, if it says to sprinkle demerara sugar or raw cane sugar on top of a cake or a pie, you can also use other coarse-grained sugars or normal caster sugar.

SUCCESS

For a recipe to be successful it is important to use the same quantity of sugar and fat as you would find in a non-vegan recipe.

VEGAN?

Beet sugar is always vegan, but sometimes refined cane sugar is not. In many areas, cane sugar is filtered using bone char made from cattle bones, and it can be difficult to find vegan white sugar in countries where cane sugar comes as standard. In that case, use raw cane sugar, or sugar that is labelled as either organic, unrefined, or natural.

In this light sponge cake (cake 1, page 92) I have added 1 teaspoon of vanilla extract and the zest of 1 lemon. It is baked in a round tin with a diameter of 20cm and covered with the glaze from page 120. Violets are edible, but are more beautiful than tasty – these are from our garden.

Caster sugar gives a nicely baked surface and a cake that melts in the mouth. The amount used here is 180g of caster sugar in a sponge cake with 180g of plain flour.

Icing sugar gives a higher cake that is lighter in colour and drier in consistency. You need to compensate for the dryness. I used 180g of icing sugar in a sponge cake with 180g of plain flour.

Light brown sugar gives a big difference in colour and a slight caramel and liquorice flavour. The amount is 180g of light brown sugar in a sponge cake with 180g of plain flour.

Agave syrup produces bubbles in the cake and gives an unpleasantly chewy and doughy texture. The amount equals 180g with 180g of plain flour. Agave burns easily compared to other sugars and will have a burned taste. Golden syrup will produce a cake of about the same colour, but not with the same chewy texture and burnt taste.

In these four cakes, everything is the same apart from the sugar that has been used. This is so you can see how this affects the result. If you develop your own recipes, you can easily adjust them.

Here, 180g of caster sugar has been replaced by the same weight of the other sugars. Agave syrup is almost twice as dense as caster sugar, so was reduced in volume but was still too wet, did not look good and had a chewy, doughy texture.

SUGARS

HOW MUCH SUGAR?

NOT ENOUGH SUGAR

0g caster sugar in a cake with 180g plain flour. Rough, bread-like surface. Large cracks in the cake.

NOT ENOUGH CASTER SUGAR

90g caster sugar in a cake with 180g plain flour – 90g less than the correct amount. The dry batter has not risen to full height as it is too firm. Large bubbles have also been created in the cake. The cake is doughy in the mouth.

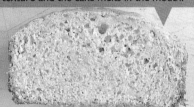

CORRECT AMOUNT OF SUGAR

180g of caster sugar in a cake with 180g of plain flour. Good texture and the cake melts in the mouth.

CORRECT AMOUNT OF SUGAR

Nice surface with an even rise. 180g caster sugar in a cake with 180g plain flour.

A LITTLE TOO MUCH SUGAR

225g of caster sugar in a cake with 180g plain flour. Slightly damp at the bottom with large air pockets; a larger amount of sugar will cause it to collapse.

A LITTLE TOO MUCH SUGAR

5g caster sugar with 80g plain flour. Gives a spongier surface. There is a bumpy, dged, darker section n the centre, which orms a dip when the ake collapses due to too much sugar.

UGAR COLLAPSE!

90g more than the correct amount of sugar. Here, there is 70g of caster sugar in cake with 180g plain flour. Spongy surface and slightly bigger cracks. The bumpy section in the middle has collapsed and the bottom is very soggy.

SUGAR COLLAPSE!

90g more than the correct amount, so 270g of caster sugar in a cake with 180g of plain flour. The bottom is doughy and unbaked, and there are large bubbles. The sponge is chewy and dough-like. With a little more sugar the cake would have collapsed like a brownie. Brownies need more sugar than flour to get their fudgey texture.

In these four cakes, everything is the same apart from the amount of caster sugar. This is to show you how an increase or decrease in sugar affects the result. If you are developing your own recipes, you will be able to adjust them more easily.

RAISING AGENTS

Baking powder

Baking powder is sodium bicarbonate (bicarbonate of soda) mixed with an acid and a little starch to prevent moisture. Baking powder as a raising agent makes sponge drier than bicarbonate of soda and gives a cake more rise, especially in the centre, since it reacts to heat and is activated as the cake is heated in the oven. You will get a quick and even reaction from baking powder by adding boiling liquid. The heat makes the baking powder react more quickly, which will make the sponge rise more evenly, instead of the cake being activated as it is heated. In that way you can get a rise in the centre. Just like the reaction between bicarbonate of soda and vinegar, the cake needs to be put in the oven quickly to prevent the bubbles in the batter from leaving the cake before they collapse. If you use baking powder that reacts with heated liquid, there is the risk that chewy bubbles will develop in the baked cake. Baking powder will keep fresh for approximately 6–8 months; if moisture gets into the pot it will be ruined and needs to be replaced. Around 1 teaspoon of baking powder per 100g of plain flour is the perfect amount in a sponge cake with a smaller amount of fat. For sponge cakes with more fat, that do not rise as much, you will need around 1 teaspoon per 200g of plain flour.

Bicarbonate of soda

Bicarbonate of soda is pure sodium bicarbonate. In contrast to baking powder, there is no added starch or acid, and acid is needed to activate the bicarbonate of soda. Vinegar, lemon juice, sparkling water, fruit or yoghurt can all activate bicarbonate of soda. Bicarbonate of soda does not give the same results as baking powder and they cannot replace one another. A combination of both bicarbonate of soda and baking powder is often perfect for dark-coloured bakes or cakes with chocolate. For these, I like to use vinegar or lemon juice to activate the bicarbonate of soda. Cocoa hides both the colour and taste of vinegar and bicarbonate of soda, so this combination gives a good result. Cocoa is slightly sour, which means that you can use bicarbonate of soda and cocoa with no other acids if you are using a larger amount of cocoa.

In light-coloured bakes, I often use yoghurt as the acid to avoid an aftertaste and colour change. The thick consistency of the yoghurt helps to stabilize the cake which is maintained after baking. A few grams of bicarbonate of soda can make the cake more spongy without adding colour or an aftertaste. In cakes containing fruit, vegetables (carrot, courgette) or a lot of spices, which hide any darker blotches on the cake, a mixture of baking powder and bicarbonate of soda might work. The taste can be even better when you add bicarbonate of soda, and both carrot cakes and banana cakes usually contain a small amount of bicarbonate of soda to achieve the traditional taste. Carrots also taste milder when you add bicarbonate of soda; the carrot flavour is stronger when just baking powder is used. In some soft gingerbreads, the bicarbonate of soda will soften the spices and is needed to get the right taste. Bicarbonate of soda gives less of a lift in bakes than baking powder and you can fill the tin to three-quarters without running the risk of it overflowing the edges or collapsing. In biscuits and cookies, the bubbles from the bicarbonate of soda make the batter spread out more compared to using baking powder.

Yeast

Yeast is a single-celled fungus species called *Saccharomyces cerevisiae*. In contrast to baking powder or bicarbonate of soda, it is a living organism that eats the sugar in the dough and creates air bubbles that expand in the heat of the oven. Yeast cannot be replaced with baking powder, but you can make bread-like bakes, such as scones or quick buns, using baking powder instead of yeast. They will be drier and the gluten in the plain flour will not develop so they have a different texture. More information on yeast can be found on pages 59 and 331.

BAKING POWDER

This recipe contains plain aquafaba. If it had been whipped, the batter could have risen by itself from the air that would have been incorporated. Halving the baking powder would not have had such a big effect on the cake as is seen here.

HALF THE AMOUNT OF BAKING POWDER
¾ tsp of baking powder in a batter of 180g of plain flour. This cake has a dense consistency that turns into a lump in the mouth. You can see that the cake has not risen evenly, but has risen in the middle.

CORRECT AMOUNT OF BAKING POWDER
Approximately 1½ tsp per 180g plain flour. The cake has an even colour and an even rise and with no dark patches of colour.

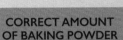

DOUBLE THE AMOUNT OF BAKING POWDER
1 tbsp of baking powder per 180g plain flour. The cake has a yellow colour and has a darker crust. The texture is also more doughy. This is why baking powder is difficult to use as an egg replacement even though many guides recommend it.

With too much baking powder the cake rises more than it can maintain when properly baked. This is why eggs never can be replaced with baking powder. The difference compared to recipes with too much sugar is that the middle of the cake does not have a ridged area in the centre where it collapses (see page 43). Here, a large air pocket has been created which has produced a hole in the middle. You can see what too much baking powder looks like on page 20, where the amount of baking powder has been increased and the cake has a dark line at the bottom and has completely collapsed.

LIGHT-COLOURED CAKE
In these three cakes, everything is the same apart from the amount of baking powder. This is so you can see how the amount of raising agent affects the result. If you are developing your own recipes you will be able to adjust the recipe more effectively.

One raising agent cannot be replaced with another raising agent even though many guides may say this is possible. Instructions often say that 1 teaspoon of baking powder = ½ teaspoon bicarbonate of soda. However, this is not true, each one is carefully chosen depending on the recipe, and if a different raising agent is used this can cause colour changes and an aftertaste, or just fail to activate. Bicarbonate of soda produces a rise with small bubbles that are distributed throughout the cake. The sponge will then be light and moist, while baking powder gives a drier result. Bicarbonate of soda needs an added acid to activate, and light-coloured bakes will take on a slight yellow colour. If there are fruit or berries in the batter, bicarbonate of soda will produce a brown colour or darker spots. Baking powder produces a rise with larger bubbles, more rise in the centre and a drier result. A combination of both usually gives a good result, but if you want a light-coloured cake you should leave out the bicarbonate of soda.

One trick when baking without eggs that has existed since the Second World War, particularly in Sweden and America, is to use bicarbonate of soda mixed with vinegar or sour milk. These cakes are made with oil and water instead of butter and milk and are usually called Depression cakes, war cakes or 'wacky cakes', as they were developed when eggs or butter were not easy to obtain. A lot of eggless baking originates from these recipes, but a few issues make them difficult to use in some types of bakes. Bicarbonate of soda and vinegar affect the flavour, consistency and colour of the cake. In light-coloured cakes this is obvious, but in bakes containing chocolate this is not apparent. The baking time affects the result and for small muffins you can sometimes use a little bicarbonate of soda with no aftertaste or yellow colour developing. However, if you use the same batter to make a layer cake it can be almost inedible. The cakes shown here are 10cm in diameter; in larger tins the colour change would have been more noticeable. Many vegan baking books say you can stop the reaction between the bicarbonate of soda and acid by dropping the cake onto a surface, but you can't pause a chemical reaction using force: what happens is that you knock the bubbles out of the cake so it looks as if the reaction has been stopped.

Apart from macarons, brownies or 'pan-banging' cookies, there are very few cakes where you need to drop the batter on the counter to improve the end result. These cakes, where the reaction has started before they are baked, need to be put in the oven as soon as possible. The batter should not be overworked, but quickly mixed together once the activating element has been added.

On the next few pages, I have made a few comparisons using baking powder and bicarbonate of soda. This shows the difference between using baking powder and bicarbonate of soda, and whether you are using enough, too much or too little. This is important as many egg replacement guides say that eggs can be replaced by more baking powder or bicarbonate of soda, which is not the case. The rise from the egg, where you can bind together large amounts of air or stabilize the cake so that it does not collapse after baking, is difficult to replace using baking powder or bicarbonate of soda. You cannot increase the amount of raising agent as it needs to be supported by something in the batter that will set while baking. If not, the rise will collapse and the cake will have be dense at the bottom. Sometimes you need to do the opposite, in other words reduce the amount of raising agent when making sponge cakes without eggs, where the egg is not there to keep the cake together. If you look at my basic sponge cakes (page 90), you will see that the more fat that is included in the recipe, the smaller amount of baking powder I use. It can also be useful to see the difference when developing your own recipes, or when using recipes where the author may not have understood that they were using too much. I often see this in older recipes, and those developed by amateurs who have baked a cake once and published their recipe straight away instead of experimenting with the quantities. I have also made a comparison between three sponge cakes where I show the results of using baking powder, a combination of both and only bicarbonate of soda. You can see that on the following pages.

It is important to combine plain flour and baking powder/bicarbonate of soda before mixing it into the wet ingredients. If you don't mix it thoroughly the texture in a sponge cake will be uneven and the distribution of bubbles and the rise in the cake will not be as good. To get the best result, you should mix the baking powder/bicarbonate of soda with the flour and sift it into the batter. Usually I don't bother with this, but you might have more patience than me!

BICARBONATE OF SODA

CAKE WITH FRUIT (BANANA)

Everything is the same in these three cakes apart from the quantity of bicarbonate of soda. This is so you can see how the amount of bicarbonate of soda affects the result. If you are developing your own recipes, you will now be able to adjust them more effectively.

HALF THE AMOUNT OF BICARBONATE OF SODA

½ tsp of bicarbonate of soda in a batter containing 180g of plain flour. It is moister and more dense than when using more bicarbonate of soda. It tastes good and melts in the mouth but has not fully risen and does not taste as good as the cake with 1 tsp bicarbonate of soda.

CORRECT AMOUNT OF BICARBONATE OF SODA

1 tsp of bicarbonate of soda per 180g plain flour. This cake could be improved by replacing half of the bicarbonate of soda with baking powder or by adding ½ tsp of baking powder.

DOUBLE THE AMOUNT OF BICARBONATE OF SODA

2 tsp of bicarbonate of soda for 180g of plain flour. The cake has a strong metallic taste and the sides and base are dark in colour.

BAKING POWDER OR BICARBONATE OF SODA?

CAKE WITH COCOA

JUST BAKING POWDER
1½ tsp of baking powder per 180g of plain flour. The texture is more compact and dry and has less flavour.

THE SAME AMOUNT OF BAKING POWDER AND BICARBONATE OF SODA
¾ tsp of each per 180g of plain flour.

DIFFERENT RAISING AGENTS
In this series of three different cakes, chocolate, light-coloured cake and fruit cake, everything is the same for each type of cake except that different raising agents have been used. This is so you can see how the raising agent affects the result. If you are developing your own recipes, you will be able to choose the right combination of raising agent more easily.

JUST BICARBONATE OF SODA
1½ tsp per 180g of plain flour. Just using bicarbonate of soda gives a different, stronger taste of chocolate. The cake is more moist, spongy with slightly less rise, but has a more even surface.

In sponge cakes containing cocoa, I think that using just bicarbonate of soda or a combination is best. The cake will have a darker colour and have a stronger chocolate flavour. In light-coloured cakes, I just use baking powder, and in fruit cakes I use a combination of both!

LIGHT-COLOURED CAKE

A nice flavour and light colour. This had the best rise out of all the light-coloured cakes and an even surface.

CAKE WITH FRUIT (BANANA)

Just baking powder gives a milder banana flavour.

JUST BAKING POWDER.
1½ tsp per 180g of plain flour.

THE SAME QUANTITY
¾ tsp of baking powder and bicarbonate of soda per 180g of plain flour.

A combination of both give you a flatter cake with a yellow colour.

JUST BICARBONATE OF SODA.
1½ tsp per 180g of plain flour.

Adding bicarbonate of soda to light-coloured cakes with no added flavour will give an unpleasant aftertaste and the sponge will take on a yellow colour. This was seen previously in the cake with half the amount of baking powder and half the amount of bicarbonate of soda.

This cake, just using bicarbonate of soda, is slightly flatter than using both raising agents. The cake has a darker colour at the bottom.

In gingerbread, carrot cake and banana bread the bicarbonate of soda is important to give the cakes the traditional flavour.

INGREDIENTS

Arrowroot

Arrowroot is a starch that can be found among the spices in most grocery shops. It can be used in some pie fillings. For custards, ice cream and frosting I use cornstarch or potato starch rather than arrowroot. Arrowroot can be replaced with most of the other starches.

Citrus fruit

Citrus fruit used in baking should be organic as you often use the peel. If you want to use citrus peel in your recipes, it is also important that you only use the outermost coloured layer as the white pith underneath can add a bitter taste. The brand Microplane sells a zester that is good for removing just the outermost citrus peel (shown in the picture opposite).

Jelly

Today there is a large selection of plant-based gelling agents that can be used to replace gelatine. The most common algae jellies are agar and carrageenan, which are produced from red algae. Carrageenan is the gelling agent in Vegegel, gelling sugar and Vegeset. Carrageenan gives a slightly softer jelly than agar and looks more like gelatine. Today you can buy different gelling agents depending on how firm you want your jelly to be; you can find these in speciality baking stores online. Read more on pages 16 and 430.

Almond paste

This contains a higher proportion of almonds than marzipan, but recent changes have meant that many producers have decreased the amount of almonds in their paste to a point where it is no longer possible to bake it in the oven. Previously, you could use any type of almond paste to make amaretti and biskvi, but now most pastes contain just 50 per cent almonds, which means it melts in the oven. I have given different recipes using almond paste, almonds or almond flour, so you can make them even if you cannot find almond paste with the right proportion of almonds.

Tapioca starch

This can be found in speciality shops or Asian grocery stores. It works like starch even though it is sometimes called flour. Tapioca starch is preferable to use in pies. Read more on page 387.

Tonka beans

These have a special flavour, a combination of bitter almonds, almonds, rum and vanilla and can be found in larger grocery shops or online. Grate into a sponge cake or use to flavour vanilla pastry cream for vanilla buns or biskvis, see page 424.

Xanthan gum

This is a thickening agent that can replace gluten but not eggs. In this book, I use it in coconut macaroons and Swedish pancakes. Mix carefully into the dry ingredients. See more on pages 52–53.

Vanilla

You can find vanilla in many different forms and all of them can be used when a recipe asks for vanilla. I usually use a pinch of vanilla powder, which is made from pure vanilla seeds. It has a strong but pleasant flavour, and the vanilla seeds add a nice look to your bakes. I have given measurements for vanilla extract throughout as it is more widely available, but it should be mixed with the other liquids in the recipe. Vanilla sugar and vanillin sugar both give a lovely, classic vanilla flavour to sponge cakes and pastries. Vanilla sugar is added with the dry ingredients.

1 tsp vanilla sugar = $\frac{1}{2}$–1 tsp vanilla extract
1 tsp vanilla sugar = $\frac{1}{2}$–1 tsp vanilla bean paste
1 tsp vanilla sugar = $\frac{1}{8}$ tsp pure vanilla powder
1 tsp vanilla sugar = 1–2 tsp vanillin sugar

Cream of tartar

Cream of tartar is used in meringues and frosting, even when using eggs, and is found in the baking section of grocery shops. Cream of tartar can be replaced with lemon juice or vinegar. It can also be used to activate bicarbonate of soda.

When grating the zest from citrus fruits, you only want the outermost layer. If you hold the grater in the position seen here, it is easier to control how deep into the skin of the fruit you go.

GLUTEN FREE

People with coeliac disease or allergies have been limited to products that don't contain wholegrains based on starch, but today there is a large selection of naturally gluten-free wholegrain products that are full of vitamins, fibre and minerals, which give a completely different result in cakes. If you want ready-mixed flour mixes in your pantry for making your old favourite recipes or new bakes, I created a list of my favourite mixes for different purposes and flavours for a big book I wrote about baking naturally gluten-free in 2014. These flour mixes are similar to the amounts of starch and protein in plain flour. Mix and store in jars with tight-fitting lids. You can always double or even triple the recipes if you want to mix bigger amounts when you have found your favourite mix.

If you want to replace plain flour in a recipe, you should make sure you use a little less of the flour mix than the quantity of plain flour. Around 60g less per 300g of plain flour, depending on the bake. The amount of time in the oven should be increased by 10–15 minutes for cookies and 15–25 minutes for sponge cakes, depending on their size, when replacing plain flour with gluten-free flour mixes. Always test bake and use a skewer. Some recipes in this book are gluten free and you can find a list on page 447.

Psyllium seed husk, linseeds, sugar beet fibre and potato fibre contain large amounts of plant-based fibre that can take up several times more than its own weight in water. This liquid is then retained in the bakes. Gluten can also retain some liquid, but not to the same extent as these plant-based fibres. These are common in gluten-free cakes and you can see the result on page 21. I do not recommend or use these in vegan cakes and I avoid them when developing gluten-free recipes as the result is not good enough. My favourite gluten replacement is xanthan gum, which you can find in the larger grocery shops or online. However, it cannot replace the egg. Xanthan gum is a natural secondary product from a bacteria that ferments vegetable material, mainly sugars, from corn, soya or wheat, for instance.

The elasticity of xanthan gum is hard to find in other gluten replacements but it can be replaced with guar gum. If you are allergic to the growth medium (wheat, soy or corn) I recommend xanthan gum, which gives the origin of fermentation. Contact the manufacturer if you are uncertain. For flour mixes with no binding agent to which you want to add your own xanthan gum, add $1/4$ teaspoon of xanthan gum per 180g of gluten-free flour mix. Bear in mind that xanthan gum cannot be added to a liquid or a dough, only to a dry mixture.

The crossed grain symbol means that a product does not contain more than 20ppm (parts per million) of gluten, which qualifies the product as gluten free. If a product contains 21–100ppm, it can be labelled as containing a very low quantity of gluten. Gluten-free flour mixes and products can contain wheat starch despite being gluten free. If you or someone you are baking for are allergic to wheat, which also includes wheat starch, it is important to find products produced in premises that do not handle wheat. According to labelling rules, ingredients such as eggs, milk, nuts, soya, gluten, wheat and other common allergens should always be labelled and can never be abbreviated. Traces of allergens that may have contaminated a product should also be labelled. For serious allergies, choose the safe option using products with guarantees that they contain no allergens. Always read the list of ingredients as this may change over time. On the Food Standards Agency website, www.food.gov. uk, there is information on labelling, intolerance and allergy. Contact the Food Standards Agency if you are unsure of labelling or standards producers have to follow.

Today, the flours and starches in my flour mixes can be found in larger grocery shops, and in Asian grocery stores you can find rice flour and sticky rice flour. You can also order them online. Make sure you buy products that are free from allergens and be careful not to contaminate any allergy friendly bakes while making them. Read more about contamination on page 56.

FLOUR MIXES

RICE FLOUR MIX

360g	wholegrain rice flour
360g	white rice flour
300g	glutinous rice flour
275g	tapioca starch or arrowroot
2 tsp	xanthan gum

This light-coloured flour mix is especially good for hard cookies, but also for sponge cakes and muffins. For dark-coloured cakes you can replace some of the wholegrain rice flour with a little teff (a traditional Ethiopian grain) to give even better wholegrain characteristics. Note that teff absorbs slightly more liquid than other flours. Mix the ingredients carefully in a bowl, put in a jar with a tight-fitting lid and keep in a cool place away from sunlight. The mixture will keep fresh for at least three months.

LIGHT-COLOURED MIX

360g	wholegrain rice flour
360g	white rice flour
240g	potato starch
240g	tapioca starch
1½ tsp	xanthan gum

A good basic flour mix that usually works for everything. However, if you are making hard cookies you should use the rice flour mix above. The wholegrain rice flour can be replaced with corn flour or jowar (white millet) flour. Mix the ingredients carefully in a bowl, put in a jar with a tight-fitting lid and keep in a cool place away from sunlight. The mixture will keep fresh for at least three months.

SORGHUM FLOUR MIX

480g	sorghum flour
640g	potato starch
400g	tapioca starch
1½ tsp	xanthan gum

This sorghum flour mix works well in rougher bakes but also gives a lift and other characteristics to most cakes. Mix the ingredients carefully in a bowl, put in a jar with a tight-fitting lid and keep in a cool place away from sunlight. The mixture will keep fresh for at least three months.

WHOLEGRAIN FLOUR

240g	wholegrain rice flour
120g	teff/sorghum flour
120g	millet/quinoa flour
240g	tapioca starch
55g	cornstarch
1 tsp	xanthan gum

The whole grain flour mix is good for chocolate bakes or rustic cookies. Teff flour absorbs quite a lot of liquid which makes it important to reduce the amount of gluten free flour mixture or add some water. Mix the ingredients carefully in a bowl, put in a jar with a tight-fitting lid and keep in a cool place away from sunlight. The mixture will keep fresh for at least three months.

NOTE

These flour mixes are not adjusted for raised gluten free doughs where you will need to rethink them to get the best result, but they work for pastry cases, cookies and sponge cakes.

Mix xanthan gum with the dry ingredients; you cannot add it after the liquid has been added.

Xanthan gum is rich in fibre, which means you should not eat large amounts of it. The recommended maximum daily intake is around 1 tablespoon (15ml).

VOLUME GUIDE FOR XANTHAN GUM

For light, sponge cakes and some cookies: ¼ tsp per 180g of flour mix.
For moist, sponge cakes and cookies: ½ tsp per 180g of flour mix.
For raised doughs: 1 tsp per 180g of flour mix.

COLOUR

There are many different edible colourings you can use for baking. You can colour batters, frostings, sugar pastes, chocolate, marzipan or paint designs on layer cakes. Red and pink are the colours that may be made from animal products as E120 is derived from crushed insects. However, E120 is prohibited in many countries, so there are many alternatives. Grocery shops used to only sell liquid food colouring, but coloured paste is now more common, and in speciality stores you can find colouring powder, metallic powder, spray colour and colouring pens.

I usually use colouring powder, which is added in very small amounts. To colour white chocolate that is not used in a chocolate buttercream, but in a ganache or a thin glaze, you need to use chocolate colouring.

To colour sugar paste or marzipan, you need to knead it carefully to spread the colour evenly. If you want to colour it completely you may want to colour it the day before, as the colour will even out more when stored overnight. I recommend wearing gloves if you want to avoid stained fingers. To colour frosting, you need to consider that powder colours or edible dust that are water-soluble may be difficult to dissolve in a frosting that contains fat. In this case, it is easier to dissolve the colour in some water or alcohol before adding it to the frosting. Colouring paste should always be handled with a clean tool, for instance a cocktail stick. This way you avoid introducing bacteria into the container. You can also colour frosting or glaze with grated beetroot or pressed blueberry juice. However, be careful with the amount of beetroot juice to avoid tainting the flavour: a little will go a long way. Beetroot coloured frosting is shown on page 199.

Icing can be coloured using colouring powder and water-soluble colours, but as aquafaba cannot bind together with fat you should not use oil-based colours in icing. This goes for meringues and macarons too. To colour meringues, put a piping bag in a large glass and paint lines with colour dissolved in water on the inside of the bag and then fill it with the meringue batter and pipe it onto the baking tray.

You can use layer cakes with sugar paste or sugar cookies with icing as a base for painting with colours, painting brushes or special colouring pens, which you can find in stores. You can also make your own watercolour or oil colour from most colours; see the instructions below. You can create patterns for layer cakes in many different ways. You can make mirrored decorations and stencils from the icing on page 324 and press it onto the sugar paste when fully set. If you need guidelines to draw from you can copy a pattern from a picture carefully onto the sugar paste, for instance by using the end of a brush. You can also use a needle to create holes to paint over on the surface of the cake.

Watercolour
Water-soluble colour + water or alcohol
Most colours are easily dissolved in water, but not all dusting powders. You can mix these with water or alcohol. Alcohol evaporates more quickly and you will get a cake where the colour is not sticky, so if you can use alcohol it usually gives a better result. There are also powders to make the colouring paste easier to paint, which is called Edible Paint Maker in speciality stores. See how I painted onto the sugar cookies with icing on page 318.

Oil-based colour
Fat-soluble colour + coconut fat, oil or shortening
Try and see which of your colours you can use for oil-based colours, as not all of them dissolve in fat. Chocolate colouring that dissolves in oil is recommended if you want to create oil-based colours. Many powder colours, known as dusting powders or lustre dust, will dissolve in fat. Oil-based colour is used, for instance, on layer cakes covered in frosting. You can also colour frosting in different colours and apply them using a spatula, for example, on a cake covered with a crumb layer of frosting.

The layer cakes in the picture are three small cakes made in 10cm tins. The smaller of the two carrot cakes on page 206 was baked in four different tins. They were each then cut into two making a total of four small cakes. They were filled and topped with coconut frosting and covered with sugar paste from Renshaw, which is vegan, delicious and smooth to work with. They were painted with colouring powder dissolved in alcohol. See also pages 190 and 318.

The meringue (opposite) was coloured using a blue water-soluble pigment. The yellow biskvi was dipped in white chocolate with yellow chocolate colouring. The pink cake pop was dipped in white chocolate coloured with pink chocolate colouring.

BEFORE YOU START

Preheat the oven, prepare the tin and weigh out all the ingredients before mixing the batter. This important step is called *mise en place*, which means 'everything in place' in French.

Be careful with the flour!

• The thing that most often goes wrong when baking is that we all measure plain flour differently. It is easy to weigh out a larger amount of plain flour than you are supposed to. Always measure quantities as carefully as you can.
• Always test bake cookies to make sure you get the best result. That way you will know if you need to add more liquid or plain flour.
• In wheat doughs, add about 60g at a time until the dough is smooth, then add about 30g at a time.
• In sponge cakes and cookies, don't overwork the batter after adding the flour.
• Always mix the dry ingredients in a bowl. When baking powder or bicarbonate of soda is not mixed carefully into the batter, the cake is more likely to crack on the outside.

Preparation

Before you begin, prepare everything you are going to use and make sure it is all close by. Read the recipe and all the instructions before mixing the ingredients. Preheat the oven to the right temperature in advance. Prepare the tin or tins that you want to use. Mix the dry ingredients and make sure everything is carefully combined. In recipes with hot liquids or vinegar, the batter should be put in the oven as soon as the liquid has been added. This is when the ingredients produce the chemical reaction that makes carbon dioxide, and if the cake is not put in the oven quickly, the air will not remain in the batter. This is why it is good to prepare the tin or tins in advance.

Contamination

If you are baking for someone with allergies, it is important to establish routines to reduce the risk of contamination with anything that might cause a reaction. If you usually bake without having to worry about allergens, there is a list of the most important things to think about when baking for someone with an allergy or intolerance. According to present labelling rules, ingredients such as eggs, milk, nuts, soya, gluten, wheat and other common allergens must be stated on the packaging, and they are not allowed to be abbreviated or written as E numbers. Common animal products and allergens in baking ingredients are, for example, milk, butterfat, lactose (milk sugar), skimmed milk powder and egg whites, which should always be included in the list. Traces of allergens that may have contaminated the product should also be labelled. Read the ingredients list carefully as contents can change over time. Products such as syrup, caster sugar, icing sugar, cocoa, baking powder, bicarbonate of soda and spices are usually gluten free and allergy friendly. It is important to check whether a product may contain traces of an allergen, which means that the product might have been contaminated during the production process. For serious allergies, choose the safe option and use products with clear labelling.

It is important to learn how to find the right products and to not contaminate the batter while baking with tools and bowls that have not been carefully washed. If you are baking for someone you don't know well and are unsure, double check about the products and production process as contamination can be dangerous: even traces of an allergen can be dangerous for someone with coeliac disease or severe allergies. The Food Standards Agency website, www.food.gov.uk, has information about labelling, intolerance and allergies. Only use clean utensils and wash for longer than usual. Try not to use utensils made of porous material that can store allergens. Glass and metal are the best materials to use; wood is the worst. Use clean plates and knives for cutting cakes. Remember never to serve allergy friendly cakes on the same plate as the ones with ingredients that need to be avoided; use paper plates or cake bases just in case. Always label a cake's ingredients, as not everyone may know that a vegan cake might contain chickpeas or soya beans, for instance.

Melting chocolate

It is easy to melt pieces of chocolate using a water bath: a bowl placed on top of a saucepan of simmering water on the hob, or over a bowl of boiling hot water. I usually use a metal colander directly over the saucepan to prevent the bowl of chocolate from touching the water so that it doesn't get hot too quickly. Don't get any water in the chocolate when melting it as that will ruin it. You can also melt the chocolate in a china or glass bowl in the microwave. Put the pieces of chocolate in the microwave for short intervals – 10–30 seconds – and mix between each interval until the chocolate is melted. Chocolate can burn and spoil easily, so keep a close eye on it.

White chocolate should not be heated over 44°C /111°F and you need to be extra careful to not place the bowl in a water bath that is too hot. The bowl of chocolate should not touch the hot water when working with white chocolate. If white chocolate turns grainy, strain through a sieve. If you are using white chocolate, you might want to freeze the bakes before dipping them in the chocolate to get the layer thick enough. This can be useful when making punsch rolls, cake pops or biskvis for example. If the chocolate is too thin you can dip it a number of times.

Test bake

Biscuits, cookies and other smaller bakes should be test baked before putting the whole tray in the oven. Then you can correct the batter or dough by adding more plain flour or more liquid to the rest of the dough if you realize something is wrong. If you are baking for an important occasion, I think you should do one test bake before the big day, but perhaps not at full size if you are making a large layer cake. Then you will know how it behaves in your oven. If you can, prepare the bake the day before the event so that you have everything ready and any potential problems can be addressed.

> **BAKING**
> Bake in the centre of the oven; it is usually cooler by the door. A skewer should go in and out of the cake with no resistance – not just come out clean. Test the edge first to see how the centre of the cake should feel when cooked.

Baking and the oven

The recipes in the book are prepared and test-baked in a fairly cool fan oven and the temperature stated should be increased by around 10 percent, or alternatively increase the baking time a few minutes if you bake in a conventional oven. Because of the differences in temperatures between ovens, the timings given here are only a guide.

It is also important to make sure that the cake is properly cooked before taking it out of the oven. The skewer should not only come out clean from sponge cakes, but should also pass through the cake with no resistance. Test the edge before the centre – that way you will know what the centre of the cake should feel like. Always use a timer or set an alarm on your mobile phone when putting the cake in the oven. Place the tin in the centre of the oven where there is no draught from the door. Only open the door if necessary and close it properly if you do. Oven cooking times vary between kitchens so it is important that you check the cake yourself and not simply follow the timings in the recipe. Handle newly baked cakes carefully and put them on a wire rack to cool.

Vinegar and heat

The recipes in this book sometimes contain vinegar, which means it is even more important to put the cake in the oven quickly. The acid in the vinegar reacts with the baking powder and bicarbonate of soda, and the air bubbles that help the cake to rise will evaporate out of the batter if you take too long. That is why you should preheat the oven and prepare all your tins before mixing the batter. Use a mild vinegar, such as apple cider, white wine or rice vinegar. Vinegar can be replaced with lemon juice or yoghurt, sparkling water, citric acid or cream of tartar. Cocoa will also react with bicarbonate of soda. You can use whatever milk you like, or even water in recipes with vinegar. It is not usually the thickened milk we are after, it is the large quantity of acidic liquid. Boiling water will also have the same effect and you need to put the cake in the oven quickly. Vinegar affects the colour of nuts when used in baking, so I use yoghurt to stop them taking on a blue or purple tint.

WHY IS THE CAKE ...

DRY?

Too much plain flour is usually the reason you get a dry cake when following a recipe. Measure carefully using the guides on your measuring cups or spoons or use a kitchen scale. The cake might also be dry if it has been baked for too long. Start with the lowest amount of time given for the recipe, but be vigilant – your oven might be warmer than the ovens I have developed the recipes in. My instructions are guiding principles, your cooking times may need to be shorter or longer. If you have developed your own recipe and your cake is dry, you may not have used enough liquid, enough oil or enough sugar. Read more about these factors on pages 34–43.

THIN?

The tin is too big, you have used too much plain flour or not enough sugar; read more on pages 38 and 40. The batter could also be over-worked. If you accidentally whip the aquafaba too much and it reaches 'ribbon stage' in recipes where the sugar and the aquafaba should be frothy, the cake may collapse and be thinner than expected. If you do whip the aquafaba too much, you can fold in the plain flour carefully as described on page 32, before adding the liquid and the fat.

SUNKEN IN THE MIDDLE?

Too much sugar causes a cake to sink in the middle as large bubbles form in the middle of the cake. Sponge cakes should contain about the same weight of sugar and flour. Too much baking powder also causes a cake to collapse in the middle; if you are using too much baking powder, try to reduce the amount. Around 1 teaspoon of baking powder per 100g of plain flour is enough. In cakes that contain a lot of fat and chocolate, the cake should be a little lower in the middle. If you accidentally whip the aquafaba to 'ribbon stage' in recipes where the sugar and the aquafaba should be frothy, the cake usually collapses and becomes dense. If you accidentally whip the aquafaba too much, you can fold in the plain flour carefully as described on page 32, before adding the liquid and the fat.

RISEN TOO MUCH IN THE MIDDLE?

Not enough sugar – increase the amount slightly. Sponge cakes should contain about the same weight of sugar and flour; see the pictures on page 43. If you have a look at my recipes, you can see approximately how much sugar you need relative to plain flour in different cakes. The original recipe you are veganizing should also have the same correlation between sugar and plain flour. In brownies, there should be more sugar than plain flour. Too much liquid or not enough oil will also produce cakes with pointed tops. See the pictures on pages 35 and 37.

BURNED ON THE TOP?

Your oven might be slightly warmer than it says on the dial. Use an oven thermometer to check the temperature or use a slightly lower temperature than given in my recipes.

NOT BAKED?

Your oven might not be hot enough or you might have taken the cake out of the oven before it was ready. Use a cake skewer to check that it is cooked in the middle. The skewer should not only come out clean but should also go through the cake with no resistance – it should go through the cake easily. Test the edges first where it will be ready before the middle. You can also get a sense of what it should feel like. To make sure that you don't get the timings wrong, always use a timer or set an alarm on your mobile phone when putting the cake in the oven.

OVERFLOWING THE TIN?

The most important thing is not to fill the tin too much, around $^2/_3$ is usually enough. Never fill it more than ¾ to stop the cake overflowing and getting ruined.

FRACTIONS!
HERE IS AN ILLUSTRATION OF SOME OF THE FRACTIONS THAT ARE MOST COMMON IN BAKING.
PEOPLE USUALLY SAY THAT YOU SHOULD FILL THE TIN TO AROUND ²/₃ OR ¾. HERE, YOU CAN SEE THAT aTHIS IS A LITTLE MORE THAN HALF. DO NOT FILL IT TOO MUCH, BECAUSE THE BATTER WILL OVERFLOW THE SIDES OF THE TIN.

One third
1 divided by 3
1/3

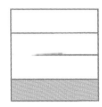

One quarter
1 divided by 4
¼

A whole
1 divided by 1
1

One half
1 divided by 2
½

Two thirds
2 divided by 3
²/₃

Three quarters
3 divided by 4
¾

MEASUREMENTS

TEST BAKING

Biscuits and cakes should be test baked before putting the whole tray in the oven. That way you can adjust the ingredients by adding more flour or more liquid if you realize something is not quite right.

¼ TSP = 1.25ML
½ TSP = 2.5ML
1 TSP = 5ML
3 TSP = 1 TBSP
1 TBSP = 15ML
3 TBSP = 45ML

CARROT
Peeled carrots have a better flavour for baking.

EGG VOLUME

One egg usually equals 50ml of liquid in a recipe. One egg yolk usually equals 1 tablespoon of liquid.

ONE BANANA?
Most of the recipes in the book do not use a particular number of bananas, but the weight of mashed banana. This is because the quantity of mashed banana from a single banana varies.

YEAST
The yeast that is usually found in shops is also called instant dry yeast. The guidelines for replacing fresh yeast with instant dry yeast is to use ¼ of the weight (and vice versa). Another type of dry yeast is active dry yeast that needs to be activated in warm water before it will work. If you replace fresh yeast with active dry yeast, you want around ½ of the weight of the dry yeast to the fresh (and vice versa).

LEMON
One medium-sized lemon contains about 50ml lemon juice. Remember to use organic, unwaxed lemons for zesting.

TINS 1

All recipes for sponge cakes are baked in metal tins. The surfaces of silicone tins do not heat up in the oven and the cakes do not rise well enough. For cheesecakes and mousse cakes, you should use a springform tin. By the recipes, I have included information about the size of tin I recommend.

Sponge cakes

The tins that I think give the best results for sponge cakes are smaller aluminium tins, preferably with a large hole in the middle so the batter is baked quickly. The thinnest of these tins are in the shape of a wreath (D), but smaller sponge cake tins of around 1 litre, with a little hole in the middle are perfect as well. One of these is shown on page 28, together with instructions for making light sponge cakes. Many of the recipes for sponge cake recipes include quantities for different sizes – one for smaller tins and one for larger tins: 180g of plain flour suits a tin of 1.2–1.5 litres; recipes with 240–300g of plain flour suit larger tins of around 2 litres. Older tins sometimes have the volume written on the outside, but if you do not know how big your tin is, you can fill it with water and measure how much it holds to find out the volume.

Among the smaller tins, there are small sponge cake tins and wreath-shaped tins with a hole in the middle. Cakes cooked in these will bake more quickly than in classic sponge cake tins.

Layer cakes

In the UK and North America, layer cakes are usually baked in several tins, one for each layer of the cake, and when you bake without eggs this is recommended. If you are making tall cakes, the result is often better if you divide the batter between several tins, and depending on how many and how large your tins are, there will be different timings and quantities for some recipes where the result is affected by which tins you use. For classic layer cakes, the Swedish cream cake and marzipan cake, you do not need several tins as they can be cut into three thin slices. The size that gives the best result for the Swedish cream cake and marzipan cake is a 15–18cm tin. It is a common size in second-hand shops as this was a standard size in the past. Tins of 24–25cm are not as good for layer cakes as you need a lot of batter to be able to slice them into layers and such a big cake will give you a lot of pieces. A 15cm cake is enough for 6–8 pieces for a cream cake, and an 18–20cm cake is enough for 8–12 pieces, depending on the occasion. If you make small layer cakes of 10cm, a batter using 60–70g of caster sugar is enough for one tin and you can adjust the recipe to the number of tins yourself. They are baked for about 25–35 minutes, depending on the amount of batter. Test with a skewer until it is properly cooked.

A = 1.5 litres, loaf tin
B = 1 litre, loaf tin
C = 1.2 litres, sponge cake tin
D = 1.2 litres, wreath-shaped tin
E = 1 liter, sponge cake tin
F = 1.5 litres, sponge cake tin
G = 2.5 litres, sponge cake tin
H = 18 cm round cake tin

Round tins are measured by diameter, e.g. 18–20cm
Several round tins are measured by diameter, e.g. 2 tins of 15cm
Rectangular loaf tins are measured in litres, e.g. 2 litres
Square tins are measured by size, e.g. 20 × 20cm

TINS 2

Grease and add crumbs

All tins should be greased and coated with crumbs, even non-stick ones as the coating does not last for long. First, grease the tin carefully with a thin layer of cooking fat. Suitable crumbs include breadcrumbs, semolina, polenta or coconut. Semolina is my favourite: the grains are small, have a nice colour and flavour when baked, and they do not stain the frosting, if using. Breadcrumbs give a golden colour but grains in the bread leave spots when the cake is covered with frosting.

If a cake gets stuck in the tin, you can put a wet towel underneath and after a few minutes you can usually turn it over and the cake will come out of the tin. The differences between plain flour, semolina and breadcrumbs is shown on pages 29, 31 and 33.

Breadcrumbs give a golden crust; semolina gives a beautiful crust but is somewhat lighter in colour and has better taste. Plain flour gives a fine, dark surface and works well for cakes with aquafaba. Breadcrumbs don't suit chocolate cakes as they give the surfaces a golden colour that looks wrong. Semolina works better for chocolate cakes.

Egg-free cakes should not be baked just using fat or fat and cocoa on the surface of the tin: the outside of the cake does not firm up as quickly without the eggs and the cake will not come cleanly out of the tin. Sponge cakes made with frothy aquafaba or baked using reverse creaming can only be greased with added plain flour, just greasing the tin doesn't generally work well. If you use paper on the sides this can keep them dark, which is good for chocolate cakes.

FOLDING A CIRCLE

Instead of greasing and applying breadcrumbs to the tins, to avoid washing up and achieve a round cake with beautiful creases around the sides, it is easy to fold baking paper to fit a round tin (shown opposite).

1. Fold the paper in half.

2. Fold the paper in half again.

3. Fold the paper in half again.

4–5. Fold the paper into a triangle and repeat.

6. Cut a slightly rounded edge on the triangle.

7. Unfold the paper and place in the centre of the tin.

8. Press down in the tin. The finished cake will have a beautiful rustic appearance and you will have less washing up!

CRUMPLED BAKING PAPER

If you take a piece of baking paper and crumple it into a ball, this gives a malleable piece of paper that will work in square, round and rectangular tins (9).

STAPLED SQUARES

In square tins, you can press in the baking paper without stapling or folding. If you do not have a suitable tin and want to make square cakes or traybakes, you can make simple tins out of baking paper by folding the edges to the right size and stapling the corners together. (A) Fold the edges in to the right size. (B) Pull the edges together and staple each corner. (C) Put the 'tin' on a baking tray before filling it with batter. For rectangular loaf tins, the cut paper method on page 64 works best (4).

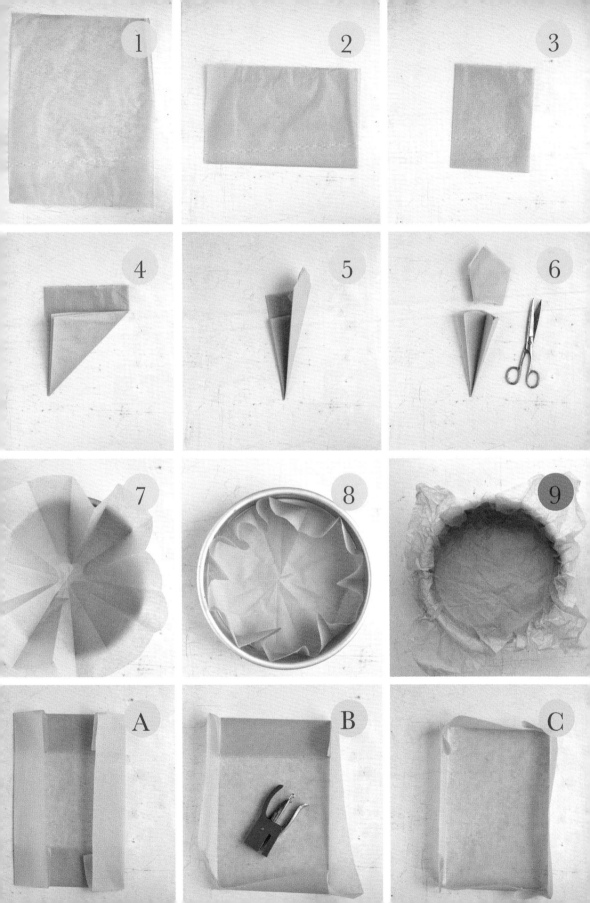

TINS 3

MUFFINS

The most effective way to bake muffins in the best shape is to use paper cases placed in a muffin tray. Muffin cases in a muffin tray (1). Paper cases placed on baking tray without a muffin tray (2) produce a flatter muffin shape. Sprinkle some uncooked rice at the bottom of each hole in the muffin tray before putting in the paper cases to stop moisture forming underneath the muffins while baking. The best way to avoid this is to take the muffins out of the tray as soon as possible and let them cool on a wire rack. If you are making muffins without a muffin tray, you should put less batter in each case to avoid the risk of the batter overflowing the edges. You can also make muffins in greased or greased and floured muffin trays. There are also mini muffin trays and mini muffin cases. One batch of batter is enough for more than 30 mini muffins, or you can halve the amount of ingredients if you are making fewer mini muffins or have a smaller baking tray. The simple muffin batter gives around 24 mini muffins, so if you have a tray with 24 holes you can use that amount of batter. Muffins should be baked for 10–15 minutes at 175°C/350°C/gas 4.

CUT PAPER FOR CAKE LAYERS

To cover the base of a layer cake with baking paper and avoid creases, cut the pieces for the bottom and the sides separately. When you cut out the bottom, add 2–3cm around the whole circle, then make cuts a few centimetres apart in from the edges. This way the paper forms a border around the sides when the baking paper is pushed down to the bottom of the tin. Then grease the tin with a thin layer of fat or water and press the paper around the sides. Paper-covered sides are good for cakes where you want the sides of the cake to remain dark, such as chocolate cakes. This is shown on page 215 where I fill a cake with mousse.

CUT PAPER FOR SQUARE TINS (3)

For square and rectangular tins, you can cut two pieces of baking paper that cover the bottom and the sides. This method also works for rectangular loaf tins (4).

GREASED AND SUGARED TINS (5)

Soufflés are traditionally baked in sugared tins and to get an even layer, first grease the sides with margarine that is very soft. Melted margarine or oil does not work very well as these do not stick to the sides evenly and do not give an even layer of sugar. In addition, when using melted fat, it is not as easy to see areas you may have missed.

MADELEINES (6)

Madeleines are baked in metal tins with shell-shaped holes. These are brushed with melted margarine, each shell is coated with plain flour and then turned upside-down to tip the excess flour out.

MINI
MUFFINS

You can also find muffin trays and cases for mini muffins. One batch of batter is usually enough for more than 30 mini muffins, which means that you can halve the amounts of all the ingredients when making mini muffins if you have a smaller mini muffin tray. The simple muffin batter gives around 24 mini muffins, which means that if you have a tray with 24 holes you can use all of the batter, or batters of the same quantity. Muffins should be baked for 10–15 minutes at 175°C/350°F/gas 4.

Muffins & other bakes

Preheat the oven in advance and prepare the muffin tray or cake tin and the ingredients before mixing the batter together. This important step is called *mise en place*, which means 'everything in place' in French.

Create your own system when adding your ingredients: make sure you add the right quantities. Focus and don't let your mind wander.

Never use flour rich in gluten (strong flour) when baking sponge cakes and muffins, since extra added gluten or flour rich in gluten will make the sponge/muffins dense. This flour should only be used in raised doughs.

Always use ingredients at room temperature. Cold ingredients can make the margarine hard and make the batter very firm.

Always add a pinch of salt to your cake and muffin batter!

Do not mix for too long; mix the ingredients together quickly if there are no other instructions. Always swipe the spatula around the bottom of the bowl when mixing the batter to make sure that all the dry ingredients have been incorporated into the batter before transferring it to the muffin tray or cake tin and baking it.

Recipes that include vinegar need to be put into the oven quickly so it does not lose its rise before baking.

Put a few grains of uncooked rice at the bottom of each hole in the muffin tray before you add the paper cases if you do not want them to be damp underneath.

To give muffins the best shape possible, use paper cases placed in a muffin tray. See page 65.

Always use a timer set for the lowest time given. Add a few minutes if the cake or muffins are not ready. Keep on testing the cake or muffins carefully using a skewer, with a few minutes in between, until ready.

SIMPLE MUFFINS

Since I started work on my first book in 2010, I have tried to veganize traditional simple muffins countless times. However many times I tried I was never satisfied – until I developed this recipe in 2017. It contains simple ingredients, the baking time is as short as it is for traditional muffins and they are baked in just the same way. They are also easy to mix together. All in all, they are better than I could have ever hoped for!

150g	plain flour
135g	sugar
1½ tsp	baking powder
1 pinch	salt
½	lemon, zest of
50ml	oil
100ml	milk
1 tsp	vanilla extract
50ml	aquafaba

Preheat the oven to 175°C/350°F/gas 4. Put 8–9 muffin cases in a muffin tray. Add the flour, sugar, baking powder and salt into a bowl and mix well. Add some grated lemon zest if you like. Add the oil, milk, vanilla extract and aquafaba to the bowl and mix until smooth without overworking. Swipe the spatula around the sides of the bowl to incorporate any leftover flour. Put the batter into the muffin cases, fill to ⅔–¾. Bake in the centre of the oven at 175°C/350°F/gas 4 for 17–19 minutes. Test with a skewer, which should come out clean from the middle of the muffin. Remove the muffins from the muffin tray when slightly cooled and leave to cool completely on a wire rack.

DOMED OR FLAT?
The simple muffin and the cupcake recipes on page 71 are classic Swedish cakes, which have a cute, domed shape, as in the picture above left. If you want to make British or American cupcakes it is better to use a recipe that gives a flatter shape, such as the flat-topped cupcake above right (see recipe on page 70). Depending on the amount of flour used, the domed cakes can be made flatter, and the flatter cakes slightly more domed than in the picture. Therefore, be meticulous with the amount of flour you use.

69

TIP!
This recipe is good for adding around 55g of chopped fruit or berries of your choice.

These muffins are also perfect as a base for a princess or frog cake (see page 194). The muffin is sliced and filled, then it is covered with cream and marzipan. Cut the middle of the pastry and press carefully if you are making frog cake. You can make frog's eyes out of marzipan or royal icing that is piped for the eyes; see an example on page 324.

FLAT-TOPPED CUPCAKES

These muffins contain slightly more fat than the simple muffins on the previous page. The recipe is similar to my favourite muffin recipe from my childhood, only it has been veganized using aquafaba and slightly less liquid. Instructions for the batter for moist sponge cakes where you fold in the flour first can be found on page 30. The muffins will be quite flat, which is good for covering with frosting. See page 73.

100g	margarine
¼–½	lemon, zest of
180g	plain flour
2 tsp	baking powder
1 pinch	salt
180g	sugar
100ml	aquafaba
100ml	milk
1 tsp	vanilla extract

Preheat the oven to 200°C/400°F/gas 6. Put 9–10 muffin cases in a muffin tray. Melt the margarine and grate the lemon zest into the margarine. Mix the flour, baking powder and salt in a bowl. Whip together the sugar and aquafaba until frothy. Carefully fold the flour mixture into the aquafaba; when it is incorporated fold in the melted margarine in three batches. Then add the milk and vanilla. Pour the batter into the muffin cases, fill them to ⅔–¾ and bake for 10–15 minutes at 200°C/400°F/gas 6. Take them out of the oven when golden. Test with a skewer, which should come out clean from the middle of the cupcake. Remove the cupcakes from the muffin tray when slightly cooled and leave to cool completely on a wire rack.

VANILLA CUPCAKES

When comparing and looking for differences between recipes, you quickly learn that many recipes for traditional cakes are similar even if they come from different parts of the world. Of course, there can also be subtle differences, and here is one version that is similar to my childhood recipe above. They are often called 'the world's best vanilla cupcakes' when baked with two eggs. Here is my veganized version, which has a slightly flat surface that is well-suited to frosting.

100g	margarine
180g	plain flour
1½ tsp	baking powder
1 pinch	salt
180g	sugar
75ml	aquafaba
75ml	milk
1 tsp	vanilla sugar or vanilla extract

Preheat the oven to 175°C/350°F/gas 4. Put 9–10 muffin cases in a muffin tray. Melt the margarine and let it cool slightly. Mix the flour, baking powder and salt in a bowl. Whip together the sugar and aquafaba until frothy. Carefully fold the flour mixture into the aquafaba; when it is incorporated, fold in the melted margarine in three batches. Then add the milk and vanilla sugar or extract. Pour the batter into the muffin cases, fill to ⅔–¾. Bake for 15–20 minutes at 175°C/350°F/gas 4. Take them out of the oven when golden and a skewer comes out clean. Remove the cupcakes from the muffin tray when slightly cooled and leave to cool completely on a wire rack.

REVERSE CUPCAKES

Rubbing in or creaming the fat into the flour before adding the eggs and the liquid is an old method for making sponge cakes in many countries. The easiest way is to combine the ingredients using your hands, but this batter can also be made in a mixer. Here, you mix the flour and the fat together first and then add the rest of the dry ingredients. Lastly, you mix in the aquafaba and the milk. Instructions for the batter can be found on page 32. Both recipes below give quite domed cupcakes.

DOMED MUFFINS

180g	plain flour
I tsp	baking powder
75g	margarine
I pinch	salt
180g	sugar
75ml	aquafaba
100ml	milk
I tsp	vanilla sugar or vanilla extract

Preheat the oven to 200°C/400°F/gas 6. Put 9–10 muffin cases in a muffin tray. Put the flour and baking powder in the bowl for the stand mixer. Dice and add the margarine and mix until the margarine is the size of peas. Add the salt and sugar and mix for 1 more minute until the mixture resembles breadcrumbs. Mix in the aquafaba, milk and vanilla carefully to make the batter well combined. Pour the batter into the muffin cases, fill to ⅔–¾. Bake for 14–16 minutes at 200°C/400°F/gas 6. Take them out of the oven when golden and a skewer comes out clean. Remove the cupcakes from the muffin tray when slightly cooled and leave to cool completely on a wire rack.

120g	plain flour
I tsp	baking powder
I pinch	salt
135g	sugar
50g	margarine
50ml	aquafaba
100ml	milk
I tsp	vanilla sugar or vanilla extract

I have veganized these cupcakes from the Hummingbird Bakery's book. Their muffins have made them well-known all over the world. It is worth trying if you like cupcakes and are looking for a new favourite recipe. Read more about the reverse creaming method on page 32.

Preheat the oven to 175°C/350°F/gas 4. Put 6–8 muffin cases in a muffin tray. Put the flour, baking powder, salt and sugar in a bowl or the bowl for the stand mixer. Dice the margarine and rub it in carefully or mix with a whisk until the margarine is the size of peas. Carefully fold the aquafaba, milk and vanilla into the batter with a spatula, electric hand mixer or in a stand mixer until well-combined. Pour the batter into the muffin cases, fill to ⅔–¾. Bake for 20–25 minutes at 175°C/350°F/gas 4. Take them out of the oven when golden and a skewer comes out clean. Remove the cupcakes from the muffin tray when slightly cooled and leave to cool completely on a wire rack.

CHOCOLATE MUFFINS

Here are two types of muffins with an intense chocolate flavour that are easy to make. The dark muffins give a flatter surface, which can be good when decorating with frosting. It is based on the traditional vinegar recipes described on page 46. The differences in flavour, colour and shape between the recipes depend mostly on the raising agent that is used.

MILD CHOCOLATE MUFFINS

120g	plain flour
30g	cocoa
135g	sugar
1½ tsp	baking powder
1 pinch	salt
¼ tsp	vanilla extract
50ml	oil
150ml	milk
50ml	aquafaba

Preheat the oven to 175°C/350°F/gas 4. Put 8–9 muffin cases in a muffin tray. Put the flour, sifted cocoa, sugar, baking powder and salt in a bowl and mix. Add the vanilla extract, oil, milk and aquafaba and mix to a smooth batter without overworking. Swipe the spatula around the sides of the bowl to incorporate any leftover flour into the batter. Pour the batter into the muffin cases, fill to ⅔–¾. Bake in the centre of the oven at 175°C/350°F/gas 4 for 17–19 minutes. Take them out of the oven when golden and a skewer comes out clean. Remove the muffins from the muffin tray when slightly cooled and leave to cool completely on a wire rack.

DARK CHOCOLATE MUFFINS

180g	plain flour
180g	sugar
40g	cocoa
1 tsp	bicarbonate of soda
1 pinch	salt
¼ tsp	vanilla extract
200ml	water
50ml	aquafaba
100ml	oil
1 tsp	vinegar

Preheat the oven to 175°C/350°F/gas 4. Put 10–12 muffin cases in a muffin tray. Mix the flour, sugar, sifted cocoa, bicarbonate of soda and salt. Add the vanilla extract, water, aquafaba, oil and vinegar. Mix the batter with a spatula until smooth. Pour the batter into the muffin cases, fill to ¾. Bake in the centre of the oven at 175°C/350°F/gas 4 for 15–17 minutes. Take them out of the oven when golden and a skewer comes out clean. Remove the muffins from the muffin tray when slightly cooled and leave to cool completely on a wire rack.

WITHOUT AQUAFABA
You can replace aquafaba with 50ml of water if you are allergic to legumes. The aquafaba gives a firmer muffin that is not as crumbly.

NEW CHOCOLATE MUFFINS

When I heard that a major test kitchen in the USA (Cook's Illustrated) said that 1 teaspoon of espresso powder in chocolate recipes makes the chocolate flavour much richer, while at the same time I read in a book that adding coffee to chocolate batter makes it even more luxurious and the chocolate flavour more complex, I developed this recipe for chocolate muffins. I have developed many muffin recipes during my years of working to veganize recipes, but this one might be the best one of all. I think they taste like the proper luxury muffins that were sold at cafés when I was little.

180g	plain flour
40g	cocoa
180g	sugar
½ tsp	bicarbonate of soda
½ tsp	baking powder
¼ tsp	vanilla extract
1 tsp	espresso powder
1 pinch	salt
100ml	aquafaba
100ml	oil
100ml	cold brewed coffee
100g	chocolate buttons (optional)

Preheat the oven to 175°C/350°F/gas 4. Put 10–12 muffin cases in a muffin tray. Mix together the flour, sifted cocoa, sugar, bicarbonate of soda, baking powder, espresso powder and salt in a bowl. In a separate bowl, whisk the oil and the aquafaba together with a hand whisk. Stir into the dry mixture together with the vanilla extract and mix the batter until smooth using a spatula. Stir in the chocolate buttons, if using. Swipe the spatula around the sides of the bowl to incorporate any leftover flour into the batter. Pour the batter into the muffin cases, fill to ⅔ full. Decorate with more chocolate buttons, if you like. Bake in the centre of the oven at 175°C/350°F/gas 4 for 15–20 minutes. Take them out of the oven when a skewer comes out clean. Remove the muffins from the muffin tray once they have cooled slightly and leave to cool fully on a rack. Store in a sealed container to give the muffins a lovely soft surface.

BANANA MUFFINS

The perfect recipe for banana muffins took me forever to develop even though it looks very simple. I started working on it for my first book in 2010, and it wasn't until 2017 that I had developed the perfect recipe. The recipe including aquafaba was not perfected until 2018 and it is both mine and my daughter's favourite. The recipe including aquafaba makes muffins that are more golden in colour than the simple recipe, which is shown in the picture opposite (aquafaba at the front and a simple banana muffin behind).

SIMPLE BANANA MUFFINS

150g	banana, peeled
180g	plain flour
135g	sugar
1 tsp	baking powder
¼ tsp	bicarbonate of soda
1 pinch	salt
150ml	milk or water
75ml	oil
	sliced banana

Preheat the oven to 175°C/350°F/gas 4. Put 8–10 muffin cases in a muffin tray. Mash the banana and leave to stand while preparing the other ingredients. Mix the flour, sugar, baking powder, bicarbonate of soda and salt in a bowl. Add and mix in the mashed banana, milk or water and oil. Pour the batter into the muffin cases, fill to ⅔–¾. You can put slices of banana on top of the batter and press them down slightly. Bake in the centre of the oven at 175°C/350°F/gas 4 for 15–25 minutes, depending on your muffin tray and your oven. Test until the skewer comes out clean. Remove the muffins from the muffin tray when slightly cooled and leave to cool completely on a wire rack.

BANANA MUFFINS WITH AQUAFABA

150g	plain flour
135g	sugar
1½ tsp	baking powder
1 pinch	salt
100g	banana, peeled
50ml	oil
¼ tsp	vanilla extract
50ml	aquafaba
50ml	water
	sliced banana

Preheat the oven to 175°C/350°F/gas 4. Put 8–10 muffin cases in a muffin tray. Mix the flour, sugar, baking powder and salt carefully in a bowl. Mash the banana. Add the mashed banana, oil, vanilla extract, aquafaba and water to the bowl and mix until smooth without overworking. Swipe the spatula around the sides of the bowl to incorporate any leftover flour into the batter. Pour the batter into the muffin cases, fill to ⅔–¾. You can put slices of banana on top of the batter and press them down slightly. Bake in the centre of the oven at 175°C/350°F/gas 4 for 17–19 minutes. Test until the skewer comes out clean. Remove the muffins from the muffin tray when slightly cooled and leave to cool completely on a wire rack.

CARROT MUFFINS

MUFFINS WITH GRATED CARROT

110g	grated carrots
100g	yoghurt
75ml	oil
135g	sugar
100g	apple sauce
180g	plain flour
1 tsp	bicarbonate of soda
½ tsp	baking powder
½ tsp	ground cinnamon
½ tsp	ground cardamom
1 pinch	salt

These muffins will be somewhat darker than the recipe that uses carrot purée, which you can see in the picture opposite.

Preheat the oven to 175°C/350°F/gas 4. Put 9–12 muffin cases in a muffin tray. Peel the carrots and grate finely with a grater, then weigh out 110g. Mix the yoghurt, oil, sugar, apple sauce and the grated carrot in a bowl. Mix the flour, bicarbonate of soda, baking powder, cinnamon, cardamom and salt in a separate bowl. Put the dry mixture into the wet and mix until smooth. Pour the batter into the muffin cases, fill to ⅔–¾. Bake at 175°C/350°F/gas 4 for 17–20 minutes. Test until the skewer comes out clean. Remove the muffins from the muffin tray when slightly cooled and leave to cool completely on a wire rack.

CARROT MUFFINS WITH CARROT PURÉE

150g	plain flour
1½ tsp	baking powder
135g	sugar
½ tsp	ground cinnamon
½ tsp	ground cardamom
1 pinch	salt
50ml	oil
50ml	carrot juice/water
125g	carrot purée
50ml	aquafaba

For these muffins, you can use baby food purée or make your own (see page 158). Carrot juice can be replaced with water. The recipe gives a lighter coloured and more orange muffin than the recipe made with grated carrot.

Preheat the oven to 175°C/350°F/gas 4. Put 6–9 muffin cases in a muffin tray. Carefully mix the flour, baking powder, sugar, cinnamon, cardamom and salt in a bowl. Add the oil, carrot juice/water, carrot purée and aquafaba into the bowl. Mix the batter until smooth and make sure that there is no leftover flour at the bottom. Pour the batter into the muffin cases, fill to ⅔. Bake in the centre of the oven at 175°C/350°F/gas 4 for 17–22 minutes. Set your timer for the shorter time first. Test until the skewer comes out clean. Remove the muffins from the muffin tray when slightly cooled and leave to cool completely on a wire rack.

PUMPKIN MUFFINS

If you find it difficult to find pumpkin purée in the shops, here is one recipe for pumpkin muffins containing shredded grated pumpkin, and one recipe that uses ready-made pumpkin purée. I always have finely grated pumpkin leftovers from when I hollow out pumpkins for decorations in the autumn. I do the last bit of scooping using a spoon, which gives me perfectly shredded pumpkin that can be used here. If the pieces are too big you can always chop them with a sharp knife. Of course, you can also grate pumpkin using a grater the same as you would to grate carrots for carrot cakes or muffins. A pumpkin muffin made from grated pumpkin and with icing eyes from page 324 is shown opposite.

PUMPKIN MUFFINS

135g	plain flour
160g	sugar
½ tsp	ground cinnamon
⅛ tsp	ground nutmeg
½ tsp	ground ginger
1 pinch	salt
¾ tsp	bicarbonate of soda
1ml	baking powder
50ml	oil
75g	yoghurt
100g	pumpkin purée

Preheat the oven to 175°C/350°F/gas 4. Put 8–10 muffin cases in a muffin tray. Mix the flour, sugar, cinnamon, nutmeg, ginger, salt, bicarbonate of soda and baking powder. Add the oil, yoghurt and pumpkin purée and quickly mix together, do not overwork the batter. Pour the batter into the muffin cases, fill to ⅔. Bake in the centre of the oven for 20–25 minutes at 175°C/350°F/gas 4. Test until the skewer comes out clean. Remove the muffins from the muffin tray when slightly cooled and leave to cool completely on a wire rack.

PUMPKIN MUFFINS WITH GRATED PUMPKIN

¼ tsp	grated nutmeg
135g	sugar
180g	plain flour
1 pinch	salt
1 tsp	bicarbonate of soda
½ tsp	baking powder
1 tsp	ground cinnamon
½ tsp	ground ginger
¼ tsp	ground cloves
110g	grated pumpkin
100g	yoghurt
75ml	oil
100g	apple sauce

Preheat the oven to 175°C/350°F/gas 4. Put 9–12 muffin cases in a muffin tray. Mix the nutmeg with the sugar, plain flour, salt, bicarbonate of soda, baking powder and the ground spices in a bowl. Add the grated pumpkin, the yoghurt, oil and apple sauce. Mix together quickly until smooth without overworking the batter. Pour the batter into the muffin cases, fill to ⅔–¾. Bake in the centre of the oven at 175°C/350°F/gas 4 for 17–22 minutes. Test until the skewer comes out clean. Remove the muffins from the muffin tray when slightly cooled and leave to cool completely on a wire rack.

CORN MUFFINS

CORN MUFFINS

210g	plain flour
165g	corn flour
1½ tbsp	baking powder
1 pinch	salt
67g	sugar
75ml	oil
250ml	milk
100g	yoghurt
50ml	aquafaba

Traditional corn bread from the southern states of the USA is well-suited for all stews. You can find really nice corn-shaped tins in America and online if you like corn bread. They can also be made in a cast iron pan if it does not have any plastic details.

Preheat the oven to 175°C/350°F/gas 4. Put 10–12 muffin cases in a muffin tray or grease the muffin tray using fat. Mix the flour, corn flour, baking powder, salt and sugar in a bowl. Add the oil, milk, yoghurt and aquafaba and mix to a smooth batter. Pour the batter into the muffin cases, fill to ¾ or almost full. They will not rise like a batter that contains more sugar, which is why they do not overflow if you fill the cases too much. Bake in the centre of the oven at 175°C/350°F/gas 4 for 15–20 minutes until a skewer comes out clean. Serve with whipped margarine from page 258.

CORN CUPCAKES

120g	plain flour
55g	corn flour
1 tsp	baking powder
75g	margarine
1 pinch	salt
160g	sugar
1 tsp	vanilla sugar or vanilla extract
75ml	aquafaba
100ml	milk
140g	fresh sweetcorn (optional) raw cane sugar

Since our family began a tradition of holding a corn party in the autumn, instead of a crayfish party, I have collected traditional corn recipes. This one comes from the southern states of America and contains corn flour and fresh corn, which can be omitted; 55g of blueberries also works for this batter. I usually sprinkle raw cane sugar on top, but you can use normal caster sugar as well. Unlike 'corn bread' or 'corn muffins' this recipe contains the same amount of sugar as traditional muffins, while corn muffins are more like a lightly sweetened bread. Instructions for the batter can be found on page 32.

Preheat the oven to 175°C/350°F/gas 4. Put 9–10 muffin cases in a muffin tray. Put the flour, corn flour, baking powder in a bowl or a stand mixer. Dice the margarine and mix until it is the size of peas. Add the salt and sugar and mix for 1 more minute until the mixture resembles breadcrumbs. Mix the vanilla sugar or extract, the aquafaba and the milk and stir carefully into a well-combined batter. Cut the sweetcorn kernels from the cob and mix into the batter. Pour the batter into the muffin cases, fill to ⅔. Sprinkle raw cane sugar on top of the muffins and bake for 18–25 minutes at 175°C/350°F/gas 4. Take them out of the oven when golden. Remove the muffins from the muffin tray when slightly cooled and leave to cool completely on a wire rack.

84

MADELEINES

These are traditional French cakes; to get a perfect madeleine you need a dome in the middle and an even surface so the stripes are clearly visible. That is exactly what this recipe does. The batter makes 24 madeleines in traditional tins, but they can also be baked in a metal madeleine tin. The batter is best after it has rested overnight, either on the madeleine tin or in a piping bag. In order to get the characteristic dome on top of the cake, the batter should be thoroughly cooled before baking, but they can also be baked immediately, if desired.

The cakes are at their best in the first couple of hours after baking as the outside is crispy and the inside is moist and light. You can prepare them in the tin and then bake them before serving. When stored in jars or in the fridge they usually become firm, which is why I recommend baking them a few hours before serving. As they are easy to prepare and it is a good idea to make them in advance, you can mix the batter or prepare the whole tin and let it sit in the fridge until you want them. However, make sure you let them cool before serving so the surface crisps up. Grease the tin with soft cooking fat, using a pastry brush or a piece of kitchen paper. Fill with plain flour. Turn the tin over and knock it carefully to get all of the excess flour out. There are pictures and more instructions on page 65.

You can replace the lemon zest and juice with orange zest and freshly squeezed orange juice.

150g	margarine
¼	lemon, zest of
180g	plain flour
1½ tsp	baking powder
1 pinch	salt
150g	sugar
100g	aquafaba
1 tsp	lemon juice

Preheat the oven to 225°C/425°F/gas 7 if you want to bake the madeleines immediately, if not, wait until shortly before baking after chilling the batter. Grease and flour the madeleine tin. Melt the margarine and grate the lemon zest into the margarine. Mix the flour, baking powder and salt in a bowl. Whip the sugar, aquafaba and lemon juice until frothy. Carefully fold in the flour and, when it is incorporated, fold in the melted margarine in three batches. Pour the batter into a piping bag and cool in the fridge for at least 1 hour or portion out one spoon into each madeleine hole, to approximately ¾, and put the tray in the fridge for at least 1 hour, preferably overnight. Put the tray in the oven that has been heated to 225°C/425°F/gas 7 and lower the temperature to 200°C/400°F/gas 6. Bake for 10–15 minutes. Take the tray out when the cakes are golden. Let them sit in the tin for a few minutes and then turn out onto a wire rack.

SWISS ROLL

The batter for Swiss roll contains more sugar than other sponge cakes, which is what allows you to roll it with a minimum of cracks. Usually there is no fat in the batter apart from the egg yolks, which for this cake I have replaced with oil. The fat in the egg yolk needs to be replaced to make a perfect cake texture, without it the cake becomes an unpleasant lump in the mouth and the cake will not have the correct texture.

You do not need a Swiss roll tin, but you can spread the batter on baking paper. I use a stainless steel Swiss roll tin of the perfect size (25 × 35cm), but if you want a clear guide, you can fold the paper so it measures 25 × 35cm so that you know how far to spread the batter. You can also staple the edges together to make a tin of the correct size – instructions on page 62. However, the batter is quite firm and will not spread so evenly if you have no edges. Brush the paper with cold water or put a damp tea towel over the cake if you cannot get the paper off the cake when it has been turned out.

120g	plain flour
1 tsp	baking powder
1 pinch	salt
100ml	aquafaba
135g	sugar
1 tbsp	oil
3 tbsp	milk
45g	sugar
50–100g	strawberry compôte, strawberry jam or apple sauce/apple butter

Preheat the oven to 225°C/425°F/gas 7. Staple a baking paper tin of around 25 × 35cm and place it on a baking sheet or put a piece of baking paper in a tin measuring 25 × 35cm. Mix the flour, baking powder and salt in a bowl. Whip the sugar and aquafaba to ribbon stage, which is described on page 26. Carefully fold in the flour mixture and, when incorporated, fold in the oil and milk together. Swipe the spatula around the sides of the bowl to incorporate any leftover flour. Spread the batter evenly onto the baking paper and bake in the centre of the oven for 12–15 minutes. Put a piece of baking paper sprinkled with the remaining 45g of sugar on the counter. Remove the cake from the oven and turn out onto the sprinkled sugar. Carefully pull the paper off and cut off the edges around the cake. Spread strawberry jam, strawberry compôte or apple sauce/butter on top. Roll the cake from the short side using the paper underneath. Let it cool in a sealed container before serving. Cut into thin slices with a bread knife.

SWISS ROLL SPONGE
If you are using a filling that cannot handle heat, like buttercream or whipped cream, the cake needs to cool down underneath a baking tray/sheet before you spread on the filling and roll up the sponge. If this is the case, you do not need to cut the edges off the cake, as it will be soft when cool. If you fill with buttercream or cream you can roll it from the long side so you don't get rolls that are too big. You can also fill your Swiss roll according to the recipe above, and pipe whipped cream on top, instead of inside the roll. If that is the case you do not need to roll it from the long side.

Swiss roll rolled with jam can be stored at room temperature for 2–3 days. Swiss roll rolled with buttercream should be stored in the fridge. You can also put the Swiss roll in the freezer and bring it out when you have unexpected guests.

CHOCOLATE SWISS ROLL

I think that 1½ tablespoons of cocoa gives the cake the best texture but you can also increase the amount to 2 tablespoons if you want a more intense chocolate flavour.

120g	plain flour
1½ tbsp	cocoa
1 tsp	baking powder
1 pinch	salt
100ml	aquafaba
135g	sugar
1 tbsp	oil
3 tbsp	milk
45g	sugar

Preheat the oven to 225°C/425°F/gas 7. Staple a baking paper tin of around 25 × 35cm and place it on a baking sheet (see page 62) or put a piece of baking paper in a tin measuring 25 × 35cm. Mix the flour, sifted cocoa, baking powder and salt in a bowl. Whip the sugar and aquafaba to ribbon stage, which is described on page 26. Add the flour mixture carefully and when it is incorporated, fold in the oil and milk together. Swipe the spatula around the sides of the bowl to incorporate any leftover flour. Pour the batter evenly onto the baking paper and bake in the centre of the oven for 12–15 minutes. Put a piece of baking paper sprinkled with the remaining 45g of caster sugar on the counter. Bring the cake out of the oven and turn out onto the baking paper. Put a wet tea towel on top, including the baking sheet. Allow to cool. Pull the paper off carefully. Spread the buttercream (see recipe below) carefully and roll the cake from the long side using the paper underneath. Let the cake sit in the fridge to help the filling firm up, then cut into thin slices with a bread knife.

TIP!
Frosting based on vegan baking margarine usually has a high melting point to make it melt in the mouth, which is why I have not previously included traditional simple recipes for frosting in my books. If you are using vegan spread, which has a lower melting point, you can actually make traditional frosting recipes like this buttercream.

BUTTERCREAM
100g	vegan spread
240–300g	icing sugar
1/8 tsp	salt
1 tsp	vanilla sugar or vanilla extract
0–3 tbsp	milk (optional)

Mix all the ingredients, except the milk, together in a bowl for several minutes to give you a light and airy frosting. You can add milk for a more airy consistency, if you like.

GREEN OR BROWN BANANAS?

Use yellow, spotted or almost brown bananas. They contain up to three times more sugar and produce a cake that is more moist, with a deeper and more complex banana flavour.

In these sponge cakes (Cake 1, page 92) it is the aquafaba that gives them their beautifully coloured surface after being cooked for 30–35 minutes. No other egg replacement gives such a beautiful colour after such a short baking time.

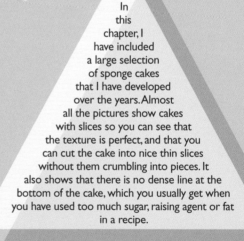

In this chapter, I have included a large selection of sponge cakes that I have developed over the years. Almost all the pictures show cakes with slices so you can see that the texture is perfect, and that you can cut the cake into nice thin slices without them crumbling into pieces. It also shows that there is no dense line at the bottom of the cake, which you usually get when you have used too much sugar, raising agent or fat in a recipe.

In this light sponge cake (Cake 1, page 92) I have folded in 55g fresh blueberries, 1 tsp of vanilla sugar/extract and the grated zest from 1 lemon to flavour the batter.

Sponge cakes

Preheat the oven in advance and prepare the tin and the ingredients before mixing the batter together. This important step is called *mise en place*, which means 'everything in place' in French.

Sift the dry ingredients, especially for large quantities, so that the risk of lumps of flour in the mixture will be reduced.

In Sweden, we traditionally make smaller batches of sponge cakes, but the amount for the smaller cakes can always be doubled. Then add 15–20 minutes to the baking time.

Never use flour rich in gluten (strong flour) when baking sponge cakes, since extra added gluten or flour rich in gluten will make the sponge dense. This flour should only be used in raised doughs (see page 331).

Always use ingredients at room temperature. Cold ingredients can make the margarine hard and make the batter very firm.

Always add a pinch of salt to your cake batters!

Do not mix for too long; mix the ingredients together quickly if there are no other instructions. Always swipe the spatula around the bottom of the bowl when mixing the batter to make sure that all the dry ingredients have been incorporated into the batter before transferring it to the tin and baking it.

Recipes that include vinegar need to be put into the oven quickly so it doesn't lose its rise before baking.

Always set a timer for the shortest time given. Add 5 minutes if the cake is not ready. Keep on testing the cake carefully using a skewer, with a few minutes in between, until ready.

In a tasting test in the big American baking bibles, the testers agreed that carrot cakes taste better if the carrots are peeled before being grated into the cake batter.

Keep sponge cakes in a cake carrier or airtight container, on a cake stand with a lid or in a plastic bag at room temperature. This will keep sponge cakes fresh for a few days.

BASIC SPONGE CAKES

In traditional books about baking there is not just one sponge cake, but several, which vary in different ways, mostly in the amount of fat in the batter and how it is incorporated. Fat gives the cake extra flavour but also affects texture. Cakes with less fat have light, airy sponges, while recipes with more fat give more moist results. The really high-fat sponge cakes (numbers 4–6) improve if they get to sit in a sealed container for a day or two before serving. The light sponge cakes I developed after three years of experimenting with aquafaba, and these are among the recipes that I am most proud of. The recipe looks like traditional sponge cake and what I noticed was that using frothy aquafaba gave the cakes different characteristics to using plain or heavily whipped aquafaba. Fat cannot be whipped until airy with the sugar and aquafaba, like it can in traditional high-fat sponge cakes using eggs. However, you can incorporate the same amount of fat into frothy aquafaba, as I discovered in 2019, and it makes all the difference if you mix in the flour before the fat. This helps the batter retain the air that has been whipped into it, even though there is a higher amount of fat. Read more about aquafaba on pages 22–33. The cakes with 125–150g of fat need to sit for a little longer before slicing. High-fat cakes cannot take too much baking powder in the recipe as they are somewhat heavier, which means that there is more rise than the cake can manage to retain after baking. Because of this the amount of baking powder decreases gradually along with the amount of fat. The different quantities of liquid give the opportunity to replace the milk with other liquids, such as saffron milk, banana, yoghurt or similar. In Cake 1, you can replace the liquid with cream for traditional 'cream cakes' that are common in America.

I have included two recipes, one smaller for 1–1.5-litre tins and one larger for tins of up to 2 litres. I think that tins of around 1.2 litres give the best result for the smaller amount of batter. Cakes 1–2 are counted as light sponge cakes, and the batter for cakes 3–6 as moist sponge cakes, according to the guides on pages 28–33.

CAKE NO. 1

SMALL	LARGE	
75g	100g	margarine
½	1	lemon, zest of
180g	270g	sugar
75ml	100ml	aquafaba
180g	270g	plain flour
2 tsp	1 tbsp	baking powder
1 pinch	1 pinch	salt
100ml	150ml	milk

CAKE NO. 2

SMALL	LARGE	
75g	100g	margarine
½	1	lemon, zest of
180g	270g	sugar
100ml	150ml	aquafaba
180g	270g	plain flour
2 tsp	1 tbsp	baking powder
1 pinch	1 pinch	salt
75ml	100ml	milk

Preheat the oven to 175°C/350°F/gas 4. Grease and add crumbs to a sponge cake tin. Melt the margarine and grate the outermost zest of the lemon. Whip the sugar and aquafaba until frothy in a stand mixer or with an electric hand mixer. Add the dry ingredients, the lemon zest, the melted margarine and the milk to the bowl and mix with a spatula until smooth without overworking. Swipe the spatula around the sides of the bowl to incorporate any leftover flour. Pour the batter into the tin and bake in the centre of the oven at 175°C/350°F/gas 4 for 30–35 minutes for the smaller cake and for 40–45 minutes for the larger cake. Test with a skewer until it comes out clean from the middle of the cake.

CAKE NO. 3

SMALL	LARGE	
100g	150g	margarine
½	1	lemon, zest of
180g	270g	plain flour
1½ tsp	2 tsp	baking powder
1 pinch	1 pinch	salt
180g	270g	sugar
100ml	150ml	aquafaba
50ml	75ml	milk

Preheat the oven to 175°C/350°F/gas 4. Grease and add crumbs to a sponge cake tin. Melt the margarine and grate the outermost zest of the lemon. Mix the flour, baking powder and salt in a bowl. Whip the sugar and aquafaba in a separate bowl until frothy. Carefully fold in the flour mixture with a spatula; when it is incorporated, fold in the melted margarine in three batches. Fold in the milk. Swipe the spatula around the sides of the bowl to incorporate any leftover flour. Pour the batter into the tin and bake in the centre of the oven at 175°C/350°F/gas 4 for 30–35 minutes for the smaller cake and for 40–45 minutes for the larger cake. Test with a skewer until it comes out clean from the middle of the cake.

CAKE NO. 4

SMALL	LARGE	
125g	200g	margarine
½	1	lemon, zest of
180g	270g	plain flour
1 tsp	1½ tsp	baking powder
1 pinch	1 pinch	salt
180g	270g	sugar
75ml	100ml	aquafaba
50ml	75ml	milk or water

Preheat the oven to 175°C/350°F/gas 4. Grease and add crumbs to a sponge cake tin. Melt the margarine and grate the outermost zest of the lemon. Mix the flour, baking powder and salt in a bowl. Whip the sugar and aquafaba in a separate bowl until frothy. Carefully fold in the flour mixture with a spatula; when it is incorporated, fold in the melted margarine in three batches. Swipe the spatula around the sides of the bowl to incorporate any leftover flour. Pour the batter into the tin and bake in the centre of the oven at 175°C/350°F/gas 4 for 30–35 minutes for the smaller cake and for 40–45 minutes for the larger cake. Test with a skewer until it comes out clean from the middle of the cake.

CAKE NO. 5

SMALL	LARGE	
125g	200g	margarine
½	1	lemon, zest of
180g	270g	plain flour
1 tsp	1½ tsp	baking powder
1 pinch	1 pinch	salt
180g	270g	sugar
100ml	150ml	aquafaba

Preheat the oven to 175°C/350°F/gas 4. Grease and add crumbs to a sponge cake tin. Melt the margarine and grate the outermost zest of the lemon. Mix the flour, baking powder and salt in a bowl. Whip the sugar and aquafaba in a separate bowl until frothy. Carefully fold in the flour mixture with a spatula; when it is incorporated, fold in the melted margarine in three batches. Swipe the spatula around the sides of the bowl to incorporate any leftover flour. Pour the batter into the tin and bake in the centre of the oven at 175°C/350°F/gas 4 for 30–35 minutes for the smaller cake and for 40–45 minutes for the larger cake. Test with a skewer until it comes out clean from the middle of the cake.

CAKE NO. 6

SMALL	LARGE	
150g	225g	margarine
½	1	lemon, zest of
180g	270g	plain flour
1 tsp	1½ tsp	baking powder
1 pinch	1 pinch	salt
180g	270g	sugar
100ml	150ml	aquafaba

Preheat the oven to 175°C/350°F/gas 4. Grease and add crumbs to a sponge cake tin. Melt the margarine and grate the outermost zest of the lemon. Mix the flour, baking powder and salt in a bowl. Whip the sugar and aquafaba in a separate bowl until frothy. Carefully fold in the flour mixture with a spatula; when it is incorporated, fold in the melted margarine in three batches. Swipe the spatula around the sides of the bowl to incorporate any leftover flour. Pour the batter into the tin and bake in the centre of the oven at 175°C/350°F/gas 4 for 30–35 minutes for the smaller cake and for 40–45 minutes for the larger cake. Test with a skewer until it comes out clean from the middle of the cake.

CLASSIC SPONGE CAKE

This recipe uses slightly different quantities than the other basic recipes and this cake is incredibly easy to make and it really melts in the mouth. It gives a slightly bigger cake than the recipes using only 180g of plain flour and 180g of sugar and the smallest tins of 1–1.2 litres cannot be used. In the picture opposite, you can see the beautiful colour on the surface that frothy aquafaba and sugar gives.

75g	margarine
225g	sugar
125ml	aquafaba
210g	plain flour
2 tsp	baking powder
1 pinch	salt
1 tsp	vanilla extract
1	lemon, zest of
100ml	milk

Preheat the oven to 175°C/350°F/gas 4. Grease and add crumbs to a sponge cake tin of 1.5–2 litres. Melt the margarine. Whip the sugar and aquafaba until frothy in a stand mixer or with an electric hand mixer. At the same time, carefully mix the flour, baking powder and salt in a separate bowl. Grate the outermost zest of the lemon. Add the dry ingredients, the lemon zest, the melted margarine, the vanilla extract and the milk to the sugar/aquafaba bowl and mix to a smooth batter with a spatula without overworking. Swipe the spatula around the sides of the bowl to incorporate any leftover flour. Pour the batter into the tin and bake in the centre of the oven at 175°C/350°F/gas 4 for 30–35 minutes. Test with a skewer until it comes out clean from the middle of the cake.

For this classic sponge cake I have used one grated tonka bean, ¼ tsp vanilla extract and the grated zest of an orange to flavour the batter.

GENOISE CAKE

I have based this recipe on my old favourite recipe for a French genoise; similar sponge goes under the name *pan di spagna* in Italy. These are suitable for layer cakes with cream and simple cakes with berries, but not for American layer cakes. There is usually no fat included except for the fat in the egg yolks and that amount of fat is replaced here; with no fat at all, the cake will be dense and rubbery. It took me about 100 test bakes to develop this recipe after the world discovered aquafaba as an egg replacement, but it will certainly be perfected over the next 100 years, as we come to understand all the possibilities and challenges of baking with aquafaba. I use a small amount of baking powder to give a softer layer cake, but you will have to test for yourself to find your favourite as you can bake the cake without a raising agent. This batter is tricky to mix, so be prepared and use the tips below and try other sponge cakes that are easier first.

150ml	aquafaba
180g	sugar
180g	plain flour
¼ tsp	baking powder
50ml	oil

TINS & BAKING TIMES
Below, you can see which tins are suitable for this cake, and how long they should be baked for.a

All tins are circular.

1 tin 15cm = 45–50 minutes
2 tins 15cm = 30–35 minutes
1 tin 18–20cm = 35–40 minutes

Preheat the oven to 175°C/350°F/gas 4. Prepare the tins with crumbs, semolina or baking paper. Whip the aquafaba and the sugar to ribbon stage, which is described on page 26. Test by drawing with your finger 0.5cm deep into the meringue, and if the sides do not collapse in immediately, it is whipped enough. It is important not to whip it too much, or to have the mixture too loose as the flour and the oil will not stay in the batter. Sift the flour and baking powder into the bowl using a sieve or a flour sifter, then fold in with a spatula, not an electric hand mixer. Fold into the batter all the way to the bottom until it is fully incorporated. You need to fold carefully to prevent knocking the air out of the batter or creating too many gluten strands. Then add the oil, which again should be carefully folded in to prevent knocking the air out of the batter. Bake in the centre of the oven at 175°C/350°F/gas 4. Times for different tins and quantities of batter are given on the left. Test with a skewer until it comes out clean from the middle of the cake.

According to the egg-genoise pros, the genoise should be turned out of the tin onto a wire rack to cool. However, I think it is okay to let the cake cool in the tin placed on a wire rack. The sides will also firm up, so if you are not going to cover the sides of the cake it helps the moisture inside the cake to reach the sides if you keep it sealed for some time. The surface will look like a meringue if it is baked for over 30–35 minutes and is then cut off.

The cake in the picture shows two layers of genoise baked in 18-cm tins. The cake is filled and decorated with whipped cream and fresh berries. Read more about aquafaba on pages 22–33. Google 'folding in flour' and 'ribbon stage' to find lots of videos with good explanations of what the ribbons in the whipped batter should look like. This is also shown on page 26.

AMERICAN BUNDT CAKE

Reverse creaming is an unusual way of baking in Sweden but it is used in some traditional recipes. The method is more common in America and instead of using a stand mixer or food processor you can use an electric mixer or rub together the fat and the flour with your fingers. In many countries, sponge cakes are larger than than the ones we bake in Sweden and I have included a recipe for a larger tin here. Both 'cream cakes' and yoghurt cakes are common and the milk in the recipes can be replaced with either cream or yoghurt. This batter will rise a lot in the oven, so make sure you don't use a tin that is too small. This is a good replacement for the creaming method, where you whip the butter and the sugar first, as that method cannot easily be veganized with aquafaba. On page 32, there is a guide for mixing the batter.

SMALL TIN

180g	plain flour
2 tsp	baking powder
75g	margarine
1 pinch	salt
180g	sugar
1 tsp	vanilla extract
75ml	aquafaba
100ml	milk

Preheat the oven to 175°C/350°F/gas 4. Grease and add crumbs to a sponge cake tin of 1–1.5 litres. Add the flour and baking powder to a bowl for the stand mixer or electric mixer. Dice the margarine and mix until the margarine is the size of peas. Add salt and sugar and mix for 1 more minute until the mixture resembles breadcrumbs. If you are using a stand mixer or an electric hand mixer you might need to make sure that everything is evenly distributed in the bowl. You will need to break up any larger lumps in the flour mixture. Add the vanilla extract, aquafaba and milk and mix thoroughly until well combined. Pour the batter into the tin and bake in the centre of the oven at 175°C/350°F/gas 4 for 50–60 minutes. Test with a skewer until it comes out clean from the middle of the cake.

LARGE TIN

360g	plain flour
4 tsp	baking powder
150g	margarine
1 pinch	salt
360g	sugar
2 tsp	vanilla extract
150ml	aquafaba
200ml	milk

Preheat the oven to 175°C/350°F/gas 4. Grease and add crumbs to a sponge cake tin of 2–2.5 litres. Add the flour and baking powder to a bowl for the stand mixer or electric mixer. Dice the margarine and mix in until the margarine is the size of peas. Add the salt and sugar and mix for a minute more until the mixture resembles breadcrumbs. If you are using a stand mixer or an electric hand mixer, you might need to make sure that everything is evenly distributed in the bowl. You will need to break up any larger lumps in the flour mixture. Add the vanilla extract, aquafaba and milk and mix thoroughly until well combined. Pour the batter into the tin and bake in the centre of the oven at 175°C/350°F/gas 4 for 40–50 minutes. Test with a skewer until it comes out clean from the middle of the cake.

LEMON & YOGHURT CAKE

A moist lemon cake for which you can make a tart, sticky syrup from the leftover lemons that you use for zesting – but you can also leave this out and serve the cake as it is, if you prefer. If you add 2–3 tablespoons of poppy seeds, you will get a classic lemon and poppy cake. This cake is perfect for adding 55–110g of blueberries before putting the batter in the tin and baking.

CAKE

150g	margarine
2–3	lemons, zest of
270g	plain flour
1½ tsp	baking powder
1 pinch	salt
270g	sugar
100ml	aquafaba
150g	yoghurt

Preheat the oven to 175°C/350°F/gas 4. Grease and add crumbs to a loaf tin of 2 litres. Melt the margarine and grate the outermost zest of the lemons. Mix the flour, baking powder and salt in a bowl. Whip the sugar and aquafaba in a separate bowl until frothy. Add the flour mixture and yoghurt carefully with a spatula; when it is incorporated, fold in the melted margarine in three batches. Swipe the spatula around the sides of the bowl to incorporate any leftover flour. Pour the batter into the tin and bake in the centre of the oven at 175°C/350°F/gas 4 for 45–50 minutes. Test with a skewer until it comes out clean from the middle of the cake.

LEMON SYRUP

2–3	lemons, juice of
50–100ml	water
45g	sugar

Squeeze the juice from the lemons and top up with water until you have 150ml of liquid. Add the sugar and carefully boil in a small saucepan until it reduces to a thick syrup. Pour the syrup over the cake as soon as it comes out of the oven. You can make a few holes with the skewer to help the cake absorb the syrup.

POPPY SEED CAKE

This is a poppy seed cake based on a traditional recipe where the poppy seeds are boiled until soft. If you put dry seeds in the cake they will not soften in the oven, which is okay when only using a tablespoon or so, but if you are using a larger quantity, as in this cake, they need to be soft for the cake to taste good. If you want a cake with less poppy seeds, read the introduction on page 100.

150ml	milk
90g	poppy seeds
150g	margarine
1	lemon, zest of
270g	plain flour
1½ tsp	baking powder
1 pinch	salt
270g	sugar
100ml	aquafaba

Preheat the oven to 175°C/350°F/gas 4. Grease and add crumbs to a sponge cake tin or a 2-litre loaf tin. Let the milk boil together with the poppy seeds, then remove from the hob. Let it sit for at least 20 minutes. Melt the margarine and grate the outermost zest of the lemon. Mix the flour, baking powder and salt in a bowl. Whip the sugar and aquafaba in a separate bowl until frothy. Add the flour mixture and milk carefully and mix with a spatula; when incorporated, fold in the melted margarine in three batches. Swipe the spatula around the sides of the bowl to incorporate any leftover flour. Pour the batter into the tin and bake in the centre of the oven at 175°C/350°F/gas 4 for 45–50 minutes. Test with a skewer until it comes out clean from the middle of the cake.

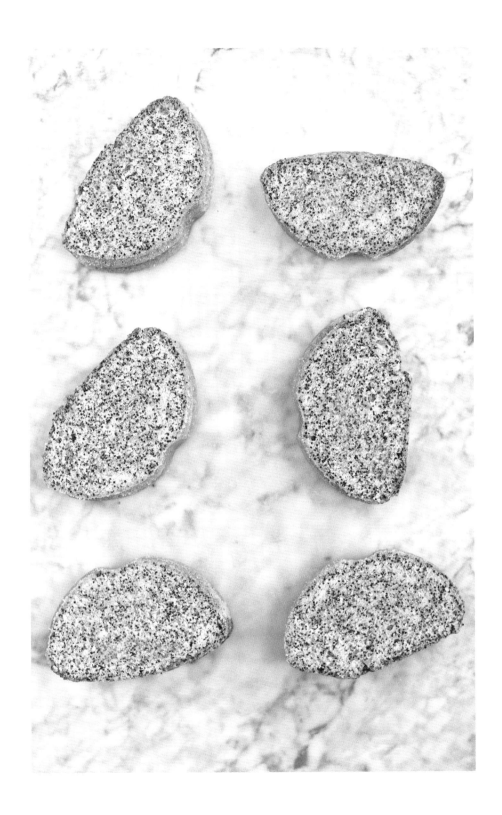

GOLDEN LEMON CAKE

This cake is adapted from a recipe by Alison Roman, which I veganized after it went viral via *The New York Times*. If you have heard of, or perhaps you are already a convert to, golden milk, this is a cake in which you can use the same spices. If you like, you can add 1 teaspoon of ground ginger to the cake batter, or you could use a pinch of all the spices in the recipe for golden milk below. If the lemons are small, you may need to use three, but if they are large, two will be enough.

125g	margarine
2–3	lemons, zest of
45g	sugar
270g	plain flour
2 tsp	baking powder
1 tsp	turmeric
1 pinch	salt
225g	sugar
150ml	aquafaba
100g	thick yoghurt
1–2 tbsp	sugar, for sprinking

Preheat the oven to 175°C/350°F/gas 4. Grease and add crumbs to a round cake tin or loaf tin that holds around 2 litres. Melt the margarine. Zest the lemon and rub the zest together with 45g of the sugar with your fingertips until the zest has turned the sugar yellow. Mix together the flour, baking powder, turmeric and salt in a bowl. Whip the remaining 225g of sugar and aquafaba until frothy in a separate bowl. Carefully stir in the flour mixture, lemon sugar and yoghurt with a spatula, and once incorporated fold in the melted margarine in in three batches. Swipe the spatula around the sides of the bowl to incorporate any leftover flour. Pour the cake batter into the tin, sprinkle the surface with sugar and bake in the centre of the oven at 175°C/350°F/gas 4C for 45–50 minutes. Test with a skewer until it comes out clean from the middle of the cake. Leave the cake to cool before cutting.

Golden milk has its roots in ayurvedic traditions, which uses a lot of turmeric for its health benefits. If you use grated fresh ginger, turmeric or crushed cardamom pods instead of using dried spices, the milk needs to be strained before serving. The coconut oil and the black pepper are important for absorbing the antioxidant and anti-inflammatory properties, so they shouldn't be left out.

GOLDEN MILK

500ml	milk
1½ tsp	ground turmeric
1 tsp	ground ginger
¼ tsp	grated ginger
½ tsp	ground cinnamon
½ tsp	ground cardamom
1 tsp	vanilla extract
¼ tsp	ground black pepper
1 tbsp	coconut oil
1 tbsp	agave syrup (optional)

Add all the ingredients to a small saucepan. Carefully whisk together on a medium heat. Bring to the boil and simmer for about 4 minutes, stirring regularly. The golden milk should be hot, but not bubbling. For a more intense flavour, you can add more turmeric and/or ginger. Serve immediately. You can keep the golden milk in the fridge for 2–3 days, and reheat before serving.

BOLO DE FUBÁ

In Brazil, this sweet corn cake is eaten for breakfast and with coffee. I usually bake this or an olive oil cake for brunch for holidays or at weekends. The original cake is made using fubá, a fine ground corn flour, so look for a really fine ground corn flour, not coarsely ground polenta. Corn flour is not the same as cornstarch, which is made from ground sweetcorn, which is why you cannot use cornstarch in this recipe.

1.5 LITRE LOAF TIN

75g	margarine
135g	sugar
75ml	aquafaba
90g	plain flour
85g	fine ground corn flour
1½ tsp	baking powder
1 pinch	salt
100ml	milk
	icing sugar

2 LITRE LOAF TIN

100g	margarine
200g	sugar
100ml	aquafaba
150g	plain flour
110g	fine ground corn flour
2 tsp	baking powder
1 pinch	salt
150ml	milk
	icing sugar

Preheat the oven to 175°C/350°F/gas 4. Grease and add crumbs to a small or a large loaf tin, depending on which batter you are making. Melt the margarine.

Whip the sugar and aquafaba in a stand mixer or using an electric hand mixer until frothy. At the same time, carefully mix the flour, corn flour, baking powder and salt in a bowl. Add the dry ingredients, the melted margarine and the milk to the mixing bowl and mix with a spatula until smooth without overworking.

Swipe the spatula around the sides of the bowl to incorporate any leftover flour. Pour the batter into the tin and bake in the centre of the oven at 175°C/350°F/gas 4 for 30–35 minutes, and 40–50 minutes for the larger tin. Test with a skewer until it comes out clean from the middle of the cake. Leave to cool and dust icing sugar on top before serving.

OLIVE OIL CAKE

An Italian cake that is good for brunch or with a cup of strong coffee. A peppery, flavoursome olive oil is suitable for this cake; once cooked the taste becomes mild and works well together with the citrus and the Amaretto. If you do not want to use the suggested alcohol you can use water or milk, which is fine as the cake is full of flavour anyway. By mixing the oil with the aquafaba you can bind the traditional amount of oil into the cake, while the amount of sugar is slightly reduced compared to my other sponge cake recipes to cope with the amount of olive oil. The olive oil will make the cake both moist and melt-in-the-mouth. Sometimes when I mix the oil and the aquafaba they turn into a firm batter and sometimes they are still quite runny. I have not found out why there is such a big difference, but my guess is that it depends on the brand of the aquafaba and different olive oils, but I know that it does not matter for the cake. As long as the oil and the aquafaba are mixed together, the recipe works.

270g	plain flour
1½ tsp	baking powder
1 pinch	salt
250g	sugar
100ml	aquafaba
180ml	extra virgin olive oil
50ml	aquafaba
1	lemon, zest of
2 tbsp	Amaretto, sweet vermouth, Grand Marnier, milk or water
	icing sugar, to dust

Preheat the oven to 175°C/350°F/gas 4. Grease and add crumbs to a tin measuring 20–22cm in diameter. Mix the flour, baking powder and salt in a bowl. Whip the sugar and 100ml of aquafaba in a separate bowl until frothy. Mix the olive oil, 50ml of aquafaba and lemon zest in another bowl until pale and fully combined. Add the flour mixture and the alcohol or milk/water to the frothy aquafaba and fold a few times with a spatula to incorporate it slightly. Then fold the olive oil mixture into the batter until combined. Run a spatula around the sides of the bowl to incorporate any remaining flour into the batter. Pour the batter into the tin and bake in the centre of the oven at 175°C/350°F/gas 4 for 40–45 minutes for a 20cm tin and 35–40 minutes for a 22cm tin. Test with a skewer until it comes out clean from the middle of the cake. Dust icing sugar on top before serving.

ORANGE & ROSEMARY

1 tbsp	fresh rosemary, chopped
270g	plain flour
1½ tsp	baking powder
1 pinch	salt
250g	sugar
100ml	aquafaba
2 tbsp	Cointreau, milk or water
180ml	extra virgin olive oil
50ml	aquafaba
1 orange	zest

Preheat the oven to 175°C/350°F/gas 4. Grease and add crumbs to a tin measuring 20–22cm in diameter. Mix the chopped rosemary with the the flour, baking powder and salt in a bowl. Whip the sugar and 100ml of aquafaba in a separate bowl until frothy. Mix the olive oil, 50ml of aquafaba and orange zest in another bowl until pale and fully combined. Stir the flour mixture and the alcohol, milk or water into the frothy aquafaba and fold a few times with a spatula to incorporate it slightly. Then fold the olive oil mixture into the batter until combined. Run a spatula around the sides of the bowl to incorporate any remaining flour into the batter. Pour the batter into the tin and bake in the centre of the oven at 175°C/350°F/gas 4 for 40–45 minutes for a 20cm tin, and 35–40 minutes for a 22cm tin. Test with a skewer until it comes out clean from the middle of the cake. Dust icing sugar on top before serving.

MARBLE CAKE

In Sweden, this cake is called tiger cake, but elsewhere it is called zebra cake or marble cake, which are also amazing names. I think that this batter with a higher amount of fat gives the best flavour when combined with cocoa, but you can also use the recipe for light sponge cake as the base. There are more versions to choose from on page 92. Use orange zest instead of lemon zest and follow the instructions for the cocoa below if that is the case.

150g	margarine
1 orange	zest
1 tsp	vanilla extract
270g	plain flour
1½ tsp	baking powder
1 pinch	salt
270g	sugar
150ml	aquafaba
75ml	water
2 tbsp	cocoa

Preheat the oven to 175°C/350°F/gas 4. Grease and add crumbs to a 2-litre loaf tin. Melt the margarine and grate the orange zest into the margarine and add the vanilla extract. Mix the flour, baking powder and salt in a bowl. Whip the sugar and aquafaba in a separate bowl until frothy. Add the flour mixture and water carefully; when it is incorporated, fold in the melted margarine in three batches. Swipe the spatula around the sides of the bowl to incorporate any leftover flour. Remove one-third of the batter to another bowl and fold in the cocoa. Pour the batter into the tin in three batches (half the vanilla/orange batter, then the chocolate/orange batter, then the remaining vanilla/orange batter) and bake in the centre of the oven at 175°C/350°F/gas 4 for 35–40 minutes. Test the cake with a skewer until it comes out clean from the middle.

CARDAMOM & COFFEE MARBLE CAKE

150g	margarine
270g	plain flour
1½ tsp	baking powder
1 pinch	salt
270g	sugar
150ml	aquafaba
1 tsp	vanilla extract
75ml	water
1 tsp	cardamom pods, crushed
1 tbsp	instant coffee
1 tsp	cocoa powder, sifted
1 tbsp	boiling water

This cake with coffee and cardamom is inspired by Ottolenghi and Goh's book *Sweet*. The cake is at its best once it has cooled completely and the flavours have developed, so it is a good idea to prepare it a day in advance. I have included their icing recipe here, but I don't think this is needed for the cake to be delicious.

Preheat the oven to 175°C/350°F/gas 4. Grease and add crumbs to a loaf tin of around 2 litres. Melt the margarine. Mix the flour, baking powder and salt in a bowl. Whip the sugar and aquafaba in a separate bowl until frothy. Carefully stir in the flour mixture, vanilla extract and the water and once incorporated, the melted margarine is folded in in three batches. Swipe the spatula around the sides of the bowl to incorporate any leftover flour. Divide the batter into two bowls. Stir cardamom into one batch. Mix the coffee powder, cocoa powder and boiling water in a small bowl, mix until disssolved and then stir into the other batch. Pour the batter into the tin in three batches (half the cardamom batter, then the coffee/chocolate batter, then the remaining cardamom batter). Bake as above.

COFEE ICING

1½ tbsp	instant coffee
50ml	hot milk
180–240g	icing sugar
25g	soft margarine

Dissolve the coffee in hot milk, then add the smaller quantity of icing sugar and the soft margarine and mix to a smooth icing. Add more icing sugar if it is too soft. Pour over the cooled cake and leave to set slightly before serving.

CHOCOLATE CAKES

This dark chocolate cake can be served with a spoon and whipped cream or a chocolate glaze from page 230.

CHOCOLATE SPONGE CAKE

75g	margarine
225g	sugar
100ml	aquafaba
180g	plain flour
20g	cocoa
1½ tsp	baking powder
½ tsp	bicarbonate of soda
1 pinch	salt
1 tsp	vanilla sugar or vanilla extract
100g	yoghurt

Preheat the oven to 175°C/350°F/gas 4. Prepare a round tin measuring 18–20cm in diameter or a loaf tin of around 1.5 litres. Melt the margarine. Whip the sugar and aquafaba until frothy in a stand mixer or using an electric hand mixer. Carefully mix the flour, sifted cocoa, baking powder, bicarbonate of soda and salt in a bowl. Add the dry ingredients, the melted margarine, the vanilla and the yoghurt to the frothy aquafaba and mix with a spatula until smooth without overworking. Swipe the spatula around the sides of the bowl to incorporate any leftover flour. Pour the batter into the tin and bake in the centre of the oven at 175°C/350°F/gas 4 for 30–35 minutes. Test with a skewer until it comes out clean from the middle of the cake.

This is an amazingly easy chocolate cake that I have been using since my first book was published in 2011. The recipe was developed from a really old classic that was the origin for many vegan sponge cakes. They were developed during rationing during the World Wars, which is why they are called war cakes, depression cakes, wacky cakes or even crazy cakes – as people thought it was crazy to bake without eggs, butter or milk. 50ml of water can be replaced with cognac, vegan red wine or brewed cold coffee for a more intense chocolate flavour. Vanilla extract can be replaced with the same amount of vanilla sugar.

AMERICAN CHOCOLATE CAKE

20g	cocoa
240g	plain flour
225g	sugar
1 pinch	salt
1 tsp	bicarbonate of soda
1 tsp	vanilla extract
100ml	oil
1 tsp	vinegar
250ml	water

Preheat the oven to 175°C/350°F/gas 4. Grease and add crumbs to a loaf tin of around 2 litres. Sift the cocoa and mix with the flour, sugar, salt and bicarbonate of soda. Add the vanilla extract, oil, vinegar and water. Mix with a spatula until smooth without overworking. Pour the batter into the tin and bake in the centre of the oven at 175°C/350°F/gas 4 for 40–45 minutes. Test with a skewer until it comes out clean from the middle of the cake. Leave to cool before removing it from the tin.

CHOCOLATE CAKE

This moist chocolate cake is baked in a round tin and ideally should be covered with a thin layer of chocolate glaze when cool or could be decorated with candy fluff (see page 228) or caramel frosting (see page 236). Here, I have used some whisky in the glaze, which you can leave out. If you are allergic to legumes the aquafaba can be replaced with 100ml of water, which gives a good result. To get a chocolate cake with a good flavour, some of the water can be replaced with red wine, whisky, coffee or stout.

40g	cocoa
180g	plain flour
180g	icing sugar
1 pinch	salt
1 tsp	bicarbonate of soda
½ tsp	baking powder
1 tsp	vanilla extract
1 tsp	vinegar
100ml	oil
150ml	water
100ml	aquafaba

Preheat the oven to 175°C/350°F/gas 4. Grease and add crumbs to a tin measuring around 18–22cm in diameter or prepare with baking paper. Sift the cocoa and mix with the flour, sugar, salt, bicarbonate of soda and baking powder in a bowl. Add the vanilla, vinegar, oil, water and aquafaba and mix with a whisk or spatula until smooth. Swipe the spatula around the sides of the bowl to incorporate any leftover flour. Pour the batter into the tin and bake in the centre of the oven at 175°C/350°F/gas 4 for 25–35 minutes depending on the size of your tin. Test with a skewer until it comes out clean from the middle of the cake. Leave to cool on a wire rack before slicing or decorating.

SOFT CHOCOLATE GLAZE

100g	margarine
250ml	cream
200g	chocolate
1 pinch	salt
1 tsp	vanilla extract
0–3 tsp	sugar (optional)
1 tbsp	whisky (optional)

Put the margarine and cream in a saucepan and remove from the hob when the margarine has melted. Break the chocolate into pieces and let it melt in the warm mixture. Add the salt and vanilla to taste. If you have used dark chocolate, you might need to sweeten the glaze with some sugar. Lastly, add whisky if using.

In the picture, the cake is covered with an extra soft chocolate glaze. It should not be chilled as it contains chocolate, but it can be stored at room temperature well-sealed for many hours. If you need to chill the cake, have a look at page 230 for more chocolate glazes and frostings that can be chilled without hardening up too much before serving.

AMBROSIA & SILVIA CAKE

Here are two traditional glazed sponge cakes with different flavours from the glazes and decorations but which are based on the same sponge cake. For the glaze for the ambrosia cake, you need freshly squeezed orange juice to get the right flavour. In the picture opposite, I have used the juice from a blood orange for the glaze.

SPONGE CAKE BASE

75g	margarine
180g	sugar
100ml	aquafaba
180g	plain flour
2 tsp	baking powder
1 pinch	salt
1 tsp	vanilla extract
75ml	milk or water

Preheat the oven to 175°C/350°F/gas 4. Grease and add crumbs to a round tin measuring 20–22cm in diameter (or prepare with baking paper). Melt the margarine. Whip the sugar and aquafaba until frothy in a stand mixer or with an electric hand mixer. Carefully mix the flour, baking powder and salt in a bowl. Add the dry ingredients, the melted margarine, the vanilla and the milk or water to the frothy aquafaba and fold with a spatula until smooth without overworking. Swipe the spatula around the sides of the bowl to incorporate any leftover flour. Pour the batter into the tin and bake in the centre of the oven at 175°C/350°F/gas 4 for 30–35 minutes. Test with a skewer until it comes out clean from the middle of the cake.

AMBROSIA GLAZE

360g	icing sugar
2–3 tbsp	orange juice
100g	candied orange peel, chopped

Let the cake cool completely. Mix the icing sugar with freshly squeezed orange juice and spread over the cake and sprinkle candied orange peel on top. Let the glaze cool to firm up.

SILVIA GLAZE

50g	margarine
120g	icing sugar
2 tsp	vanilla sugar or vanilla extract
2 tsp	cream
	desiccated coconut

Let the cake cool completely. Melt the margarine and let it cool a little. Mix with the icing sugar, vanilla and cream. Spread over the cake and sprinkle desiccated coconut on top.

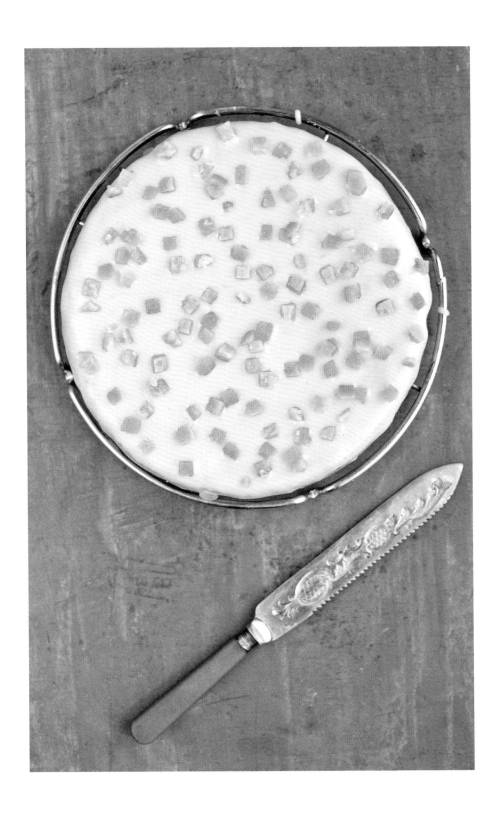

TOSCA CAKE

This is a classic that is not as difficult to make as it looks and which is worth the extra effort. If you are allergic to almonds, you can use the same amount of pumpkin seeds in the tosca topping.

SPONGE CAKE

100g	margarine
180g	sugar
100ml	aquafaba
180g	plain flour
1 tsp	baking powder
1 tsp	vanilla extract
1 pinch	salt
50ml	milk or water

Preheat the oven to 175°C/350°F/gas 4. Grease and add crumbs to a round tin measuring 20–22cm in diameter (or prepare with baking paper). Melt the margarine. Whip the sugar and aquafaba until frothy in a stand mixer or with an electric hand mixer. Carefully mix the flour, baking powder and salt in a bowl. Add the dry ingredients, the melted margarine, the vanilla and the milk or water to the frothy aquafaba and mix with a spatula until smooth without overworking. Swipe the spatula around the sides of the bowl to incorporate any leftover flour. Pour the batter into the tin and bake in the centre of the oven at 175°C/350°F/gas 4 for 20 minutes. While it bakes, prepare the tosca topping.

TOSCA TOPPING

50g	margarine
45g	sugar
1 tbsp	milk
1 tbsp	plain flour
50–75g	flaked almonds

Put the margarine, sugar, milk and plain flour in a saucepan and let the mixture simmer for a few minutes until it is slightly thickened and does not stick to the sides. Spread the tosca batter over the baked cake straight from the oven, then put it back in the centre of the oven at 175°C/350°F/gas 4 for around 15 minutes, or until the tosca has a nice colour. Leave to cool completely before slicing.

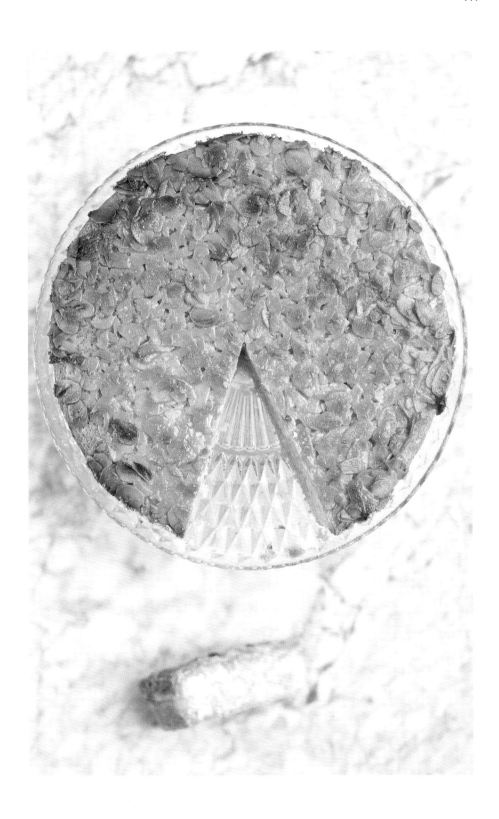

ALMOND CAKES

ALMOND CAKE WITH GLAZE

5	bitter almonds or
1 tsp	almond extract
25g	almond flour
75g	margarine
180g	sugar
75ml	aquafaba
150g	plain flour
1 tsp	baking powder
1 pinch	salt
100ml	milk or water

Preheat the oven to 175°C/350°F/gas 4. Grease and add crumbs to a round tin measuring 20–22cm in diameter (or prepare with baking paper). Grate the bitter almonds with a grater or in an almond grinder, if using. Mix with the almond flour. Melt the margarine. Whip the sugar and aquafaba until frothy in a stand mixer or with an electric hand mixer. Carefully mix the flour, almond flour mixture, baking powder and salt in a bowl. Add the dry ingredients, the melted margarine and the milk or water (and almond extract, if using) to the frothy aquafaba and mix with a spatula until smooth without overworking. Swipe the spatula around the sides of the bowl to incorporate any leftover flour. Pour the batter into the tin and bake in the centre of the oven at 175°C/350°F/gas 4 for 25–30 minutes. Test with a skewer until it comes out clean from the middle of the cake.

GLAZE

180g	icing sugar
2–3 tbsp	water
	colouring (optional)

Mix the icing sugar with the water and spread on top of the cooled cake. You can split the mixture into two bowls and colour one of them using colouring. Pour both of them into separate piping bags and pipe the glaze in lines over the cold cake.

ALMOND CAKE WITH FLAKED ALMONDS

50g	margarine
180g	sugar
100ml	aquafaba
120g	plain flour
50g	almond flour
1 tsp	baking powder
1 pinch	salt
1 tsp	vanilla extract
100ml	milk or water
	flaked almonds

Preheat the oven to 175°C/350°F/gas 4. Grease and add crumbs to a round tin measuring 20–22cm in diameter (or prepare with baking paper). Melt the margarine. Whip the sugar and aquafaba until frothy in a stand mixer or with an electric hand mixer. Carefully mix the flour, almond flour, baking powder and salt in a separate bowl. Add the dry ingredients, the melted margarine, the vanilla and the milk or water to the frothy aquafaba and mix with a spatula until smooth without overworking. Swipe the spatula around the sides of the bowl to incorporate any leftover flour. Pour the batter into the tin, sprinkle the flaked almonds on top and bake in the centre of the oven at 175°C/350°F/gas 4 for 25–30 minutes. Test with a skewer until it comes out clean from the middle of the cake.

This cake was decorated with glaze coloured with red colouring powder that does not contain E120. Read more about colouring for frosting on page 54.

NUT SPONGE CAKES

TORTA DI MANDORLE

100g	almond flour
50g	margarine
180g	sugar
100ml	aquafaba
150g	plain flour
1 tsp	baking powder
1 pinch	salt
50ml	milk

Torta di mandorle is an Italian almond cake from Liguria. It is similar to the French gateau Breton and the consistency should be quite dense. Sometimes the recipe contains ¼ teaspoon of ground cinnamon, which is mixed in with the flour and the other dry ingredients.

Preheat the oven to 175°C/350°F/gas 4. Grease and add crumbs to a small sponge cake tin of 1.2 litres. Use 100g of almond flour or make your own from 100g of sweet almonds. Blanch the almonds for a few minutes in boiling water and remove the skins. Leave to dry. Process or blend the almonds to make the flour. Melt the margarine. Whip the sugar and aquafaba until frothy in a stand mixer or with an electric hand mixer. Mix the flour, almond flour, baking powder and salt in a separate bowl. Add the dry ingredients, the margarine and the milk to the frothy aquafaba and mix with a spatula until smooth without overworking. Swipe the spatula around the sides of the bowl to incorporate any leftover flour. Pour the batter into the tin and bake in the centre of the oven at 175°C/350°F/gas 4 for 35–45 minutes. Test with a skewer until it comes out clean from the middle of the cake. The cake will develop a deeper flavour and consistency by sitting overnight.

HAZELNUT CAKE

125g	blanched hazelnuts
50g	margarine
180g	sugar
100ml	aquafaba
150g	plain flour
1 tsp	baking powder
1 pinch	salt
50ml	milk

Preheat the oven to 175°C/350°F/gas 4. Grease and add crumbs to a small sponge cake tin of 1–1.2 litres. Process, blend or finely grind the hazelnuts or use 125g of hazelnut flour. Melt the margarine. Whip the sugar and aquafaba until frothy in a stand mixer or with an electric hand mixer. Mix the hazelnut flour, plain flour, baking powder and salt in a separate bowl. Add the dry ingredients, the melted margarine and the milk to the frothy aquafaba and mix with a spatula until smooth without overworking. Swipe the spatula around the sides of the bowl to incorporate any leftover flour. Pour the batter into the tin and bake in the centre of the oven at 175°C/350°F/gas 4 for 35–45 minutes. Test with a skewer until it comes out clean from the middle of the cake. The cake will develop a deeper flavour and consistency by sitting overnight.

PASSION FRUIT & LEMON CAKE

In countries close to the equator, passion fruit is often used in baking. In South America and Brazil, where passion fruit come from, these cakes are called bolo de maracuja, but they are also popular in Australia and New Zealand where passion fruit is now widely cultivated. It is also possible to buy the fruit pulp frozen into cubes, which can be easier to use than the fresh fruit. 100g of passion fruit pulp is the equivalent of about five passion fruit. If you get too little out of the fruit, you can always add milk or yoghurt to get the right quantity. You can strain the pulp to remove the seeds if you prefer.

100g	margarine
1	lemon, zest of
270g	plain flour
2 tsp	baking powder
1 pinch	salt
270g	sugar
150ml	aquafaba
100g	passion fruit pulp

Preheat the oven to 175°C/350°F/gas 4. Grease and add crumbs to a round cake tin that holds 1–1.2 litres (or prepare with baking paper). Melt the margarine and add the lemon zest. Stir and set aside. Mix the baking powder and salt in a bowl. Whip the sugar and aquafaba until frothy in a separate bowl. Add the dry ingredients and the passion fruit pulp to the frothy aquafaba with a spatula, and once incorporated, fold in the melted margarine and lemon mixture in three batches. Swipe the spatula around the sides of the bowl to incorporate any leftover flour. Pour the batter into the tin and bake in the centre of the oven at 175°C/350°F/gas 4 for 45–50 minutes. Test with a skewer until it comes out clean from the middle of the cake. Leave the cake to cool before cutting.

PASSION FRUIT ICING

50g	passion fruit pulp
180g	icing sugar

Mix the passion fruit pulp with enough icing sugar to make the icing thick, and spread over the cake once completely cool. Leave to set slightly before serving.

CLEMENTINE CAKE

This moist clementine cake is amazingly aromatic because it contains the whole fruit – peel and all. It is a classic that has many versions in Southern Europe but I like it best using clementines. Make sure you use organic fruit, as it contains the whole fruit. Also, be sure to use fruit with a thin peel; if you are using fruit with a rind that is too thick, the cake will not be as good, and both the taste and consistency will suffer. The cake is best the day after baking, so I recommend you let it sit overnight to even out the flavours from the citrus. This cake is prepared with folded baking paper, which is shown on page 63.

3–4 (200g)	clementines
	milk, if required
100g	margarine
270g	sugar
150ml	aquafaba
270g	plain flour
1 tbsp	baking powder
1 pinch	salt

Preheat the oven to 175°C/350°F/gas 4. Grease and add crumbs to a round tin measuring 20–22cm in diameter, or prepare with baking paper. Put the whole clementines in a small saucepan and remove the stalk from the top of each. Add water to halfway up the fruit, cover and let them simmer for 30 minutes. The water should not be allowed to evaporate as the fruit will burn. Remove the fruit from the saucepan, cut into pieces and remove the pips. Do this on a plate to save the liquid for the purée. Blend the whole fruit and the juice from the plate into a smooth purée. Remove any pips that you might have missed. Pour into a measuring jug and if you do not have 150ml, top up with milk to the right amount.

Melt the margarine and mix with the fruit purée; mix to a fully emulsified purée. Whip the sugar and aquafaba until frothy. Carefully mix the flour, baking powder and salt in a separate bowl. Add the dry ingredients and the fruit mixture to the frothy aquafaba and mix with a spatula until smooth without overworking. Swipe the spatula around the sides of the bowl to incorporate any leftover flour. Pour the batter into the tin and bake in the centre of the oven at 175°C/350°F/gas 4 for 35–45 minutes. Test with a skewer until it comes out clean from the middle of the cake.

CITRUS CAKE

I have included two slightly tart glaze recipes to cover this cake so that you can choose one of them. The citrus syrup is poured over the warm cake and absorbed into the sponge, the glaze is poured over the cold cake and will create a beautiful, light-coloured, tart layer on top. Prepare the cake in a tin lined with baking paper, which will prevent the glaze from running off the cake. For this cake, the tin is lined with folded baking paper, which is shown on page 63.

100g	margarine
1	lemon, zest of
1	lime, zest of
270g	sugar
150ml	aquafaba
270g	plain flour
1 tbsp	baking powder
1 pinch	salt
100ml	milk

Preheat the oven to 175°C/350°F/gas 4. Grease and add crumbs to a round tin measuring 20–22cm in diameter (or prepare with baking paper). Melt the margarine and grate the outermost zest of the lemon and lime. Whip the sugar and aquafaba in a stand mixer or with an electric hand mixer until frothy. Carefully mix the flour, baking powder and salt in a separate bowl. Add the dry ingredients, the melted margarine and the milk to the frothy aquafaba and mix with a spatula until smooth without overworking. Swipe the spatula around the sides of the bowl to incorporate any leftover flour. Pour the batter into the tin and bake in the centre of the oven at 175°C/350°F/gas 4 for 35–45 minutes. Test with a skewer until it comes out clean from the middle of the cake.

GLAZE

| 2–3 tbsp | mixed lemon and lime juice |
| 120g | icing sugar |

Mix the icing sugar with citrus juice until smooth and combined; make holes all over the cooled cake and pour the glaze over it. If you leave it to harden, you can remove the lining paper without the glaze running off.

CITRUS SYRUP

50ml	water
45g	sugar
50ml	citrus juice

Boil the water, sugar and citrus juice together in a small pan; when the sugar is dissolved, you can remove the saucepan from the hob. Pour the syrup over the cake when it comes out of the oven. Make holes in the cake with a skewer first to help the cake absorb the syrup faster and more deeply into the cake.

CLASSIC APPLE CAKES

APPLE CAKE

50g	margarine
180g	plain flour
135g	sugar
2 tsp	baking powder
I pinch	salt
150ml	milk
45g	sugar
2 tsp	ground cinnamon
1–2	eating apples

If you want a slightly more airy apple cake, you can replace 50ml of the milk with plain aquafaba, which gives a good result in this flat cake. In the classic apple sponge cake, the aquafaba is whipped until frothy, which makes it rise slightly more.

Preheat the oven to 200°C/400°F/gas 6. Grease and add crumbs to a round tin measuring 18–22cm in diameter (or prepare with baking paper). Melt the margarine and let it cool slightly. Mix the flour, sugar, baking powder and salt in a bowl. Add the milk and melted margarine. Carefully fold the batter until smooth and pour into the tin. Mix the sugar and cinnamon. Cut thin slices of the apples and fold into the sugar and cinnamon mixture. Arrange the slices on top of the cake batter, sprinkle over the leftover cinnamon sugar and bake in the centre of the oven at 200°C/400°F/gas 6 for 25–30 minutes.

CLASSIC APPLE SPONGE CAKE

2–3	eating apples, diced
I tsp	cinnamon
2 tbsp	sugar
75g	margarine
180g	sugar
75ml	aquafaba
180g	plain flour
2 tsp	baking powder
I pinch	salt
100ml	milk

Preheat the oven to 175°C/350°F/gas 4. Grease and add crumbs to a round tin measuring 20–22cm in diameter, or a loaf tin. Peel, core and slice or dice the apples and fold in the cinnamon and sugar. Set aside. Melt the margarine. Whip the sugar and aquafaba until frothy in a stand mixer or with an electric hand mixer. Carefully mix the flour, baking powder and salt in a separate bowl. Add the dry ingredients, the melted margarine and the milk to the frothy aquafaba and mix the batter until smooth without overworking. Swipe the spatula around the sides of the bowl to incorporate any leftover flour. Pour the batter into the tin, add the diced apple or apple slices, sprinkle the leftover cinnamon sugar on top, and bake in the centre of the oven at 175°C/350°F/gas 4 for 30–35 minutes. Test with a skewer until it comes out clean from the middle of the cake.

CIDER CAKE

300ml	cider
75g	margarine
½ tsp	grated nutmeg
225g	sugar
125ml	aquafaba
210g	plain flour
2 tsp	baking powder
½ tsp	ground cinnamon
I pinch	salt
I tsp	vanilla extract
60g	walnuts, chopped

Preheat the oven to 1175°C/350°F/gas 4. Reduce 300ml of cider in a saucepan on a low heat until 100ml remains. If it has reduced too much you can add a little more cider so you have the right volume. Grease and add crumbs to a round tin that holds 1.5–2 litres. Melt the margarine. Grate the nutmeg and measure out ½ teaspoon. Whip the sugar and aquafaba until frothy in a stand mixer or with an electric hand mixer. Carefully mix the flour, baking powder, grated nutmeg, cinnamon and salt in a separate bowl and stir until everything is combined. Add the dry ingredients, the margarine, vanilla and cider to the mixing bowl and stir until the batter is smooth without overmixing. Swipe the spatula around the sides of the bowl to incorporate any leftover flour. Stir in the walnuts, pour the batter into the tin and bake in the centre of the oven at 175°C/350°F/gas 4 for 35–40 minutes. Test using a skewer until it comes out clean from the middle of the cake.

MORE APPLE CAKES

This recipe was the first sponge, before we had aquafaba, where I managed to make a light-coloured cake with no aftertaste from the bicarbonate of soda and other egg replacements. Even though I have a simpler recipe today, which includes aquafaba, I have included this recipe to show that a similar sponge can be made without aquafaba and legumes. The first apple cake on page 130 can also be made without aquafaba. This recipe was developed using some of the sugar in the form of icing sugar so that the right amount of sugar can be used with the cornstarch to stabilize the cake. Sadly, you cannot use it for layer cakes as you cannot cut it into thin slices, but it is perfect for apple cakes! The apples can be replaced with pears or rhubarb. Pears go well together with ground cardamom instead of cinnamon, while rhubarb pairs best just with sugar and no additional spices.

BASIC RECIPE FOR APPLE CAKE WITHOUT AQUAFABA

100g	soft margarine
135g	sugar
60g	icing sugar
200ml	room-temperature cream
30g	cornstarch
2 tsp	baking powder
210g	plain flour
¼ tsp	salt
1 tsp	vanilla extract
2–3	eating apples, peeled, cored and diced
2 tbsp	sugar
2 tsp	ground cinnamon

Preheat the oven to 200°C/400°F/gas 6. Grease and add crumbs to a springform tin measuring 22–24cm in diameter. For a cake like the one opposite, use a tin measuring 22cm in diameter. Mix the margarine, sugar and icing sugar in a bowl until light and airy. Mix the cream and the cornstarch in a small bowl until smooth. Mix the baking powder with the flour and salt in a separate bowl, then add to the batter, along with the cornstarch mixture and the vanilla extract. Do not overwork the batter but mix until just combined. Pour the batter into the tin. Mix the diced apples with the sugar and cinnamon and spread over the top of the cake batter. Make sure they are spread out evenly and press them down slightly. Bake at 200°C/400°F/gas 6 for 45–55 minutes. Test with a skewer until it comes out clean from the middle of the cake.

FRENCH APPLE CAKE

3 tbsp	rum
150g	room-temperature yoghurt
2–3	eating apples, peeled, cored and diced

Follow the basic recipe, but replace the 200ml of cream with the rum and yoghurt. Fold the diced apples into the batter before pouring it into the tin and bake according to the basic recipe.

SAFFRON APPLE CAKE

¼–½g	saffron

Follow the basic recipe above, but first let the cream and the saffron simmer together. I usually leave out the cinnamon in this recipe but it is up to you. Bake according to the basic recipe.

SUNKEN APPLE CAKE

Versunkener Apfelkuchen is a German cake with a high proportion of apples in the mix. For the apple to become soft in the oven it is soaked in lemon and thinly sliced down to the core. Do not cut the apple in half, it is important that the slices of apple are a little thinner than half an apple. Use small, compact apples if you can, such as coxes. It is also important that the apples have time to soak in the lemon juice as this softens the apples and allows them to bake more quickly. Serve with a small scoop of vanilla ice cream, vanilla cream or whipped cream. There are many different spices in the old German recipes, some of them have a little cinnamon or cardamom and many recipes use neither lemon zest nor vanilla. I think the lemon zest is suitable as the lemon juice is used with the apples. Read about the batter on page 32.

20cm	25cm	
3–4	4–6	small eating apples
2–3 tbsp	3–4 tbsp	lemon juice
2 tbsp	45g	sugar
180g	270g	plain flour
2 tsp	1 tbsp	baking powder
75g	100g	margarine
1 pinch	1 pinch	salt
180g	270g	sugar
75ml	100ml	aquafaba
100ml	150ml	milk
1 tsp	2 tsp	vanilla extract
1	1–2	lemons, zest of

Peel the apples, keeping them whole. Place one apple on your work surface, base downwards, and carefully cut into it on either side of the core. Remove the core. Next, slice each side of the apple as thinly as you can so it resembles a hasselback potato. Repeat for the other apples. Mix the apples, lemon juice and sugar in a bowl and leave to soak while preparing the rest of the ingredients.

Preheat the oven to 175°C/350°F/gas 4. Prepare a round tin measuring 20 or 25cm in diameter, depending on how much batter you have. Mix the flour and baking powder in a stand mixer or an electric hand mixer. Dice the margarine and mix until the margarine is the size of peas. Add the salt and sugar and mix for a few more minutes, until the mixture resembles breadcrumbs. If you are using a stand or hand mixer, you might need to make sure that everything is evenly mixed in the bowl. Add the aquafaba, milk, vanilla extract and lemon zest and mix thoroughly to a well-combined batter. Pour the batter into the tin and even it out, then put the lemon-soaked apples in a circle 1.5cm from the edges, possibly with half an apple in the centre, and bake at 175°C/350°F/gas 4 for 40–50 minutes. Bring it out when the cake is golden on top and a skewer comes out clean.

CAKES WITH GRATED APPLE

Apple cakes with grated apples in the batter make a different type of cake to the classic versions in the book that use larger pieces of apple. Instead of muscovado sugar you can use soft brown sugar; both the light and dark versions work. The recipe for spicy apple cake was veganized from a recipe by Mary Berry.

SPICY APPLE CAKE

165g	finely grated apples
190g	muscovado sugar
240g	plain flour
1 pinch	salt
½ tsp	bicarbonate of soda
1½ tsp	baking powder
1 tsp	cinnamon
50ml	apple juice
50ml	aquafaba
100ml	oil
100g	apple sauce
60–70g	raisins
60g	chopped hazelnuts

Preheat the oven to 175°C/350°F/gas 4. Prepare a round tin measuring 20–22cm in diameter (or prepare with baking paper). Finely grate the apples, measure the amount, then press out the juice and save 50ml for the batter. Set aside. Mix the sugar, plain flour, salt, bicarbonate of soda, baking powder and cinnamon in a bowl. Add the grated apple, the juice from the grated apples, the aquafaba, oil, apple sauce, raisins and nuts and mix to a smooth batter with no lumps using a spatula. Do not overwork the batter, which can make the cake chewy. Swipe the spatula around the sides of the bowl to incorporate any leftover flour, pour into the tin and bake in the centre of the oven at 175°C/350°F/gas 4 for 35–45 minutes. Test with a skewer until it comes out clean from the middle of the cake.

LIGHT-COLOURED APPLE CAKE

55g	coarsely grated apples
75g	margarine
180g	sugar
75ml	aquafaba
180g	plain flour
2 tsp	baking powder
1 pinch	salt
75ml	apple juice or cider

Preheat the oven to 175°C/350°F/gas 4. Grease and add crumbs to a springform tin measuring 18–20cm in diameter (or prepare with baking paper). Peel the apples and grate with the coarse end of the grater. Measure out 55g. Melt the margarine. Whip the sugar and aquafaba until frothy in a stand mixer or with an electric hand mixer. Mix the flour, baking powder and salt in a separate bowl. Add the dry ingredients, the melted margarine, the grated apple and the apple juice or cider to the frothy aquafaba and mix with a spatula until smooth without overworking. Swipe the spatula around the sides of the bowl to incorporate any leftover flour. Pour the batter into the tin and bake in the centre of the oven at 175°C/350°F/gas 4 for 30–35 minutes. Test with a skewer until it comes out clean from the middle of the cake.

FRUIT CRUMBLE CAKE

Based on my simple sponge cake, I have veganized a wonderful cake from Nick Malgieri's book *Bake!* The fruit helps the crumble stay dry without soaking in the sponge cake batter and the crumble works nicely with the thin fruit layer. The banana flavour in the banana version is different to other banana cakes where the banana is mashed into the batter. Choose one of the crumbles. You could also try the recipe using a different fruit.

SPONGE CAKE BATTER

150g	plain flour
135g	sugar
1 pinch	salt
1½ tsp	baking powder
50ml	oil
100ml	milk
50ml	aquafaba

BANANA CRUMBLE

90g	plain flour
2 tbsp	sugar
1/8 tsp	baking powder
1 pinch	salt
40g	almond flour or dried coconut flakes
60g	margarine
1–2	bananas

APPLE CRUMBLE

90g	plain flour
2 tbsp	sugar
½ tsp	ground cinnamon
1 pinch	salt
30g	porridge oats
60g	margarine
1–2	eating apples
1 tsp	ground cinnamon
2 tbsp	sugar

Preheat the oven to 175°C/350°F/gas 4. Prepare a tin measuring 20–22cm in diameter with baking paper at the bottom and around the sides. Start with the crumble by mixing all the dry ingredients in a bowl and dicing the margarine. Rub the ingredients together to form a crumbly dough. Peel and cut the bananas into 5–7mm-thick rounds, or peel and core the apples and cut into thin slices, then dip in the cinnamon mixed with the sugar.

Now prepare the batter. Mix the flour, sugar, salt and baking powder in a bowl. Add the oil, milk and aquafaba to the bowl and mix with a spatula until smooth without overworking. Swipe the spatula around the sides of the bowl to incorporate any leftover flour. Pour the batter into the tin and even it out. Cover the cake with the crumble mixture in an even layer and bake in the centre of the oven at 175°C/350°F/gas 4 for 30–35 minutes. Test with a skewer until it comes out clean from the middle of the cake.

STRAWBERRY CAKE

This is a sweet and summery cake filled with strawberries. The tin for the cake was lined with baking paper at the bottom and had two strips of baking paper on the sides; see page 64. If you are using a sponge cake tin or a loaf tin, it needs to hold around 2 litres. The cake can also be baked in a smaller tin of 25 × 35cm, with a baking time of about 35–50 minutes. If you roast the strawberries according to the instructions on page 412, you can increase the quantity to 500–600g. Then use 10 per cent of the weight of the strawberries in sugar, i.e. 50–60g of sugar depending on how much fruit you used. The strawberries roast in around 2–3 hours. If you do roast the strawberries, save some fresh strawberries for the top, otherwise they will become too well-baked.

200–300g strawberries

100g	margarine
270g	sugar
125ml	aquafaba
300g	plain flour
1 tbsp	baking powder
2 tsp	vanilla sugar or vanilla extract
1 pinch	salt
150g	room-temperature yoghurt
1	lime, zest of (optional)
	raw cane sugar or nibbed sugar

Preheat the oven to 175°C/350°F/gas 4. Prepare a round tin measuring 20–25cm in diameter or a roasting tin of 20 × 30cm by greasing and adding crumbs or using baking paper.

Hull the strawberries and dice into pieces. Reserve 3–5 strawberries and cut them into slightly larger pieces to put on top of the cake.

Melt the margarine. Whip the sugar and aquafaba until frothy in a stand mixer or using an electric hand mixer. Mix the flour, baking powder and salt in a separate bowl. Add the dry ingredients, the melted margarine, the yoghurt, vanilla, lime zest, if using, and the diced strawberries to the frothy aquafaba and mix with a spatula until smooth without overworking. Swipe the spatula around the sides of the bowl to incorporate any leftover flour. Pour the batter into the tin, spread your reserved strawberries on top and sprinkle raw cane sugar or nibbed sugar evenly over the cake. Bake in the centre of the oven at 175°C/350°F/gas 4 for 40–50 minutes for a tin of 20cm, or 35–45 minutes for larger tins. Test with a skewer until it comes out clean from the middle of the cake.

CHERRY CAKE

In the picture below I have used both black and red cherries, but you can also use the same quantity of raspberries, blueberries or any of your favourite berries. If you are using rhubarb, you should peel and dice it and roll it in some sugar before baking.

110g	sweet cherries
75g	margarine
180g	sugar
75ml	aquafaba
180g	plain flour
2 tsp	baking powder
1 pinch	salt
100ml	milk
	flaked almonds or nibbed sugar

Preheat the oven to 175°C/350°F/gas 4. Grease and add crumbs to a tin (or prepare with baking paper) measuring 20–22cm in diameter, or a rectangular loaf tin.

Remove the stones from the cherries and weigh out 110g.

Melt the margarine. Whip the sugar and aquafaba until frothy in a stand mixer or using an electric hand mixer. Mix the flour, baking powder and salt in a separate bowl. Add the dry ingredients, the melted margarine and the milk to the frothy aquafaba and mix with a spatula to a smooth batter without overworking. Swipe the spatula around the sides of the bowl to incorporate any leftover flour. Pour the batter into the tin and sprinkle the cherries and the flaked almonds or nibbed sugar on top. Bake in the centre of the oven at 175°C/350°F/gas 4 for 30–35 minutes. Test with a skewer until it comes out clean from the middle of the cake.

CLASSIC
BANANA BREADS

Moist, sweet banana breads have, just like many recipes in this book, been part of my repertoire since my very first books. I have included two versions, one simple banana bread and one spiced banana bread, which in my book means adding coffee and cinnamon. When I started, my recipes included a specific number of bananas instead of going by weight, but as bananas come in different sizes I now just use weight in almost all my banana recipes. Both 250g and 300g of bananas makes a good cake. You can reduce the batter to half the amount and bake it in a small tin of 1–1.5 litres or use two smaller tins. The margarine can be replaced with 115ml of oil with good results. The picture opposite shows the simple batter on the left and the spiced batter on the right; both have been baked in larger tins of around 2 litres.

SIMPLE

250–300g	mashed bananas
125g	margarine
300g	plain flour
270g	sugar
1 tsp	bicarbonate of soda
1 tsp	baking powder
1 pinch	salt
150ml	milk

SPICED

250–300g	mashed bananas
125g	margarine
300g	plain flour
270g	sugar
1 tsp	bicarbonate of soda
1 tsp	baking powder
1 pinch	salt
100ml	milk
50ml	cold espresso
½–1 tsp	ground cinnamon

Preheat the oven to 175°C/350°F/gas 4. Grease and add crumbs to a loaf tin of 1.5–2 litres or prepare with baking paper. Mash the bananas well and set aside while the batter is prepared. Melt the margarine. Mix the flour, sugar, bicarbonate of soda, baking powder and salt in a bowl. Add the mashed banana, melted margarine and the milk (and the espresso and cinnamon for the spiced cake). Fold to a smooth batter with no lumps using a whisk or a spatula without overworking, as otherwise the cake will be chewy. Swipe the spatula around the sides of the bowl to incorporate any leftover flour, then pour the batter into the tin and bake in the centre of the oven at 175°C/350°F/gas 4. Timings for different tins and quantities of batter are shown opposite. Leave it to cool on a wire rack before removing from the tin.

RIPE?

The riper the bananas are, the more flavour the cake will have.

TINS & BAKING TIMES
Below, are details of the tins suitable for this cake and how long they should be baked for.

Half the batter in a 1–1.5-litre tin = 30–40 minutes
All the batter in a 2-litre loaf tin = 50–60 minutes

CARAMEL BANANA BREAD

For this cake you can use five large bananas in the batter without it giving a doughy cake with too much liquid. You do this by heating the peeled bananas in the microwave to remove most of the liquid so that they reduce down to a smaller quantity. After it is reduced the liquid tastes like caramelized banana. The recipe comes from the TV show *America's Test Kitchen*. That particular recipe also includes 50g of pecan nuts and 1 teaspoon of ground cinnamon, but I think that the cake is delicious with just the flavour from the brown sugar and bananas. However, you can add both cinnamon and nuts if you think that gives a better flavour. As the bananas are heated whole I have used whole bananas in this recipe. If you are using very small bananas you might need 6 bananas. You can also sprinkle caster sugar on top of the cake before baking if you do not have raw cane sugar.

5	ripe bananas
125g	margarine
270g	plain flour
1 tsp	bicarbonate of soda
1 pinch	salt
1 tsp	vanilla extract
150g	brown sugar
100ml	aquafaba
1	banana
	raw cane sugar

Put the 5 bananas in a microwave-safe bowl. Do not mash them but leave them as they are in the bowl. Cover with a lid to avoid losing the banana liquid, but do not seal it properly. Microwave on full power for 4–6 minutes, by which time the bananas should have released a large amount of liquid. Put the liquid in a small saucepan and put the bananas in a sieve and let them drain over the saucepan for 10–15 minutes. Then mash the bananas in the sieve and collect the liquid for the reduction. All the banana liquid should now be reduced on a low heat to about 50–75ml. Be careful towards the end not to burn the reduction as the liquid thickens. The total weight of the mashed bananas should be 200g, but up to 250g also works.

Preheat the oven to 175°C/350°F/gas 4. Grease and add crumbs to a 2-litre loaf tin or a square tin measuring 20 × 20cm. You can also prepare with crinkled or cut baking paper according to the instructions on page 63. Melt the margarine. Mix the flour, bicarbonate of soda and salt in a bowl. Add the banana reduction, the mashed bananas, melted margarine, vanilla extract, brown sugar and aquafaba. Mix to a smooth batter with no lumps using a whisk or a spatula without overworking, as this will make the cake chewy. Swipe the spatula around the sides of the bowl to incorporate any leftover flour and pour the batter into the tin. Decorate with sliced banana, either cut lengthways or as rounds, and sprinkle a thin layer of raw cane sugar over the cake. Bake in the centre of the oven at 175°C/350°F/gas 4 for 40–50 minutes in the loaf tin and for 25–30 minutes in the square tin. Test the cake with a skewer and let it cool before slicing.

MORE
BANANA BREADS

BANANA BREAD WITH NUTS AND CINNAMON

180g	plain flour
135g	sugar
1 tbsp	ground cinnamon
½ tsp	baking powder
½ tsp	bicarbonate of soda
1 pinch	salt
60g	walnuts
200g	peeled bananas
100ml	oil
200g	yoghurt

This is a simple recipe for banana bread where the walnuts in the batter give it a totally different flavour. The cinnamon can be omitted if you want a pure banana flavour.

Preheat the oven to 175°C/350°F/gas 4. Prepare a sponge cake tin or a loaf tin of about 1.5 litres. Mix the flour, sugar, cinnamon, baking powder, bicarbonate of soda and salt in a bowl. Chop the walnuts coarsely and mix with the dry ingredients. Mash the bananas with a fork and add to the bowl with the oil and yoghurt. Fold all the ingredients together with a spatula. Swipe the spatula around the sides of the bowl to incorporate any leftover flour and pour the batter into the tin. Bake in the centre of the oven at 175°C/350°F/gas 4 for 45–55 minutes. Test the cake with a skewer that should come out clean from the cake. Leave the cake to cool before removing it from the tin.

AMERICAN BANANA BREAD

180g	plain flour
150g	soft brown sugar
1 tsp	baking powder
½ tsp	bicarbonate of soda
1 pinch	salt
200g	peeled bananas
100g	yoghurt
75ml	oil
1 tsp	vanilla extract
½	banana, cut lengthways
1–2 tsp	raw cane sugar

Darker sugar, vanilla extract and half a banana on top make a banana bread that stands out from classic banana breads. The crispy top from the raw cane sugar, or other caster sugar that is caramelized while baking, gives the cake extra character. Here, I have used bicarbonate of soda and yoghurt together to replace the functions of the egg, which results in a perfect sponge cake. As I am using bananas and the right amount of yoghurt, no other stabilizing ingredients are needed, like starch or one part icing sugar, to give the cake a nice consistency. Besides, the yoghurt activates the bicarbonate of soda, which gives a more spongy and moist result than just using baking powder. The cake is shown opposite.

Preheat the oven to 175°C/350°F/gas 4. Prepare a sponge cake tin or a loaf tin of about 1–1.5 litres. Grease and add crumbs or prepare with crinkled baking paper if you are using a loaf tin. Mix the flour, brown sugar, baking powder, bicarbonate of soda and salt in a bowl. Mash the bananas (save one extra half for the topping) and add to the bowl with the yoghurt, oil and vanilla extract. Fold all the ingredients together with a spatula, then pour the batter into the tin, put the halved banana on top and sprinkle over the raw cane sugar. Bake in the centre of the oven at 175°C/350°F/gas 4 for 50–60 minutes. Test with a skewer that should come out clean from the cake. Leave the cake to cool before removing it from the tin.

BANANA SPONGE CAKES

It is possible to double the amount of batter for these cakes if you have a large tin that holds 2–2.5 litres. Then the time in the oven increases by up to 20 minutes.

LIGHT-COLOURED BANANA SPONGE CAKE

75g	margarine
180g	plain flour
2 tsp	baking powder
1 pinch	salt
75ml	aquafaba
180g	sugar
100g	mashed bananas
1 tsp	vanilla extract

Preheat the oven to 175°C/350°F/gas 4. Grease and add crumbs to a 1.2–1.5 litre loaf tin or prepare a round tin measuring 18–20cm in diameter with baking paper. Melt the margarine. Carefully mix the flour, baking powder and salt in a bowl. Whip the aquafaba and sugar until frothy in a separate bowl. Fold in the dry ingredients, the melted margarine, vanilla extract and the mashed banana and carefully mix the batter until smooth without overworking. Swipe the spatula around the sides of the bowl to incorporate any leftover flour. Pour the batter into the tin and bake in the centre of the oven at 175°C/350°F/gas 4 for 30–35 minutes. Test with a skewer that should come out clean from the middle of the cake.

DARK BANANA SPONGE CAKE

100g	margarine
180g	plain flour
1½ tsp	baking powder
1 tsp	vanilla sugar or vanilla extract
1 pinch	salt
190g	soft brown sugar
75ml	aquafaba
100g	mashed bananas

Preheat the oven to 175°C/350°F/gas 4. Grease and add crumbs to a 1.2–1.5 litre loaf tin or prepare a round tin measuring 18–20cm in diameter with baking paper. Melt the margarine and leave it to cool while preparing the rest of the ingredients. Mix the flour, baking powder, vanilla and salt in a bowl. Whip the sugar with the aquafaba until frothy in a separate bowl. Carefully fold in the flour mixture with a spatula; when it is incorporated, fold in the melted margarine in three batches. Fold in the mashed banana. Swipe the spatula around the sides of the bowl to incorporate any leftover flour. Pour the batter into the tin and bake in the centre of the oven at 175°C/350°F/gas 4 for 35–45 minutes. Test with a skewer that should come out clean from the middle of the cake.

MY FAVOURITE BANANA CAKE

75g	margarine
210g	plain flour
1 tsp	baking powder
½ tsp	bicarbonate of soda
1 pinch	salt
1 tsp	vanilla sugar or vanilla extract
125ml	aquafaba
180g	sugar
150g	mashed bananas

Preheat the oven to 175°C/350°F/gas 4. Grease and add crumbs to a 1.5–2 litre loaf tin or prepare a round tin measuring 22cm in diameter with baking paper. Melt the margarine. Carefully mix the flour, baking powder, salt and vanilla sugar or extract in a bowl. Whip the aquafaba and sugar until frothy in a separate bowl. Fold in the dry ingredients, the melted margarine and the mashed banana and carefully mix the batter until smooth without overworking. Swipe the spatula around the sides of the bowl to incorporate any leftover flour. Pour the batter into the tin and bake in the centre of the oven at 175°C/350°F/gas 4 for 35–45 minutes. Test with a skewer that should come out clean from the middle of the cake.

RAISING AGENT & COLOUR
The colour variation in these cakes is mainly due to the type of raising agent that has been used. Baking powder by itself will give a cake that is light in colour, while a combination of the two will make the cake slightly darker. Brown sugar will also give a dark cake. Read more about both raising agents and sugar in the introduction.

UPSIDE-DOWN BANANA CAKE

Using simple sponge cake as the base, I have created a sticky upside-down cake based on caramel and banana. Serve soon after baking, or the same day. However, it will keep well-sealed for a day or two. The bananas can be replaced with almost any fruit, for instance apples, pears, kiwi, plums or pineapple, but I like the banana version best. The most important thing is to slice the fruit thinly so that it has time to bake through in the oven. You can replace the muscovado sugar with soft brown sugar.

BANANA CARAMEL

50g	margarine
55g	light muscovado sugar
1 tbsp	rum
1 tsp	vanilla extract
2–3	bananas

SPONGE CAKE BATTER

150g	plain flour
135g	sugar
1½ tsp	baking powder
1 pinch	salt
50ml	oil
100ml	milk
50ml	aquafaba

Preheat the oven to 175°C/350°F/gas 4. Prepare a tin measuring 20–22cm in diameter with baking paper on the sides and on the bottom; be careful of the paper at the bottom coming too far up the sides. Heat the margarine and sugar together until both are melted, then add the rum and mix together. Remove from the hob and add the vanilla extract. Pour the caramel into the tin. Peel and slice the bananas into rounds or lengthways and put them facing sliced-side down into the tin. Try to cover the bottom of the tin with banana.

Prepare the batter. Mix the flour, sugar, baking powder and salt in a bowl. Add the oil, milk and aquafaba and fold with a spatula until smooth without overworking. Swipe the spatula around the sides of the bowl to incorporate any leftover flour. Pour the batter on top of the caramel bananas and bake in the centre of the oven at 175°C/350°F/gas 4 for 25–35 minutes. Remove the cake from the oven and immediately turn it upside-down onto a serving board or plate; l let it cool for a few minutes before removing from the tin.

GINGER CAKES

AMERICAN GINGER CAKE

SMALLER/LARGER

SMALLER	LARGER	
75g	150g	soft margarine
75g	150g	soft brown sugar
50g	100g	yoghurt
50ml	100ml	aquafaba
180g	360g	plain flour
1 tsp	2 tsp	ground ginger
½ tsp	1 tsp	ground cinnamon
¼ tsp	½ tsp	ground cloves
¼ tsp	½ tsp	grated nutmeg
1 tsp	2 tsp	cocoa
1 pinch	¼ tsp	salt
½ tsp	1 tsp	bicarbonate of soda
½ tsp	1 tsp	baking powder
100ml	200ml	milk
75ml	150ml	golden syrup

I developed this recipe from *Baking Illustrated*, which is a fantastic baking bible published in the USA. The original recipe uses a larger quantity of batter and is baked in a tin measuring 20 x 30cm. My recipe has been adapted to fit a smaller sponge cake tin, or a small square tin measuring 20 x 20cm. I have also included a larger quantity for a bigger cake tin, or a small frying pan as in the original recipe, which fits perfectly with frosting on the top.

Preheat the oven to 175°C/350°F/gas 4. Grease and line or add crumbs to your chosen tin. Whisk together the margarine and soft brown sugar in a bowl, add the aquafaba and whisk to combine. Mix together the dry ingredients in a separate bowl, pour into the margarine and sugar mixture, and then add the milk and the syrup. Stir until the mixture is well-combined. Swipe the spatula around the sides of the bowl to incorporate any leftover flour. Pour the batter into your chosen tin and bake in the centre of the oven at 175°C/350°F/gas 4. The smaller quantity should baked for 30–40 minutes, the larger quantity for 45–55 minutes. Test with a skewer that should come out clean from the middle of the cake.

GINGER CAKE WITH STOUT

75ml	reduced stout (from 300–400ml stout)
75g	margarine
150g	soft brown sugar
100ml	aquafaba
180g	plain flour
2 tsp	baking powder
1 tbsp	ground ginger
1 tbsp	grated fresh ginger
1 pinch	salt

Here you can use stout, Christmas ale, porter or Guinness. If you do not want to use beer, you can use water, ginger juice, ginger beer or milk. You can also leave out the step where you reduce the beer, but you lose a lot of flavour. In the picture opposite, the frosting was coloured using food-grade activated carbon.

Preheat the oven to 175°C/350°F/gas 4. Grease and line or add crumbs to a 1.2–1.5 litre loaf tin or a round tin measuring 18–20cm in diameter. Start by reducing the stout, if using. Put 300–400ml of beer in a saucepan and simmer on a medium heat until there is 75ml left. If you accidentally reduce it too much, you can top it up with water. Set aside to cool. Melt the margarine. Whip the brown sugar and aquafaba until frothy using a stand mixer or an electric hand mixer. Carefully mix the flour, baking powder, ground ginger and salt in a separate bowl. Add the grated fresh ginger, the melted margarine and the reduced beer, then add this and the dry ingredients to the frothy aquafaba and mix with a spatula to a smooth batter without overworking. Swipe the spatula around the sides of the bowl to incorporate any leftover flour. Pour the batter into the tin and bake in the centre of the oven at 175°C/350°F/gas 4 for 30–35 minutes. Test with a skewer that should come out clean from the middle of the cake.

CHRISTMAS CAKE

Christmas cake is a must for many during the holidays, but in Sweden our fruit cakes are more like sponge cake, and very few of our older traditional cookery books include classic British or American fruit cakes with this much fruit in them. I think that the quantity of fruit is slightly on the generous side, but many recipes include up to 900g dried fruit; if you want to try using more fruit you may need to increase the baking time.

700–800g	dried fruit
75ml	brandy
200g	soft margarine
200g	dark muscovado sugar
150ml	aquafaba
240g	plain flour
½ tsp	ground cinnamon
½ tsp	ground cardamom
½ tsp	ground ginger
½ tsp	ground cloves
1 pinch	salt
100g	mixed chopped nuts
20–30g	peeled whole almonds or preserved cherries (optional)

Week 1: Chop any larger pieces of fruit into chunks. Mix the fruit with brandy in a jar, seal and store in a cool, dry place.

Week 2–4: Preheat the oven to 150°C/300°F/gas 2. Grease and line a tin, measuring 20cm in diameter, with baking paper. Line the inside with double or triple layers, and make sure the paper extends high above the sides of the tin.

Melt the margarine in a saucepan, remove from the heat and set aside to cool. In a bowl whip together the sugar and aquafaba until light and frothy. In a separate bowl, mix together the flour, spices and salt and stir to combine. Sift the flour mixture into the frothy aquafaba and fold in thoroughly using a silicone spatula to make sure no pockets of flour remain.

Stir in the melted margarine, 50ml at a time. Add the fruit and chopped nuts to the batter and mix to combine. Pour the batter into the tin and level out using the spatula.

Make a shallow depression in the centre of the cake, around one-third of the cake's diameter and no deeper than 1cm, to help it bake evenly. You can skip this step, but it is a commonly used method.

Decorate with almonds, other nuts or preserved cherries, if you like.

Bake in the centre of the oven at 150°C/300°F/gas 2 for 1½–2½ hours. Test with a skewer until it comes out clean from the middle of the cake. Leave the cake in the tin to cool completely.

If you like you can feed the cake with alcohol, according to the instructions opposite, every few days. The cake can be prepared several weeks in advance of serving if it is fed with alcohol and is stored in a cool place in an air-tight container.

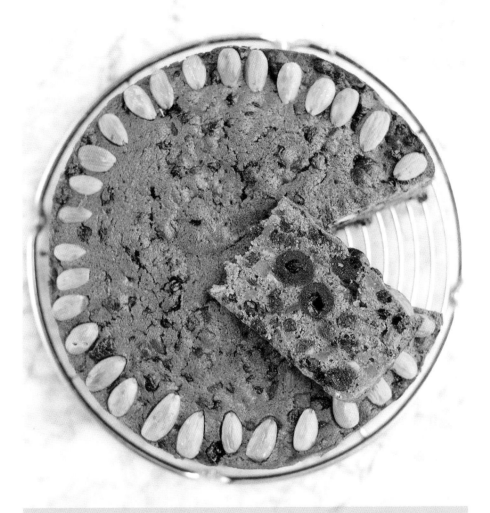

You can leave out the step of leaving the fruit to soak in alcohol for a week and instead let it soak for a couple of hours or just quickly boil the fruit with 100ml of alcohol (instead of 75ml) and another 50ml of water. You can also use 100ml of tea instead. The cake can be served when it has cooled, but traditionally it is baked a few months before Christmas and fed with a tablespoon of alcohol every week until Christmas. The cake should then be sealed inside several plastic bags or the equivalent so that it does not dry out during the feeding process. The baking time and temperature will depend on how hot your oven is. My oven is hot and distributes the heat very efficiently so I use 125°C/250°F/gas ½, but if you notice that the recipes in this book take longer to cook than the longest baking time given, you may need to bake at 150°C/300°F/gas 2. If you notice that the top of the cake is starting to burn, you can turn down the temperature to 125°C/250°F/gas ½.

CLASSIC CARROT CAKE

This one of my oldest recipes, and I have improved it each time I have included it in my books. Because it appeared in my latest layer cake book, I have included quantities for two sizes, and baking times for tins of different sizes if you want to make a simple layer cake.

If you like cardamom you can add a teaspoon of that too. The yoghurt in the recipe can be replaced with the same amount of milk mixed with 1 teaspoon of vinegar. I have used yoghurt to stop the walnuts from becoming discoloured. The picture opposite shows a plain carrot cake made using the larger quantity of batter in two tins measuring 18cm. It has been decorated with rolls of thinly sliced carrot made using a traditional potato peeler.

SMALLER QUANTITY

110g	carrot, finely grated
¼ tsp	grated nutmeg
225g	sugar
240g	plain flour
1 pinch	salt
1 tsp	bicarbonate of soda
1½ tsp	baking powder
1 tsp	ground cinnamon
100g	yoghurt
100ml	oil
100g	apple sauce
100g	walnuts, chopped (optional)

LARGER QUANTITY

165g	carrot, finely grated
½ tsp	grated nutmeg
340g	sugar
360g	plain flour
1 pinch	salt
1½ tsp	bicarbonate of soda
2 tsp	baking powder
1–2 tsp	ground cinnamon
150g	yoghurt
150ml	oil
150g	apple sauce
150g	walnuts, chopped (optional)

Preheat the oven to 175°C/350°F/gas 4. Grease and line or add crumbs to your chosen tin or tins, or prepare with baking paper. Peel the carrots and grate them using the finest side of your grater. Set aside. Mix the nutmeg with the sugar, flour, salt, bicarbonate of soda, baking powder and cinnamon in a bowl. Add the carrots, yoghurt or milk, vinegar (if using), oil, apple sauce and walnuts, if using. Quickly mix to a smooth batter using a spatula. Do not overwork as the cake will become chewy. Swipe the spatula around the sides of the bowl to incorporate any leftover flour. Pour the batter into the tin or tins and bake in the centre of the oven at 175°C/350°F/gas 4. Timings for tins of different sizes are given below. Test with a skewer that should come out clean from the middle of the cake. Let cool in the tin on a wire rack before cutting or decorating.

TINS & BAKING TIMES
Below, suitable tins for different quantities of batter are given, together with the relevant baking times.

2 tins 15cm: smaller quantity = 35–45 minutes
1 tin 18–20cm: smaller quantity = 40–50 minutes

1 tin 24cm: larger quantity = 35-45 minutes
2 tins 18–20cm: larger quantity = 25–35 minutes
3 tins 15cm: larger quantity = 35–45 minutes

CARROT CAKE WITH PURÉE

This recipe using carrot purée was developed for my layer cake book that was published in 2016. You can leave out the vinegar if you would like a light, orange-coloured cake with no discoloration in the walnuts, but vinegar in the batter will makes the cake slightly lighter. It is also common to include 60–70g of raisins in carrot cakes, but I usually use currants as they are smaller and work better in a cake. The carrot cake opposite has been decorated with light-coloured frosting with added lemon zest and lemon juice.

250g	carrot purée
270g	plain flour
270g	sugar
1 pinch	salt
½ tsp	grated nutmeg
1 tsp	ground cinnanmon
1 tsp	ground cardamom
1 tsp	bicarbonate of soda
1 tsp	baking powder
100ml	oil
100ml	carrot juice or water
2 tsp	vinegar (optional)
100 g	walnuts, chopped (optional)

You can buy pure carrot purée from the baby and child section of the supermarket or make your own by boiling or steaming peeled carrots until they are really soft and blending them to a smooth purée with a hand hand blender and allowing them to cool before mixing into the batter.

Preheat the oven to 175°C/350°F/gas 4. Grease and line or add crumbs to a tin measuring 18–20cm in diameter. Mix the flour, sugar, salt, spices, bicarbonate of soda and baking powder together in a bowl. Add the oil, carrot juice or water, carrot purée, vinegar and walnuts, if using, and mix until smooth with no lumps, using a whisk or a spatula. Do not overwork as this will make the cake chewy. Swipe the spatula around the sides of the bowl to incorporate any leftover flour. Pour the batter into the tin and bake in the centre of the oven at 175°C/350°F/gas 4 for 45–50 minutes. Test with a skewer that should come out clean from the middle of the cake. Let the cake cool in the tin on a wire rack before cutting or decorating.

RECIPE WITH AQUAFABA

200g	carrot purée
270g	sugar
125ml	aquafaba
270g	plain flour
1 pinch	salt
½ tsp	grated nutmeg
1 tsp	ground cinnamon
1 tsp	ground cardamom
1 tsp	bicarbonate of soda
1 tsp	baking powder
100ml	oil
100g	walnuts, chopped (optional)

Preheat the oven to 175°C/350°F/gas 4. Grease and line or add crumbs to a tin measuring 18–20cm in diameter. Whip the sugar and aquafaba together in a bowl until frothy. Mix the flour, salt, spices, bicarbonate of soda and baking powder together in a separate bowl. Add the dry ingredients together with the oil, carrot purée, and walnuts, if using, to the frothy aquafaba and mix until smooth with no lumps, using a whisk or a spatula. Do not overwork as this will make the cake chewy. Swipe the spatula around the sides of the bowl to incorporate any leftover flour. Pour the batter into the tin and bake in the centre of the oven at 175°C/350°F/gas 4 for 45–55 minutes. Test with a skewer that should come out clean from the middle of the cake. Let the cake cool in the tin on a wire rack before cutting or decorating.

CARROT CAKE

My most recent recipe for carrot cake has been developed since I gained a better understanding of aquafaba and the best way to use it in sponge cakes. If you whip aquafaba until frothy together with the sugar, you will get a very light sponge and the finely grated carrot looks beautiful in this light-coloured cake.

180g	sugar
100ml	aquafaba
210g	plain flour
1 tsp	baking powder
1 tsp	bicarbonate of soda
1 tsp	ground cinnamon
¼ tsp	grated nutmeg (optional)
1 pinch	salt
100ml	oil
140g	carrot, finely grated

Preheat the oven to 175°C/350°F/gas 4. Grease and line or add crumbs to a 1.5-litre loaf tin or a round tin measuring 18–20cm in diameter. Whip the sugar and aquafaba until frothy using a stand mixer or an electric hand mixer. Carefully mix the flour, baking powder, bicarbonate of soda, cinnamon, nutmeg (if using) and salt in a separate bowl. Add the dry ingredients, together with the oil and the grated carrot, and fold until smooth with a spatula without overworking. Swipe the spatula around the sides of the bowl to incorporate any leftover flour. Pour the batter into your chosen tin and bake in the centre of the oven at 175°C/350°F/gas 4 for 45–50 minutes for a tin measuring 18–20cm and 35–45 minutes for a tin measuring 22cm. Test with a skewer that should come out clean from the middle of the cake.

CARROT CAKE CRUMBLE

This is a crumble that is suitable for many sponge cakes, such as chocolate, banana and carrot cake. The recipe for carrot cake with crumble is based on a Christmas recipe from Jamie Oliver's magazine, and it also appeared in my Christmas book, as carrot cakes are particularly good for baking during the autumn and winter when carrots are in season.

CRUMBLE

45g	plain flour
1 tbsp	soft brown sugar
40g	margarine
1 pinch	salt
30g	sesame seeds or poppy seeds

Mix all the ingredients and rub together until they resemble breadcrumbs, then sprinkle on top of your chosen cake before baking according to the instructions.

BANANA CARROT CAKE

If you like carrot cake and banana cake, this might be your new favourite. The consistency is perfect and the combination of spices, banana and carrot creates a very special flavour. The recipe can be made without emulsifying the oil if you would prefer not to, but this will improve the cake and you will get a better texture and more of a rise if you mix the aquafaba and oil before adding it to the batter. Read more on how emulsions affect sponge cakes on pages 24 and 36. Here the tin has been covered with two pieces of baking paper according to the instructions on page 65. It makes a lot of batter, so make sure that your tin is big enough, or use two smaller tins. You can also bake the cake in a round tin measuring 22–25cm in diameter. This will need to be baked for around 45–55 minutes. Be careful not to fill the tin to more than ¾; it is better to leave some of the batter in the mixing bowl than for it to overflow the sides of the tin. The cake is topped with a soft cream cheese frosting, with some lemon zest for added flavour, from page 226.

200g	mashed bananas
110g	carrots, coarsely grated
300g	plain flour
270g	sugar
1 tsp	bicarbonate of soda
1 tsp	baking powder
1 tsp	ground cinnamon
1 tsp	ground cardamom
1 tsp	ground ginger
¼ tsp	grated nutmeg (optional)
1 pinch	salt
150ml	oil
100ml	aquafaba
100ml	milk

Preheat the oven to 175°C/350°F/gas 4. Prepare two small 1–1.2-litre tins or one large 2-litre loaf tin with crumbs or baking paper according to the instructions on page 63. Mash the bananas thoroughly in a bowl. Peel the carrots and grate using the the coarse side of your grater. Add to the mashed banana and mix to combine. Mix the flour, sugar, bicarbonate of soda, baking powder, spices and salt in a separate bowl. Mix the oil and aquafaba in another bowl and add to the dry ingredients together with the banana and carrot mixture and the milk. Fold until smooth using a spatula without overworking as this can make the cake chewy. Swipe the spatula around the sides of the bowl to incorporate any leftover flour. Pour the batter into the tin and bake in the centre of the oven at 175°C/350°F/gas 4 for 30–40 minutes for two tins, or 50–60 minutes for a large tin. Let the cake cool in the tin on a wire rack before removing it from the tin.

GINGERBREAD CAKE

.

This is a classic Swedish gingerbread cake, using traditional spices, and is an old recipe that is traditionally baked without eggs. I have test baked many different versions of the recipe and found that traditional gingerbread cake usually contains a high proportion of sugar and that the texture and the taste is improved by reducing the quantity of sugar, which is what I have done here. Now I think the texture is perfect!

CLASSIC GINGERBREAD CAKE

150g	margarine
210g	plain flour
225g	sugar
1½ tsp	ground cinnamon
1½ tsp	ground ginger
¼ tsp	ground cloves
1 tsp	bicarbonate of soda
½ tsp	baking powder
1 pinch	salt
200g	yoghurt

Preheat the oven to 175°C/350°F/gas 4. Grease and line or add crumbs to a 2-litre cake or loaf tin. Melt the margarine and leave to cool. Mix the flour, sugar, cinnamon, ginger, cloves, bicarbonate of soda, baking powder and salt in a bowl. Add the yoghurt and the melted margarine. Mix the batter until smooth and pour into the tin. Bake in the centre of the oven at 175°C/350°F/gas 4 for 40–50 minutes. Test with a skewer that should come out clean from the middle of the cake. Leave the cake to cool before removing it from the tin.

My grandmother often baked a version of this cake, not just at Christmas time. In old cookery books, cakes like this using soured cream and lingonberry jam appear as traditional gingerbread from northern Sweden. For instance, I found a recipe that is similar to the one I have used in this book in *Goda pepparkakor & annat gott* ('Tasty gingerbread & other good things') from the 1930s. Perhaps this was where my grandmother found the recipe.

GRANNY'S LINGONBERRY CAKE

270g	plain flour
225g	sugar
1½ tsp	ground cinnamon
1½ tsp	ground ginger
¼ tsp	ground cloves
1½ tsp	bicarbonate of soda
1 pinch	salt
100g	margarine
150ml	milk
50ml	cream
150g	lingonberry jam

Preheat the oven to 175°C/350°F/gas 4. Grease and line or add crumbs to a 2-litre cake tin or a loaf tin. Melt the margarine and leave to cool. Mix together the flour, sugar, cinnamon, ginger, cloves, bicarbonate of soda and salt in a bowl. Add the melted margarine, milk, cream and lingonberry jam. Fold the batter until smooth with a spatula and pour into the tin. Bake in the centre of the oven at 175°C/350°F/gas 4 for 40–50 minutes. Test with a skewer that should come out clean from the middle of the cake. Leave the cake to cool before removing it from the tin.

SAFFRON CAKES

SAFFRON SPONGE CAKE

100ml	milk
¼–½g	saffron
180g	sugar
75ml	aquafaba
180g	plain flour
2 tsp	baking powder
1 pinch	salt
75g	margarine
	nibbed sugar (optional)

Preheat the oven to 175°C/350°F/gas 4. Grease and line or add crumbs to a sponge cake tin of 1.2–1.5 litres or a round tin measuring 18–20cm in diameter. Boil the milk and saffron together in a small pan. Set aside to cool. Whip the sugar and aquafaba until frothy using a stand mixer or an electric hand mixer. Carefully mix the flour, baking powder and salt in a separate bowl. Melt the margarine. Add the dry ingredients, the melted margarine and the saffron milk to the frothy aquafaba and fold with a spatula until smooth without overworking. Swipe the spatula around the sides of the bowl to incorporate any leftover flour. Pour the batter into the tin, sprinkle nibbed sugar on top if you have used a round tin and bake in the centre of the oven at 175°C/350°F/gas 4 for 30–35 minutes. Test with a skewer that should come out clean from the middle of the cake.

RAISIN AND SAFFRON SPONGE CAKE

100ml	milk
¼–½g	saffron
180g	sugar
75ml	aquafaba
180g	plain flour
2 tsp	baking powder
1 pinch	salt
60–70g	raisins
75g	margarine

Preheat the oven to 175°C/350°F/gas 4. Grease and line or add crumbs to a sponge cake tin of 1.2–1.5 litres. Follow the instructions for the saffron sponge cake recipe and mix the raisins into the flour mixture. Pour the batter into the tin and bake in the centre of the oven at 175°C/350°F/gas 4 for 30–35 minutes. Test with a skewer that should come out clean from the middle of the cake.

SAFFRON SPONGE CAKE WITH ALMOND PASTE

100ml	milk
¼–½g	saffron
180g	sugar
75ml	aquafaba
180g	plain flour
2 tsp	baking powder
1 pinch	salt
75g	margarine
75g	almond paste

Preheat the oven to 175°C/350°F/gas 5. Grease and line or add crumbs to a sponge cake tin of 1.2–1.5 litres. Follow the instructions for the saffron sponge cake recipe and add the coarsely grated almond paste when the batter is ready to pour into the tin. Bake according to the instructions for the saffron sponge cake recipe.

Traybakes

All sponge cakes, like fruit cakes, banana cakes, carrot cakes and the soft gingerbread in the book can also be baked as squares. A batter using 180g of plain flour is suitable for a tin measuring 20 × 20cm. For recipes using around 240–300g of flour, a tin measuring 20 × 30cm works best. For thinner squares, a tin measuring 25 × 35cm is used. If you do not have 20 × 20cm, 20 × 30cm or 25 × 35cm tins, I usually recommend making your own out of baking paper. Fold in the sides to the correct measurements, then staple them together to make it stable enough to put on a baking tray. I show you how to do this on page 63.

Preheat the oven and prepare the tin and the ingredients before mixing the batter together. This important step is called *mise en place,* which means 'everything in place' in French.

Sift the dry ingredients, especially in large batters, so the risk of lumps of flour in the mixture will be reduced.

Create your own system when adding your ingredients: make sure you add the right quantities. Focus and don't let your mind wander.

Never use flour rich in gluten (strong flour) when baking sponge cakes, since extra added gluten or flour rich in gluten will make the sponge dense. This flour should only be used in raised doughs (see page 331).

Always use ingredients at room temperature. Cold ingredients can make the margarine hard and make the batter very firm.

Always add a pinch of salt to your cake batters!

Do not mix things for too long; mix the ingredients together quickly if there are no other instructions. Always swipe the spatula around the bottom of the bowl when mixing the batter to make sure that all the dry ingredients have been incorporated into the batter before transferring it to the tin and baking it.

Always set a timer for the lowest stated time. Add 5 minutes if the cake or bake is not ready. Keep on testing carefully using a skewer, with a few minutes in between, until it is ready.

CRUMBLE CAKE

I have been looking for a traditional recipe for the American 'crumble' cake and I fell for and veganized this old recipe in which reverse creaming is used for the batter, and where the nut layer using walnuts in the batter and almonds in the crumble give the cake a fantastic flavour. For a crumble without almonds, you can use the recipe on page 174.

Read more on how this kind of batter is prepared on page 32. Also note that batters using reverse creaming rise a lot in the oven, so make sure you have a tin with tall sides.

You can make blueberry crumble cake by adding 110g of fresh blueberries to the batter instead of the nut layer. If so, it is a good idea to add lemon zest to the batter.

NUT LAYER

100g	roasted walnuts
2 tbsp	sugar
½ tsp	ground cinnamon

CRUMBLE

60g	plain flour
50g	almond flour
45g	sugar
1 pinch	salt
75g	margarine

SPONGE CAKE BATTER

270g	plain flour
1 tbsp	baking powder
100g	margarine
1 pinch	salt
270g	sugar
1 tsp	vanilla extract
100ml	aquafaba
150g/ml	yoghurt or milk

Preheat the oven to 175°C/350°F/gas 4. Prepare a round tin measuring 25cm, or a tin measuring 20 × 30cm or 25 × 25cm with baking paper. Start by roasting the nuts if they are unroasted. Spread them out on a baking tray and roast for 5–10 minutes in the centre of the oven. Watch the nuts carefully as they burn easily in the oven. Let the nuts cool and then mix them with the sugar and cinnamon, breaking them up as you mix, until there are only a few larger pieces left. Then mix all the dry ingredients for the crumble in a bowl and dice the margarine. Rub the ingredients together until they form a firm but crumbly dough with just a few crumbs left.

For the sponge cake batter, put the flour and baking powder in the bowl of a stand mixer or in a mixing bowl. Dice the margarine into the bowl and mix until the margarine is the size of peas. Add the salt and sugar and mix for another minute until the fat is evenly distributed. If you are using a stand mixer or an electric hand mixer you might need to make sure that everything is spread out evenly in the bowl as any larger lumps need to be broken down into the flour mixture. Add the vanilla extract, aquafaba and the yoghurt or milk and mix thoroughly to a well-combined batter. Swipe the spatula around the sides of the bowl to incorporate any leftover flour. Pour half of the batter into the tin and spread it out evenly; add the nut layer over the top and then spread the rest of the batter on top of that. Now spread the crumble mixture evenly on top of the batter and bake in the centre of the oven at 175°C/350°F/gas 4 for 30–35 minutes. Test with a skewer until it comes out clean from the middle of the cake.

ROASTING NUTS

The nuts will taste better when roasted. Spread the nuts on a baking tray and roast for 5–10 minutes in the centre of the oven at 175°C/350°F/gas 4. Watch the nuts carefully as they burn easily in the oven. You can also roast them in a dry frying pan.

BERRY SQUARES

Here are two versions of sponge cakes with fruit or berries that are best served with vanilla cream or vanilla ice cream. You can roll the berries in plain flour if they are damp to prevent them from sinking to the bottom of the cake in version number 1. This batter is not as firm and gives a lighter cake. Version number 2 has a firmer batter where larger pieces of fruit and berries are held up more easily.

VERSION NO. 1

20×20cm	20×30cm	
75g	100g	margarine
180g	270g	sugar
100ml	150ml	aquafaba
180g	270g	plain flour
2 tsp	1 tbsp	baking powder
1 tsp	2 tsp	vanilla extract
1 pinch	1 pinch	salt
75ml	100ml	milk
55–110g	110–165g	berries

Preheat the oven to 175°C/350°F/gas 4. Grease and add crumbs to a square or rectangular tin and line with baking paper. Melt the margarine. Whip the sugar and aquafaba until frothy in a stand mixer or with an electric hand mixer. Carefully mix the flour, baking powder and salt in a separate bowl. Add the dry ingredients, the melted margarine, vanilla extract and the milk to the frothy aquafaba and fold with a spatula until smooth without overworking. Swipe a spatula around the sides of the bowl to incorporate any leftover flour. Add the berries dusted with some plain flour and fold in; some berries can be reserved to put on top of the cake, if you like. Pour the batter into the tin and top with the berries. Bake in the centre of the oven at 175°C/350°F/gas 4 for 30–35 minutes. Test with a skewer until it comes out clean from the middle of the cake. Serve with a scoop of vanilla ice cream or vanilla sauce.

VERSION NO. 2

20×20cm	20×30cm	
180g	270g	plain flour
2 tsp	1 tbsp	baking powder
75g	100g	margarine
180g	270g	sugar
1 tsp	2 tsp	vanilla extract
1 pinch	1 pinch	salt
75ml	100ml	aquafaba
100ml	150ml	milk
55–110g	110–165g	berries

Preheat the oven to 175°C/350°F/gas 4. Grease and add crumbs to a square or rectangular tin and line with baking paper. Put the flour and baking powder in the bowl for the stand mixer or in a mixing bowl. Dice the margarine and mix or rub into the flour until the margarine is the size of peas. Add the sugar, vanilla extract and salt and mix or rub in for another minute until the fat is evenly distributed. If you are using a stand mixer or an electric hand mixer you might need to make sure that everything is spread out evenly in the bowl and any larger lumps are broken down into the flour mixture. Mix the aquafaba and milk thoroughly until well-combined and add to the mixture. Swipe a spatula around the sides of the bowl to incorporate any leftover flour. Add the berries dusted with some plain flour and fold in; some berries can be reserved to put on top of the cake, if you like. Pour the batter into the tin and top with the berries. Bake in the centre of the oven at 175°C/350°F/gas 4 for 35–45 minutes. Test with a skewer until it comes out clean from the middle of the cake. Serve with a scoop of vanilla ice cream or vanilla sauce.

RHUBARB SQUARES

This is a fantastic rhubarb cake with a crumble topping that is cut into squares and can be served like a sponge cake or with a scoop of vanilla ice cream or vanilla sauce. It is perfect if you cannot decide whether you want to make a cake or a pie using the first rhubarb of the season. If you are baking the cake in a tin measuring 20 × 30cm, the baking time is closer to 40–50 minutes. For a smaller tin, there will be a little too much crumble. You can halve the recipe or choose not to use all of it. Use any leftover crumble dough to make a couple of biscuits using the instructions on page 282. If you are using a tin measuring 20 × 30cm, you will not need more than 300g of rhubarb.

300–400g rhubarb
2–3 tbsp sugar

CRUMBLE
120g plain flour
2 tbsp sugar
¼ tsp salt
75g margarine
1 tbsp water or aquafaba
(optional)

SPONGE CAKE
100g margarine
270g sugar
150ml aquafaba
300g plain flour
1 tbsp baking powder
1 pinch salt
150g room-temperature yoghurt
2 tsp vanilla extract

Preheat the oven to 175°C/350°F/gas 4. Prepare a tin measuring 25 × 35cm. Place baking paper of the right size in the tin or make a tin out of baking paper by folding the sides in a few centimetres from the edges and then stapling the corners together (see page 62). Put the paper tin on a baking tray or in a roasting tin.

Trim the rhubarb, strip off any stringy ribs, then dice and mix with the sugar.

Prepare the crumble. Mix the flour, sugar and salt in a bowl. Dice in the margarine and rub together to a crumble. If the dough is too crumbly, you can add the water or aquafaba to make a nice dough that stays together. Set aside

For the sponge cake, melt the margarine. Whip the sugar and aquafaba until frothy in a stand mixer or with an electric hand mixer. Carefully mix the flour, baking powder and salt in a separate bowl. Add the dry ingredients, the melted margarine, vanilla extract and the yoghurt to the frothy aquafaba and fold with a spatula until smooth without overworking. Swipe a spatula around the sides of the bowl to incorporate any leftover flour. Add half the rhubarb, without any of the liquid from the bowl. Pour the batter into the tin and sprinkle the rest of the rhubarb on top, also without any of the liquid. Then sprinkle the crumble evenly on top of the cake. Bake in the centre of the oven at 175°C/350°F/gas 4 for 35–40 minutes until the surface is golden. Test with a skewer until it comes out clean from the middle of the cake.

AUTUMN SQUARES

This recipe works with both finely grated carrot and coarsely grated apple, and makes moist squares perfect for autumn. I've included two different types of icing: the classic one for silvia squares, which works well for both; and a caramel icing that is especially good with the apple cake. The carrot cake also works well with a cream cheese frosting or a classic one with lemon.

270g	sugar
150ml	aquafaba
300g	plain flour
1½ tsp	baking powder
1 tsp	bicarbonate of soda
1 tsp	ground cinnamon
1 tsp	ground cardamom
¼ tsp	grated nutmeg (optional)
1 pinch	salt
165g	apple or carrot, grated
150ml	oil

Preheat the oven to 175°C/350°F/gas 4. Line a 20 × 30cm or 25 × 35cm tin with baking paper or make a case from baking paper following the instructions on pages 62 and 63. Whip the sugar and aquafaba until frothy in a stand mixer or with an electric hand mixer. Mix the flour, baking powder, bicarbonate of soda, cinnamon, cardamom, nutmeg (if using) and salt thoroughly in a separate bowl. Peel the carrots or apples; grate the carrot on the fine side of the grater, and the apple on the coarse side. Add the dry ingredients, the oil and the apple or carrot to the frothy aquafaba and fold with a spatula until smooth without overworking. Swipe a spatula around the sides of the bowl to incorporate any leftover flour. Pour the cake batter into the tin and bake in the centre of the oven at 175°C/350°F/gas 4 for 30–40 minutes for a 20 × 30cm tin and 20–25 minutes for a 25 × 35cm tin. Test with a skewer until it comes out clean from the middle of the cake. Leave the cake to cool completely.

CLASSIC ICING

75g	vegan spread
210g	icing sugar
2 tsp	vanilla sugar or vanilla extract
1 tbsp	single cream

desiccated coconut, for sprinkling

Melt the vegan spread and leave to cool slightly. Mix with icing sugar, vanilla sugar or extract and cream. Spread over the cooled cake and sprinkle with desiccated coconut.

CARAMEL ICING

75g	vegan spread
55g	soft brown sugar
1½ tbsp	single cream
150g	icing sugar

desiccated coconut, for sprinkling

Melt the vegan spread together with the brown sugar in a saucepan on a low heat. Simmer until the brown sugar has dissolved, stirring. Add the single cream, remove the pan from the heat and leave to cool slightly. Mix with the icing sugar, spread over the cooled cake and sprinkle with desiccated coconut.

LOVE TREATS

We have many names for the things we love and these squares have many names in Sweden, such as mocha squares, 'snoddas' and love treats. I have included two recipes, my older recipe with vinegar and bicarbonate of soda (No. 2) and my newer recipe with aquafaba (No. 1). For cake No. 1 you can use a tin measuring 20 × 30cm for both the quantities of batter, with a baking time of 18–25 minutes. The smaller amount of batter will give thinner squares and the larger amount will give thick squares like the ones in the picture opposite. For cake No. 2, a tin measuring 20 × 30cm is perfect.

CAKE NO. 1 SMALLER
20 × 20cm

30g	cocoa
120g	plain flour
1½ tsp	baking powder
1 tsp	vanilla extract
135g	sugar
1 pinch	salt
50ml	oil
150ml	water
50ml	aquafaba

CAKE NO. 1 LARGER
25 × 35cm

60g	cocoa
240g	plain flour
1 tbsp	baking powder
1 tsp	vanilla extract
270g	sugar
¼ tsp	salt
100ml	oil
300ml	water
100ml	aquafaba

CAKE NO. 2
20 × 30cm

2 tbsp	cocoa
210g	plain flour
180g	sugar
1 tbsp	cornstarch
1 tsp	baking powder
½ tsp	bicarbonate of soda
1 tsp	vanilla extract
1 pinch	salt
50ml	oil
1 tsp	vinegar
250ml	milk

Preheat the oven to 175°C/350°F/gas 4. Place baking paper of the right size in the tin or make a tin out of baking paper by folding the sides in a few centimetres from the edges and then stapling the corners together (see page 62). Put the paper tin on a baking tray or in a roasting tin. Sift the cocoa and mix with the dry ingredients, then add the wet ingredients and fold it in without overworking the batter; it only needs to be smooth with no lumps. Swipe a spatula around the sides of the bowl to incorporate any leftover flour. Pour the batter into the tin and bake in the centre of the oven at 175°C/350°F/gas 4 for 14–18 minutes. Test with a skewer until it comes out clean from the middle of the cake.

MOCHA GLAZE

20 × 20cm	25 × 35cm	
50g	75g	vegan spread
180g	240g	icing sugar
3 tbsp	4 tbsp	cocoa
2–3 tbsp	3–4 tbsp	cold brewed coffee

desiccated coconut, for sprinkling

The smaller quantity of glaze is enough for cakes of 20 × 20cm and 20 × 30cm, but for a 25 × 35cm cake you need the larger quantity.

Let the cake cool completely. Melt the vegan spread. Mix the icing sugar, cocoa and coffee with the melted margarine until smooth. Spread over the cake and sprinkle with coconut flakes. Put it somewhere cold to set.

CHOCOLATE SQUARES

These chocolate squares are darker than the love treats on page 178, and are served with a thick chocolate glaze on top. I have piped the chocolate frosting with a piping nozzle like the nozzle number 7 on page 225. In the picture opposite, the cake is covered with the soft chocolate frosting from page 230, but I have included a simpler chocolate glaze recipe here that goes very well with this chocolate cake and is easier to mix together.

20×20cm	25×35cm	
40g	80g	cocoa
120g	240g	plain flour
½ tsp	1 tsp	baking powder
¾ tsp	1½ tsp	bicarbonate of soda
160g	315g	sugar
1 pinch	¼ tsp	salt
75ml	150ml	oil
150ml	300ml	water
50ml	100ml	aquafaba

Preheat the oven to 175°C/350°F/gas 4. Prepare a square or rectangular tin using baking paper or make a tin out of baking paper by folding the sides in a few centimetres from the edges and then stapling the corners together (see page 62). Put the paper tin on a baking tray or in a roasting tin. Sift the cocoa into a bowl and mix with the dry ingredients, add the wet ingredients without overworking the batter; it only needs to be mixed until smooth with no lumps. Pour the batter into the tin and bake in the centre of the oven at 175°C/350°F/gas 4 for 20–25 minutes. Test with a skewer until it comes out clean from the middle of the cake.

The glaze on the cake on page 114 and the recipe below are perfect for covering these chocolate squares as they are easy to mix together quickly. For the cake opposite, I used the soft chocolate frosting from page 230 as it is easily piped and can be chilled without getting too stiff, but the recipe below gives a slightly softer glaze, which is easier to mix together. It can also be chilled without the glaze becoming too firm for serving, but you cannot pipe it. The glaze below is shown on top of the courgette cake on page 187.

CHOCOLATE GLAZE

100g	vegan spread
50g	vegan crème fraîche
1 tbsp	strong brewed coffee
180g	icing sugar
40g	cocoa
1 pinch	salt

Melt the vegan spread and add crème fraîche and coffee. Sift the icing sugar and cocoa into the coffee mixture and add the salt. Mix the glaze until smooth. The glaze can be spread when soft, but if it is too soft you should chill it slightly. Then you can beat it until fluffy before spreading.

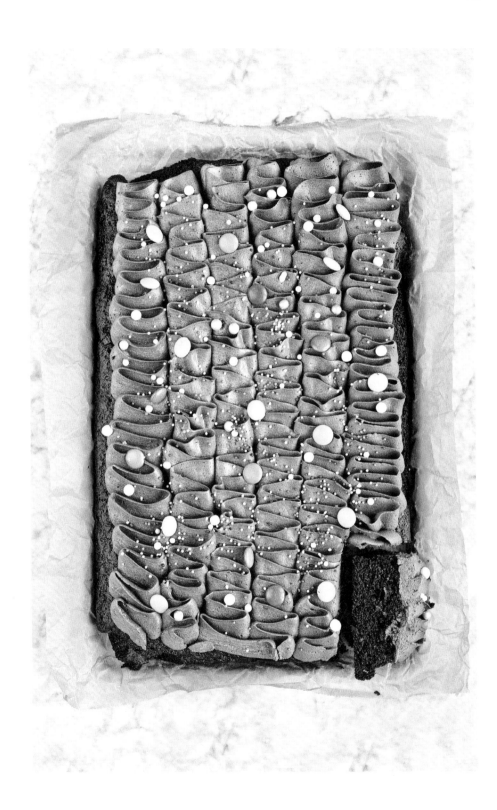

BANANA SQUARES

SPICED BANANA SQUARES

300g	mashed bananas
270g	sugar
300g	plain flour
1 tsp	bicarbonate of soda
1 tsp	baking powder
1 pinch	salt
½ tsp	ground cinnamon
½ tsp	ground cardamom
¼ tsp	grated nutmeg
100g	chopped walnuts
100ml	milk
125ml	oil
50ml	aquafaba

I like to use 300g of mashed banana but that is quite a large amount. You can also use 250g if that is what you have. The cake is good on its own but you can decorate it with frosting or add 100g of chopped walnuts to the batter. These are the squares that are shown in the picture opposite. If you do not have a baking tin of the right size, you can staple together baking paper according to the instructions on page 63.

Preheat the oven to 175°C/350°F/gas 4. Prepare the tin (see below) with baking paper. Mash the bananas and set aside while preparing the other ingredients. Mix the sugar, plain flour, bicarbonate of soda, baking powder, salt, cinnamon, cardamom, nutmeg and walnuts in a bowl. Add the mashed bananas, the milk, oil and aquafaba to the bowl of dry ingredients. Using a whisk or a spatula, quickly mix to a smooth batter with no lumps, without overworking it, as this can make the cake chewy. Swipe a spatula around the sides of the bowl to incorporate any leftover flour, then pour the batter into the tin and bake in the centre of the oven at 175°C/350°F/gas 4. Timings for different tin sizes are given below.

LIGHT-COLOURED BANANA SQUARES

200g	bananas, mashed
240g	plain flour
180g	icing sugar
1½ tsp	baking powder
¼ tsp	bicarbonate of soda
1 pinch	salt
150ml	milk or water
50ml	aquafaba
100ml	oil

Preheat the oven to 175°C/350°F/gas 4. Prepare the tin (see below) with baking paper. Mash the bananas and set aside while preparing the other ingredients. Mix the flour, icing sugar, baking powder, bicarbonate of soda and salt in a bowl. Add the mashed bananas, milk or water, aquafaba and oil and mix to a smooth batter. Pour the batter into the tin and bake in the centre of the oven at 175°C/350°F/gas 4 according to the times given below.

TINS & BAKING TIMES

Below, you can see which tins are suitable for this cake and how long they should be baked for.

20 × 20cm =	40–50 minutes
20 × 30cm =	30–40 minutes

TIP!

If you are allergic to aquafaba, or do not have any at home, you can just use milk in both of these recipes. Leave out the aquafaba and increase the quantity of milk by 50ml. The aquafaba gives squares that are slightly lighter and more moist, but the recipe using all milk makes good banana squares too.

CARROT SQUARES

There are lots of different types of carrot cakes in this book and that is because you can vary the way carrots are prepared so much. Finely grated, coarsely grated, carrot purée and carrot juice can all be used in carrot cakes. This combination of grated carrot, raisins or currants and cardamom is my latest version. You can use freshly ground cardamom. If you want a spicier carrot cake, you can include ½ teaspoon of grated nutmeg.

The icing sugar increases the amount of oil that can be included in the batter together and here I have managed to bind the traditional amount of oil used in old recipes. Read more about the difference between baking with caster sugar and icing sugar on page 40. I think that this cake is best served as it is, but a frosting with lemon zest always works well with all carrot cakes. The small carrots on top of the squares were made with royal icing and were left to dry out on a piece of baking paper, which means that they can be kept for a long time in a sealed jar. They will stay firm and will not melt on the frosting. You can find the recipe for royal icing on page 324.

In tasting tests in the big American baking bibles, the testers thought that carrot cakes tasted better when the carrots were peeled before being grated into the batter.

100ml	aquafaba
240g	icing sugar
240g	plain flour
1 tsp	ground cinnamon
1 tsp	ground cardamom
1 tsp	baking powder
1 tsp	bicarbonate of soda
1 pinch	salt
150–160g	carrots, peeled and finely grated
100g	walnuts, chopped (optional)
60–70g	raisins or currants
1 tsp	vanilla extract
150ml	oil

Preheat the oven to 175°C/350°F/gas 4 and prepare a tin measuring 20 × 30cm with baking paper. Whip the aquafaba and icing sugar until frothy in a bowl. In a separate bowl, mix the flour, cinnamon, cardamom, baking powder, bicarbonate of soda and salt. Fold the dry ingredients, carrot, walnuts (if using), the raisins or currants, vanilla extract and the oil into the frothy aquafaba with a spatula. Fill the tin and bake in the centre of the oven for 35–40 minutes. Check that the cake is cooked through using a skewer. If you want to cover the cake with frosting, let it cool completely first.

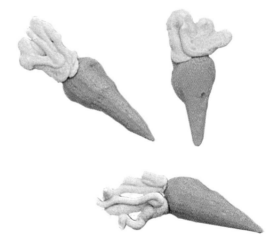

COURGETTE CAKES

The grated courgette helps to make this cake really moist where the frothy aquafaba and icing sugar would otherwise have resulted in a drier cake. You can use both yellow and green squash or courgettes for these two recipes. For the light coloured cake, you will get the best results if you use a pestle and mortar to crush the cardamom seeds instead of using ready ground cardamom.

CHOCOLATE COURGETTE CAKE

100ml	aquafaba
240g	icing sugar
150g	plain flour
60g	cocoa
2 tsp	baking powder
1 pinch	salt
1 tsp	vanilla sugar or vanilla extract
150ml	oil
2 tbsp	aquafaba
150g	grated courgette

Preheat the oven to 175°C/350°F/gas 4 and prepare a tin measuring around 20 × 30cm with baking paper. Whip the aquafaba and icing sugar until frothy in a bowl. In a separate bowl, mix the flour, sifted cocoa, baking powder and salt. Mix the vanilla sugar or extract, oil and aquafaba in a small bowl. Squeeze out as much liquid as possible from the courgettes and discard the liquid. Mix all the ingredients together using a spatula. Fill the tin and bake in the centre of the oven at 175°C/350°F/gas 4 for 30–40 minutes. Check that the cake is cooked through using a skewer. Let the cake cool completely before covering with frosting.

> The cake opposite was covered using the soft chocolate glaze from page 180. It mixes together easily and works well for the moist courgette cake.

COURGETTE CAKE

100ml	aquafaba
240g	icing sugar
240g	plain flour
1 tsp	ground cinnamon
1 tsp	ground cardamom
2 tsp	baking powder
1 tsp	vanilla sugar or vanilla extract
1 pinch	salt
150ml	oil
2 tbsp	aquafaba
150g	grated courgettes
100g	walnuts (optional)

Preheat the oven to 175°C/350°F/gas 4 and prepare a tin measuring around 20 × 30cm with baking paper. Whip the aquafaba and icing sugar until frothy in a bowl. In a separate bowl, mix the flour, cinnamon, cardamom, baking powder, vanilla sugar or extract and salt. Mix the oil and aquafaba. Squeeze out as much liquid as possible from the courgettes and discard the liquid. Roughly chop the walnuts, if using. Fold all the ingredients together using a spatula. Fill the tin and bake in the centre of the oven at 175°C/350°F/gas 4 for 35–45 minutes. Check that the cake is cooked through using a skewer. Let the cake cool completely before covering with frosting.

> The combination of cinnamon and cardamom together with walnuts gives a light-coloured cake with a lot of flavour.

APPLE SQUARES

I have tried to find the maximum quantity of apples that it is possible to put in an apple cake and here is my best result. They will be perfectly baked at the bottom even though there is a large amount of diced apples on top of the batter. The bottom of the cake is shown in the picture below. The larger quantity of batter can also be baked in a round tin measuring around 25cm in diameter or a square tin measuring 25 × 25cm.

20 × 20cm	20 × 30cm	
165–220g	220–275g	apples, diced
2 tbsp	3 tbsp	sugar
2 tsp	1 tbsp	ground cinnamon
180g	270g	plain flour
180g	270g	sugar
2 tsp	1 tbsp	baking powder
75g	100g	margarine
1 pinch	1 pinch	salt
75ml	100ml	aquafaba
100ml	150ml	milk
1 tsp	2 tsp	vanilla extract

Preheat the oven to 175°C/350°F/gas 4. Grease and add crumbs to the square or rectangular tin or prepare the tin with baking paper.

Peel, core and dice the apples and mix with the sugar and cinnamon.

Put the flour and baking powder in the bowl of a stand mixer or in a mixing bowl. Dice the margarine in and mix or rub in until the margarine is the size of peas. Add the salt and sugar and mix or rub in for another minute until the fat is evenly distributed. If you are using a stand mixer or an electric hand mixer you might need to make sure that everything is spread out evenly in the bowl and any larger lumps are broken down into the flour mixture. Add the aquafaba, milk and vanilla extract and mix thoroughly to a well-combined batter. Swipe the spatula around the sides of the bowl to incorporate any leftover flour. Pour the batter into the tin and spread the diced apples evenly on top of the cake. Bake in the centre of the oven at 175°C/350°F/gas 4 for 35–45 minutes. Test with a skewer until it comes out clean from the middle of the cake. Serve with a scoop of vanilla ice cream or vanilla sauce.

AMERICAN APPLE SQUARES

This cake is based on a very old recipe from the USA and it's baked using a large quantity of apples. They are worked into the batter for a few minutes, and that way the liquid from the apples is absorbed by the batter, meaning that the cake doesn't get too soggy when it is baked. The apples can be peeled if you like, but it's also fine to just dice the apples and leave the skins on.

100g	walnuts
400g	apples, diced (8–9 apples)
270g	plain flour
300g	soft brown sugar
1½ tsp	bicarbonate of soda
1 tsp	ground cinnamon
¼ tsp	grated ginger
¼ tsp	grated nutmng
½ tsp	salt
100g	margarine
100ml	aquafaba

Preheat the oven to 175°C/350°F/gas 4. Grease and add crumbs to a tin measuring either 20 × 30cm or 25 × 35cm or line with baking paper.

Lightly roast the walnuts on a baking tray in the for 6–8 minutes. Peel, core and dice the apples (you can leave the skins on if you prefer).

Add the flour, soft brown sugar, bicarbonate of soda and spices to a bowl. Dice in the margarine and either use a mixer or rub together with your fingers until the margarine has been evenly distributed. If you are using a mixer, you may need to double check that everything is evenly distributed throughout the bowl; larger lumps may need breaking up in the flour mixture. Stir in the aquafaba, diced apple and walnuts, and beat or stir thoroughly with a wooden spoon to that the batter is thoroughly combined and wet. It can take 2–3 minutes for the apples to release enough moisture. Pour the cake batter into the tin and spread it out evenly. Bake in the centre of the oven at 175°C/350°F/gas 4 for 35–40 minutes for the smaller tin, and 25–25 minutes for the larger tin. Test with a skewer until it comes out clean from the middle of the cake. Leave the cake to cool completely.

ICING

100g	margarine
150g	soft brown sugar
1 pinch	salt
50ml	milk
240g	icing sugar
2 tsp	vanilla sugar or vanilla extract

Melt the margarine together with the soft brown sugar and the salt in a sauce pan on a low heat, stirring, until the sugar has dissolved. Stir in the milk, bring to the boil and leave to cool for around 10 minutes. Mix with the icing sugar and the vanilla sugar or extract. Spread over the cooled cake immediately as the mixture can set fairly quickly. Leave the icing to set before serving.

PAINTING

This anatomical-style heart was painted using colouring powder dissolved in alcohol. I sketched it out with a cocktail stick in in the sugar paste using gentle strokes before painting. Read more on page 54.

Layer cakes

LAYER CAKE GUIDE FOR SUGAR PASTE

SIZE	SLICES	AMOUNT OF SUGAR PASTE
10cm	4–6 slices	150–200g
15cm	8–12 slices	350–450g
20cm	14–28 slices	550–750g
25cm	21–42 slices	750–850g

This guide is suitable for round layer cakes around 10cm high. For taller cakes or square cakes, the amount needs to be increased by 20–30 per cent. Around 70 per cent of the sugar paste will be used on top of the cake. That is why it may be useful to prepare any figures or details after covering the cake, as there will always be leftovers. The number of slices is not given for cream cakes and marzipan cakes that give fewer slices.

I have divided the layer cakes and fillings, creams and frostings into different sections in the book. That way they serve as elements you can put together yourself and my choices will not stand in the way of your imagination. For some recipes I have written down which frosting I have used in the pictures. You can assemble cakes depending on your own taste or based on the ingredients you have at home.

The number of slices in a cake depends on what type of occasion it is baked for: at weddings you usually serve the smallest slices; for a party the slices will be slightly bigger; and for smaller coffee parties you will need larger slices. Cream cakes give fewer slices as they are sliced in triangles and are looser. You cannot put cream cakes on top of one another like other filled and covered cakes because they need a stand for each layer. For covered cakes, marzipan is traditionally used, but sugar paste can be used as a replacement if anyone is allergic to almonds.

BANANA LAYER CAKE

The banana-shaped cake was made in a loaf tin. It is easiest to cut it into three slices before creating the banana shape. Cut into a triangle shape on the top and bottom edges on one side. Do this on the right or the left, depending on which way you want the banana to bend. Move the pieces that are cut off to the opposite side to create the ends of the banana. Then fill and cover the cake, for instance, with banana curd, sliced banana and vanilla pastry cream. The cake is covered with yellow marzipan. The brown markings are made by drizzling over melted dark chocolate.

CREAM CAKE

The strawberry cake is filled with vanilla pastry cream for one layer and mashed strawberries in the second layer. The cake is then covered with firmly whipped cream (see page 409) and decorated with fresh strawberries.

PUMPKIN CAKE

This can be made with, for instance, vanilla pastry cream and crushed raspberries or raspberry jam as the filling. Here, the cake was covered with orange marzipan and green marzipan was used to make the stalk.

CLASSIC LAYER CAKE

If you want a lighter cake, you can reduce the amount of fat to 50g in the smallest version and increase the amount of milk to 100ml, or use 75g of fat and 150ml of milk in the larger recipe for round and rectangular tins. If you want to make the cake in a roasting tin for a larger cake or to make a stable sponge for shaped cakes, use the quantity that is suitable for a baking tray. For the baking tray you can use double the amount for the same baking time. For the double quantity you will also need a large bowl when mixing the batter. These cakes are usually cut into two slices and are suitable for princess cakes, see below.

ROUND	15-cm		20-cm		BAKING TRAY	
ANGULAR	1.5 LITRES		2 LITRES		25 × 35cm	
	75g	margarine	100g	margarine	125g	margarine
	180g	sugar	270g	sugar	360g	sugar
	100ml	aquafaba	150ml	aquafaba	200ml	aquafaba
	180g	plain flour	270g	plain flour	360g	plain flour
	2 tsp	baking powder	1 tbsp	baking powder	4 tsp	baking powder
	1 pinch	salt	1 pinch	salt	1 pinch	salt
	75ml	milk	100ml	milk	200ml	milk

Preheat the oven to 175°C/350°F/gas 4. Grease and line or add crumbs to a round or rectangular tin or a baking tray. Melt the margarine. Whip the sugar and aquafaba until frothy in a stand mixer or with an electric hand mixer. Carefully mix the flour, baking powder and salt in a separate bowl. Add the dry ingredients, the melted margarine and the milk to the frothy aquafaba and fold with a spatula until smooth without overworking. Swipe a spatula around the sides of the bowl to incorporate any leftover flour. Pour the batter into the tin and bake in the centre of the oven at 175°C/350°F/gas 4 according to the times given below. Test with a skewer until it comes out clean from the middle of the cake. Slice when the cake is cool.

TINS & BAKING TIMES

Below, suitable tins for different quantities of batter are given, together with the relevant baking times.

3 tins 10cm: smaller amount = 20–25 minutes
15cm: smaller amount = 30–40 minutes
18cm: smaller amount = 30–35 minutes
20cm: larger amount = 30–40 minutes
18cm: larger amount = 35–45 minutes
25 × 35cm: amount = 30–35 minutes for baking tray

MORE SUGGESTIONS FOR CAKES

* You can make an Easter cake with lemon curd and vanilla pastry cream. You can colour the marzipan yellow.
* You can make a Christmas cake using white or red marzipan. The cake can be filled with orange or clementine curd and vanilla pastry cream.
* Princess cake lengths are made by using a cake baked in a baking tray measuring 25 × 35cm. Cut the cake into three lengths and cut in half again to give six thin lengths. These can be used to make two long princess cakes that give around 14–16 slices. Fill like the princess cake on page 194; you will need 400–500g of marzipan for each length.
* Blueberry cake is made with blueberry vanilla pastry cream and blueberry jam. You can colour the marzipan purple or blue.

PRINCESS CAKE

Outside Sweden, cakes are often covered with fondant, sugar paste or sugary frosting, but marzipan cakes and cream cakes are the most popular cakes in Sweden. 'Green cake' appeared for the first time in *The Princesses' New Cook Book* that was published in 1948, and even though the recipe has changed slightly since then it is still our favourite. Traditionally, princess cakes are coloured pistachio green, which is a mix of green and yellow, which gives them the bright green colour. If you cannot find pistachio green, you can combine green and yellow colouring yourself to get a similar shade. White and pink cakes are usually called opera cakes, and yellow marzipan cakes are sometimes called king's cakes. I recommend concentrated powders or pastes that are mixed with water or alcohol, as these will distribute evenly throughout the marzipan. If you are using water-based colouring, you can add some icing sugar to the marzipan to make it firm again. Knead thoroughly to spread the colour evenly. You might benefit from wearing gloves to avoid discoloured hands. Today you can find ready-rolled marzipan sheets in shops, but these are too thin and stiff to make smooth, even marzipan cakes. A few creases are not the end of the world though, so if you do not want to roll out the marzipan yourself, you can use the ready-made sheets. However, be careful of red and pink marzipan that often contains E120, made from crushed insect scales. Read more on vegan colouring and how to colour marzipan on page 54.

3	sponge cake layers
	crushed fresh raspberries or raspberry jam
1 batch	vanilla pastry cream from page 424
250ml	whipped cream, firmly whipped (see page 409)
400–500g	marzipan

You can prepare the marzipan cake completely or partly the day before serving. It is always better if it has time to sit. I usually fill the cake with raspberries or jam and vanilla cream, seal it with clingfilm and chill overnight in the fridge to let the sponge soak up the flavours. I cover the cake with cream and marzipan on the day of serving. However, you can colour the marzipan the day before covering the cake for a more even effect.

1. Put the underside of one cake layer facing upwards and the sliced surface facing downwards on the plate. That way the raspberries will colour the cooked surface and the base of the cake will not be dark. Spread raspberry jam or crushed fresh raspberries over the cake. (If you are worried about possible norovirus in frozen raspberries, boil them before using.) Put the next cake layer on top and spread vanilla cream over it. You can then put a thicker layer of whipped cream on top of the vanilla cream before placing the last cake layer on top, as shown opposite. Then you only need a thin layer of whipped cream to cover the cake.

2. Spread a thin layer of cream all over the cake. You can add a little more whipped cream on top to give it a dome-like effect if the top layer was not previously filled with extra cream.

3. Roll out the marzipan until it is 3–4mm thick. If it is too thin it will crack when you are covering the cake. To prevent the marzipan from sticking to anything, you can roll it between two pieces of baking paper or two pieces of clingfilm, and you can also sprinkle over some icing sugar. Roll the marzipan onto the rolling pin and lay it out over the cake. To avoid creases, smooth your hands around the cake and gently pat down the marzipan on the sides. Work your way from the top to the bottom of the cake. Any creases can be stretched out from the bottom. Work with the marzipan from the top down, just like the sugar paste on page 219. Do not cut the marzipan too close to the bottom as it can contract. It is better to cut off too little and cut it again later.

18-CM GENOISE

HERE, I FORGOT MY OWN ADVICE ABOUT TURNING THE CAKE THE OTHER WAY UP.

YOU CAN PREPARE UP TO THIS STAGE, WRAP CLINGFILM AROUND THE CAKE AND CHILL

MINI CAKES

Having written two books about layer cakes, I have realized that my favourite size of cake is 10cm in diameter, which is perfect for a small birthday celebration. The layers bake perfectly in these small tins. You can make them quickly and they do not create too much washing up as everything goes into one bowl. They bake quickly, they cool quickly, they can be decorated quickly and they give 4–8 slices. Mini cakes are also perfect if you want to take a small cake to a party where the party host is unsure how to bake vegan for their guests. These recipes can, of course, also be used for cream cakes and layer cakes with frosting.

MINI VANILLA

60g	plain flour
60g	icing sugar
¾ tsp	baking powder
1 pinch	salt
¼ tsp	vanilla sugar or vanilla extract
2 tbsp	aquafaba
2 tbsp	milk
2 tbsp	oil

Preheat the oven to 175°C/350°F/gas 4. Grease and line or add crumbs to a 10cm diameter tin. Mix the flour, icing sugar, baking powder, salt and vanilla sugar or extract in a bowl. Add the aquafaba, milk and oil and mix using a spatula. Pour into the tin and bake at 175°C/350°F/gas 4 for 25–30 minutes. Test with a skewer that should come out clean from the middle of the cake. Let it cool in the tin before removing the cake and cutting into three thin layers. Then follow the instructions for assembling the cake layers on page 194.

MINI CHOCOLATE

2 tbsp	cocoa
60g	plain flour
60g	icing sugar
¼ tsp	baking powder
½ tsp	bicarbonate of soda
1 pinch	salt
2 tbsp	oil
2 tbsp	aquafaba
50ml	water
¼ tsp	vanilla extract
½ tsp	vinegar

Preheat the oven to 175°C/350°F/gas 4. Grease and add crumbs to a 10cm diameter tin. Sift the cocoa and mix with the flour, icing sugar, baking powder, bicarbonate of soda and salt in a bowl. Add the oil, aquafaba, water, vanilla extract and vinegar and fold to a smooth batter using a spatula. Swipe the spatula around the sides of the bowl to incorporate any leftover flour. Pour into the tin and bake at 175°C/350°F/gas 4 for 30–35 minutes. Test with a skewer that should come out clean from the middle of the cake. Let it cool in the tin before removing the cake and cutting into three thin layers. Then follow the instructions for assembling the cake layers on page 194.

If you are adapting recipes for cake layers in 10cm tins, a batter using around 70g sugar is suitable for one tin and you will have to adjust the recipe to suit the number of tins you have. These are baked for 25–35 minutes depending on the quantity of batter. Test with a skewer along the way. For some cake recipes, baking times are given for for 10-cm cakes, but you will need to reduce the quantity of batter or bake in 4–6 small tins. 10cm tins can be found in most cake shops online.

You will need around 150–200g of marzipan or sugar paste to cover a mini cake. A cake covered with frosting only needs one batch of frosting made with 50–100g of fat. This means that you can reduce my frosting recipes accordingly when making a mini cake.

AMERICAN LAYER CAKE

This kind of recipe includes more fat and gives a denser cake with more flavour compared to the layer cakes traditionally made in Sweden. You can also use the reverse creaming batters from page 98, which are also common in America. The cakes are always baked in several tins and are not cut into layers, but you can cut off the top to give a flatter surface. The cake opposite was decorated with a classic frosting coloured with beetroot juice. Read more about colouring on page 54. The cake was baked using the larger amount of batter baked in three tins measuring 15cm in diameter.

SMALLER

150g	margarine
2 tsp	vanilla extract
270g	plain flour
2 tsp	baking powder
1 pinch	salt
270g	sugar
150ml	aquafaba
75ml	milk

LARGER

225g	margarine
3 tsp	vanilla extract
405g	plain flour
1 tbsp	baking powder
¼ tsp	salt
405g	sugar
200ml	aquafaba
100ml	milk

Preheat the oven to 175°C/350°F/gas 4. Grease and line or add crumbs to the tins. Melt the margarine and mix with vanilla extract. Mix the flour, baking powder and salt in a bowl. Whip the sugar and aquafaba until frothy in a separate bowl. Carefully fold in the flour mixture. When almost incorporated, fold in the melted margarine in three batches. Fold in the milk.

Swipe the spatula around the sides of the bowl to incorporate any leftover flour, pour the batter into the tin or tins and bake in the centre of the oven at 175°C/350°F/gas 4. Baking times for different tins and amounts of batter are given below. Test with a skewer that should come out clean from the middle of the cake.

Let the cake cool in the tin on a wire rack before cutting or decorating. The top of the cake is removed to make it level when assembling the cake.

TINS & BAKING TIMES
Below, suitable tins for different quantities of batter are given, together with the relevant baking times.

2 tins 15cm: smaller amount = 35–45 minutes
1 tin 20cm: smaller amount = 35–45 minutes
3 tins 15cm: larger amount = 35–45 minutes
2 tins 18cm: larger amount = 30–35 minutes

DARK CHOCOLATE LAYER CAKE

After 10 years of developing recipes, I have many chocolate cake layers in my repertoire and I have included many versions in this book. All of them have an intense chocolate flavour. The American and the Australian cakes are slightly more stable than the dark chocolate version on this page. If you mix aquafaba with oil as in the newer recipe, the texture will be better, which is described on page 36. I recommend you use separate tins for perfectly baked layer cakes, rather than cutting one cake to make several layers. A high proportion of cocoa can make the cake rather porous, so if you want a firmer texture, you can replace 20g of cocoa with the same quantity of flour.

NEWER

60g	cocoa
270g	plain flour
315g	sugar
¼ tsp	salt
1 tsp	bicarbonate of soda
1 tsp	baking powder
1–2 tsp	vanilla extract
1 tsp	vinegar
250ml	water
150ml	oil
100ml	aquafaba

SIMPLE

60g	cocoa
270g	plain flour
315g	sugar
¼ tsp	salt
1 tsp	bicarbonate of soda
1 tsp	baking powder
1–2 tsp	vanilla extract
1 tsp	vinegar
350ml	water
150ml	oil

Preheat the oven to 175°C/350°F/gas 4. Grease and add crumbs to the tin or tins or prepare with baking paper if you want the sides to be chocolate-coloured. Sift the cocoa and mix with the flour, sugar, salt, bicarbonate of soda and baking powder. Add the vanilla extract, vinegar, water and oil (mixed with aquafaba if using the newer recipe) and mix until smooth. Swipe a spatula around the sides of the bowl to incorporate any leftover flour, pour into the tin or tins and bake in the centre of the oven at 175°C/350°F/gas 4. Baking times for different tins and quantities of batter are given below. Test with a skewer that should come out clean from the middle of the cake. Let the cake cool in the tin on a wire rack before cutting or decorating. The top of the cake is removed to make it level when assembling the cake.

TINS & BAKING TIMES
Below, suitable tins for different quantities are given, together with the relevant baking times.

6 tins 10cm = 30–35 minutes
2 tins 15cm = 45–55 minutes
3 tins 15cm = 30–35 minutes
1 tin 18–20cm = 60–70 minutes
2 tins 18–20cm = 35–45 minutes
1 tin 25cm = 45–55 minutes

TIP!
For extra flavour, some of the water can be replaced with red wine, whisky, coffee or stout.

CHOCOLATE LAYER CAKES

These cakes are slightly more stable than the simple dark layer cake on the previous pages and they contain yoghurt; the Australian cake layer also includes melted chocolate in the batter. I recommend using several tins for perfectly baked layers. In the picture opposite, the cake is covered and filled with the chocolate mousse from page 234.

AMERICAN

60g	cocoa
300g	plain flour
315g	sugar
1½ tsp	bicarbonate of soda
¼ tsp	salt
100g	yoghurt
200ml	oil
250ml	water
1 tsp	vinegar

AUSTRALIAN

60g	cocoa
300g	plain flour
315g	sugar
1½ tsp	bicarbonate of soda
¼ tsp	salt
100g	yoghurt
100ml	oil
100g	dark chocolate
250ml	water
1 tsp	vinegar

Preheat the oven to 175°C/350°F/gas 4. Grease and add crumbs to the tin or tins or prepare with baking paper if you want the sides to be chocolate-coloured. Sift the cocoa and mix with the flour, sugar, bicarbonate of soda and salt in a bowl.

For the American cake layer, pour the yoghurt, oil, water and vinegar into the dry ingredients and mix until smooth without overworking, preferably with a spatula.

For the Australian cake layer, heat the yoghurt and oil in a pan until they just start to simmer, then take the saucepan off the hob. Break the chocolate into pieces and add to the oil mixture. Mix until the chocolate melts. The mixture will curdle, but it will bind together when the batter is mixed. Add the melted chocolate mixture, water and vinegar to the dry mixture. Mix until smooth without overworking, preferably with a spatula.

Swipe the spatula around the sides of the bowl to incorporate any leftover flour, pour it into the tin or tins and bake in the centre of the oven at 175°C/350°F/gas 4. Baking times for different tins and quantities are given below. Test the cake with a skewer which should come out clean from the middle of the cake. Let the cake cool in the tin on a wire rack before cutting or decorating. The top of the cake is removed to make it level when the cake is assembled.

TINS & BAKING TIMES
Below, suitable tins are given together with the relevant baking times.

2 tins 15cm = 40–50 minutes
3 tins 15cm = 30–40 minutes
2 tins 18–20cm = 30–35 minutes
1 tin 18cm = 65–75 minutes
1 tin 20cm = 55–65 minutes
1 tin 22–25cm = 45–55 minutes

FUDGE LAYER CAKE

The chocolate layers in these cakes are very moist with an intense chocolate flavour. This recipe has been inspired by what are called mayonnaise cakes in America, as the oil is emulsified before adding it to the cake, which makes it extra moist. In the picture opposite, the cake is covered with the soft chocolate frosting from page 230.

100g	cocoa
210g	plain flour
315g	sugar
¼ tsp	salt
2 tsp	bicarbonate of soda
150ml	oil
50ml	aquafaba
300ml	water
1–2 tsp	vanilla sugar or vanilla extract

Preheat the oven to 175°C/350°F/gas 4. Grease and add crumbs to the tin or tins or prepare with baking paper if you want the sides to be chocolate-coloured. Sift the cocoa and mix with the flour, sugar, salt and bicarbonate of soda. Mix the oil and aquafaba until pale and slightly thicker in a separate bowl. Add the oil mixture, water and vanilla to the dry ingredients and mix until smooth. Swipe a spatula around the sides of the bowl to incorporate any leftover flour, then pour the batter into the tin or tins and bake in the centre of the oven at 175°C/350°F/gas 4. Baking times for different tins and quantities are given below. Test the cake with a skewer which should come out clean from the middle of the cake. Let the cake cool in the tin on a wire rack before cutting or decorating. The top of the cake is removed to make it level when the cake is assembled.

TINS & BAKING TIMES
Below, the suitable tins are given, together with the relevant baking times.

2 tins 18–20cm = 25–35 minutes
2 tins 15cm = 40–50 minutes
3 tins 15cm = 25–35 minutes
1 tin 25cm = 35–45 minutes

CARROT LAYER CAKE

This cake is one of my favourites and the carrot cake that is best for a layer cake, preferably together with the coconut frosting on page 228 and with desiccated coconut on the sides. You can use all the other carrot cakes in the book to build layer cakes and there are instructions for several tins in the recipe for classic carrot cake on page 156. You can find instructions on how to make carrot purée on page 158.

SMALLER

270g	plain flour
270g	sugar
1 tsp	ground cinnamon
1 pinch	salt
1 tsp	bicarbonate of soda
1 tsp	baking powder
100ml	oil
100ml	carrot juice or water
250g	carrot purée (baby food)
2 tsp	vinegar (optional)
100g	chopped walnuts (optional)

Preheat the oven to 175°C/350°F/gas 4. Grease and add crumbs to the tin or tins or prepare with baking paper. Mix the flour, sugar, cinnamon, salt, bicarbonate of soda and baking powder in a bowl. Add the oil, carrot juice or water, carrot purée, and the vinegar and walnuts, if using, and quickly mix until smooth using a whisk or a spatula. Do not overwork as this can make the cake chewy. Swipe the spatula around the sides of the bowl to incorporate any leftover flour, pour the batter into the tin or tins and bake in the centre of the oven at 175°C/350°F/gas 4. Baking times for different tins and quantities are given below. Test the cake with a skewer which should come out clean from the middle of the cake. Let the cake cool in the tin on a wire rack before cutting or decorating. The top of the cake is removed to make it level when the cake is assembled.

LARGER

390g	plain flour
405g	sugar
1–2 tsp	ground cinnamon
¼ tsp	salt
1½ tsp	bicarbonate of soda
1½ tsp	baking powder
150ml	oil
150ml	carrot juice or water
375g	carrot purée (baby food)
1 tbsp	vinegar (optional)
150g	chopped walnuts (optional)

TINS & BAKING TIMES
Below, suitable tins for different quantities are given, together with the relevant baking times.

6 tins 10cm: smaller amount = 30–35 minutes
2 tins 15cm: smaller amount = 40–45 minutes
3 tins 15cm: smaller amount = 30–35 minutes
1 tin 18–20cm: smaller amount = 45–55 minutes

3 tins 15cm: larger amount = 40–45 minutes
2 tins 18–20cm: larger amount = 35–45 minutes
1 tin 22–24cm: larger amount = 45–55 minutes

15CM

This cake has been made using the larger amount of batter in three tins. The frosting is coloured using juice from a grated beetroot. The cake is decorated with candy UFOs and sprinkles.

HUMMINGBIRD CAKE

Hummingbird cake is a classic cake from the southern states of America and traditionally contains cinnamon, banana, pecan nuts and pineapple. If you are allergic to pecan nuts you can leave them out, of course, or replace them with a nut or seed that you can eat. You can replace caster sugar with soft brown sugar for more flavour. All versions of the vanilla frosting on page 226 are perfect for this moist cake. The American custard frosting also works with this recipe. The picture shows the batter baked in two tins measuring 15cm in diameter, covered with the soft cream cheese frosting from page 226, flavoured with lemon zest from half a washed organic lemon. The top of the cake is decorated with dried pineapple sprinkles and old 'cake toppers' from America bought from Etsy.

50g	pecan nuts
200g	bananas, mashed
100g	pineapple, crushed
125g	margarine
150ml	room-temperature milk
300g	plain flour
270g	sugar
1 tsp	bicarbonate of soda
1 tsp	baking powder
½ tsp	ground cinnamon
1 pinch	salt

Preheat the oven to 175°C/350°F/gas 4. Grease and add crumbs to the tin or tins or prepare with baking paper. Chop the nuts finely and weigh out 50g. Mash the bananas thoroughly in a bowl and add the crushed pineapple and nuts. Melt the margarine and add to the fruit together with the milk. Mix the flour, sugar, bicarbonate of soda, baking powder, cinnamon and salt in a separate bowl. Using a spatula fold the dry ingredients with the liquid until smooth, then swipe the spatula around the sides of the bowl to incorporate any leftover flour. Pour the batter into the tin or tins and bake in the centre of the oven at 175°C/350°F/gas 4. Baking times for different tins and quantities are given below. Test the cake with a skewer which should come out clean from the middle of the cake. Let the cake cool in the tin on a wire rack before cutting or decorating. The top of the cake is removed to make it level when the cake is assembled.

TINS & BAKING TIMES

Below, suitable tins for different quantities are given together with the relevant baking times.

2 tins 15cm =	40–50 minutes
3 tins 15cm =	30–40 minutes
2 tins 18–20cm =	30–35 minutes
1 tin 18cm =	65–75 minutes
1 tin 20cm =	55–65 minutes
1 tin 22–25cm =	45–55 minutes

ROASTING NUTS

If you want to decorate the cake with pecan nuts, they taste best when roasted. Spread the nuts on a baking tray and roast lightly in the centre of the oven at 175°C/350°F/gas 4 for 5–10 minutes. Watch the nuts carefully since they burn easily. They can also be roasted in a dry frying pan for a few minutes.

LEMON LAYER CAKE

This is a classic layer cake that I like to pour some lemon juice over before assembling. You can also pour over the lemon syrup from page 100 before assembling. Use a cream cheese frosting, classic frosting or a custard frosting with added lemon zest and some lemon juice. Here I added some poppy seeds, but you can also add blueberries or raspberries to this cake. The cute carousel horse is a candle.

SMALLER

150g	margarine
2	lemons, zest of
270g	plain flour
2 tsp	baking powder
I pinch	salt
270g	sugar
100ml	aquafaba
150g	yoghurt

LARGER

225g	margarine
3	lemons, zest of
405g	plain flour
I tbsp	baking powder
¼ tsp	salt
405g	sugar
150ml	aquafaba
200g	yoghurt

Preheat the oven to 175°C/350°F/gas 4. Grease and add crumbs to the tin or tins or prepare with baking paper. Melt the margarine and add the lemon zest. Mix the flour, baking powder and salt in a bowl. Whip the sugar and aquafaba until frothy in a separate bowl. Add the flour mixture and yoghurt carefully, and when incorporated, fold in the melted margarine in three batches. Fold with a spatula until smooth, then swipe the spatula around the sides of the bowl to incorporate any leftover flour. Pour the batter into the tin or tins and bake in the centre of the oven at 175°C/350°F/ gas 4. Baking times for different tins and quantities are given below. Test the cake with a skewer which should come out clean from the middle of the cake. Let the cake cool in the tin on a wire rack before cutting or decorating. The top of the cake is removed to make it level when the cake is assembled.

TINS & BAKING TIMES
Below, suitable tins for different quantities are given, together with the relevant baking times.

2 tins 18cm: smaller amount = 30–35 minutes
2 tins 15cm: smaller amount = 35–40 minutes

3 tins 15cm: larger amount = 35–40 minutes
3 tins 18cm: larger amount = 30–35 minutes

PUMPKIN LAYER CAKE

This classic North American layer cake is made a lot during the autumn months and especially during Halloween, where pumpkin is used a lot more in baking and cooking. The easiest way to use pumpkin is to find pumpkin purée in cans, but you can also boil or steam pumpkin flesh and mix to a smooth purée. It is important not to make it watery as it needs to be quite firm. Well-stocked grocery shops will have pumpkin purée in the world foods section. The picture opposite shows the larger amount of batter baked in three tins measuring 15cm in diameter The cake is covered and filled with a maple syrup frosting made using 400g of soft vegan spread, 300g of icing sugar, 75ml of maple syrup and ¼ teaspoon of ground cinnamon. See the instructions for the classic frosting on page 226. The top of the cake is decorated with candy rocks.

SMALLER

⅛ tsp	grated nutmeg
270g	plain flour
315g	sugar
1 tsp	ground cinnamon
¼ tsp	ground ginger
1 pinch	salt
1 tsp	bicarbonate of soda
1 tsp	baking powder
100ml	oil
150g	yoghurt
200g	pumpkin purée

LARGER

¼ tsp	grated nutmeg
400g	plain flour
450g	sugar
1½ tsp	ground cinnamon
½ tsp	ground ginger
¼ tsp	salt
1½ tsp	bicarbonate of soda
1½ tsp	baking powder
150ml	oil
250g	yoghurt
300g	pumpkin purée

Preheat the oven to 175°C/350°F/gas 4. Grease and add crumbs to the tin or tins or prepare with baking paper. Grate the nutmeg with a grater and measure out the correct amount. Mix the flour, sugar, cinnamon, nutmeg, ginger, salt, bicarbonate of soda and baking powder in a bowl. Add the oil, yoghurt and pumpkin purée and fold until smooth using a whisk or a spatula. Do not overwork it as the cake can end up chewy. Swipe the spatula around the sides of the bowl to incorporate any leftover flour. Pour the batter into the tin or tins and bake in the centre of the oven at 175°C/350°F/gas 4. Baking times for different tins and quantities are given below. Test the cake with a skewer which should come out clean from the middle of the cake. Let the cake cool in the tin on a wire rack before cutting or decorating. The top of the cake is removed to make it level when the cake is assembled.

TINS & BAKING TIMES

Below, suitable tins for different quantities are given, together with the relevant baking times.

2 tins 15cm: smaller amount = 45–50 minutes
3 tins 15cm: smaller amount = 35–40 minutes
1 tin 18–20cm: smaller amount = 50–60 minutes

3 tins 15cm: larger amount = 45–50 minutes
2 tins 18–20cm: larger amount = 40–50 minutes
1 tin 22–24cm: larger amount = 50–60 minutes

MOUSSE & CURD FILLING

MOUSSE

If you want thick, stable layers of filling that are still light and airy, a mousse is perfect. The mousse needs to set in the fridge for several hours, preferably overnight, which means that you need to prepare the mousse filling in advance. Chocolate mousse can also be used to cover cakes, but cakes covered in chocolate mousse can be hard to cut if not served cold or covered with sugar paste or marzipan. That is why I recommend covering them with sugar paste or using a different frosting.

When filling a cake with mousse, you need to use the tin it was baked in or a cake ring of the same size as the cake layers. Some cake rings can be adjusted to fit most cakes. Cover the inside with baking paper, clingfilm or food-safe plastic made from acetate. The one you choose will depend on whether you are making a naked cake or if you are covering it. When using acetate to cover the sides of the cake, the mousse will not be pushed out at the sides and the layers will be even enough to be served as a naked cake. You can bake cake layers that are slightly larger than the tin and trim off the edges with a knife for naked cakes filled with mousse, like the cakes from the bakery Milk Bar (see opposite). Using baking paper in the tin that is cut to fit the bottom and the sides, you will get a more even mousse that can be served naked. Baking paper is softer than acetate, which makes it bulge slightly more. Brushing some oil on the inside of the cake ring will help the paper to stick to the sides. Using clingfilm will give the mousse a rough surface as the mousse is pushed easily out to the sides, but clingfilm is easy to use and works well for covered cakes. When covering a tin with clingfilm you can put in two strips to make a cross. Place the first cake layer in the centre of the cross, and when the cake is assembled, you can lift the cake out of the tin by lifting the strips of clingfilm. This will cover the tin in clingfilm on all sides.

1. Start by preparing a tin with clingfilm or baking paper of the same size as the cake layers.

2. Remove the top of each cake layer to level and cut the cakes into as many layers as you need.

3. Put the first cake layer into your prepared tin, then cover with mousse and put the next cake layer on top. If you want to fill more layers with mousse, then keep going. You can check the surface is even using a spirit level if you are using multiple layers.

4. Cover the cake layers so that the cake is completely sealed and put in the fridge overnight or for at least 8 hours to let the mousse set.

5. If you are covering the cake with frosting or sugar paste, you can remove any excess mousse now and cover with the crumb coat according to the instructions on page 216.

CURD

If you want a tart or softer filling in a cake with a lot of layers, you can pipe a ring of firm frosting around each layer so that the filling does not come into contact with the sugar paste or is pushed out when the heavier cake layers are put on top. For marzipan cakes with a thin layer of crushed raspberries or raspberry jam, this edge is not needed and a thin layer can be spread between the layers.

TIP!
The cakes shown opposite were baked in three tins measuring 15cm in diameter. The first cake was filled with blackberry mousse from page 234. The cake on the bottom right was filled with rhubarb curd from page 262.

15CM

ke baked with the
arger amount of
merican batter in
3 tins.

After
8 hours in
the fridge.

MILK
BAR-STYLE

Milk Bar, the bakery belonging to restaurant chain Momofuku, uses imaginative flavours and makes naked layer cakes that are usually prepared like the ginger cake, below, left. The cake is cut to the right size and plastic made from acetate is used on the sides of the tin to keep the lemon mousse in place and to get straight sides. Acetate can be found in baking shops.

FILLED AND COVERED CAKES

A cake with straight sides is a lot easier to cover than an uneven cake. So, if a cake is going to be covered with sugar paste or marzipan the groundwork is important. For naked layer cakes that are either just filled with frosting or covered with a crumb coating, you should use baking paper to line the tin as breadcrumbs can make the cake crumbly. You can also bake the cake using semolina and then brush off the excess before covering the cake with frosting. The quantity of frosting needed for different sized cakes depends on the height of the cake layers and whether the cake is going to be decorated with piped details. See page 221 for a guide.

For cakes with multiple layers, it is important that the cakes are even: a small spirit level is the perfect tool. Check every layer and cut the layer with a sharp knife if it is not straight.

If the cake is going to be covered or needs straight edges, even without sugar paste on top, chocolate ganache is one of the best things to work with.

1. Start by slicing the cooled cake into as many layers as you need. If you have made several cakes, cut off the top of each layer to level. I always cut around the whole cake with a knife before slicing the layers. Cut the top off the cake even if you are not slicing it; this gives you a flatter cake that is not at risk of cracking in the middle when the layers are placed on top of one another, and you will get a more even cake. Place the bottom layer on a plate or a cake stand.

2. Cover each layer with a thick layer of the frosting of your choice and stack them on top of one another. Make sure that each layer is even before spreading over the next layer of frosting. Remember that if you put too much frosting in between the layers, the cake will be unstable. You can fill the layer(s) with a thick layer of mousse; see instructions for filling a cake with mousse on page 214.

3. Cover the cake in a very thin layer of what is called crumb-coat frosting. The crumb coat bonds any crumbs together so that the final layer of frosting is crumb-free.

4. Let the cake chill slightly so that the crumb coat can set if you are covering the cake with frosting.

5. After the crumb coat, you can cover your cake in a thicker layer of frosting. If you are piping frosting over the cake, the crumb coat usually provides enough of a base.

6. To give an even surface, the spatula or scraper needs to go over the cake several times and between each stroke the tool needs to be rinsed in warm water. Smooth over the whole cake to make it even: first work on the sides to make them completely straight and then even out the top.

TIP!
If you want a completely smooth cake covered in frosting, the easiest way is to use either a curved spatula, which makes it easy to hold in the right position, or a scraper that is the same height as the cake. For a tall cake, for example, you can use a thoroughly washed ruler. Curved spatulas are shown on page 223. The cake shown here is a carrot cake made with purée (see page 206), baked in three tins measuring 15cm in diameter. For a perfect naked cake, springform tins are not used as they often make a little dent at the bottom of the cake. These dents can be seen opposite, before the cake was covered by a thicker layer of frosting.

1

2

3

4

A naked cake is a cake that either has no frosting on the sides or a very thin layer, like this one.

5

6

15CM

Cake baked with the larger amount of carrot cake batter in 3 tins.

USING SUGAR PASTE

First of all, find a sugar paste that you like. There are many vegan sugar pastes, and my favourite is the one from Renshaw, which is an award-winning British sugar paste. However, not all their pastes are vegan, so make sure you check the ingredients – there is a vegan label. Many sugar pastes are either too firm or don't taste that good. Sugar paste should not be used on cream cakes but should be put over a high-fat frosting to prevent it from melting. However, sugar paste can be used on top of a cream cake if the sugar paste is brushed with oil.

First, make sure that the sugar paste is warm. Knead it thoroughly or warm larger quantities of paste in the microwave in short bursts to make it soft and flexible. If the paste is too cold and firm it will crack more easily when it is rolled out. Tall cakes are considerably harder to cover without creases, as a larger part of the lid needs to be evened out around the sides.

You can put leftover sugar paste or marzipan in the freezer if it has not been in contact with the frosting. It can be kept for a few months and used for making figures or for the next cake that needs to be covered. It might be wise to create figures and details after covering the cake since there are always leftovers. Around 70 per cent of the paste will be needed for the cake.

It is important not to roll the paste out too thin as you won't be able to correct the lid at all; a thicker layer can be smoothed out. Lids that are too thick are not good to eat, so they should be rolled out to 3–4mm.

1. Start by covering the cake with frosting or ganache. If the cake is covered in ganache, it can be brushed with some boiled and cooled water to make it easier to correct the sugar paste and press out any bubbles when the sugar paste is smoothed out.

2. Dust your surface with icing sugar or cornstarch to prevent the paste from sticking.

Roll out the sugar paste (or marzipan) to the correct size. You can measure the cake so that it is not too small. The total diameter of the rolled-out covering will be equal to the sum of the height of two sides of the cake plus the diameter of the top. In order to be able to stretch out the sugar paste (or marzipan) it is important that it is thick enough (but not too thick). If it is rolled out too thinly, you will not be able to correct it when it is in place. A slightly thicker lid can be smoothed out by stretching or pressing it around the creases.

3. Carefully put the lid on top of the cake. If the lid is large, you can pick it up with a rolling pin to make it easier to move. For cakes with square edges, it is important to shape the rolled-out paste at each corner quickly so that the weight of the paste does not tear around the sides. Even out the cake from the top using your hands, working your way down to create a smooth surface. If creases do appear, they can be evened out from underneath by pressing together or stretching the paste while smoothing it out and down from the top with your hands. Work your way down the cake one section at a time, without pulling down the sugar paste. You may need to dust your hands with icing sugar or cornstarch to help them move smoothly over the surface.

4. Use one or two finishing tools, called icing smoothers, to make the cake smooth (see the picture opposite, below left). For square edges, you will need two smoothers and press them against one another, one from the top and the other from the side, all the way around the cake. Be careful when using dark chocolate underneath a light coloured lid as the chocolate can make marks in the sugar paste.

5. Do not cut the lid too close to the cake, as it usually contracts after the excess paste is cut off. It is better to cut it several times; if you are not happy with the bottom edge, you can cover it with a row of sugar paste balls, a rolled-out strip of paste or icing.

3–4MM
Sugar paste

4–5MM
Sugar paste for
beginners

HOW MUCH
SUGAR PASTE
IS ENOUGH?

This all depends on how tall your cake is, which is why this question
is hard to answer. If you are a beginner, it is also better to use a larger
amount so that it is easier to cover the cake. The quantity given here
is suitable for cakes around 10cm high. If you are making taller cakes,
you need to increase the quantity. If you are making square cakes, you
should increase the quantity by around one-third. See the guide on
page 191. If you are a beginner or like thick layers of sugar paste,
you can double the amount of sugar paste in the illustrated guide.
There will always be sugar paste left over, but you can use it
to fill in holes, cracks or to smooth out so-called 'elephant
skin' on the cake. Unfortunately, this is not possible
with marzipan as it is not as flexible.

15CM
Cake is baked with the
smaller amount of
batter in 2 tins.

MELTING CHOCOLATE

The easiest way to melt chocolate is to use a water bath: a bowl containing pieces of chocolate set on top of a saucepan of simmering water on the hob, or on a bowl of hot water. Make sure you don't get any water in the chocolate when melting it over a water bath. White chocolate should not be heated over 44°C/111°F and you need to be extra careful not to place the bowl of chocolate over a water bath where the water is too hot. The bottom of the bowl should not be in contact with the water when melting chocolate. You can also melt chocolate in the microwave in a bowl made of porcelain or glass. Put the pieces of chocolate in the microwave for short bursts, 10–30 seconds, and mix in between until the chocolate has melted completely. Chocolate burns easily so watch it closely.

CLASSIC CHOCOLATE FROSTING

A curved spatula (see page 223) was used to spread this frosting.

Frosting & fillings

FROSTING

These are rough estimates for filling and covering cakes that are 10cm tall. The amount of fat given refers to the solid or liquid fat that is added to the frosting, as that is easier to control than the total weight of the frosting. These amounts are only guidelines as it varies depending on the thickness of the layer covering the cake. Leftover frosting can usually be put in the freezer and thawed at a later date. You will have to whip it again after it has thawed completely.

10cm cake = 50–100g fat
15cm cake = 200–300g fat
18–20cm cake = 300–500g fat
25cm cake = 400–600g fat

LEMON & CARROT
Carrot cakes go well with lemon frosting. You can grate the zest of ½–1 organic, unwaxed lemon and add to all the light-coloured frostings on page 226. Taste and add as much lemon zest as you like. If you want a frosting that is more tart, you can also add some lemon juice, but be careful not to add too much. If the frosting contains liquid, you can replace it with the same amount of lemon juice.

SOFT MARGARINE
Always make sure you take the vegan spread out of the fridge before making frosting. It needs to be at room temperature.

PIPING TIPS

1. Prepare all your equipment.

2. Cut off the corner of the piping bag if it is a disposable one. Do not cut off too much; it is better to have to cut the bag twice than it is to cut off too much and not be able to use it.

3. Insert your chosen nozzle and cut off a little more of the bag if you need to.

4. Roll up the bottom of the bag or use a clip so that you do not have to worry about the contents of the bag escaping.

5. Fold out the edges of the bag so that you can fill it without getting frosting on the outside. You can also place the bag in a jug or a large glass so you can fill the bag more easily. You can buy special piping bag racks to help you do this, but I think a large glass works perfectly well. If the frosting is very soft, it can be helpful to put a clip on the bottom of the bag even before you have finished filling it.

6. Fill the bag. Make sure it the bag is not too full and you can hold it comfortably in your hand. If the bag is too full it can be difficult to hold it steady and apply an even pressure.

7. Try not to get air bubbles in the bag as this will make it difficult to pipe evenly. Eliminate any air bubbles from the bag before you start piping.

8. Put a clip at the end of the bag so that the contents do not escape before you have pushed all the frosting down to the end of the bag. Never squeeze the piping bag in the middle as it is hard to apply a steady pressure. If you are not using a clip there is also the risk of the frosting escaping from the piping bag. Always squeeze from the top down. Use your thumb and index finger to hold the bag at the point where you you have spun it to push the frosting together. Then press down gradually using more fingers to do so. Remember to always push from the top downwards. Use a clip from the outset (as in the picture opposite) so you don't have to worry about anything else while you are piping. Hold one hand at the end of the bag to guide it, and the other above so you so can squeeze from above. The piping bag can get warm if you are piping for a long time, and the frosting can become too soft for piping. If this happens, put the bag in the fridge until the frosting has firmed up again.

To achieve smooth, round swirls on cupcakes and muffins it is important for the frosting to be very soft. If the frosting is too firm, your swirl will not end neatly and instead will 'break off' when you lift the piping nozzle. White chocolate buttercream and meringue buttercream are the softest frostings in this book and they are perfect for making round swirls on cupcakes or for piping flowers.

Picture 9 opposite shows a selection of tools. To change nozzles without changing the piping bag, you can use nozzle holders (the white tools in the picture). Piping bags are available in many sizes and materials. Straight and curved spatulas are useful for making cakes, icing and decorations. If you want to pipe many colours at once, converters are available (bottom right corner). The following pages show some of the most common nozzles and how they can be used.

Flowers

The basic technique for making piped flowers is to place a dot of frosting on a flower needle, which is then used to attach a small piece of baking paper about the same size as the plate of the needle, to the top of the needle plate. Then pipe your flower onto the baking paper disc, and when you are finished, carefully lift off the baking paper and place the flower in the fridge or freezer to firm up. When the flower is firm, you can place it on the cake without it breaking. It is possible to make flowers without using a flower needle, but as well as making the flowers easier to handle a flower needle allows you to work all around the flower with the piping bag.

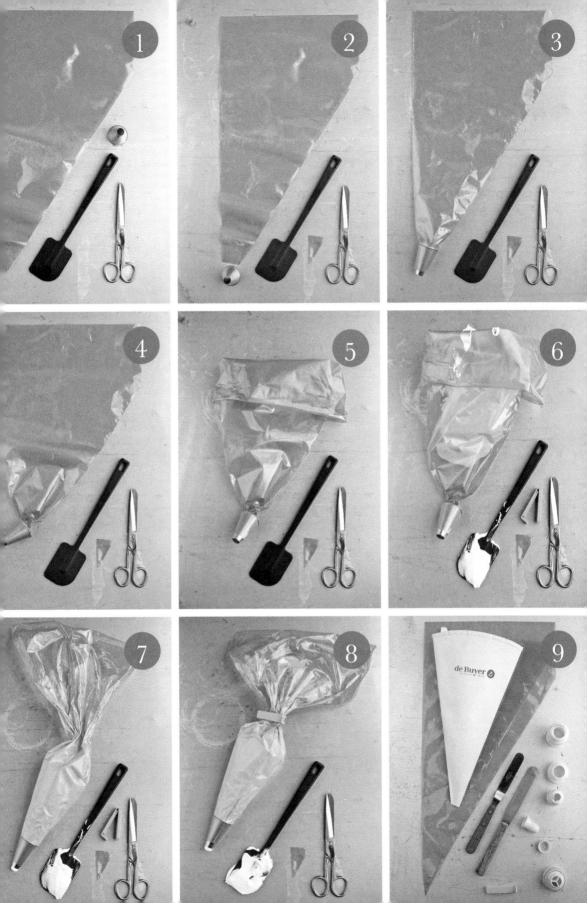

PIPING NOZZLES

1. **Round**. Small round nozzles are used for writing; 8–12mm nozzles to pipe round toppings for cupcakes and biskvis.
2. **Star.** A standard classic nozzle that is used for many different decorations.
3. **Eclair.** This is wide star nozzle that is used for eclairs and decorations.
4. **Closed star.** Used in a similar way to the nozzle above, but has more defined ridges and is often used for roses.
5. **Ruffle.** Used for ruffles, tassels and borders; comes in many different styles.
6. **Leaf.** These come in many different styles and sizes; they can also be used for ruffles.

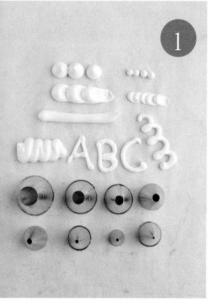

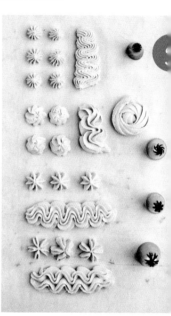

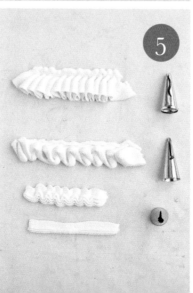

7. **St Honoré.** Used for piping meringue or cream onto pies. Pipe with the base almost touching the surface that is to be decorated.

8. **Curved.** These are used for ruffles and decorations. The bottom nozzle is similar to the rose tip or St Honoré, but is slightly curved. Use with the wide base almost touching the surface that is to be decorated.

9. **Straight and slightly waved.** Ribbon nozzles (straight) can also be used to pipe carnations. For flowers, a decoration nail is useful.

10. **Grass.** Grass nozzles with varying hole sizes are used to pipe grass and animal fur.

11. **Petal.** Used for flowers or St Honoré. The opening is teardrop-shaped. For flowers, a flower nail is useful.

12. **Speciality.** The star ribbon/serrated border nozzle is used for cream cakes and decorations. The injection nozzle is used for filling cream buns or doughnuts. The flower nail or decoration nail is used for flowers. The pipe cleaner is used to clean nozzles.

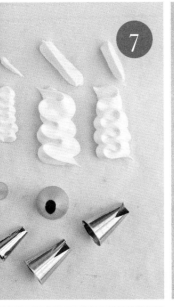

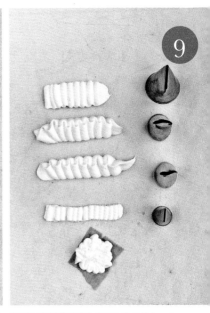
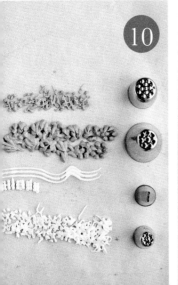

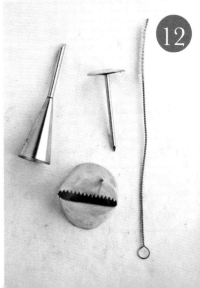

VANILLA FROSTING

CLASSIC FROSTING

Frostings based on vegan baking margarine often have a melting point that is too high for the frosting to have a good flavour, which is why I have not previously included these recipes for frosting. If you use vegan spread that is soft with a lower melting point, it will work perfectly well for classic frosting recipes like this and for the white chocolate buttercream on page 228.

200g	vegan spread
240–480g	icing sugar
$^1/_8$ tsp	salt
I tsp	vanilla extract or vanilla sugar
0–3 tbsp	liquid (milk, lemon juice)

Beat together all the ingredients in a bowl, adding the icing sugar to taste and beating for several minutes to make a light and airy frosting. Add liquid if needed.

AMERICAN CUSTARD FROSTING

This is a custard frosting developed from a traditional American cookbook. To make the frosting gluten free, replace the flour with cornstarch. Recipes based on corn are usually called German buttercreams and they have, like the American custard frosting, a very soft, light texture. The frosting is not stable enough to provide a thick filling layer in a tall layer cake.

SOFT	FIRM	
30g	30g	plain flour
250ml	250ml	cream
225g	225g	sugar
250g	350g	vegan spread
I pinch	I pinch	salt
I tsp	I tsp	vanilla extract or vanilla sugar

Heat the flour, cream and sugar in a saucepan and stir until thickened. Stir continuously to avoid lumps. Remove the saucepan from the hob after having simmered it for a few seconds and the mixture has thickened. Leave to cool completely, preferably covered with clingfilm to prevent a skin forming on top of the cream. Beat the soft margarine with the salt and vanilla in a separate bowl. Add the cold custard, a little at a time, and beat thoroughly for a light-coloured, fluffy frosting.

COCONUT OIL FROSTING

Frosting based on coconut oil is incredibly fluffy and melts in the mouth but is firm when cold from the fridge. If you need to chill the bake, you should not use a frosting with coconut oil. This is shown in the photo opposite.

200ml	coconut oil
200g	soft margarine
300–480g	icing sugar
I pinch	salt
I tsp	vanilla extract or vanilla sugar

Beat the soft or melted coconut oil with the soft margarine until fluffy. Add the icing sugar to taste together with the salt and vanilla. Beat for several minutes to make it fluffy.

CREAM CHEESE FROSTING

Using a slightly higher proportion of margarine in the recipe makes this frosting a little more airy and firmer in consistency; for a softer frosting use a lower proportion of margarine. The sweet version is based on traditional American recipes for cream cheese frosting that use icing sugar. If the frosting separates, add a little more cream cheese until it comes together again. If I use this frosting for carrot cakes, I usually add some lemon zest. Note that some vegan cream cheeses become runny when combined with sugar and can't be used to make frosting.

SOFT	FIRM	SWEET	
100g	150g	150g	soft margarine
120g	120g	480–600g	icing sugar
200g	200g	200g	cream cheese
250g	350g		vegan spread
I pinch	I pinch	I pinch	salt
I tsp	I tsp	I tsp	vanilla extract

Beat together the margarine and icing sugar in a bowl. Stir in the cream cheese, a little at a time, together with the salt and vanilla extract and whisk until light and fluffy.

FLAVOURED FROSTING

WHITE CHOCOLATE BUTTERCREAM

This is a luxurious, light-coloured frosting. There is one version that is perfect for piping decorations that are supposed to be moved but is slightly too firm to be served chilled, and another version in a larger quantity that can be served slightly cooler. Depending on which white chocolate you use and how much cocoa butter it contains, you may not need to add cream to make the frosting soft. White chocolate is extra sensitive to heat; it should not be heated over 44°C/111°F. If it does become granular, you can strain using a sieve. Read more about this on page 57.

PIPING   CHILLING

100g	100g	dairy-free white chocolate
125g	250g	vegan spread
120–180g	240–360g	icing sugar
2–3 tbsp	50–100ml	double cream
1 pinch	1 pinch	salt
½ tsp	½ tsp	vanilla extract or vanilla sugar

Melt the white chocolate carefully over a water bath and let it cool. Beat the margarine until fluffy in a bowl and add the icing sugar and the cooled melted chocolate. Beat thoroughly to a soft and fluffy buttercream, add the cream to give the consistency of your choice and then add the salt and vanilla.

COCONUT FROSTING

Nowadays you can usually find coconut cream with at least 25 per cent fat in ordinary grocery shops. If you can only find coconut milk, buy the full fat version and chill the can. One 400g can will give varying amounts of coconut cream depending on the brand and fat percentage, but be aware you may need more than one can. Discard the thin milk underneath that is not needed for this recipe. Make sure that the coconut cream comes to room temperature, otherwise the frosting will split easily. When I use this frosting I like to cover it with a thin layer of desiccated coconut. This works well, especially for a carrot cake.

200g	firm coconut cream
250g	vegan spread
180–360g	icing sugar
1 pinch	salt
1 tsp	vanilla extract
1–2 tsp	coconut essence (optional)

Chill the coconut milk (or cream if you can find it) in advance. Scoop out 200g of the firm coconut cream and leave until it reaches room temperature again. Beat the margarine in a bowl until soft, add the coconut cream and beat until smooth and fluffy, then add icing sugar to taste. Add the salt, vanilla extract and coconut essence, if using, to boost the coconut flavour.

PEANUT FROSTING

For this it is best to use an organic peanut butter that is made almost exclusively from peanuts. That is what this recipe was created with.

200g	smooth peanut butter
100g	vegan spread
180g	icing sugar
50–100ml	double cream

Beat the peanut butter, soft margarine and icing sugar thoroughly until the frosting is fluffy. Add double cream to your preferred consistency.

CANDY FLUFF

Nowadays, you can find many kinds of vegan jelly candy and foam candy in ordinary grocery shops, and with these you can make a soft candy fluff for decorating muffins, cakes, brownies and layer cakes.

65g	foam candy or jelly candy
250ml	cream

Cut the candy into pieces and put into a small saucepan together with the cream. Melt the candy on a low heat while stirring – the cream should not boil as vegan cream normally cannot cope with high temperatures. When all the candy has melted, cool the mixture before whipping thoroughly to a firm consistency.

Here banana muffins with aquafaba were baked in a mini muffin tray at 175°C/350°F/gas 4 for 13–15 minutes. Candy fluff made from melted fluffy banana candy was piped using a round 1-cm piping nozzle.

CHOCOLATE FROSTING

SOFT CHOCOLATE FROSTING

This is one of the most delicious frostings for cakes if you want a strong chocolate flavour. What is unique about this recipe is that it is soft even when chilled, which is usually difficult when using melted chocolate. My simple chocolate frosting on this page is another soft recipe. It does not include any melted chocolate but has a lot of cocoa and it stays soft in the fridge. Here, you can also use margarine with a good result.

400ml	water
270g	sugar
60g	cocoa
I tsp	vanilla extract or vanilla sugar
85g	cornstarch
150g	vegan spread or margarine
150g	chocolate
I pinch	salt

Boil 300ml of the water with the sugar, cocoa and vanilla in a saucepan. Beat the cornstarch in the remaining water and add to the simmering mixture. Keep stirring all the time and remove from the hob when thickened. Allow to cool, preferably covered with clingfilm to prevent a skin forming on top. Beat the vegan spread and cooled, melted chocolate until fluffy. Add the salt and then the custard, a little at a time; mix until smooth. Mix for several more minutes until fluffy.

CLASSIC CHOCOLATE FROSTING

100g	milk or dark cooking chocolate
200g	room-temperature vegan spread
60–120g	icing sugar
20g	cocoa
I pinch	salt
I tsp	vanilla extract

Melt the chocolate and let it cool slightly to avoid melting the vegan spread. Beat the soft vegan spread and 60g of the icing sugar, cocoa, salt and vanilla. Mix in the cooled chocolate, a little at a time. Beat the frosting for 5–10 minutes to make it really fluffy. Add more icing sugar if the frosting is too soft or if you want it sweeter.

SIMPLE CHOCOLATE FROSTING

This frosting is based on my classic frosting where I use vegan spread and includes a large amount of cocoa which gives an incredible chocolate frosting, almost like a truffle or unbaked brownie batter. It also stays soft in the fridge as it does not contain any melted chocolate. If you are using the frosting for a large cake, you need to double the recipe. It is also perfect on top of kladdkaka and brownies. Start out using 180g of icing sugar, but if you want your chocolate buttercream sweeter, you can add a little more. This is shown in the picture opposite.

100g	vegan spread
180–240g	icing sugar
I pinch	salt
I tsp	vanilla extract or vanilla sugar
3–4 tbsp	cream or milk
100g	cocoa

Mix together all the ingredients, apart from the cocoa, in a bowl. Beat for a few minutes and then add the cocoa, a little at a time. When all the cocoa has been added, continue beating to make the frosting light and fluffy. You can add more liquid for an even fluffier consistency.

CHOCOLATE GLAZE

If you want a thinner chocolate glaze for covering your cake or a chocolate ganache for covering a cake, but you have not had time to prepare the ganache on page 238, you can use this recipe. I have divided it according to the percentage of cocoa solids in the chocolate.

40–60%	70–80%	
250ml	300ml	cream
200g	200g	dairy-free chocolate
I pinch	I pinch	salt

Follow the instructions for the chocolate ganache (on page 238) but chill the glaze to the right consistency. Glaze that is poured on top of the cake only needs to cool slightly, while it needs to cool a little more to be spreadable.

Dark chocolate muffins baked in a mini muffin tray at 175°C/350°F/gas 4 for 13–15 minutes. The simple chocolate frosting was piped using a round 1-cm piping nozzle.

MERINGUE BUTTERCREAM

Meringue buttercream has a very soft consistency and is perfect for piping details. In Italian meringue buttercream the syrup is heated to a high temperature. The syrup heats the raw egg white and kills any harmful bacteria. Swiss meringue buttercream is often made in a water bath to dissolve the sugar crystals and heat the egg white. The meringue buttercreams included here are more like an American version as the quantities of sugar are slightly higher than in the traditional recipes. In these vegan versions, there is no need to worry about bacteria. All the ingredients need to be at room temperature and if the mixture splits, continue mixing and it will come together again. If the meringue is added too hot and the cream splits because the margarine has melted, you can cool it slightly. If the margarne is added too cold, a little of the buttercream can be heated in the microwave and returned to the bowl. This will heat the meringue buttercream more quickly than just mixing for a few more minutes, which will also work. If you are using a light yellow margarine, the buttercream will become pale yellow, which means that it is not ideal for white cakes or white details. If you can find 'shortening', you can use half vegan margarine and half shortening to give a whiter meringue buttercream.

ITALIAN MERINGUE BUTTERCREAM

340g	sugar
75ml	water
200ml	aquafaba
$1/8$ tsp	cream of tartar
300g	room-temperature margarine
1–2 tsp	vanilla extract

Put the sugar and water in a saucepan and boil to 130°C/266°F. You will need to use a thermometer. In the meantime, using a stand mixer, whip the aquafaba and cream of tartar to a firm foam. Try to time this so that you get a firm foam at around the same time as the syrup reaches the correct temperature. If the foam gets firm before that, just decrease the speed of the mixer – meringue made using aquafaba is not as sensitive as egg whites when it comes to over-mixing. Add the warm syrup to the foam slowly, and whip the meringue until cold, firm and shiny, which can take up to 10 minutes. The meringue needs to be completely cold when the diced margarine is added, otherwise the margarine will melt. Add a little at a time, until incorporated. The meringue buttercream may split at some point, but it will come together again if you continue mixing. Add the vanilla extract and whisk for a further 5–10 minutes until you get a fluffy buttercream. Chill the buttercream slightly if it becomes too soft.

SWISS MERINGUE BUTTERCREAM

300ml	aquafaba
340g	sugar
$1/8$ tsp	cream of tartar
300g	room-temperature margarine
1–2 tsp	vanilla extract

Reduce the aquafaba to 200ml in a saucepan on a medium to low heat. Add the sugar to the aquafaba and mix until the sugar crystals have dissolved, and then let it cool completely. Beat the reduced aquafaba and cream of tartar in a stand mixer using a wire whisk. When the meringue is fluffy, white and shiny, add the diced margarine a little at a time, until incorporated. The meringue buttercream may split at some point, but it will come together again if you continue mixing. Add the vanilla extract and beat thoroughly for a further 5–10 minutes until you get a fluffy buttercream. Chill the buttercream slightly if it becomes too soft.

THANKS LINDA!!!

MOUSSE

A chocolate mousse is firm because of the high proportion of cocoa butter. I use coconut oil in my fruit mousse as it firms up in the fridge and you get a mousse that is firm enough without using chocolate. Plant-based double cream usually has a lower percentage of fat than dairy double cream, but together with the coconut oil the percentage of fat will be about the same as the dairy version. It gives a light, fluffy but firm mousse that you can use to fill layer cakes. The custard cannot be chilled in the fridge and agar will eventually set at room temperature, which is why you should not let the custard cool too much. Fill the layer cakes with mousse according to the instructions on page 214.

CHOCOLATE MOUSSE FILLING

I have divided the recipe according to the percentage of cocoa solids in the chocolate.

WHITE	40–60%	70–80%	
200ml	300ml	400ml	double cream
300g	300g	300g	dairy-free chocolate
$1/8$ tsp	$1/8$ tsp	$1/8$ tsp	salt
I tsp	I tsp	I tsp	vanilla extract

Take the cream out of the fridge in advance to bring it to room temperature. Melt the chocolate carefully, white chocolate is extra sensitive and should not be heated over 44°C/111°F. Add the salt and vanilla extract to the chocolate and let it cool. Beat the cream slightly and add the cooled chocolate, a little at a time, while contuning to whisk.

FRUIT MOUSSE FILLING

Use whatever fruit purée you want, including mashed banana. Blackberry mousse is shown on page 215.

200g	unsweetened fruit purée
45g	sugar
I tsp	cornstarch
I tbsp	agar powder
150ml	room-temperature coconut oil
200ml	room-temperature double cream

Boil the fruit purée together with the sugar, cornstarch and agar powder. Remove the pan from the hob when the mixture has thickened and immediately add the coconut oil. If the coconut oil is not ready, the custard will cool and it will be difficult to make it come together. Mix until the coconut oil is incorporated. You can use a hand blender to ensure the mixture is smooth, then let it cool until lukewarm. The custard cannot be chilled in the fridge and cannot sit for too long as the agar will set. Whip the cream until firm using an electric hand mixer, then add it to the custard, a little at a time, while mixing carefully.

LEMON MOUSSE FILLING

100ml	lemon juice, plus zest
50ml	water
I tsp	cornstarch
I tbsp	agar powder
67g	sugar
125ml	room temperature coconut oil
200ml	room temperature double cream

Grate the zest of the lemon, slice them in half and squeeze out the juice. Boil the lemon juice, zest, water, cornstarch, agar powder and sugar in a saucepan while stirring. Remove the pan from the hob when thickened and immediately add the coconut oil. If the custard starts to cool too much, it will be difficut to make it come together. Mix with a hnad blender until the coconut oil is incorporated. You can use a mixer to ensure the mixture is smooth, then let it cool until lukewarm. The custard cannot be chilled in the fridge and cannot sit for too long as the agar will set. Whip the cream until firm, then add it to the custard, a little at a time, while mixing carefully.

MOUSSE

The quantities given for the mousses are enough to fill 15-cm layer cakes with two layers of mousse and also fill layer cakes up to 18–20cm with one or two layers of mousse. Larger cakes will need a larger amount of mousse.

CARAMEL

Caramel can be used as decoration for both cakes and ice cream. You can make beautiful decorations with honeycomb or crumble it into vanilla or caramel ice cream. Salted caramel frosting goes well with kladdkaka, chocolate cakes, muffins and large layer cakes; it also makes an amazing filling for biskvis. Take care not to get caramel on your skin – it is extremely hot and can cause a nasty burn. It's a good idea to keep other people and pets out of the kitchen while you are working with caramel.

SALTED CARAMEL FROSTING
400ml   cream
360g   sugar
500g   vegan spread
120–240g icing sugar
½ tsp   salt

Boil the cream in a saucepan and set aside. Put 45g of the sugar in a another saucepan on a high heat. When melted, add another 45g of sugar and continue until all the sugar has melted. Let the melted sugar become dark brown in colour without burning. Add the warm cream, a little at a time (it will spit!), then remove from the hob and stir until all the caramel has melted. Let it boil for a few more minutes while stirring if there are any hard pieces still left in the mixture. Let it cool completely in the fridge, stirring frequently to prevent the surface from hardening or clingfilm over the surface while it is cooling. Beat the soft margarine and icing sugar in a bowl using an electric hand mixer until light-coloured and fluffy. Add the caramel, a little at a time, and beat for several minutes. Add salt to taste.

BURNT CARAMEL SAUCE
100ml   cream
50g   margarine
⅛ tsp   salt
135g   sugar

Boil the cream, margarine and salt in a saucepan and set aside. Put 45g of the sugar in a another saucepan on a medium heat. When melted, add another 45g of sugar and repeat until all the sugar has melted. Let the melted sugar become dark brown in colour without getting burned. Add the warm cream mixture, a little at a time (it will spit!), remove from the hob and stir until all the caramel has melted. Let it boil for a few more minutes while stirring if there are hard pieces still left in the mixture. Pour into a clean jar.

CARAMEL SAUCE
250ml   cream
50ml   milk
90g   sugar
140g   golden syrup
1 pinch salt

Boil the cream, milk, sugar, syrup and salt to in a saucepan. Let it simmer for 10–20 minutes until the sauce has thickened. It should also have a nice and light caramel colour. If the sauce is too firm when it thickens, you can boil it again and add more cream or milk. Serve warm or cold. Store in a sealed jar.

HONEYCOMB
70g   agave, maple or your favourite syrup
70g   golden syrup
135g   sugar
2 tsp   bicarbonate of soda

Prepare a baking tray with baking paper. If you want a tall honeycomb you can line a tin measuring 20 × 20cm or create a tin using baking paper that is stapled together at the sides and then placed on the baking tray. Mix the syrups and sugar in a saucepan and boil on a medium heat until golden and it can stand a breaking test, which is described in the box on page 434, or when it reaches 150°C/300°F. Remove the saucepan from the hob and add the bicarbonate of soda. Mix carefully to avoid a bitter aftertaste but work quickly. Pour the mixture into the tin while still bubbling and mind your hands. Let it harden. Break or cut into pieces.

Are there lumps in your caramel? Adding too much cream at once will cool the caramel and create lumps. If this happens, you can put the caramel back on the hob until the lumps have dissolved. If you are left with any lumps, you can strain the caramel through a metal sieve when it is cooling. To clean, fill the saucepan with hot water to dissolve the caramel left in the pan.

These banana muffins were baked in a greased muffin tray without paper cases.

GANACHE

GANACHE

This ganache is perfect for giving square edges to layer cakes both with and without sugar paste. It is important to work with the cake layers and to serve the cake at room temperature. Depending on the percentage of cocoa solids your chosen chocolate contains, you will need different amounts of cream. Below, I have given two amounts for the two different percentages of cocoa solids. The lower amount needs less cream. I recommend you test bake the ganache using the chocolate you want to use before baking for a special event, so you know how much cream your chocolate needs. If it is allowed to set for 24 hours, the consistency will change, so make sure that you give yourself enough time.

40–60%	70–80%	
200–250ml	300–350ml	cream
400g	300g	chocolate
1/8 tsp	1/8 tsp	salt

Heat the cream and remove the saucepan from the hob when it is lukewarm. Melt the chocolate according to the instructions on page 57. Let the chocolate cool slightly before adding it, a little at a time, to the lukewarm cream with the salt. Ganache should be allowed to harden and set at room temperature for at least 24 hours and should not be stored in the fridge before that. When it has set, it can be stored in the fridge or in the freezer; it must be allowed to thaw completely before use. The risk of lumps in the ganache is lowest if it is allowed to set in a bowl where the chocolate is no deeper than 5cm. Make sure that you do not cover cakes in a layer of ganache that is too thin, as the ganache can crack easily on top of the cake.

GANACHE DRIP

Make sure that the cake is cold but not too chilled so that the ganache creates drips but does not set too quickly. The ganache should be cool enough that the base on top of the cake does not melt from the heat of the ganache. Tricky – but practice makes perfect!

50g	margarine
75g	dark chocolate

Melt the margarine in a saucepan. Melt the chocolate in a heatproof bowl according to the instructions on page 57. Carefully mix in the melted margarine, a little at a time, and let the ganache cool at room temperature until slightly thicker. Stir it often if put in the fridge. If it sets, you can place the bowl over some hot water to melt it again. Make sure the cake you are dripping over is cold but not chilled, so the frosting you are pouring the ganache over does not melt, and the ganache will set in nice drips. If the cake is too cold, the ganache will set too quickly. I start by putting a little ganache in the centre of the cake and spreading it out over the edges, but many people make the drips around the edges first and then spread the ganache over the top.

WHITE & COLOURED GANACHE DRIZZLE

White chocolate easily splits when mixed with other liquids, but this ganache is made with a neutral-flavoured oil that gives a nice soft ganache, which is stable to work with. If you want a really white ganache, there is colouring for white chocolate, which is often slightly yellow or beige. Read more on colouring on page 54. The quantity given here is suitable for cakes up to 18cm in diameter; for bigger cakes you will need to increase the amount.

50g	white chocolate
50ml	neutral-flavoured room-temperature oil
	chocolate colouring (optional)

Chop or break the chocolate into pieces and melt it carefully together with the oil and colouring, if required, according to the instructions on page 57. The ganache should cool slightly before it is poured over the cake as it will be very runny and hot. In the fridge, it will cool quickly, but if you do not have time to let it cool at room temperature for 1–3 hours, you can cool it in the fridge for short intervals and stir frequently. The ganache will quickly go from runny to firm and lumps may form. If it becomes too hard, you can place it over some hot water and it will melt again. It is important that the cake you are pouring the ganache over is cold so that the frosting you are pouring it over will not melt, and the ganache will set in nice drips. Pour over the ganache as above.

The Easter cake in the picture is 15cm in diameter. It has been covered with ganache and then with white chocolate ganache drip coloured using yellow chocolate colouring, and finally with sprinkles, a marzipan chick and a dark chocolate egg. Cake pops can be found on page 328 and macarons on page 288. Cake boxes can be found in baking stores online.

GANACHE DRIP

This is used to cover the top of a cake and run down the sides. It is important that the cake you are covering is cold but not chilled, as well as the ganache drip, so that the frosting that you are pouring over does not melt and the ganache sets in nice drips. If the cake is too cold, the ganache will set too quickly. I usually drop the cake gently onto a surface or tap it to bring the ganache further down the sides before it is completely set. This will also help the top to even out slightly, but don't tap it too hard.

ON THE LEFT ARE PANCAKES MADE WITH
NOEGG AND ABOVE ARE PANCAKES MADE
WITH AQUAFABA. ON THE RIGHT ARE
FLUFFY PANCAKES.

ALL ARE FRIED WITHOUT USING FAT IN
A NON-STICK FRYING PAN.

WHIPPED VEGAN SPREAD CAN BE
FOUND ON PAGE 258.

Brunch

Here, you can find bakes that are perfect for brunch, but don't forget the brioche, milk bread, conchas, bagels, chocolate bread and the overnight raised simple rolls in the chapter of raised doughs (see page 331). An olive oil cake or a few shortbreads are also perfect for a brunch. The apple butter on page 404 goes well with both pancakes and scones.

SWEDISH PANCAKES

These Swedish pancakes are very similar to French crêpes. It is a universal truth that the first pancakes made always turn out badly, which is why you should not lose hope if these are ruined. In the first two recipes, your pancakes will be more flexible if you add 30g of cornstarch. Makes 15–20 pancakes.

50g	margarine
210g	plain flour
¼ tsp	salt
500ml	milk

Melt the margarine and let it cool. Mix the flour and salt in a large bowl and add the milk and cooled margarine. Mix to a smooth pancake batter. Ideally, let the batter stand for 30 minutes. Fry on a medium heat; 75–100ml of batter per pancake is usually enough depending on the size of your frying pan. Add some oil and spread it out over the pan. Then add the batter, tilt the pan around so that the batter covers the whole pan. Test fry one pancake first. If the batter is too thin, add a few extra tablespoons of plain flour. Add more milk for a thinner batter. The batter at the bottom is usually thicker, so you might need to add some liquid at the end anyway.

AQUAFABA PANCAKES

150ml	aquafaba
50ml	oil
400–500ml	milk
240g	plain flour
¼ tsp	salt

Mix the aquafaba, oil and 200ml of the milk in a bowl, preferably using a hand blender. Add the flour and salt and mix to a smooth batter with no lumps. Then add the remaining milk. Start with the lower amount and see if that gives a thick enough batter. Ideally let the batter stand for 30 minutes. Fry on a medium heat; 75–100ml of batter per pancake is usually enough depending on the size of your frying pan. Add some oil and spread it out over the pan. Then add the batter, tilt the pan around so that the batter covers the whole pan. Test fry one pancake first. If the batter is too thin, add a extra few tablespoons of plain flour. Add more milk for a thinner batter. The batter at the bottom is usually thicker, so you might need to add some liquid at the end anyway.

GLUTEN-FREE PANCAKES

900ml	milk
2 tbsp	vinegar
110g	cornstarch or whole-grain rice flour
120g	sorghum flour
80g	potato starch
55g	tapioca starch
4 tsp	baking powder
¼ tsp	xanthan gum
4 tbsp	sugar
¼ tsp	salt
100ml	oil

These different flours can often be found in well-stocked grocery shops but can also be ordered online. Makes 25–35 pancakes.

Mix the milk and vinegar in a bowl and set aside for a few minutes. Mix the cornstarch or wholegrain rice flour, sorghum flour, potato starch, tapioca starch, baking powder, xanthan gum, sugar and salt in a separate bowl. Add the milk mixture and the oil and mix until smooth. Fry on a medium heat; 75–100ml of batter per pancake is usually enough depending on the size of your frying pan. Add some oil and spread it out over the pan. Then add the batter, tilt the pan around to make the batter cover the whole pan. Test fry one pancake first. If the batter is too thin, add a few extra tablespoons of corn flour or wholegrain rice flour. Add more milk for a thinner batter. The batter at the bottom is usually thicker, so you might need to add some liquid at the end anyway.

PANCAKES

To make pancakes that are perfectly cooked on both sides you should only turn them over once and you need cook them at a temperature so that by the time the first bubbles appear on the surface, it means that the pancake should be turned over and will be golden on the other side. Test fry one pancake until golden and make sure that it is cooked through to the middle, if not adjust the temperature. However, note that the first pancake is almost always ruined, so do the test on the second pancake. This is tricky at first, but you will learn quickly both about the temperature and the consistency of the batter. The vanilla extract can be replaced with a teaspoon of vanilla sugar or a pinch of vanilla powder. The top picture on page 240 shows pancakes made with aquafaba. You can make pancakes using just 300ml of milk, but with yoghurt, the pancakes are thicker and fluffier. If you use 200g of yoghurt and 100ml of milk, they are slightly fluffier. This recipe makes 10 large pancakes made using 75–100ml of batter or 15–20 small pancakes when using around 50ml of batter.

PANCAKES WITH AQUAFABA

100ml	aquafaba
45g	sugar
240g	plain flour
1 tbsp	baking powder
1 pinch	salt
1 tsp	vanilla extract
200ml	milk
100g	yoghurt
50ml	oil

Whip the aquafaba and sugar in a bowl until pale and frothy using an electric hand mixer. Mix the flour with the baking powder and salt in a separate bowl, and the vanilla extract, milk, yoghurt and oil in another. Add both mixtures to the frothy aquafaba. Fold together until just combined. Lumps in the batter do not matter, a less worked batter will make thicker and fluffier pancakes than an overworked batter. Fry without cooking fat (in a non-stick frying pan) for pancakes with an even brown colour on both sides – the classic American look – or with cooking fat if you want spotty pancakes (see page 247).

PANCAKES WITH NoEgg

50g	margarine
240g	plain flour
30g	cornstarch
1 tbsp	sugar
1 pinch	salt
1½ tbsp	baking powder
50ml	water
30g	NoEgg
1 tsp	vanilla extract
350–400ml	milk

Melt the margarine and let it cool. Mix the flour, cornstarch, sugar, salt and baking powder in a bowl. Whip the water with the NoEgg in a separate bowl. It should be thick and fluffy, but you don't need to use an electric hand mixer, you can use a hand whisk. Add the melted margarine, vanilla extract, the NoEgg mixture and 350ml of the milk to the flour mixture. The batter will be firmer than a traditional pancake batter. This is because the 'egg effect' has been reached using the NoEgg mixture before frying and not when it is in the frying pan as it does when using eggs. The batter is fluffy and does not give heavy or dense pancakes. If you think it is too thick when test frying one pancake, add the extra milk – the batter should spread out slightly when frying.

FLUFFY PANCAKES

100ml	aquafaba
45g	sugar
240g	plain flour
1 tbsp	baking powder
1 pinch	salt
300g	yoghurt
1 tsp	vanilla extract
50ml	oil

Whip the aquafaba and sugar in a bowl to a soft meringue using an electric hand mixer. Mix the flour with the baking powder and salt in a separate bowl. In another bowl, whisk together the yoghurt, vanilla extract and oil until well-combined. Add both mixtures to the meringue. Carefully fold all the ingredients together using a spatula, but don't stir too much. Lumps in the batter do not matter, a less worked batter will make thicker and fluffier pancakes than an overworked batter. For best results, transfer the batter to a piping bag. Fry without fat over a low to medium heat. Pictured on page 241.

For what are called birthday pancakes, add 1–2 tablespoons of coloured sprinkles to the batter that melt into colourful dots.

For blueberry pancakes, add 55g of fresh berries to the batter. If your berries are frozen, it is better to add them when the batter is put into the frying pan, otherwise they will make the whole batter purple.

For strawberry pancakes, add 55g of diced strawberries to the batter.

BANANA PANCAKES

FLUFFY BANANA PANCAKES

100g	bananas, mashed
100ml	aquafaba
45g	sugar
360g	plain flour
1 tbsp	baking powder
1 pinch	salt
300ml	milk
2 tbsp	oil

This recipe makes 10 large or 15–20 smaller pancakes.

Mash the bananas. Whip the aquafaba and sugar in a bowl until pale and frothy using an electric hand mixer. Mix the flour with the baking powder and salt in a separate bowl and then fold into the aquafaba mixture with the milk, oil and mashed banana. Fold carefully to prevent any air leaving the aquafaba. Fry around 50ml of batter at a time, using a 50ml measure if you have one. Fry without fat or oil (in a non-stick frying pan) for pancakes with an even brown colour on both sides – the classic American look. Fry with with fat or oil if you want the surface to be speckled, like the classic Swedish pancakes opposite.

SIMPLE BANANA PANCAKES

GRAMS	QUANTITY	
200g	1	banana
350ml	150ml	milk
210g	90g	plain flour
2 tsp	1 tsp	baking powder
1 pinch	1 pinch	salt

If I only have one banana, I make the batter according to the quantity of banana I have. If I have plenty of bananas, I use the full recipe.

Mash the banana with a fork in a bowl until there are no lumps left. Mix the mashed banana with milk. Carefully mix the flour, baking powder and salt in a separate bowl. Add the flour mixture to the wet mixture and mix with a fork or something similar to make a smooth batter. Fry without without fat or oil (in a non-stick frying pan) for pancakes with an even brown colour on both sides – the classic American look – or fry with with fat or oil if you want the surface speckled, like classic Swedish pancakes.

GLUTEN-FREE BANANA PANCAKES

1	ripe banana
150ml	milk
60g	wholegrain rice flour
30g	cornstarch
1 tsp	baking powder
1 pinch	salt

Here, you can replace the wholegrain rice flour with almost any gluten-free flour you like, depending on your favourite. Teff flour and oat flour will absorb more liquid than wholegrain rice flour, which means you will have to increase the amount of milk if using one of those. To make these pancakes, follow the instructions for simple banana pancakes above.

These pancakes have been fried using fat and have a speckled surface. Page 245 shows the even colour achieved when frying pancakes without fat in a non-stick frying pan.

CRISPY & SOFT WAFFLES

SOFT WAFFLES

100g	margarine
240g	plain flour
¼ tsp	salt
1 tsp	baking powder
500ml	milk
75ml	aquafaba

Here, the aquafaba replaces the function of the egg and gives soft waffles. The recipe makes 10–12 waffles.

Melt the margarine and let it cool. Mix the dry ingredients in a large bowl. Add half of the milk and mix until smooth. Add the rest of the milk, the aquafaba and the margarine and mix until smooth. Preheat a waffle maker and brush with melted fat or oil for the first batch. Fill using 75–100ml of batter for each waffle, depending on the size of the waffle maker. Cook the waffles in the hot waffle maker to a nice colour. Put the freshly made waffles on a wire rack and serve.

CRISPY WAFFLES

100g	margarine
180g	plain flour
1 tsp	baking powder
¼ tsp	salt
400ml	milk

Melt the margarine and let it cool. Mix the flour with the baking powder and salt in a bowl, then mix in the milk. Add the melted margarine and mix until smooth. Use 75–100ml of batter for each waffle, depending on the size of the waffle maker. Cook the waffles in the hot waffle maker to a nice colour. Put the freshly made waffles on a wire rack and serve.

GLUTEN-FREE CRISPY WAFFLES

100g	margarine
60g	wholegrain rice flour
90g	sorghum flour
120g	potato starch
¼ tsp	salt
2 tsp	baking powder
400–500ml	room-temperature milk

Melt the margarine and let it cool. Mix the wholegrain rice flour, jowar flour, potato starch, salt and baking powder in a bowl. Add the melted margarine and milk, and mix until smooth. Let the batter stand for a few minutes; you may need to add more milk for a smoother batter. A 100-ml measure is usually perfect as the scoop for most waffle makers. Cook the waffles to a nice colour and transfer to a wire rack. Grease the waffle maker between each batch. Serve fresly made.

BELGIAN WAFFLES

These waffles are best when made using a Belgian waffle maker that heats to 225–250°C/435–480°F. You can find these in many stores, but you can also cook Belgian waffles in a regular waffle maker if you can get it to the right temperature. Make sure you grease the waffle maker; this is more important the deeper the pattern is as the waffles can easily get stuck. The recipe with yeast makes my favourite kind of waffles, but many people love the quicker version that includes baking powder. Even though these can be a bit time-consuming to make, they are really good. You can heat them up in the oven, the toaster or the microwave if you have leftovers.

WAFFLES WITH YEAST

100g	margarine
500ml	milk
1 tsp	vanilla extract
100g	yoghurt
25g/6g	fresh/dried yeast
420g	plain flour
½ tsp	salt
75ml	aquafaba
45g	sugar

Makes about 10 large waffles

Melt the margarine in a saucepan and add the milk, vanilla extract and yoghurt; when the mixture is lukewarm, stir in the yeast. Mix the flour and salt in a bowl. Whip the aquafaba and sugar in a separate bowl until pale and frothy. Add the margarine mixture to the dry ingredients and mix the batter until smooth. Carefully fold in the aquafaba until smooth. Let the batter sit for 20–30 minutes. Grease the preheated waffle maker before each batch and cook until golden, then put the waffles on a wire rack. In my waffle maker, they are ready in 3 minutes if I cook them at 225–250°C/435–480°F.

WAFFLES WITH BAKING POWDER

100ml	oil
1 tsp	vanilla extract
500ml	milk
300g	plain flour
1 tbsp	baking powder
¼ tsp	salt
100ml	aquafaba
45g	sugar

Makes about 8 large waffles

Mix together the oil, vanilla extract and milk in a bowl. In another bowl, mix the flour with the baking powder and salt. Add the flour mixture to the milk mixture and stir to make an almost smooth batter. It is important not to overwork it, so just stir until almost all the lumps have dissolved. Whip the aquafaba with the sugar in a separate bowl until white and frothy. Fold into the batter and mix or fold the bubbles in carefully. Let the batter sit for a few minutes before baking the waffles. Grease the waffle maker and cook until golden, then put the waffles on a wire rack. In my waffle maker they are ready in 3 minutes if I cook them at 225–250°C/435–480°F.

LIÈGE WAFFLES

There are two versions of waffles from Belgium that are known all over the world, 'Belgian' waffles. and Liège waffles. Belgian waffles are made using a batter containing yeast. They are baked like most of the waffles we are familiar with. Liège waffles are made with a brioche-like dough. Both versions are cooked in a Belgian waffle maker. When made properly, these waffles are baked with Belgian nibbed sugar, but as this is not available in Sweden; I used Swedish nibbed sugar with great results.

For waffles that are left to rise overnight, you should use cold milk and cold aquafaba. Liège waffles need to be served warm, otherwise the caramelized sugar on the surface is too hard. If they do get too cold, you can warm them in a toaster, the oven or the microwave.

12g/3g	fresh/dried yeast
100ml	aquafaba
250ml	room-temperature milk
1 tbsp	sugar
½ tsp	salt
540–660g plain flour	
250g	soft margarine
225g	nibbed sugar or Belgian nibbed sugar

Mix the crumbled yeast with the aquafaba, milk, sugar and salt in a bowl. Add a little plain flour at a time until you have a sticky dough. Dice the margarine, add it in and work the dough for at least 5 minutes. Add the flour until the dough is smooth. It should still be soft and not firm.

Let the dough rise for 30 minutes, then knead in the nibbed sugar. Shape 12–15 balls of dough of around 100g each and leave to rise for at least 2 hours at room temperature or in the fridge overnight. Cook in a Belgian waffle maker at 175–180°C/350°F for 3–5 minutes. Keep the waffles warm and soft in the oven at 100°C/212°F before serving, as the caramelized sugar will harden quickly when it cools.

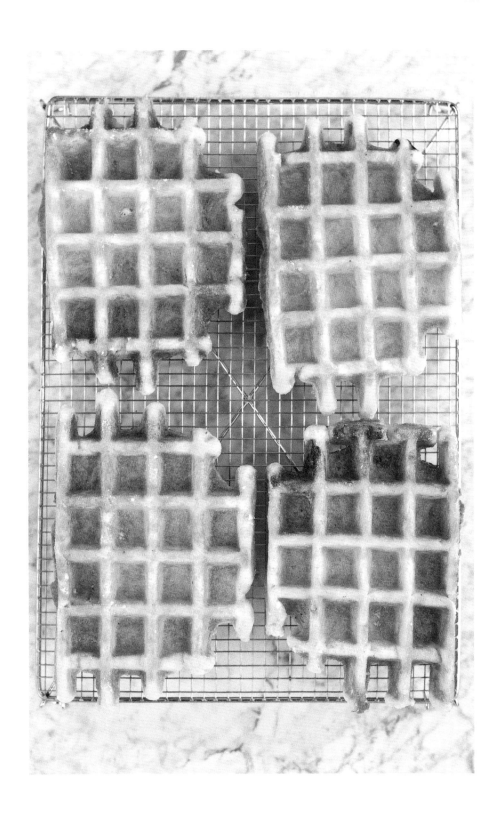

FRENCH TOAST

In America, batter for French toast usually only consists of eggs, milk and some spices, but in Sweden, we usually add some plain flour to the batter, which is why I developed that type of recipe. The batter sets perfectly when frying and forms a nice surface. I serve my French toast with maple syrup but cinnamon and icing sugar is a classic. My tip is to make French toast out of day-old cinnamon buns or saffron buns cut in half! Leftover sponge cake can also be made into French toast. Makes 5–6 slices.

5–6 slices white bread

BATTER
100ml	aquafaba
150ml	milk
1 tsp	sugar
1 pinch	salt
60g	plain flour
¼ tsp	vanilla extract (optional)

Mix together all the batter ingredients in a bowl and dip the slices of bread into the batter. Only dip the number of slices that can fit in your frying pan to avoid having them sitting in the batter. Melt cooking fat in a frying pan on a medium heat and fry until golden on both sides. Serve hot.

PIKELETS

Pikelets are Australian pancakes and there is a lot of variation among the recipes. The base is fairly similar to classic pancakes, but the batter isn't as airy. Usually the batter includes some bicarbonate of soda, which helps to make them fluffy. They are usually served with jam and whipped cream. This recipe makes 7–9 pikelets.

25g	margarine, plus extra for frying
75ml	aquafaba
75–100ml	milk
45g	sugar
1 pinch	salt
150g	plain flour
1 tsp	baking powder
¼ tsp	bicarbonate of soda
¼ tsp	vanilla extract

Melt the margarine. Leave to cool slightly. Mix the melted margarine with the aquafaba and the smaller amount of milk in a bowl. In a separate bowl, mix together the sugar, salt, plain flour, baking powder and bicarbonate of soda. Then whisk the wet and dry ingredients together, and add the vinegar extract and 1–2 tbsp more milk if you want to make the batter thinner. Melt a small amount of fat in a frying pan over medium heat, add a ladleful of batter, and fry on both sides until golden. Repeat until all the batter has been used.

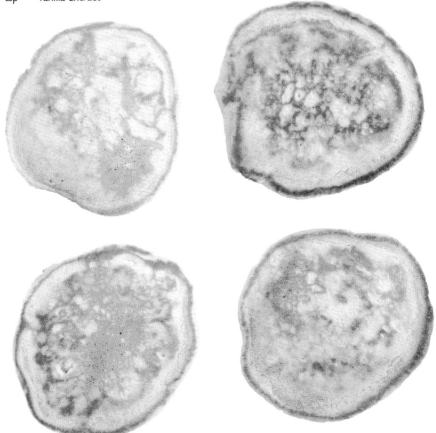

BAGHRIR

Baghrir are Moroccan pancakes, which by themselves are vegan, but they are often served with honey and butter. Also known as 'thousand holes' they are fried carefully just on one side, so don't turn up the heat too high!

This recipe uses dry yeast as this is what is usually used, but you can also use 12g of fresh yeast. I think you get thicker, lighter baghrir using fresh yeast. Before they have cooled, the baghrir are sticky, so leave them to cool separately, after this they will no longer stick together.

My vegan baghrir are served with a dollop of a luxurious vegan spread, possibly the whipped version from page 258, and agave or maple syrup. You can also melt the fat together with the syrup for a more traditional way to serve them. This recipe makes 15–20 bahirir.

600ml	warm water	
90g	plain flour	
320g	semolina	
1½ tsp	dried fast action yeast	
2 tsp	baking powder	
1 tsp	sugar	
¼ tsp	vanilla extract	
¼ tsp	salt	

Use warm (37°C/99°F) water or slightly warmer if you are using dried yeast, which can take up to 40°C/104°F. Mix together all the ingredients in a bowl. Blend with a hand blender for at least 1 minute, until you have a smooth batter. Leave to rise for 35–60 minutes; the batter should have already started to rise and develop bubbles when you stir the batter. The batter should be fairly runny, but if it is too runny when you test fry, you can add a little more flour. If the batter is too thick, add a little water. Cook in a frying pan without fat over a medium heat. Add a ladleful of batter at a time; once the surface has set, the pancake should also be cooked underneath. Baghrir are not fried on both sides, only on one, so you will have to test to find the optimum temperature for a perfectly cooked baghrir.

SYRUP DRIZZLE

50g	margarine
50g	agave or maple syrup

Use a really delicious vegan spread and a flavoursome syrup. Serve in a small bowl and drizzle over the baghrir.

Melt the margarine and syrup together in a small saucepan over a low heat. The mixture should just melt and doesn't need to boil.

SCONES

CLASSIC SCONES

75g	margarine
300g	plain flour
1 tbsp	baking powder
¼ tsp	salt
200g/ml	yoghurt, milk or water

Rub together the margarine, plain flour, baking powder and salt using your hands, a pastry blender or a stand mixer. Add the yoghurt, milk or water when the margarine is well distributed and knead the dough. Do not overwork it or the scones will be chewy. Roll the dough out to 2–3cm thick, press out the scones using a round cutter, place on a baking tray and bake in the middle of the oven at 250°C/480°F/gas 9 for 10–15 minutes. The dough can also be rolled out to make one scone round that is baked for a few more minutes than the smaller scones; the scone round should be thoroughly baked on the surface. Cut it into wedges for serving. Scones need to be served fresh since they become dry quickly when stored, even for a short time.

CORN SCONES

220g	fine ground corn flour
1 tbsp	baking powder
¼ tsp	salt
50g	cold margarine
200g/ml	yoghurt or milk

These simple, luxurious, yellow scones are made from fine ground corn flour. Corn flour is not the same as cornstarch and cannot replace it in recipes. These scones are gluten free when using gluten-free corn flour.

Mix the corn flour, baking powder and salt in a bowl. Dice the margarine, add it to the bowl and rub the ingredients together until the fat is well distributed in the flour mixture. Add the yoghurt or milk, mix to a dough, then form scones to your liking, for example, by making a scone round marked into triangles, or smaller scones made using a round cutter. Bake on a baking tray in the middle of the oven at 250°C/480°F/gas 9 for 12–15 minutes. Scones need to be served freshly made as they become dry quickly when stored even for a short time.

WHIPPED VEGAN SPREAD

100g	vegan spread
1 pinch	salt
1–3 tsp	cream (optional)

A classic trick in hotels and restaurants is to whip butter or margarine until fluffy, possibly with a little added cream, and put it in a nice cup. This makes any breakfast or brunch feel luxurious and is worth the extra effort (shown on page 240).

Whip the margarine in a stand mixer or with an electric hand mixer until fluffy, then add the salt. If you want the vegan spread to be softer, you can add the cream.

CHOCOLATE SPREADS

A tasty chocolate spread can be based on many different things. Here, I have included three versions with either chocolate, hazelnut butter or tahini as the base. They are perfect for a luxurious brunch to accompany toast, brioche, waffles and pancakes.

CHOCOLATE SPREAD

90g	sugar
1 tbsp	cocoa
50ml	water
150g	margarine
100g	dark chocolate

Boil the sugar, cocoa and water in a saucepan and remove from the hob. Add the margarine and the chocolate and stir until melted. Put it into a clean jar and store in the fridge. Take it out of the fridge in advance before serving so the spread can soften.

CHOCOLATE HAZELNUT SPREAD

200g	hazelnuts
60g	icing sugar
1 tsp	vanilla sugar or vanilla extract
20g	cocoa
1 pinch	salt
1–2 tbsp	oil

If your nuts are already roasted you can skip the roasting step, but if they are not, it is easy to roast them in the oven for 8–10 minutes at 175°C/350°F/gas 4. Rub off the skins when the nuts are cool. Blend the hazelnuts to a soft hazelnut butter in a food processor or blender. Add the icing sugar, vanilla sugar or extract, sifted cocoa, salt and oil and mix thoroughly. You may need to add another tablespoon of oil if the chocolate hazelnut spread is too firm. Put in a clean jar and store in the fridge.

CHOCOLATE TAHINI

200g	tahini
60g	icing sugar
1 tsp	vanilla sugar or vanilla extract
40g	cocoa
1 pinch	salt
50ml	oil

Use a relatively firm tahini, preferably wholegrain. If you are using a looser tahini, you can omit the oil to start with and add some later if the chocolate tahini is firmer than you want it to be.

Stir the tahini around in the jar before measuring out 200g. Mix all the ingredients in a bowl until smooth and combined. Put in a clean jar and store in the fridge.

TAHINI

CHOCOLATE
HAZELNUT

CHOCOLATE
SPREAD

CURD

LEMON CURD

Since I love lemon, my lemon curd is extremely tart. If you want your curd less tart you can, without spoiling the recipe, replace up to 100ml of lemon juice with water.

250ml	lemon juice + zest (3–5 lemons)
30g	cornstarch
135g	sugar
100g	margarine, diced

First, zest and juice the lemons. Slice the lemon in half and squeeze out the juice. Then put 100ml of lemon juice aside for dissolving the cornstarch. Boil the 150ml that is left of the lemon juice together with the zest and then strain the zest out of the juice. Add the cornstarch and the sugar and boil while stirring until thickened. Remove from the hob when thickened and add the margarine. Blend with a hand blender until the margarine has been emulsified and put in a clean jar. Cool and refrigerate. The curd will take a few hours in the fridge to set so be sure to give yourself enough time.

BANANA CURD

Banana curd is good both on a slice of bread and in cakes. If you fill a pastry case with banana curd and top it with cream you get a classic 'banana cream pie'. Bases are usually made with digestive biscuits like the recipe on page 408.

2 tbsp	lemon juice
2 tbsp	water
2 tbsp	cornstarch
200g	mashed banana
90g	sugar
100g	margarine, diced

Mix the lemon juice, water and cornstarch in a saucepan, add the mashed banana and bring to the boil, stirring. Remove the saucepan from the hob when thickened. Add the sugar and margarine. Blend with a hand blender until the margarine has been emulsified and then put into a clean jar. Cool and refrigerate. The curd will take a few hours in the fridge to set so be sure to give yourself enough time.

FRUIT CURD

250g	unsweetened fruit purée
30g	cornstarch
180g	sugar
100g	margarine, diced

Bring the fruit purée and cornstarch to the boil in a saucepan, while stirring. Remove from the hob when thickened and add the sugar and margarine. Blend with a hand blender until fullly emulsified, then put in a clean jar. Cool and refrigerate. The curd will take a few hours in the fridge to set so be sure to give yourself enough time.

RHUBARB CURD

300g	diced rhubarb
180g	sugar
30g	cornstarch
50ml	water
100g	margarine, diced

Simmer the rhubarb until soft in a pan together with the sugar for 10–15 minutes. Press through a sieve. Mix the cornstarch with water, then add to the rhubarb purée. Boil, stirring and remove from the hob when thickened. Add the margarine and blend with a hand blender until melted, then put in a clean jar. Cool and refrigerate.

PASSION FRUIT CURD

1	lemon, zest and juice
250g	passion fruit pulp
30g	cornstarch
180g	sugar
100g	margarine, diced

First, zest and juice the lemon. If you want a curd with no seeds, strain the passion fruit using a sieve. Heat the lemon zest, lemon juice, fruit pulp, cornstarch and sugar in a saucepan and bring to the boil. Remove the pan from the heat when the mixture has thickened and add the diced margarine. Stir the mixture using a hand whisk (or a hand blender if you have strained out the seeds) until the margarine has melted and everything is properly combined, then pour into a clean jar. The curd will take a few hours in the fridge to set so be sure to give yourself enough time.

RHUBARB

BANANA

CHERRY

CURD

My recipes for curd contain a larger amount of fruit than traditional curd recipes as I have replaced the eggs with more fruit. The curd takes a few hours to set in the fridge, so make sure you give yourself enough time. I think that the curd works best when it is mixed with a hand blender after adding the fat to the custard, otherwise the thickener and the fat may not become fully emulsified. However, you can mix it thoroughly without a mixer. The recipes give 400–500g of curd. Instructions for filling a layer cake with curd can be found on page 214.

LEMON

A KLADDKAKA WITH AQUAFABA
(LEFT) AND A WHITE KLADDKAKA
WITH RHUBARB (BELOW)

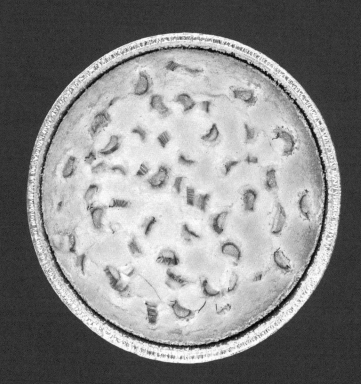

Chocolate

Here is a collection of classic chocolate recipes from a number of different countries. There are several versions of the Swedish classic kladdkaka: a brownie-like cake that is baked in a round tin with a small amount of cocoa compared to most chocolate cakes. It is underbaked so that it gets really fudgy. Kladdkaka is best served with whipped cream or ice cream. I have also included several different brownies together with French classics, such as chocolate fondant, soufflé and a really rich chocolate cake. The French recipes were incredibly difficult to veganize and these were the last recipes I worked out reliable methods for when working on this book.

Cook's Illustrated and America's Test Kitchen, two large test kitchens in the USA, say you should always add 1–2 teaspoons of instant espresso powder in chocolate recipes to enhance the taste. It does not make the finished cakes taste of coffee, but rather boosts the chocolate flavour, making it more intense and complex.

Another unexpected ingredient that enhances taste is miso paste, which Nicole Bermensolo wrote about in *The Wall Street Journal*. Shiro miso is the best type to use in chocolate recipes, but saikyo miso is also good. The latter works really well in ice cream and with caramel to enhance flavours. However, both can be used in baking. They are often sold under the name 'white miso paste'. In brownies and other really chocolate-rich bakes, you can add 1–2 tablespoons. In vegan baking, where we sometimes lack some of the flavours, this is really a revolutionary new ingredient.

KLADDKAKA

My recipes are designed for springform tins measuring around 22cm in diameter, but the kladdkaka with aquafaba can be baked in a tin of up to 25cm. Before aquafaba was discovered and I developed the method of whipping aquafaba until frothy, I used several different ingredients to make a successful kladdkaka; this recipe, just called 'kladdkaka' appears below. Kladdkaka is served warm or cold, with whipped cream or ice cream, and eaten with a spoon.

KLADDKAKA WITH AQUAFABA

100g	margarine
100ml	aquafaba
270g	sugar
150g	plain flour
40g	cocoa
1 pinch	salt
1 tsp	vanilla extract

Preheat the oven to 200°C/400°F/gas 6. Grease and add crumbs to a tin measuring 22–24cm in diameter (or prepare with baking paper). Melt the margarine. Whisk the aquafaba and sugar until pale and frothy in a stand mixer or with an electric hand mixer. Fold the flour, sifted cocoa and salt together and add to the frothy aquafaba with the melted butter and vanilla extract. Use a spatula to make sure that everything is thoroughly mixed. Do not overwork the batter. Pour the batter into the tin and bake in the middle of the oven at 200°C/400°F/gas 6. For a 22–24cm tin, bake for 12–18 minutes; for a 18–20cm tin, bake for 17–18 minutes.

KLADDKAKA

125g	margarine
100g	room-temperature yoghurt
1 tsp	vanilla extract
180g	sugar
120g	icing sugar
150g	plain flour
1 tbsp	cornstarch
4 tbsp	cocoa
¼ tsp	baking powder
¼ tsp	salt

I have tried many different ways of replacing the eggs and still being able to bind together the right quantity of fat and sugar in the cake, for instance, by using one part of the sugar as icing sugar, which is more stable in cakes. The liquid provided by the eggs has been replaced with yoghurt, which makes the mixture more stable compared to milk or water. I have also included some cornstarch for even more stability. See also pages 14 and 16.

Preheat the oven to 200°C/400°F/gas 6. Grease and add crumbs to a tin measuring 22cm in diameter. Melt the margarine and mix with the yoghurt and vanilla extract in a bowl. Mix together with the sugar, icing sugar, plain flour, cornstarch, sifted cocoa, baking powder and salt. Pour the batter into the tin and bake in the middle of the oven at 200°C/400°F/gas 6 for 18–20 minutes.

DARK CHOCOLATE KLADDKAKA

150g	dark chocolate (70% cocoa solids)
100g	margarine
1 tsp	vanilla extract
100ml	aquafaba
180g	icing sugar
60g	plain flour
30g	cocoa
1 pinch	salt

Preheat the oven to 175°C/350°F/gas 4. Grease and add crumbs to a tin measuring 18–20cm or 22cm in diameter. Melt the margarine in a saucepan and remove from the heat. Break the chocolate into pieces, add it to the pan with the margarine and let it melt. Add the vanilla extract. Whisk together the aquafaba and icing sugar in a stand mixer or with an electric whisk until pale and frothy. This happens quickly with such a high proportion of icing sugar, so take care not to over-mix. Next fold in the flour, sifted cocoa and salt. Add the chocolate mixture in three batches. Use a spatula to make sure everything is thoroughly mixed. Do not overwork the batter. Pour the batter into the tin and bake in the middle of the oven at 175°C/350°F/gas 4. For a 22cm tin bake for 15–18 minutes; for a 18–20cm tin, bake for 17–20 minutes.

FRUIT KLADDKAKA

If you want a fudgy cake, use the shorter baking time. The cake will be not quite set when it comes out of the oven but it will set in the fridge. The kladdkaka will keep its shape and can be served warm. You can replace the aquafaba with 150g of yoghurt and 1 teaspoon of baking powder. The baking powder should be mixed with the flour first, the sugar is not whipped and instead everything is mixed together in a bowl. This kladdkaka is amazing with diced rhubarb that goes well with the sweet chocolate. This is shown at the bottom of page 264.

FRUIT OR BERRY KLADDKAKA

100g	margarine
100g	white chocolate
1	lemon, zest of
2 tbsp	rum or milk
180g	sugar
100ml	aquafaba
150g	plain flour
½ tsp	salt
55g	prepared fresh fruit or berries

Preheat the oven to 200°C/400°F/gas 6. Grease and add crumbs to a tin measuring 20–22cm in diameter, or prepare with baking paper. Melt the margarine. Break the chocolate into pieces and mix into the margarine until melted. Grate the zest of the lemon and add, if using. Mix the sugar and aquafaba until pale and frothy in a stand mixer or with an electric hand mixer. Carefully fold in the flour, salt and the melted margarine mixture. Lastly, fold in the fruit or berries. Pour the batter into the tin and bake in the middle of the oven at 200°C/400°F/gas 6 for 12–20 minutes depending on the size of the tin and the oven. When I am baking in a 20cm tin I usually bake it for 15 minutes; in a larger tin, the shorter amount of time may be enough, but make sure that the cake has a golden colour. Serve warm or cold.

SAFFRON KLADDKAKA

For saffron kladdkaka, use the above recipe as the base. Start by melting the margarine and then add the saffron to the saucepan and let it dissolve in the heated liquid. Another method is to mix the saffron with 2 tablespoons of alcohol, for instance, the rum in the recipe, and let it sit for a while; ¼–½g of saffron is enough for a flavoursome, golden kladdkaka.

FRENCH CHOCOLATE CAKE

This extra luxurious chocolate cake is basically just melted chocolate. It uses the emulsifying qualities of aquafaba, and the melted chocolate is bound together with the fat and the aquafaba. A small amount of plain flour is then enough to make a perfectly gooey chocolate cake despite the short baking time. For a long time, I thought that recipes like this with such a high proportion of fat and only a tiny bit of flour, would be impossible to achieve after all my failed test bakes, but on my thirty-sixth birthday I had a craving for chocolate batter and thought that if I was going to eat the batter anyway, I might just as well try out a recipe that was doomed to fail once more. I swapped the sugar from my original recipe for icing sugar (read more on page 40), and at the last minute I decided to not whip the aquafaba until fluffy, but instead try to emulsify the whole amount of fat (read more on page 36) together. This was the result!

18–20CM TIN

100g	margarine
¼ tsp	vanilla extract
150ml	single cream
300g	dark chocolate (70% cocoa solids)
150ml	room-temperature aquafaba
½ tsp	salt
120g	icing sugar
60g	plain flour

Preheat the oven to 175°C/350°F/gas 4. Line an 18–20cm springform cake tin with baking paper. Melt the margarine, vanilla extract and single cream in a pan on a low heat, remove from the heat once the margarine has melted. Break the chocolate into chunks and leave to melt in the margarine mixture. Once melted, add the room-temperature aquafaba and carefully blend to a smooth batter using a hand blender. Mix the salt, icing sugar and plain flour together in a bowl and then fold into the melted chocolate mixture. Use a silicone spatula to make sure everything is thoroughly combined. Pour the batter into the tin and bake in the centre of the oven at 175°C/350°F/gas 4 for 20 minutes for a 20-cm tin and 25 minutes for an 18-cm tin. Carefully take out of the tin and place on a rack. Leave the cake to cool before cutting. To get nice slices, leave the cake to set in the fridge for at least 1 hour.

20–22CM TIN

125g	margarine
1 tsp	vanilla extract
200ml	single cream
400g	dark chocolate (70% cocoa solids)
200ml	room-temperature aquafaba
½ tsp	salt
150g	icing sugar
80g	plain flour

Preheat the oven to 175°C/350°F/gas 4. Line a 20–22cm springform cake tin with baking paper. Melt the margarine, vanilla extract and single cream in a pan on a low heat, remove from the heat once the margarine has melted. Break the chocolate into chunks and leave to melt in the margarine mixture. Once melted, add the room-temperature aquafaba and carefully blend to a smooth batter using a hand blender. Mix the salt, icing sugar and all the flour together in a bowl and then fold into the melted chocolate mixture. Use a silicone spatula to make sure everything is thoroughly combined. Pour the batter into the tin and bake in the centre of the oven at 175°C/350°F/gas 4 for 25 minutes for a 20-cm tin and 20 minutes for a 22-cm tin. Carefully take out of the tin and place on a rack. Leave the cake to cool before cutting. To get nice slices, the leave the cake to set in the fridge for at least 1 hour.

BROWNIES

These recipes are classics and only work because you fold the flour in first, which stabilizes the aquafaba. The older recipes for brownies usually include walnuts and you can mix 50–100g of chopped walnuts into the batter before pouring it into the tin, if you like. If you want a smooth brownie, you can shake the tin slightly and gently drop it on the counter a few times after taking it out of the oven. It will then even out before setting and the edges will drop. If you want a completely smooth brownie, you can take it out of the oven after 15 minutes and shake until the edges drop down.

BROWNIES

300g	dark chocolate
175g	margarine
1 tsp	vanilla extract
300g	icing sugar
150ml	room temperature aquafaba
180g	plain flour
¼ tsp	salt
40g	cocoa

Preheat the oven to 175°C/350°F/gas 4 and prepare a tin measuring 20 × 20 or 20 × 30cm with baking paper. If you have a tin of the right size, you can prepare it using two strips of baking paper (see pages 64 and 65), or by folding the paper into the corners. You can also create a tin of the right size using baking paper secured using staples (see pages 62 and 63). Break the chocolate into pieces and melt the margarine and chocolate in the microwave in short bursts or in a saucepan on a low heat, then add the vanilla extract. Whisk the icing sugar and aquafaba in a bowl until pale and frothy, then carefully fold in the flour. Fold in the sifted cocoa. Lastly, add the chocolate to the mixture. Pour the batter into the tin. Bake in the middle of the oven at 175°C/350°F/gas 4 for 25 minutes for a 20 × 20cm tin, and 20 minutes for a 20 x 30cm tin. It will be sticky when it comes out of the oven but it will firm up when cooled. Store and serve at room temperature.

FUDGE BROWNIES

200g	chocolate
100g	margarine
1 tsp	vanilla extract
100ml	cold aquafaba
135g	sugar
120g	plain flour
¼ tsp	salt

When a company like Guittard, which has been making chocolate since 1868, believes this is the best recipe for brownies and I realized that it was easier to veganize than the 'original' recipe for brownies that uses a large amount of fat and sugar, I developed this recipe. This recipe is based around the chocolate, so choose one that you like, preferably with around 40–50 per cent cocoa solids.

Preheat the oven to 175°C/350°F/gas 4 and prepare a tin measuring 20 × 20cm with baking paper. If you have a tin of the right size you can prepare it using two strips of baking paper (see pages 64 and 65), or by folding the paper into the corners. Melt the chocolate and margarine together and add the vanilla extract. Let this cool while preparing the rest of the ingredients. Whisk the aquafaba and sugar in a bowl until frothy, then carefully fold in the flour and salt. Fold in the melted chocolate mixture using a spatula. Pour the batter into the tin. Bake in the middle of the oven at 175°C/350°F/gas 4 for 15–20 minutes. After 15 minutes, the brownie will be loose and will look like fudge-brownie, after 20 minutes it will look more like a cake-brownie.

COCOA BROWNIES

This cocoa batter makes a slightly larger batch than the two previous brownie recipes on page 272. It is made without melted chocolate, which is a new way of imitating the ready-made packets of brownie mix you can buy in the shops, which are really popular. Brownies tend to be very chocolate-rich to ensure they are gooey enough. This recipe uses a large quantity of fat instead, which is incorporated with help from emulsification with the aquafaba. Using 1–2 teaspoons of instant espresso powder will enhance the chocolate flavour without adding any coffee flavour, but you can leave this out without affecting the texture.

225g	margarine
450g	sugar
1 tsp	vanilla extract
200ml	aquafaba
180g	plain flour
150g	cocoa powder
1 tsp	baking powder
1–2 tsp	espresso powder
1 tsp	salt
100–200g	chocolate buttons (optional)
100g	walnuts, chopped (optional)

Preheat the oven to 175°C/350°F/gas 4 and line a tin measuring 25 × 35cm with baking paper. If you have a tin of the right size, you can prepare it using two strips of baking paper (see pages 64 and 65), or by folding the paper into the corners. You can also create a tin of the right size using baking paper secured using staples (see pages 62 and 63).

Melt the margarine in a saucepan on a low heat and stir in the sugar, vanilla extract and aquafaba. Remove from the heat and carefully blend the mixture using a hand blender. Mix together the flour, cocoa powder, baking powder and salt in a bowl and sift into the blended mixture. Carefully fold in the dry ingredients and add chocolate buttons and walnuts, if you want. Pour the batter into the tin and bake in the centre of the oven at 175°C/350°F/gas 4 for 20–25 minutes. Test with a skewer until it comes out almost clean from the middle of the cake. Leave the cake to cool before placing the tin in the fridge to cool completely. When the cake is cold, cut into squares.

CHOCOLATE SOUFFLÉ

This recipe has been designed for soufflé tins measuring 8–9cm in diameter or three slightly bigger tins. The soufflés need to be served immediately, but you can prepare them in advance and bake them just before serving. Prepared tins can also be chilled for a while and put in the oven just before serving, but the baking time might need to be increased by an extra minute or so. If the soufflé is not baked enough, it will be deliciously runny, and if it is perfectly cooked, the whole soufflé will be like a baked chocolate mousse. Both are amazing, but if you prefer one to the other and are serving soufflé, I recommend you test bake it in advance, then you see what timings give the best results. It is important to be precise about the measurements for the ingredients. The aquafaba needs to be cold to produce the best result. I recommend using chocolate with 70 per cent cocoa solids.

100g	dark chocolate
75ml	water
25g	margarine
1 pinch	salt
1 tsp	vanilla extract
100ml	cold aquafaba
60g	icing sugar
45g	plain flour

Grease and sugar three or four tins; see the guide on page 64. Make sure that the sugar reaches all the way to the edges. Preheat the oven to 175°C/350°F/gas 4. Break the chocolate into pieces and put in a bowl or a saucepan with the water and margarine. Melt in the microwave in short bursts or in a saucepan on a low heat. Mix until all the chocolate has melted. Add the salt and vanilla. Let it cool slightly. Whisk the aquafaba and icing sugar in a bowl until frothy and the whisk leaves marks in the mixture. Add the flour, mix until incorporated, but do not overwork the batter. Carefully fold in the melted chocolate mixture in three batches. Pour the batter into the tins and fill them to the top. Bake in the middle of the oven just before serving at 175°C/350°F/gas 4: 12–15 minutes for four tins; and 15–18 minutes for three tins. Serve immediately as they will collapse soon after baking.

CHOCOLATE FONDANT

This is one of the most difficult recipes that I have managed to veganize for this book and the first time I did is successfully was on New Year's Eve 2020. It was the perfect way to end the year. The recipe is designed for 4–6 tins that hold around 100ml and the batter shouldn't be filled to more than ¾. You can bake them in both metal tins and ceramic pots; small, pretty coffee cups will work perfectly too. You can prepare the fondants in advance and leave the filled tins out to be baked shortly before serving. It's good if they're left to rest for a couple of minutes before they are turned out, but they shouldn't be left for too long. Prepared tins can also be refrigerated for a while before baking, but if that is the case you may need to add a minute or so to the baking time. If the fondant is underbaked it will be lovely and runny, and if it is overbaked it will be like a soft chocolate cake. Both are good, but if you want them to turn out perfectly, you should test bake the recipe in the tins that you will be using, then you can see which time will give the best result. The aquafaba needs to be at room temperature so that the batter does not set when it is added. For the best result, use a chocolate with 70 per cent cocoa solids. Here, I have baked my fondants in metal tins that hold 100ml; if your tins are larger or smaller you will need to adjust the baking times accordingly. This recipe makes five fondants for this size of tin. The edges bake more quickly in metal, so if you are using a thicker ceramic pot, you may also need to add some extra time. Both 175°C/350°F/gas 4 and 200°C/400°F/gas 6 work in my oven, but it will depend on how your oven works and how hot it is. I bake for 1–2 minutes less at the higher temperature and leave the fondants to rest for at least 3 minutes before turning them out. For narrow fondant tins that hold 150ml, the baking time is about the same. Test in your own oven to find the timings that work for you.

100g	margarine
¼ tsp	vanilla extract
50ml	single cream
100g	dark chocolate
100ml	room-temperature aquafaba
60g	icing sugar
60g	plain flour
¼ tsp	salt

Preheat the oven to 175°C/350°F/gas 4. Grease the tins with a thick layer of margarine. I usually use soft margarine on my index finger to grease the sides of the tins to give an even layer with no bare patches. Dust the insides of the tins with cocoa powder and make sure that the whole inside surface is covered. Hold the tins upside-down and tap lightly to remove any excess cocoa powder.

Melt the margarine with the vanilla extract and the single cream in a small pan on a low heat. Remove from the heat. Break the chocolate into chunks, add to the margarine mixture and leave to melt. Add the room-temperature aquafaba and carefully blend to a smooth batter using a hand blender. Mix the icing sugar, plain flour and salt together in a separate bowl and then fold into the melted chocolate mixture. Fill the tins to ¾ and bake in the centre of the oven at 175°C/350°F/gas 4 for 8–12 minutes (slightly longer if you are using thick ceramic pots). Remove from the oven and leave to cool for 4–5 minutes. Run a sharp knife around the sides of each tin and turn out the fondants. You can also serve the fondants without turning them out onto a plate; this is especially nice if you have baked them in small, pretty coffee cups.

Cookies

Always test bake your cookies as it will tell you whether you need to add more liquid or more plain flour.

I always bake my cookies on baking paper even though this is not always written in the instructions.

Depending on the size you make your cookies the number from a batch varies, but the recipes for smaller cookies/biscuits usually give you at least 25–40 cookies/biscuits. Larger bakes, such as mazarines, cookies, macaroons or almond cookies yield between 14–20 pieces.

Cookies dipped in melted chocolate should never be placed directly onto a plate as they are likely to stick. Always use baking paper for this. When dipping cookies in chocolate, it is often easier to add 1–2 tablespoons of neutral-flavoured oil to make the chocolate runny. However, this is not the case for white chocolate, which is usually runnier when melted. When the bakes are dipped, carefully shake off any excess over the bowl of chocolate to avoid a coating that is too thick. If the cookies are not frozen, it will look better if you first place it on some baking paper and then, before the chocolate has set, move it slightly so you don't get a pool of chocolate.

When making cookies like cake pops, punsch rolls or biskvis, freeze them for a short time first, so that the chocolate sets immediately.

COOKIES

Many cookies can be made with shortcrust pastry and here are three versions. The smooth ones are those that are usually baked with an egg yolk or an egg. They give a firmer cookie and the smooth shortcrust pastry with aquafaba is my favourite. Chill for at least 30 minutes, preferably overnight, before baking for a good result. Also test bake one cookie before baking the whole batch. I think the cookies are best when thoroughly baked and slightly golden underneath.

CLASSIC SHORTCRUST PASTRY		SMOOTH SHORTCRUST PASTRY		SMOOTH SHORTCRUST PASTRY	
200g	room-temperature margarine	200g	room-temperature margarine	270g	plain flour
90g	sugar	2 tbsp	aquafaba	90g	sugar
270–300g	plain flour	90g	sugar	200g	margarine
1 pinch	salt	270–300g	plain flour	1 tbsp	oil
1 tsp	vanilla sugar or vanilla extract	1 pinch	salt	1 tbsp	cornstarch
		1 tsp	vanilla sugar or vanilla extract	1 pinch	salt
				1 tsp	vanilla sugar or vanilla extract

Mix all the ingredients into a dough using your hands or in a food processor. Mix the dough quickly and do not overwork it after bringing it together. Wrap and chill the dough for at least 30 minutes, but preferably longer, before baking. Cut into preferred sizes and bake in the middle of the oven at 175°C/350°F/gas 4 until golden, around 8–15 minutes, depending on size and your oven.

SHORTBREAD

300g	room-temperature margarine
135g	sugar
300g	plain flour
1 pinch	salt
1 tsp	vanilla extract
165g	rice flour, corn flour, skrädmjöl or oat flour

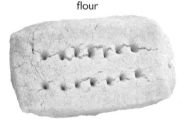

There are many recipes for shortbread. Some use half caster sugar and half icing sugar, others use corn flour instead of rice flour. The cookies are short, made with a high proportion of fat to flour, which is where the name shortbread comes from. Chill the dough thoroughly before baking and the cookies will keep their shape. If you put them in the freezer for a short time the edges will stay straight too.

Mix all the ingredients into a dough with your hands or in a food processor. Mix it quickly and do not overwork it after bringing it together. Put the dough on a piece of baking paper and roll out to a rectangle measuring 20 × 25cm and about 2cm thick. Let the dough chill in the fridge for at least 30 minutes, but preferably longer. Cut out rectangular cookies measuring 2 × 5cm and prick with a fork. Transfer (on the baking paper) to a baking sheet. Bake in the middle of the oven at 175°C/350°F/gas 4 until golden, for around 15–20 minutes, depending on the size and your oven.

Thumb-print cookies (above) are made by rolling balls and making an indentation in the middle of each that is filled with jam or fruit compôte. Many recipes include 1 teaspoon of baking powder mixed in with the flour. Bake the cookies paper cases for up to 18 minutes.

Flower cookies (above) are made by attaching small edible flowers on top of the cookies. Brushing a little aquafaba or cream on top of each cookie will help the flower to stick to it. Wild pansies are edible, for instance.

Butter biscuits are made with 90–180g of sugar that is coloured with a few drops of colouring in a bowl or bag. The shortcrust pastry rolls are rolled in sugar and sliced. You can also roll them in nibbed sugar.

Chequered squares (above) are made by colouring one half of the dough with 1–2 tablespoons of cocoa (and preferably 1–2 tablespoons of coffee liqueur, chocolate liqueur, whisky or other alcohol). Leave the dough to chill. Roll out the halves of dough into two equal squares about 1–2cm thick. Before putting the two layers together, you can brush them with a little aquafaba or cream to help them stick together better. Place one layer on top of the other and cut into lengths 1–2cm wide. Build the lengths up together, with the colours alternating, so that a chequer board pattern is formed. Form a length of compressed squares in alternating colours of about 5–10 rows in length and height. Chill the dough again if it has become warm. Then cut into squares and bake according to the instructions opposite.

Finnish sticks (above) are made by rolling rolls of the smooth shortcrust pastry made with aquafaba and cutting them into 4–5-cm pieces. They are brushed with cream and pressed into a mixture of chopped almonds and nibbed sugar. Bake according to the instructions opposite.

PIPED COOKIES

To make the best piped cookies you need a fixed piping tube. I recommend the type shown opposite where you turn a handle to pipe the dough, as it can be hard to get the cookies right otherwise. Look for second hand ones or online and you should probably find one quite easily. Test bake one cookie before baking the whole batch. Both recipes can be piped straight, in a variety of shapes or in circles filled with jam. The Strasbourger dough gives incredibly delicate cookies that melt in the mouth, while the piped almond cookies are firmer. I prefer the almond dough and think that when these are piped and filled with jam they are irresistible.

STRASBOURGER

100g	room-temperature margarine
30g	icing sugar
75g	plain flour
80g	potato starch
1 pinch	salt
¼ tsp	vanilla extract
	jam (optional)
	melted chocolate (optional)

Preheat the oven to 175°C/350°F/gas 4. Mix the margarine with the icing sugar in a bowl until fluffy, then add the other ingredients and mix to a smooth dough. Pipe strips of dough and form to your liking. Strasbourgers are usually made into rectangles, and are sometimes slightly curved, like the cookies dipped in chocolate at the top of the picture opposite, but they are also perfect filled with jam. For these, pipe a circle, flatten out the middle, and then fill with jam. You can also use dough to create a small flat disc, and then pipe the dough in a circle around it, before filling with jam. Bake in the middle of the oven until golden, for around 10–15 minutes, depending on the size and your oven.

PIPED ALMOND COOKIES

125g	room-temperature margarine
70g	sugar
50g	almond flour
210g	plain flour
1 pinch	salt
¼ tsp	vanilla extract
50ml	aquafaba
	jam (optional)

Preheat the oven to 175°C/350°F/gas 4. Mix the margarine with the icing sugar in a bowl until fluffy, then add the dry ingredients, vanilla extract and aquafaba and mix to a smooth dough. Form into a roll that fits the piping tube. Pipe out strips in your preferred shape. The almond cookies are usually made in wavy lines like the ones in the middle of the picture opposite, but they are also perfect filled with jam. For these, pipe a circle, flatten out the middle, and fill with jam. You can also use dough to create a small flat disc, and then pipe the dough in a circle around it, before filling with jam. Bake in the middle until golden, for 10–15 minutes, depending on the size and your oven.

MERINGUES

As when beating egg whites, in order to whip air into aquafaba it is very important for there not to be any fat in the bowl. Cream of tartar is used to give a more stable whipped meringue. Read more on page 50. You can clean the bowl you are going to use for whisking by wiping the bowl with a cloth or paper towel moistened with vinegar. Eton mess, made for more than a century, consists of strawberries, cream and meringue. A Swedish version uses meringue, whipped cream and chocolate sauce. Nowadays, there is often vanilla ice cream in both.

MERINGUES

75ml	aquafaba
1/8 tsp	cream of tartar
90g	sugar

Preheat the oven to 100°C/212°F/gas 1/4. Whip the aquafaba with the cream of tartar in a bowl until soft peaks form – this can take a few minutes. Then add the sugar, a tablespoon at a time, while continuing to mix. Continue beating until you have really stiff peaks. If you want to pipe coloured meringues (see page 54) you need to prepare piping bags with coloured strips. Put a piping bag into a large glass with the tip of the piping bag facing downwards and fold the top of the bag over the edges of the glass so it can stand up by itself. Then use a brush and colouring powder (dissolved in a little water) or colouring paste to brush lines of colouring on the inside of the piping bag, all the way around. Put the meringue into the piping bag, cut off the tip and pipe your meringues onto baking paper on a baking sheet. Bake small meringues in the middle of the oven at 100°C/212°F/gas 1/4 for around 1 hour, and larger meringues for up to 1 1/2 hours. Small meringues burn easily, so do keep an eye on them. They will come off the baking paper easily when cool.

ITALIAN MERINGUES

340g	sugar
75ml	water
200ml	aquafaba
1/8 tsp	cream of tartar

This is a classic Italian meringue with a hot syrup that is suited for making glace au four (baked Alaska) or lemon meringue pie (see page 406) with browned meringue. For an even more stable version, see page 406. For this, you brown the meringue using a blowtorch.

Put the sugar and water in a saucepan and boil to 130°C/265°F – you will need a sugar thermometer. Meanwhile, whip the aquafaba and cream of tartar to a stiff foam in a heatproof bowl. The goal is for the foam to get to the right consistency when the syrup has heated to the correct temperature, but if the foam is stiff before that, just reduce the speed of the whisk to low. Meringue made with aquafaba is not as sensitive when it comes to over-whipping as meringue made with egg whites. Add the hot syrup slowly into the foam, mixing constantly, then mix the meringue until completely cool, firm and shiny, which can take up to 10 minutes. Pipe and bake the meringues according to the instructions above.

MARÄNGSVISS
Whipped cream
Vanilla ice cream
Bananas, peeled
Meringue, crushed
Chocolate sauce

Whip the cream and take the ice cream out of the freezer so it is easy to scoop. Slice the bananas. Mix the cream, ice cream, banana slices, crushed meringue and chocolate sauce. Serve immediately.

ETON MESS
Whipped cream
Vanilla ice cream
Strawberries
Meringue, crushed

Whip the cream and take the ice cream out of the freezer so it is easy to scoop. Slice the strawberries and mix together the cream, ice cream, strawberries and crushed meringue. Serve immediately if you want crispy meringue.

MACARONS

Macarons are hard to make and it takes a lot of practice to get them perfect. All the stages need to be precise and you need to learn how to heat your oven to exactly the right temperature, so be patient and do expect mishaps. Meringues and sponge cakes were the first recipes I worked with when aquafaba was discovered, but Charis Mitchell in England (@floralfrostingbakes) started with macarons. Her recipe is so amazing that I asked if I could use it in my books and fortunately she said yes. Google a few instruction videos and you see what the consistency should look like. Charis's films will help you to perfect your vegan macarons!

180ml	aquafaba
100g	almond flour
65g	icing sugar
100g	sugar
	colouring (optional)

Reduce the aquafaba in a small saucepan from 180ml to around 80ml. I usually use a medium heat which takes a few minutes. Let it cool.

Prepare the dry ingredients. The almond flour and the icing sugar should be mixed in a food processor or blender and then sifted at least once to be as fine as possible with no lumps. So, pulse the almond flour, add the icing sugar and pulse again, then sift into a bowl. Preferably repeat once more and set aside while preparing the meringue.

Put the cooled, reduced aquafaba into a bowl, preferably in a stand mixer, but an electric hand mixer is also fine. Add the caster sugar and colouring, if using, and whip thoroughly until the meringue is thick and shiny (see page 26). Sift half the almond sugar powder into the meringue and carefully fold it into the batter using a spatula, without overworking it (this is very important for the end result). Then sift and carefully fold in the rest of the almond sugar powder.

The next step is called 'macronage' and involves folding and pressing the batter in the bowl. Google a few videos to help you see how it should look. Fold the batter like this about 19–20 times to get the right consistency.

Fill a piping bag with the batter and pipe out the macarons with an even pressure directly onto baking paper on two baking trays. When one tray is ready, lift it up and drop it gently onto the surface from a height of 10–15cm three times to remove any bubbles. Next, allow to set and dry at room temperature for 2–3 hours. Put one baking tray in a cold oven, set the heat to 100°C/212°F/gas ¼ and bake for 20–25 minutes, although it can take up to 30 minutes. The macarons should come cleanly off the paper when you gently lift them off the baking tray. Turn off the oven and leave for 15 minutes.

Take the baking tray out of the oven and let it cool before repeating the same procedure with the second baking tray. Let it cool. Choose two halves the same size and fill with your favourite frosting (and jam or curd in the middle if you like), press them together and put in the fridge to set for at least 24 hours. If you want to keep the macarons for a long time, you can freeze them, but take them out at least 30 minutes before serving.

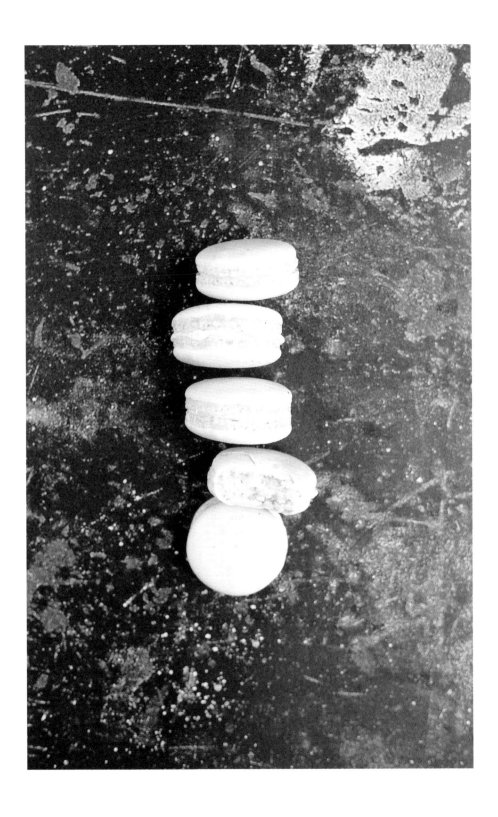

NUT TARTLETS

There are many nut tartlets in Sweden with origins from around the world: leipziger lerche, congresses, helena pastry and polynés – the difference between these bakes depends on the type of case and the nut filling you use.

Helena pastry is baked with a classic case and almond filling.

Polynés are baked with a shortcrust case and the nut filling of your choice.

Leipziger lerche are baked with almond filling, sometimes with a puff pastry case and sometimes with a shortcrust pastry case. They are similar to polynés.

Congresses are baked with a puff pastry case and hazelnut filling.

For the almond filling, you can use 100g of almond flour instead of grinding your own. The filling will then be light coloured as the almonds are blanched and peeled. For a darker almond filling, you can use almonds with the skins left on.

1 packet of ready-made puff pastry, shortcrust pastry case (see below), or a classic American pie crust (see page 394)

SHORTCRUST PASTRY CASE
100g	cold margarine
180g	plain flour
45g	sugar
2 tbsp	cream or
aquafaba	

NUT FLLING
120g	icing sugar
75ml	aquafaba
45g	plain flour
100g	nut flour
1 pinch	salt

For the shortcrust pastry case, dice the cold margarine and rub together with plain flour, sugar and cream or aquafaba in a bowl to make a dough. Wrap and chill for at least 30 minutes (this also applies to the classic pastry case, if using).

Preheat the oven to 200°C/400°F/gas 6. Roll out or press out your chosen pastry into mazarin tins. If you are using metal tins, you should grease them with some cooking fat before pressing in the dough. Disposable tins do not need greasing. Roll out the offcuts of dough and cut strips to place on top of the pastry cases when filled. Make the nut filling. Whip the icing sugar and aquafaba in a bowl until frothy. Carefully fold in the flour, then the nut flour and salt, and fill the tins with the filling slightly more than halfway, but never more than ⅔ full. Use the strips of pastry to make a cross on the top of each one and then bake at 200°C/400°F/gas 6 for 15–20 minutes. Test bake one cake to make sure that you have the right amount of filling.

MAZARINS

Mazarins are Swedish almond tarts. Like mini frangipane tarts with a glaze. I have included three versions depending on whether or not you want to use aquafaba, and if you want to use almond paste or almond flour. If you cannot find almond paste with a high percentage of almonds, you can add up to 45–60g of plain flour, or use the recipe with almond flour. For apple mazarins, put one or two slices of peeled and cored eating apple in the batter and sprinkle both ground cinnamon and sugar on top of the cakes before baking. Catalans are baked just like mazarins but using puff pastry instead of shortcrust pastry. You can buy ready-made puff pastry. Before spreading icing sugar glaze on the catalans, you spread a layer of raspberry jam.

USE ALMOND PASTE THAT CONTAINS AT LEAST 55% ALMONDS

SHORTCRUST PASTRY CASE
100g	cold margarine
180g	plain flour
45g	sugar
2 tbsp	cream or aquafaba

ALMOND FILLING NO. 1
100g	room-temperature margarine
50ml	cream
30g	cornstarch
250g	almond paste

ALMOND FILLING NO. 2
75g	room-temperature margarine
100ml	aquafaba
200g	almond paste
45g	plain flour
½ tsp	baking powder

ALMOND FILLING NO. 3
50g	margarine
120g	icing sugar
75ml	aquafaba
45g	plain flour
100g	almond flour
1 pinch	salt

GLAZE
180g	icing sugar
2–3 tbsp	water

For the pastry case, dice the cold margarine and rub together with the flour, sugar and cream or aquafaba in a bowl to make a dough. Wrap and chill for at least 30 minutes. Roll out or press into mazarin tins. If you are using metal tins, you should grease them with some cooking fat before pressing the dough into place. Disposable cases do not need greasing. Chill again for at least 30 minutes in the fridge.

You can use a food processor to make fillings 1 and 2. Combine all the ingredients and mix to a smooth batter. Otherwise, for the first filling, you can mix margarine, cream and cornstarch. Finely grate the almond paste and mix with the rest of the ingredients to a smooth batter.

For the second almond filling, beat the margarine with the aquafaba, finely grate the almond paste and mix to a loose batter. Then fold in the flour mixed with the baking powder.

For filling number 3, melt the margarine and let it cool slightly. Whip the icing sugar and aquafaba in a bowl until frothy. Carefully fold in the flour, then the almond flour and salt, and lastly the melted margarine.

Test bake one mazarin and add some plain flour to the batter if the filling is too loose and collapses. Fill the lined tins to ⅔ with the filling of your choice and bake at 200°C/400°F/gas 6 for 15–20 minutes until golden. Let the mazarins cool.

For the glaze, mix the icing sugar and water to a smooth paste in a bowl. Put some glaze on top of each mazarin and spread into an even layer with a knife or a spoon.

BISKVI BASES

Biskvis are complicated as there are so many steps, but they are amazing and definitely worth the effort. Here, I have included three different bases. It is important to use an almond paste with at least 55 per cent almonds, to avoid the bases melting in the first two recipes. As the result depends on the type of almond paste, it might be worth test baking one cake before baking the whole tray, then you will know whether you need to add extra aquafaba, if you need to increase the amount of almond paste or almond flour, or perhaps add some plain flour to the batter. If the cakes melt completely, you can add 3 tablespoons of plain flour to the dough. You can choose a classic vanilla filling, lemon filling or make a chocolate filling for Sarah Bernhardt pastry. The salted caramel frosting on page 236 is also perfect for biskvis. The instructions for filling and assembling can be found below.

USE ALMOND PASTE THAT CONTAINS AT LEAST 55% ALMONDS

BISKVI BASES NO. I

500g	almond paste
30g	icing sugar
I tsp	baking powder
4 tbsp	cornstarch
2 tbsp	cream

Preheat the oven to 150°C/300°F/gas 2. Coarsely grate the almond paste. Mix the icing sugar, baking powder, cornstarch and cream in a separate bowl, then mix together with the almond paste. Form into round balls with slightly wet hands and press them out on a baking tray to the shape of your choice. Bake the cakes for 15–30 minutes. Mini biskvis are baked for 15–20 minutes while the standard-sized cakes may take up to 35 minutes.

BISKVI BASES NO. 2

SMALLER	LARGER	
300g	400g	almond paste
2 tbsp	50ml	aquafaba
2 tbsp	45g	sugar

Here, I have given two different quantities, depending on how much almond paste you are using. Preheat the oven to 150°C/300°F/gas 2. Coarsely grate the almond paste and mix with the aquafaba and sugar. Form into round balls with slightly wet hands and press them out on a baking tray to the shape of your choice. Bake for 15–30 minutes depending on the size. Mini biskvis are baked for 15–20 minutes while standard-sized cakes can take up to 35 minutes.

PIPED BASES

150g	almond flour/blanched almonds
120g	icing sugar
75ml	aquafaba

Preheat the oven to 175°C/350°F/gas 4. If you are not using ready-made almond flour, process the nuts in a food processor until finely ground, or grate them in an almond grinder. Mix the icing sugar and aquafaba in a bowl until frothy and carefully fold in the almond flour or ground/grated almonds. Put the batter in a piping bag and pipe flat bases on the baking tray. Bake the cakes in the middle of the oven for 12–15 minutes. The smaller the cakes are the less time they need in the oven. Let them cool on the baking tray.

BISKVI FILLING

VANILLA FILLING

150g	vegan spread
30g	icing sugar
1 tsp	vanilla sugar or vanilla extract
1 batch	vanilla pastry cream (see page 424, the smaller amount)

If you are using very soft vegan spread, you might need to slightly reduce the amount of vanilla pastry cream. Add and mix in different batches and decide how much vanilla pastry cream is needed for a really soft and creamy vanilla filling. The tonka bean pastry cream on page 424 works amazingly well for making tonka bean biskvis and is used instead of the vanilla cream.

Mix the vegan spread with the icing sugar and vanilla sugar or extract until fluffy. Add the vanilla cream, 1 tablespoon at a time, and mix between each spoonful. Mix for a few minutes for a soft, smooth filling.

LEMON FILLING

100g	vegan spread
120g	icing sugar
100–150g	lemon curd (see recipe on page 262)

For a milder lemon pastry cream, you can also make the vanilla filling above and add the zest from an unwaxed lemon to the filling. With this recipe, you can also use whatever curd you like to make a fruit biskvi.

In a bowl mix the vegan spread with the icing sugar. Add the lemon curd 1 tablespoon at a time, until the filling has the taste and consistency of your choice. Mix in between each spoonful. Mix for a few more minutes for a soft, smooth filling.

CHOCOLATE FILLING

150ml	cream
2 tbsp	golden syrup
200g	chocolate

Heat the cream and syrup in a small saucepan, then remove from the hob when it reaches the boil. Break the chocolate into pieces and stir into the hot cream mixture until melted. Let the filling cool until it is the right consistency for spreading.

ASSEMBLING

200g	chocolate
1–2 tbsp	oil

For white chocolate, you can freeze the biskvis with the filling before dipping them in the melted chocolate. This will give a thick and even coating. It is important not to heat the white chocolate over 44°C/111°F to get a good result, not to mix in more than 1–2 tablespoons of oil per 100g of chocolate, and not to colour it using normal colouring but using chocolate colouring.

Spread or pipe the filling on the cold biskvi bases. If you spread the filling with the bowl of the spoon, the curve will help you to give the filling a good shape. You can also pipe the filling, like the smaller biskvis in the picture. It is easier to dip the biskvis in the melted chocolate if you add 1–2 tablespoons of oil per 200g of chocolate after melting it according to the instructions on page 57. After dipping each biskvi in the melted chocolate, you can shake it slightly so that any excess chocolate runs back into the bowl. This will give you a thinner chocolate coating.

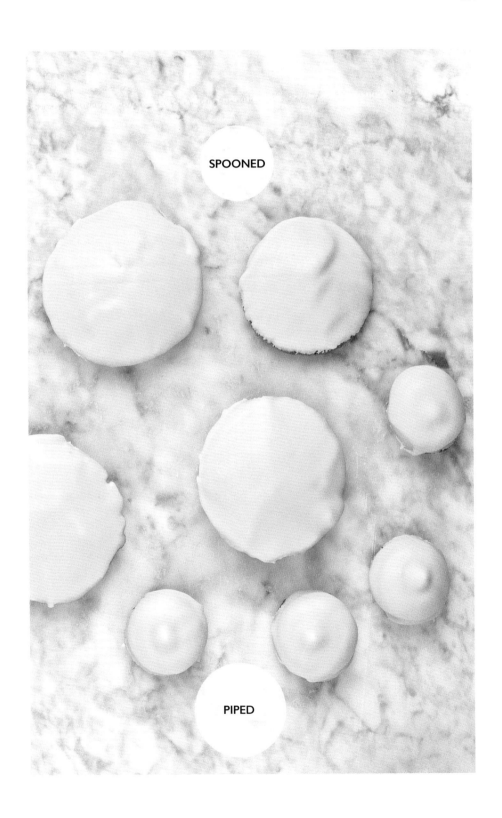

SPOONED

PIPED

ITALIAN ALMOND COOKIES

The result you get from these almond cookies will depend on the type of almond paste you use. It is worth test baking one cookie before baking the whole tray. If the cookie melts, you can add almond paste or plain flour; if the cookie is too firm, you can add aquafaba. If you cannot find good-quality almond paste for the pignoli, you can use the recipe for almond cookies below, add the zest from one lemon and then roll them in 100g of pine nuts instead of flaked almonds. These are then baked like the almond cookies at 175°C/350°F/gas 4 for a slightly shorter time.

USE ALMOND PASTE THAT CONTAINS AT LEAST 55% ALMONDS

PIGNOLI

300g	almond paste
50–75ml	aquafaba
45g	sugar
½	lemon, zest of
I pinch	salt
100g	pine nuts

Preheat the oven to 150°C/300°F/gas 2. Work the almond paste together with 50ml of the aquafaba, the sugar, lemon zest and salt in a bowl. Test bake one cookie rolled in pine nuts before baking the whole tray (see above). Form into 14–16 round balls with slightly wet hands and roll the balls in the pine nuts. Place on a lined baking tray and bake for 25–35 minutes, depending on the size and your oven.

For this recipe, you can use almond paste with any percentage of almonds, but as the result does depend on this it is always good to test bake one first.

ALMOND COOKIES

400g	almond paste
50ml	aquafaba
45g	sugar
60g	plain flour
I pinch	salt
flaked almonds, for rolling	

Preheat the oven to 175°C/350°F/gas 4. Mix the almond paste, aquafaba, sugar, plain flour and salt together in a bowl. Form into 15–16 round balls with slightly wet hands and roll the balls in the flaked almonds. Test bake one cookie before baking the whole tray (see above). Bake the cookies for 15–25 minutes, depending on the size and your oven.

This is an almond cookie that originated in Siena. It is similar to amaretti but baked with icing sugar instead of caster sugar. Both lemon peel and orange peel work well as a flavouring. You can roll the cakes in flaked almonds before rolling them in icing sugar.

RICCIARELLI

250g	almond flour or sweet almonds
150g	icing sugar
75ml	aquafaba
I	lemon/orange, zest of
icing sugar, for rolling	

Preheat the oven to 175°C/350°F/gas 4. If you do not have ready-made almond flour, blitz the nuts in a food processor until they are finely chopped or grind into flour in an grinder. Whisk together the icing sugar and aquafaba in a bowl until pale and frothy, then carefully fold in the almond flour and lemon or orange zest. Form into 20–25 balls, roll in icing sugar, shape into rectangles or squares and place on a lined baking tray. Bake the cookies in the middle of the oven at 175°C/350°F/gas 4 for 14–18 minutes. The smaller the cookies, the less time they will need in the oven. Leave to cool on the baking tray.

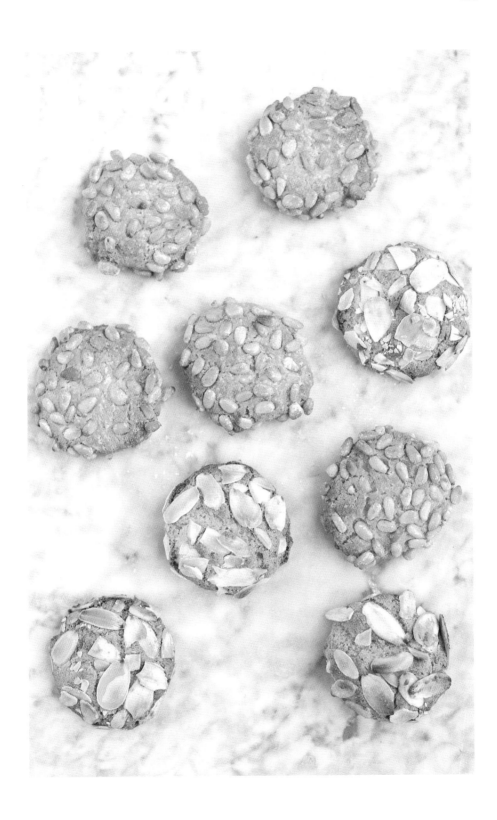

COCONUT MACAROONS

Luxurious coconut macaroons are made using the same weight of coconut flakes as sweetened condensed coconut milk. I usually use Nature's Charm so if you are using a different brand you might need to adjust the amount slightly. In that case, test bake one cake to see whether you need to add more coconut flakes, or perhaps add some more condensed milk or liquid to make them softer. The macaroons can be dipped in melted chocolate when they have cooled down.

LUXURIOUS RECIPE

320g	coconut flakes
320g	sweetened condensed coconut milk

Preheat the oven to 175°C/350°F/gas 4. Mix the coconut flakes and condensed milk in a bowl and let the batter swell for 10–15 minutes. Shape into tops and place on baking paper on a baking tray. Bake the coconut tops in the middle of the oven 4 for 10–15 minutes, depending on the size of your tops. Take them out of the oven when golden. Let them cool completely before removing them from the baking tray – they are brittle when warm.

SIMPLE RECIPE

180g	icing sugar
75ml	aquafaba
200g	coconut flakes
100g	almond flour

Preheat the oven to 175°C/350°F/gas 4. Whisk the icing sugar and aquafaba in a bowl until frothy and carefully fold in the coconut flakes and the almond flour. Let the batter swell for 10–15 minutes. Shape into tops and place on baking paper on a baking tray. Bake the coconut tops in the middle of the oven at 175°C/350°F/gas 4 for 12–18 minutes, depending on the size of your tops. Take them out of the oven when golden. Let them cool completely before removing them from the baking tray – they are brittle when warm.

COCONUT MACAROOONS

50g	margarine
120g	icing sugar
30g	cornstarch
¼ tsp	xanthan gum
200g	coconut flakes
100ml	cream

Preheat the oven to 175°C/350°F/gas 4. Melt the margarine and let it cool. Mix the icing flour, cornstarch, xanthan gum and coconut flakes in a bowl. Add the cooled margarine and the cream and mix to a sticky dough. Allow to rest for at least 10–15 minutes to allow the moisture to soak into the coconut flakes. Dip your fingers in water so that the batter does not stick to your hands and make the tops too tall. Shape the mixture into tops and place on baking paper on a baking tray. Bake the coconut tops in the middle of the oven at 175°C/350°F/gas 4 for 10–25 minutes, depending on the size of your tops. Take them out of the oven when golden. Let them cool completely before removing them from the baking tray – they are brittle when warm.

FORTUNE COOKIES

Fortune cookies should contain little slips of paper containing intriguing prophecies. They are perfect for New Year's Eve or at theme parties when you want to put in some extra effort making both the notes and the baking. The cakes take slightly more time to bake as you can only bake a few at a time.

> **YOU WILL ALSO NEED:**
> 20–25 paper strips
> imagination
> patience
> nimble fingers

50g	margarine
90g	sugar
120g	plain flour
2 tbsp	cornstarch
1 tsp	vanilla sugar or vanilla extract
1 pinch	salt
150ml	water
2 tbsp	aquafaba

Preheat the oven to 150°C/300°F/gas 2. Write messages on the paper strips and fold once.

Melt the margarine. Mix the sugar, plain flour, cornstarch, vanilla sugar or extract and salt in a bowl and add the melted margarine and water. When the batter is smooth, add the aquafaba. Put 1–3 tablespoons of batter on a piece of baking paper on a baking tray, 1 tablespoon for each cookie, using a measuring spoon. To begin with it might be good to bake one cookie at a time until you get the idea. Using the back of the measuring spoon, spread the batter to make a circle of around 8–10cm in diameter. Try to make the batter an even thickness as the cookie will not bake as well if the edges are thinner than the middle. Bake in the middle of the oven at 150°C/300°F/gas 2 until the edges start to brown, about 14–16 minutes.

Remove from the oven. Pick up one cookie at a time using a spatula and put it face down on a clean tea towel.

Put a message in the centre and fold the cookie in half. Then bend the cookie over the edge of a glass or a bowl while still holding onto the edges. Let the cookies cool in a muffin tray, for example, to prevent them from losing their bend. Store somewhere dry.

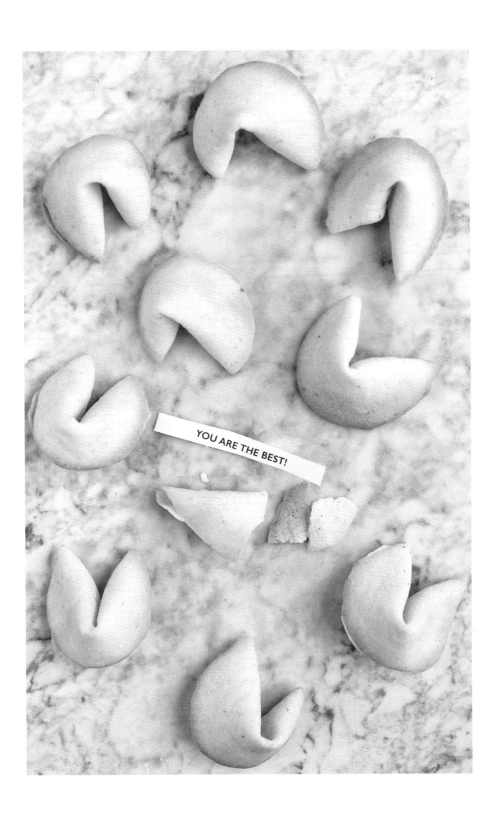

YOU ARE THE BEST!

SLICED CHOCOLATE COOKIES

CHOCOLATE DOUGH NO. 1

200g	soft margarine
225g	sugar
70ml	golden syrup
I tsp	vanilla sugar/extract
40g	cocoa
330g	plain flour
I tsp	baking powder
¼ tsp	salt

CHOCOLATE DOUGH NO. 2

200g	soft margarine
225g	sugar
I tsp	vanilla sugar/extract
4 tbsp	cocoa
330g	plain flour
I tsp	baking powder
¼ tsp	salt
3 tbsp	aquafaba

cream, for brushing
nibbed sugar, for decorating

These two versions give similar results. Syrup is used in the first recipe to give a crispy consistency and aquafaba is used in recipe number 2.

Preheat the oven to 200°C/400°F/gas 6. Mix the margarine, sugar, syrup (if using recipe number 1), vanilla and sifted cocoa. Add the flour, baking powder, salt and aquafaba (if using recipe number 2) and knead to a smooth dough. Divide the dough into 3–4 pieces and shape them into rolls that are as long as the baking tray. Place two rolls on each baking tray. Flatten out the rolls, brush cream on top and sprinkle them with nibbed sugar. Bake in the middle of the oven at 200°C/400°F/gas 6 for 14–17 minutes. Cut the rolls diagonally into cookies 3–4cm thick while they are still hot.

CARAMEL COOKIES

180g	sugar
300g	plain flour
I tsp	bicarbonate of soda or baking powder
I tsp	vanilla sugar/extract
I tsp	ground ginger (optional)
¼ tsp	salt
200g	margarine
4 tbsp	syrup

You can either use I teaspoon of bicarbonate of soda or I teaspoon of baking powder in this recipe. Baking powder gives slightly thicker cookies.

Preheat the oven to 175°C/350°F/gas 4. Mix the sugar, plain flour, bicarbonate of soda, vanilla, ginger, if using, and salt in a bowl or a mixer bowl. Add the diced margarine and syrup. Rub the ingredients together to a form a smooth dough and then divide into four pieces. Shape two pieces into long rolls, put them on baking paper on a baking tray and flatten out using a fork. Bake in the middle of the oven for 12–15 minutes. Cut the lengths diagonally into cookies 3–4cm thick as soon as they are taken out of the oven. Repeat for the two other pieces of dough.

THIN FRENCH CLASSICS

Almond tuiles are thin almond biscuits that, in contrast to most other thin biscuits, use a large amount of egg white in the batter. The flaked almonds can either be mixed into the batter or be sprinkled over it once it has been spread out into rounds on a baking tray. If you sprinkle the almonds over the batter, you will use a slightly smaller quantity of flaked almonds. These biscuits are classics from France and are served both as they are, as an accompaniment to other desserts and as decoration. The biscuits are often cooled around something curved, and you can often find tuile curving sheets at flea markets if you know what to look for. The batter for tuiles can also be used for making cylinders that are served with ice cream and other desserts and you can use them to make your own ice cream wafers. If the biscuits become soft due to moisture in the air, you can bake them for a couple of minutes before serving and they will crisp up again.

ALMOND TUILES

50g	margarine
75ml	aquafaba
90g	sugar
60g	plain flour
¼ tsp	vanilla extract
I pinch	salt
70–100g	flaked almonds

Preheat the oven to 150°C/300°F/gas 2. Line a baking tray with baking paper. Melt the margarine in a saucepan on a low heat. Remove from the heat and set aside. Mix the aquafaba with the sugar in a bowl and whisk together using a hand whisk; you don't want to whip air into the batter, it just needs to be thoroughly combined. Add the flour, vanilla extract and salt and whisk to a smooth batter. Stir in the melted margarine. It's a good idea to leave the batter to expand for 20–30 minutes. Either stir in the flaked almonds at this stage, or sprinkle over the rounds of batter once they have been spread out on the baking paper on the baking tray. Make dollops the size of a tablespoon with the batter and spread out into large rounds on the tray using the spoon. Bake in the centre of the oven at 150°C/300°F/gas 2 for 12–18 minutes or until golden, depending on your oven and the thickness of the tuiles. Using a spatula, immediately transfer the tuiles onto a tuile curving sheet if you have one, or place the biscuits over a rolling pin or a bottle to cool to the right shape. The tuiles can also be cooled flat.

Langues de chat, or cats' tongues, are very similar to tuiles but are oblong in shape and are usually baked with icing sugar in the batter. The batter is cooled to make it easier to pipe or spread out to the required shape. Just like tuiles, they should be very thin and crispy, and if they soften while they are being stored you can bake them again for a few minutes to crisp them up. Sandwiched with chocolate filling (see page 296) or melted chocolate they are known as Milano cookies.

CATS' TONGUES

50g	margarine
50ml	aquafaba
90g	icing sugar
60g	plain flour
¼ tsp	vanilla extract
I pinch	salt

Preheat the oven to 175°C/350/gas 4. Follow the instructions for tuiles above. Once the batter is mixed it should be chilled for at least 30 minutes, but preferably for longer. Fill a piping bag with a nozzle of around 0.5cm and pipe out lengths of 5–8cm or spread out teaspoon-sized dollops of batter. Bake in the centre of the oven for 12–15 minutes or until golden, depending on your oven and the size of the biscuits.

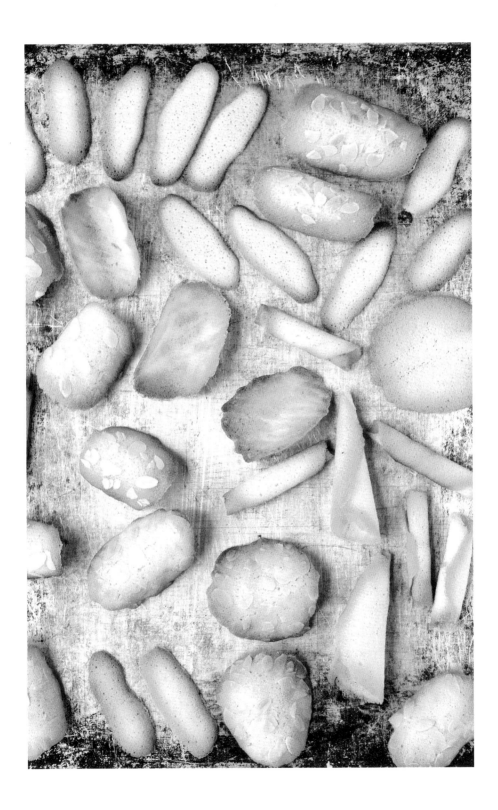

AMARETTI

USE ALMOND PASTE THAT CONTAINS AT LEAST 55% ALMONDS

RECIPE WITH ALMOND PASTE

75g	whole sweet almonds
200g	almond paste
70g	sugar
1 tbsp	aquafaba
1 approx.	lemon, zest of
120g	icing sugar, for dusting

This is a Swedish version of these classic chewy Italian almond cookies made with almond paste. This makes 18 rectangular amaretti or 10 'pinched' cookies. Test bake one cookie to make sure that you are using the right amount of aquafaba. If they are too soft, add a little almond paste or plain flour, and if they are too firm, add more aquafaba. If you add lemon zest to the batter it is known as *amaretti al limone*. Both blanched almonds and almonds with the skin left on work well for this recipe.

Preheat the oven to 175°C/350°F/gas 4. Grind the almonds until coarse. Mix the almond paste, sugar and aquafaba in a bowl, add the ground almonds and the lemon zest. Divide the dough into 18 pieces for rectangular amaretti or 10 pieces for 'pinched' cookies. Make 18 rolls of around 4–5cm long, or 10 round balls; roll in icing sugar. Pinch the balls at the top using three fingers to get this particular shape. Place the cookies on a baking tray lined with baking paper. Bake in the middle of the oven at 175°C/350°F/ gas 4 for 12–15 minutes. If you are making the larger 'pinched' cookies, bake for 15–17 minutes. The amaretti are supposed to have a nice, light golden colour when ready.

RECIPE WITH WHOLE NUTS

1–3	bitter almonds or
½ tsp	almond extract
250g	sweet almonds/ almond flour
135g	sugar
50ml approx.	aquafaba
120g	icing sugar, for dusting

This is a more Italian-type recipe using ground almonds or mixed sweet almonds and some bitter almonds, if available. You can also add some lemon zest according to the instructions above. I like to bake them with lemon zest and use almonds with the skin on, but you can also use blanched almonds or almond flour for light-coloured cookies. For one of my absolute favourite bakes, replace the almonds with hazelnuts, and leave out the bitter almonds. Instead of rolling in icing sugar, these are baked without decoration, although sometimes a hazelnut is pressed into the top. They are then baked like the amaretti. These are seen below.

Preheat the oven to 175°C/350°F/gas 4. Blitz all the nuts in a food processor until finely ground or grind them in an almond grinder. Add the sugar and aquafaba and mix together. Form the mixture into 20–25 tops or balls and roll in icing sugar. Place on a baking tray lined with baking paper. Bake the cookies in the middle of the oven at 175°C/350°F/gas 4 for 14–18 minutes, depending on the oven and the size. Let them cool on the baking tray.

BISCOTTI

This is a classic Italian cookie, firmer than a rusk, that should be dipped in strong coffee or dessert wine to give it the perfect consistency. I have included two recipes, one older recipe that has appeared in my books since 2011, and one newer recipe that I developed when I started to use aquafaba. In my early books, I used 100g of apple sauce instead of the aquafaba, so if you are allergic to aquafaba, you can use that instead for the first recipe. The older recipe makes biscotti that are harder than the others, which I think are perfectly crispy. Nowadays, biscotti are usually a little softer than the Italian ones, and if you want to make more 'modern' biscotti that do not need to be dipped in liquid before eating, use the newer recipe and add the smaller amount of sugar. You can increase the amount of nuts to up to 120g in the new recipe if you are prepared for the extra work of creating rolls with more nuts in the dough. For saffron biscotti let ¼–½g of saffron dissolve in aquafaba before adding it to the dough. The older biscotti is shown above, with the more recent biscotti shown below.

OLDER RECIPE

60g	whole sweet almonds
75ml	aquafaba
135g	sugar
2 tbsp	oil
240g	plain flour
¼ tsp	salt
2 tsp	baking powder

Preheat the oven to 175°C/350°F/gas 4. Chop the almonds coarsely. In a bowl mix the aquafaba and sugar slightly using a whisk. Then mix together with the oil. Mix the flour, salt and baking powder together, then fold into the dough. Fold in the chopped almonds. The dough will be slightly sticky but if you work it together and leave for a minute it will become smooth. You will be able to roll it with slightly wet hands, or put some plain flour on the table when rolling out. Divide the dough into two pieces and roll out lengths on the baking tray. Flatten out the lengths slightly and bake in the middle of the oven at 175°C/350°F/gas 4 for 20–25 minutes. Bring the baking tray out, let it cool for 5 minutes and then cut the biscotti in diagonal slices. Arrange on the baking tray with the cut sides facing up. Lower the temperature to 100°C/212°F/gas ¼ and bake for 45 minutes more.

NEW RECIPE

90–120g	whole sweet almonds
100ml	aquafaba
135g	sugar
240–300g	plain flour
¼ tsp	salt
1 tsp	baking powder
2 tbsp	oil
1 tsp	vanilla extract

Use 225g sugar for the harder Italian biscotti.

Preheat the oven to 175°C/350°F/gas 4 Chop the almonds coarsely. Whip the aquafaba and sugar until frothy. Mix 240g of the flour, the salt and baking powder in a bowl and fold half of this into the frothy aquafaba. Fold in the chopped almonds together with the oil and vanilla extract. Then fold in the rest of the flour mixture and tip onto a flour-dusted surface. Knead the dough until it comes together. You might need to add some plain flour to make it firm enough. Divide the dough into two pieces and form two lengths on the baking tray. Flatten out the lengths slightly and bake in the middle of the oven at 175°C/350°F/gas 4 for 25–30 minutes. Bring the baking tray out and lower the temperature to 150°C/300°F/gas 2. Allow to set for 5 minutes, then cut into rectangular slices. Bake at 150°C/300°F/gas 2 for 15 minutes more.

CHOCOLATE CHIP COOKIES

These cookies are not hard, like Swedish cookies, but a little crispy around the edges and soft and chewy in the middle. Chocolate chip cookies were among the recipes that were hard to veganize in order to achieve a ball of dough that melted perfectly to create a crinkled cookie. Since aquafaba appeared it has become much easier, even though it took me over a year after the discovery of aquafaba until I was happy with the recipe. I like to let the dough chill for 12–36 hours to get a nicer colour while baking and a more developed flavour. This is something that even Ruth Graves Wakefield, who came up with the original recipe in 1938, was supposed to have done.

250g	room-temperature margarine
2 tsp	vanilla extract
190g	soft brown sugar
90g	sugar
75ml	aquafaba
360–390g	plain flour
1 tsp	baking powder
1 tsp	bicarbonate of soda
¼ tsp	salt
150g	chocolate chips

Preheat the oven to 175°C/350°F/gas 4. Mix the margarine, vanilla extract and both sugars until well combined, then add the aquafaba and mix until well combined. Mix the flour, baking powder, bicarbonate of soda and salt in a separate bowl. Fold into the batter and add the chocolate chips. Shape the dough into balls and place on a baking tray and bake in the middle of the oven. For a smaller ball of dough around 3cm in diameter, 6–8 minutes is enough. For larger balls of 5–6cm, the cookies need to be baked for 10–13 minutes. Test bake one cookie. If they become too thin, add more plain flour; if they are too thick, add more aquafaba. They cannot be over-baked; they are supposed to be soft in the middle but still crispy around the edges. This means practice makes perfect. I usually wait until the ball of dough has melted and become flat. After that, the middle of the cookie should rise slightly, which means that the batter in the middle is warm. This is when they should come out of the oven. Preferably eat them freshly baked. They will stay nice and soft in a sealed jar for about a day. Store in the fridge.

DOUBLE CHOCOLATE CHIP COOKIES

250g	room-temperature margarine
2 tsp	vanilla extract
265g	soft brown sugar
100ml	aquafaba
300g	plain flour
40g	cocoa
1 tsp	baking powder
1 tsp	bicarbonate of soda
¼ tsp	salt
150g	chocolate chips

Preheat the oven to 175°C/350°F/gas 4. Mix the margarine, vanilla extract and sugar in a bowl until well combined, add the aquafaba and mix until well combined. Mix the flour, cocoa, baking powder, bicarbonate of soda and salt together. Fold into the batter and add the chocolate chips. Shape the dough into balls and place on a baking tray. Bake in the middle of the oven at 175°C/350°F/gas 4. See opposite for baking times and tips. Preferably eat the cookies freshly baked. They will stay nice and soft in a sealed jar for about a day. Store in the fridge.

RYE & WHISKY CHOCOLATE CHIP COOKIES

250g	room-temperature margarine
2 tsp	vanilla extract
1–2 tsp	whisky or bourbon
190g	soft brown sugar
90g	sugar
75ml	aquafaba
300g	plain flour
90g	fine rye flour
1 tsp	baking powder
1 tsp	bicarbonate of soda
¼ tsp	salt
150g	chocolate chips

Preheat the oven to 175°C/350°F/gas 4. Mix the margarine, vanilla extract, whisky or bourbon and the sugars until well combined, then add the aquafaba and mix well. Mix the flour, rye flour, baking powder, bicarbonate of soda and salt together. Fold into the batter and add the chocolate chips. Shape the dough into balls and place on a baking tray. Bake in the middle of the oven at 175°C/350°F/gas 4. See opposite for baking times and tips. Preferably eat the cookies freshly baked. They will stay nice and soft in a sealed jar for about a day. Store in the fridge.

TIP!
The whisky flavour in these cookies is most prominent on the day of baking. If they are stored overnight, the flavour is lost.

CLASSIC CHOCOLATE CHIP COOKIES

Here, I have included three well-known versions of classic cookies. One of them comes from the bakery Ovenly, which has developed a recipe that uses oil instead of butter, and does not include eggs. Ovenly calls it 'accidentally vegan'. I have added vanilla extract, but it is optional and not in the original recipe. I have also written down some instructions on how to make the batter smooth using extra water. Opposite I have included a recipe using strong bread flour with extra resting time.

CHOCOLATE CHIP COOKIES WITH OIL

250g	plain flour
1 tsp	baking powder
¾ tsp	bicarbonate of soda
½ tsp	salt
150g	chocolate chips
150ml	oil
65ml	water
2 tsp	vanilla extract, optional
110g	soft brown sugar
100g	sugar
50–100ml water	

Mix the flour, baking powder, bicarbonate of soda and salt in a bowl. Add the chocolate chips. Mix the oil, 50ml of water, vanilla and the sugars in a separate bowl. Dissolve any lumps of brown sugar. Add the flour mixture and knead to a smooth dough. Add some more water to make the dough smooth, if needed. Chill in the fridge for at least 12 hours and up to 24 hours and then form the dough into balls. If the batter is too dry, you can add more water. Preheat the oven to 175°C/350°F/gas 4. Place the dough balls on a baking tray and bake in the middle of the oven. For a smaller ball of dough around 3cm in diameter, 6–8 minutes is enough. For a ball of dough of 4cm, 8–10 minutes is enough. For larger balls of 5–6cm, the cookies need to be baked for 10–13 minutes. Test bake one cookie. If they become too thin, add some flour; if they are too thick, add some water. They should not be over baked; they are supposed to be soft in the middle but still crispy around the edges. This means that practice makes perfect.

CHOCOLATE CHIP COOKIES WITH PROTEIN MILK & 36 HOURS RESTING TIME

300g	room-temperature margarine
3 tsp	vanilla extract
225g	soft brown sugar
225g	sugar
100ml	aquafaba
300g	plain flour
240g	strong bread flour
1½ tsp	baking powder
1¼ tsp	bicarbonate of soda
½ tsp	salt
200g	chocolate chips
	sea salt

Mix the margarine, vanilla extract and sugar together well in a bowl. Add the aquafaba and mix well. Mix both flours, baking powder, bicarbonate of soda and salt together. Fold into the batter and then add the chocolate chips. Let the dough chill for 36 hours. Preheat the oven to 175°C/350°F/gas 4. Shape the dough into balls, place on a baking tray and bake in the middle of the oven. See opposite for baking times and tips. Preferably eat the cookies freshly baked. They will stay nice and soft in a sealed jar for about a day. Store in the fridge.

TAHINI CHOCOLATE CHIP COOKIES

125g	room-temperature margarine
100g	tahini
1 tsp	vanilla extract
112g	soft brown sugar
90g	sugar
50ml	aquafaba
180–210g	plain flour
¾ tsp	bicarbonate of soda
½ tsp	salt
150g	chocolate chips

Depending on whether you want a thin or a thick result for your cookies, you will need to adjust the quantity of plain flour depending on the consistency of your tahini. You might need up to 240g of plain flour. I have used thin tahini and here I have used 210g of plain flour. Make sure you mix the tahini in the jar thoroughly before measuring it so that it is evenly mixed. Test bake one cookie before putting the dough to set in the fridge overnight. This will make it easier to adjust the dough before it has chilled.

Mix the margarine, tahini, vanilla extract and sugars together well in a bowl. Add the aquafaba and mix well. Mix the flour, bicarbonate of soda and salt together. Fold into the batter and then add the chocolate chips. Chill the dough in the fridge overnight. Preheat the oven to 150°C/300°F/gas 2. Shape the dough into balls, place on a baking tray and bake in the middle of the oven. See opposite for baking times and tips. Preferably eat the cookies freshly baked. They will stay nice and soft in a sealed jar for about a day. Store in the fridge.

BROWNIE COOKIES

Chocolate cookies, fudge cookies or brownie cookies ('brookies'), are classic American cookies that are traditionally made from brownie batter baked into cookies. In the past, it wasn't possible to veganize these cookies as they contain too much fat and chocolate, but by emulsifying these ingredients together I have managed to veganize them with a perfect result. They are incredibly fudgy and will keep nice and soft for a long time. Using ½ teaspoon baking powder makes thick cookies like the ones in the picture opposite, but if you use 1 teaspoon baking powder you get larger, thinner cookies, like the ones you get in cafés.

200g	dark chocolate with 70% cocoa solids
50g	margarine
100ml	aquafaba
1 tsp	vanilla extract
180g	icing sugar
120g	plain flour
20g	cocoa powder
½ tsp	baking powder
1 pinch	salt
50g	chocolate buttons (optional)

Preheat the oven to 175°C/350°F/gas 4. Line a baking tray with baking paper.

Melt the margarine and chocolate in a bowl in the microwave or over a water bath on the hob. Once melted, carefully blend in the aquafaba and vanilla extract using a hand blender.

Mix together the icing sugar, plain flour, sifted cocoa powder, baking powder and salt in a bowl and fold into the melted chocolate mixture. Leave the dough to rest for 10–20 minutes; it should firm up so that you can shape it into balls with your hands.

Shape the dough into balls and place on the baking tray. If you are using 1 teaspoon of baking powder to make thinner cookies the balls should be well spaced out. Bake in the centre of the oven at 175°C/350°F/gas 4. For a 4cm ball of dough, 8–10 minutes is about right. For larger balls, around 5–6cm, bake for around 10–12 minutes.

It's a good idea to test bake a cookie. If they end up too thin, work in a bit more flour. Leave to cool on the tray, as they are very soft when they come out of the oven.

SNICKERDOODLES

These are classic American cookies that are chewy in the middle and crinkled around the edges, just like chocolate chip cookies. The recipe was originally created before baking powder was developed, when bicarbonate of soda was mixed with cream of tartar, an acid, to make the bicarbonate of soda react. Baking powder has an added acid which means you can use 1 tablespoon of baking powder instead of the original mixture. You can make traditional cookies using the original ingredients, which do have a sour flavour from the acid, but I think that baking powder works well. The snickerdoodles opposite were baked with baking powder. Cream of tartar can usually be found in the baking section of well-stocked grocery shops. I like to let the dough rest in the fridge for 12–24 hours for a more developed flavour. This is also an excellent recipe to start with if you want to make cookies with a flavour other than cinnamon. Use baking powder and add 2 teaspoons of vanilla extract for classic drop sugar cookies. Adding sprinkles makes them extra festive. The cookies on the bottom row below have been made without sprinkles to show how using sugar on the surface affects the result. The cookie on the left was made without being rolled in sugar, while the one on the right was rolled in sugar. You can also roll the cookies in icing sugar after rolling them in sugar, which gives them a lovely white, cracked surface. The dough makes 15–20 cookies.

250g	soft margarine
340g	sugar
75ml	aquafaba
420g	plain flour
1 tbsp	baking powder
¼ tsp	salt
70g	sugar
2 tbsp	ground cinnamon

Mix the margarine, sugar and aquafaba together well in a bowl. Knead in the flour mixed with the baking powder and salt until smooth. Preferably let the dough rest in the fridge for at least 12 hours and up to 24 hours. Preheat the oven to 200°C/400°F/gas 6. Roll the dough into balls the size of golf balls, and then roll in a mixture of sugar and cinnamon. Do not place them too close to one another on the baking tray as the balls will spread out into large cookies while baking. Test bake one cookie. If they become too thin, add some flour; if they are too thick, add some aquafaba. Bake in the middle of the oven at 200°C/400°F/gas 6 for 8–10 minutes. Let them cool on the baking tray for a few minutes, then move to a wire rack.

SUGAR COOKIES

Sugar cookies are the American's classic for decorating and they are a little thinner and crispier than other decorated cookies they are developed from. According to me – and Martha Stewart – they are best when you use whisky instead of milk in the batter, but this is not compulsory! The cat and the rabbits below were painted with colouring powder dissolved in alcohol. Read more about this on page 54.

300g	plain flour
¼ tsp	salt
½ tsp	baking powder
125g	room-temperature margarine
225g	sugar
50ml	aquafaba
2 tbsp	whisky or milk
½ tsp	vanilla extract

Mix the flour, salt and baking powder in a bowl. Mix the margarine and sugar together well in a separate bowl, then add the aquafaba, whisky or milk and vanilla and mix to a batter. Mix thoroughly; when light-coloured and fluffy, add the dry ingredients. Form into a smooth dough without working the batter too much. Divide into two pieces and flatten out slightly, cover in clingfilm and chill for at least 1 hour in the fridge. Preheat the oven to 175°C/350°F/gas 4. Roll the dough out to 2–3mm thick on a floured surface, cut out shapes, place on a baking tray and bake for 8–10 minutes.

1 batch	royal icing (see page 324)

To be able to spread the icing evenly over the sugar cookies, you need to use two icings of different thicknesses. The thicker icing is used for making the edges and the thinner for flooding the surface; both are piped on top of the cookies. Prepare both before starting so that you can flood the surface using the thinner icing straight after piping the edges; this will make them blend nicely together. It is important that the thicker icing is firm enough to create a stable edge, but not so firm it doesn't stick to the cookie. The thin icing should spread evenly, but you might need to use a slightly wet spatula to even it out further. Look online for videos of a pro making the icing. This will make it easier for you.

GINGERBREAD

SIMPLE GINGERBREAD

150ml	water
140g	golden syrup
360g	sugar
1 tbsp	ground cloves
1 tbsp	ground cinnamon
1 tbsp	ground ginger
300g	margarine
2 tsp	bicarbonate of soda
780–840g	plain flour

Boil the water, syrup, sugar and spices together in a pan. Remove from the hob and stir in the margarine. Let it cool. Mix the bicarbonate of soda with 60g of the flour and add to the batter. Add the rest of the flour and mix to a smooth batter. Allow to rest in the fridge for at least 24 hours, preferably for several days. Preheat the oven to 225°C/425°F/gas 7. Roll out the dough and cut out the shapes. Place on a baking tray. Bake in the middle of the oven for 4–5 minutes.

THIN GINGERBREAD

250g	room-temperature margarine
180g	sugar
210g	golden syrup
1½ tbsp	ground cinnamon
1 tbsp	ground clove
1 tsp	ground ginger
2 tsp	ground cardamom
2 tsp	ground bitter orange peel
1/8 tsp	ground allspice
1½ tsp	bicarbonate of soda
420–480g	plain flour

This gingerbread was developed after looking at lots of older recipes, partly to achieve a really thin gingerbread, but also to find traditional Swedish spices. The flavour is based on bitter orange, allspice and cardamom in addition to the simple spices, as older recipes commonly used all these spices in gingerbread.

Mix the margarine and sugar in a bowl until well combined. Add the syrup, cinnamon, cloves, ginger, cardamom, bitter orange and allspice. Mix to a smooth batter. Mix the bicarbonate of soda with 60g of plain flour and add to the batter. Add enough of the flour to the batter to become slightly firm. Allow to rest in the fridge for at least 24 hours, but preferably for several days. Preheat the oven to 200°C/400°F/gas 6. Roll the dough out on a piece of baking paper and cut out the shapes. Place on a baking tray. Bake in the middle of the oven for 5–8 minutes.

AMERICAN GINGER COOKIES

780–900g	plain flour
1 tsp	bicarbonate of soda
½ tsp	baking powder
225g	room-temperature margarine
185g	soft brown sugar
1½ tbsp	ground ginger
1½ tbsp	ground cinnamon
1½ tsp	ground cloves
1 tsp	freshly ground black pepper
1 tsp	salt
75ml	aquafaba
350g	golden syrup,

I veganized this classic gingerbread recipe from Martha Stewart by removing the eggs that are usually included in American cookies. Rather than the name 'gingerbread', in Swedish we would call these 'pepper cookies', focusing instead on the black pepper that was often included in the recipe.

Mix together the flour, bicarbonate of soda and baking powder in a bowl and set aside. In a separate bowl, whisk together the margarine, soft brown sugar, spices and salt until the mixture is fluffy. Pour in the aquafaba and syrup, while continuing to whisk, and then add the flour mixture, stirring gently, until everything is incorporated. Divide the dough into two halves and refrigerate, well-sealed for at least 1 hour. Preheat the oven to 175°C/350°F/gas 4. On a lightly floured baking sheet, roll out the dough to a thickness of 3–7mm, depending on the type of cookies you want to make, and return to the fridge for 20–30 minutes. Cut out your preferred sizes and bake in the middle of the oven for 10–15 minutes, or until the cookies are golden.

GINGERBREAD HOUSE

When making gingerbread houses, a dough containing less sugar than normal gingerbread is often used as it is the sugar that causes the gingerbread to melt and become thin. Dough adjusted to suit larger figures and houses can swell slightly more, but you can roll it out really thinly to make perfect details. For instance, you can cut doors and windows where the cut pieces fit perfectly into the cut holes. I always cut the pieces out before putting them in the oven because I think that gives the best result, but that is a matter of taste. I also always put the pieces together using melted sugar, but the royal icing with aquafaba also works, even though the build is not as stable. Use a knife with a straight, sharp edge, not rounded, to make the cuts meet precisely. Use baking paper to make your templates as normal paper will stick to the dough. Cut your pieces on the baking tray and the baking paper but roll out the dough thinly on a flour-dusted surface before putting it onto the baking paper. If the dough is rolled too thinly on the baking paper without flour, the dough will stick to the paper and the paper will wrinkle during baking from the tension in the dough. It is better to roll the dough out thinly, move it over onto the baking paper on the baking tray, and then cut out the figures. Make a base from the leftover dough. This will make it easier to assemble the house and make it stable. Bake to a nice colour, otherwise the pieces might become too damp from the moisture in the air and collapse. This is why you should make sure the dough is an even thickness to allow it to bake properly without burning. Do not bake using hot baking trays as that might cause bubbles in the figures; let the trays cool between batches. When the pieces are newly baked, they can be moved carefully and put on a flat surface to flatten out if they have become bent on the baking tray.

GINGERBREAD HOUSE & LARGE FIGURES

270g	sugar
280g	golden syrup
100g	margarine
1 tbsp	ground cinnamon
1 tbsp	ground ginger
300ml	milk
1 tbsp	bicarbonate of soda
900–1.02kg	plain flour

Heat the sugar, syrup, margarine and spices in a pan until they start to simmer. Remove from the hob and add the milk. Let it cool. Add the flour and mix to make a slightly firm dough. Chill in the fridge for at least 24 hours. Preheat the oven to 175°C/350°F/gas 4. Work the dough until smooth and roll out to 3–4mm thick, or slightly thinner if you want even figures. See above for tips on rolling out. Cut out into shapes or figures. Bake in the middle of the oven at 175°C/350°F/gas 4 for 12–15 minutes until the pieces are well baked. Remove from the baking paper while still warm but leave to cool on the baking tray.

I think frosting using melted sugar is the best way of assembling gingerbread houses. It sticks quickly and it keeps the shape for a long time. You can assemble houses using the aquafaba icing but it is trickier and is not as stable.

ASSEMBLING

270g	sugar

Melt the sugar for assembling on low heat in a frying pan. Remove from the heat. Dip the edges of the pieces in the melted sugar and put them together immediately. Put the frying pan back on the hob if the sugar starts to harden. Be careful of your fingers and others nearby as the sugar will be very hot. To clean, put hot water into the frying pan when you are finished, and the melted sugar will dissolve.

DECORATION

You can read more about colourings for icing on page 54. Vegan rainbow chocolate beans are available online. Royal icing can be found on page 324.

HOUSE DOUGH

I have used this dough all my life and the book with the original recipe is well-thumbed and very worn. Similar recipes for large figures or gingerbread houses can be found in really old books. What is special about the dough is that it is not as sweet and does not spread out like thin gingerbread. This is why it is more stable and does not absorb moisture so easily, meaning that it is less likely to break.

ROYAL ICING

Royal icing is often used for decoration, details and as the 'glue' in traditional baking. This recipe is smooth and works both as glue and for decorating gingerbread houses, covered cakes, figure cakes or for making figures out of the icing itself. Traditionally, an acid is added to the icing for gingerbread, so I like to add some vinegar or lemon juice for this purpose. This recipe makes a large batch that is designed to make thick icing for decorations for gingerbread houses, for instance, or separate decorations like carrots and decorative eyes that are shown opposite, below right. Two thinner icings, one with and one without aquafaba to decorate gingerbread, are given below.

ROYAL ICING

75ml	aquafaba
½ tsp	vanilla extract, lemon juice or ¼ tsp vinegar
approx. 480g	icing sugar

This icing can be made and is similar to traditional icing made with egg whites, acid and icing sugar.

Whip the aquafaba and vanilla extract, or acid in a bowl, until thick and firm. Add 60g of the icing sugar at a time until the batter can be piped; add a little more water if it is too thick, or increase the amount of icing sugar if it is too runny. Sometimes two batches of different textures are needed: a thicker one for edges and for details; and a thinner one for flooding the surface. You can control the thinner one by making patterns in the icing in the bowl, if it is thin enough, these patterns should disappear within 10 seconds – what is called 'run-out icing'. If it takes longer, add a drop of water. If the icing is too thin, add more icing sugar. Royal icing should keep its shape, but the tip should bend slightly, which is often called 'off-peak icing'. This is soft enough for piping but will keep its shape when dry. Correct with water or icing sugar if it is too firm or too soft. This off-peak icing can be used for houses and details, for instance, the diamonds on the doughnut tower on page 349, the unicorns and rainbows on the left and icing eyes. Make them on a piece of baking paper and dry them completely before use. When dry, they can sit on top of a glaze and frosting for a long time.

THIN ICING NO. 1

2 tbsp	aquafaba
¼ tsp	lemon juice
180–240g	icing sugar

Mix the aquafaba and lemon juice in a bowl and then add the icing sugar, 60g at a time, until you have a firm icing. If it is too firm, add some aquafaba or a little lemon juice; if it is too soft, increase the amount of icing sugar.

THIN ICING NO. 2

180g	icing sugar
2 tsp	glucose syrup
1–3 tbsp	milk

Mix the icing sugar, glucose syrup and enough milk together in a bowl until it reaches a consistency that can be piped. Add more milk or icing sugar to achieve the right consistency.

THREE DIFFERENT CONSISTENCIES

The consistency required for your royal icing will depend on what you are using it for. For icicles on a gingerbread house or thick details, such as Christmas trees, a really firm icing is needed. For details on gingerbread and on houses that are supposed to run out and have smooth edges, you can use a softer icing. If you are decorating cookies and filling out between lines using icing you need a runny icing that will fill out the area evenly. Read more about icing opposite.

CHRISTMAS TREES

These Christmas trees are made using ice cream cones turned upside-down and piped with royal icing. You can spread the icing using a spatula like the two Christmas trees in the back to the left. The tree second from the front on the right has been piped using a star-shaped nozzle. The trees at the front have been piped using a round nozzle, starting from the bottom and working up; the trees on the right at the back, and the second tree from the front on the left have been piped in the same way, but I have spread out each layer of icing with a spatula/spoon before piping the next row.

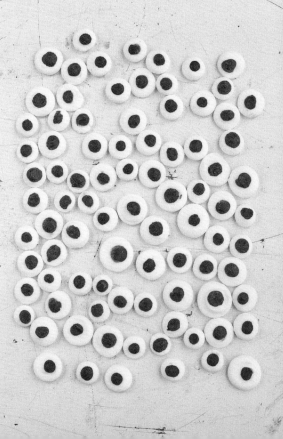

CHOCOLATE BALLS & PUNSCH ROLLS

Since I stopped using dairy products in my teens, I only attempted to make chocolate balls once. I tried using normal baking margarine and realized that the melting point was too high to get a good flavour; I thought about a solution for this for a decade, until I realized that vegan spread is soft enough. This is what I now use in all frostings and pastry creams where butter is used in traditional baking. Read more about this on page 36. I have tried many different margarines for spreading and the higher the percentage of fat, the better the result. These are shown on page 280.

CHOCOLATE BALLS
105–140g oats
2–3 tbsp cold brewed coffee
100g vegan spread
90g sugar
1 tsp vanilla extract
20g cocoa

Desiccated coconut, nibbed sugar or sprinkles

Start by using the lower amount of oats and coffee and mix all the ingredients together in a bowl. Then increase the quantities until you have the perfect flavour and consistency. If the batter is too sticky, add oats; and if it is too dry, add some coffee. Let the mixture cool in the fridge for a smoother batter and then shape into small balls and roll in the decorations of your choice.

WHITE CHOCOLATE BALLS
80g dairy-free white chocolate
100g vegan spread
30g icing sugar
140g oats
1 tsp vanilla extract

Decoration as above

Melt the white chocolate carefully according to the instructions on page 57 and let it cool. Beat the margarine until fluffy in a bowl and add the icing sugar and the cooled melted chocolate. Mix thoroughly to make a soft, fluffy buttercream. Add the rest of the ingredients and mix well. If the batter is too sticky, add more oats. For a batter that is easier to work with, ideally let the mixture cool in the fridge and then shape into small balls and roll in the decorations of your choice.

COCONUT CARAMEL BALLS
105–140g oats
100g vegan spread
70g coconut sugar
1 tsp vanilla extract

Decoration as above

I developed these coconut caramel balls together with my son and they are the whole family's favourite among the recipes on this page. If you want to use sweetened condensed coconut milk instead of coconut sugar, you can do that as well. Replace the coconut sugar with 150g of sweetened condensed coconut milk and increase the quantity of oats to 140–175g.

Start by using the lower amount of oats and mix all the ingredients together. Then increase the quantity of oats until you have the perfect flavour and consistency. If the batter is too sticky, add oats; if it is too dry, add some vegan spread. Let the mixture cool in the fridge for a smoother batter and then shape into small balls and roll in the decorations of your choice. The caramel balls taste best after they have set in the fridge for a few hours.

Punsch rolls are a classic treat in Sweden, originally made from offcuts and leftovers at bakeries flavoured with punsch or arrack. They are basically marzipan-covered cake pops, without the stick. They are also called vacuum cleaners because of their resemblance to old-style machines, but also because they were made from crumbs. It is a luxury to be able to find really good arrack for punsch rolls. I recommend the arrack essence from Stockholms Aete & Essencefabrik, but fortunately, the arrack essence you find in baking shops and online also works. Punsch was used in older recipes developed from leftover cake. The flavour is not as strong as when using essence or extract, but you can use both. For the biscuits in the first recipe, I usually use digestives. Pistachio green is most commonly used, if you can find it. It is a mixture of green and yellow and you can read about it on page 194. For Easter punsch rolls I use yellow marzipan and dip the ends in white chocolate. When using white chocolate it is very important to freeze or chill the rolls so that the chocolate hardens quickly and creates a thick layer. If you want rolls that look like the ones from a bakery, after dipping them in the chocolate and placing them on a piece of baking paper, move them around a few times before they set to get nice smooth ends. Read more about this on page 281.

PUNSCH ROLL FILLING WITHOUT LEFTOVER CAKE

100–150g	crushed biscuits
70g	oats
100g	almond paste
75g	margarine
45g	sugar
2 tbsp	cocoa
3–5 tsp	arrack essence or punsch

OLDER BAKERY FILLING

400g	cake crumbs
150g	margarine
20–40g	cocoa (not needed if using chocolate cake crumbs)
75–100ml	punsch
3–5 tsp	arrack essence

ASSEMBLING

500g	marzipan (with colouring if required)
200g	melted chocolate (see page 57)
1–2 tbsp	oil

First, blend the biscuits and oats or cake crumbs until fine before adding the rest of the ingredients into the food processor in smaller batches. Start with the smaller measurements and adjust the taste or texture along the way. Mix to a smooth dough, adding arrack essence or punsch and arrack essence to taste. If the dough is too dry, add more arrack/punsch or a little margarine. If the dough is too wet, add some more biscuit crumbs or oats. You can also adjust the older filling using oats for a filling to your taste. Divide the dough and the marzipan in two sections. Wrap the strip of marzipan around the roll of dough and seal the edges together. Cut the roll into pieces, dip the ends in melted chocolate, possibly mixed with some oil, and place on a piece of baking paper. Leave to cool in the fridge. Once set, punsch rolls are best stored in a sealed container in the fridge overnight. This will help the flavours to develop.

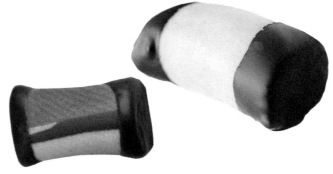

CAKE POPS

Cake pops are luxurious mini bakes that can be created out of leftover cake, much like punsch rolls. Leftover sponge cake or cake made for an event and not bought or eaten can be mixed with frosting to make a mixture that you can shape, and that is not too sticky, and then form into cake pops. For instance, I always save the cut tops from cake layers in a sealed bag in the freezer. You can buy sticks for the cake pops in baking stores online.

YOU NEED:
Lolly sticks
Leftover sponge cakes or cut cake layers
Ganache or frosting
Melted chocolate for dipping
Neutral-flavoured oil (1–2 tbsp per 100g chocolate)

Carefully knead together the sponge cake and ganache or frosting. This can be done by hand, in a food processor or with a stand mixer. If the mixture is too firm, add some cream or more ganache or frosting. If the batter is too soft, you can add more sponge cake if you have any or some extra melted chocolate (if the cake pop contains chocolate), or chill the mixture slightly. Form into balls or shapes and stick them on the lolly sticks, or leave without sticks for truffle-like cake pops.

Place on a baking paper-lined tray. Freeze for at least 1–2 hours, preferably until they are completely frozen. If the cookies are frozen, it will be easier to dip them in melted chocolate as the chocolate will set faster and more evenly. Melt the chocolate and add some oil for a runnier and smoother chocolate. For the best results, you want a thin layer of chocolate.

Dip the cake pops in the chocolate, and then spin or shake them over the chocolate bowl so that any excess chocolate comes off the lolly.

Press in any decorations before the chocolate hardens. Put the cake pops somewhere to harden, like a glass or a jar filled with sugar so they stand up.

You can make both light-coloured and dark-coloured cake pops. For light-coloured cake pops you can use light-coloured frosting or 100g of vegan spread mixed with some cream and an extra teaspoon of vanilla extract, vanilla sugar or $1/4$ teaspoon of vanilla powder.

You can also use the second recipe for punsch rolls on page 327 where the batter is made of cake crumbs, punsch and margarine to make a batter that you can shape. The punsch can be replaced with cream or other suitable liquids.

QUANTITIES
The proportions of crumbled cake to frosting will vary depending on how dry or moist the cake is, but I estimate that you need around 10 muffins or one sponge cake for around 200g of frosting. If you do not have any frosting, you can boil 100ml of cream and add 100g of dark chocolate, then stir until melted and combined for a good ganache.

REMEMBER!

It is important that the milk mixture is not hotter than 37°C/98.6°F for the yeast to develop. If it is warmer than that, the yeast will die and the dough will not rise. The liquid should feel lukewarm to the touch.

PLAIN FLOUR

Add just a little of the flour at a time to prevent the dough from becoming too stiff. Never start by adding all of the flour stated in the recipe, half is probably enough. Then add 60g at a time until you have a smooth dough.

BRIOCHE PAGE 350

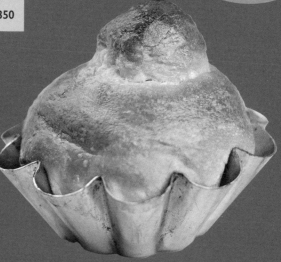

BREAD GLAZE

Heat 1 tbsp of potato starch and 200ml of water in a saucepan until thickened. Stir constantly to prevent the mixture from burning at the bottom and remove from the hob when thickened. Do not whip as this will create a foam. Brush on the bread dough before baking to give a shine.

SUGAR SYRUP

If you want extra shiny buns, you can do what pastry chefs do and brush over a thin layer of sugar syrup immediately after baking. For the syrup, boil 100ml of water and 90g of granulated or cane sugar and brush a thin layer on top of the newly baked buns straight from the oven. However, if you roll the buns on an unfloured surface and brush with cream, I do not think anything else is needed and they will be as shiny as the picture above.

Raised doughs

Wheat bread with no egg wash will not become golden as quickly as loaves brushed with egg and they will not take on the same dark colour. Consequently, they should be taken out of the oven before they become dark gold, otherwise they will be over-baked and dry. This has given wheat bread baked without eggs and milk an undeserved reputation of being a dry imitation. If you are used to baking with eggs, you need to practice and then you will learn how to judge when they are ready. My grandmother always says that if the buns are lightly golden underneath they are ready. You can also use this as an indicator, but you will need to watch your fingers!

Fresh yeast is sold all over Sweden and is what I use most often. If you are using dried yeast make sure the dough has risen to the double size for the first rise, which might take a bit longer with dried yeast. Fresh yeast lasts for a couple of weeks in the fridge if it is kept sealed. There are two types of dry yeast: active dry yeast and instant dry yeast. Active dry yeast is mixed in with the liquid for the dough, while instant dry yeast is mixed in the dry ingredients. Dry yeast survives at slightly higher temperatures. 50g of fresh yeast corresponds to 15g of instant dry yeast. Guidelines for conversion are generally to use around ¼ of the weight when you are converting fresh yeast to instant dry yeast (and vice versa); if you are converting fresh yeast to active dry yeast, you should use about ½ the weight of dry yeast to fresh (and vice versa). You can use lukewarm liquid (37°C/98.6°F) for fresh yeast and slightly warmer for dry yeast (40–45°C/104–113°F).

Using soft margarine instead of melted margarine is an amazing tip that means you do not need as much plain flour to make the dough pliable.

For really shiny buns, you should not roll out your buns for semlor, brioches or saffron buns on an unfloured surface. If you roll and shape the buns on a clean worktop they will be shiny. To be able to do this, you have to knead the dough well to make it smooth. Brush the buns with cream, bread glaze or sugar syrup. I almost always use cream made from soya to give the buns a nice surface. If you brush the buns using melted margarine when they come out of the oven, they will look nice and shiny.

Depending on the size you make your yeasted bakes the number from a batch varies greatly, but the recipes usually yield 12–20 buns/pastries.

CINNAMON BUNS

Even classic cinnamon buns are better when made using soft cooking fat rather than melted. In Sweden we celebrate Cinnamon bun day on October the 4:th. If you want to bake the buns in a pan (35x25-40x30cm) you need to lower the temperature to 200°C/400°F/gas 6 and bake for 20-25 minutes. If you don't have cardamom seeds, use ground cardamom. Strong bread flour can also be used. These recipes make 15–20 buns.

DOUGH

1–2 tsp	cardamom seeds
175g	room-temperature margarine
50g/12g	fresh/dried yeast
500ml	room-temperature milk
135g	sugar
1 tsp	salt
720–800g plain flour	

cream, for brushing the buns
nibbed sugar

Grind the cardamom seeds. Dice the margarine. Crumble the yeast and mix with the cardamom, milk and margarine in a bowl or a stand mixer. Add the sugar, salt and some of the flour. Knead the dough for 15 minutes in the stand mixer with a dough hook or for 20 minutes by hand. Add more flour until the dough is smooth, but be careful not to add too much. Start with a smaller amount and add more gradually until the dough is pliable. The flour needs to be added gradually as the dough needs more flour the more it is kneaded. Allow the dough to rise for 1 hour or until doubled in size. Put the dough on a lightly floured surface and follow the instructions for either buns or knots. Allow to rise for 30 minutes and preheat the oven to 225°C/425°F/gas 7. Brush the buns with cream and sprinkle nibbed sugar on top. Bake in the centre of the oven for 8–12 minutes.

FILLING

200g	room-temperature margarine
45–90g	sugar
2–3 tbsp	ground cinnamon

FOR BUNS

Mix the margarine, sugar and cinnamon. Roll the dough out to a rectangle 0.5cm thick and spread the filling on top. Roll the dough into a roll. Slice into rounds and put on a baking tray.

FOR KNOTS

Mix the margarine, sugar and cinnamon. Roll out the dough to a rectangle 0.5cm thick and spread the filling on top. Fold the dough over itself once so that the filling is covered. Cut 1,5-2cm strips and twist them a couple of times. Wind the strips around 3 fingers to form the bun. Put the end of the strip underneath the bun.

SEMLA

The Swedish cream bun, semla, is a classic that should really only be eaten on Shrove Tuesday but is now eaten during the first months of the year. This recipe gives 12–17 semlor depending on how big you make them. You can also make half the quantity of dough. In my wheat dough for semlor, I use a dough where the fat is melted with a large amount of sugar because I want my buns to be really light and fluffy. If they are too moist, I think the buns turn out too heavy. This dough should barely be kneaded at all and it is important not to add too much plain flour. It should be soft and smooth but not be kneaded until smooth for a long time. See page 409 for information on how I whip the cream until extra stiff. If you do not have any cardamom seeds at home, you can use ground cardamom.

DOUGH

1–2 tsp	cardamom seeds
100g	margarine
400ml	milk
50g/12g	fresh/dried yeast
135g	sugar
½ tsp	salt
600–720g	plain flour

cream, for brushing

ASSEMBLING

200g	almond paste or almond-free paste, grated
2 tbsp	water
1–2 pots	double cream lemon juice/vinegar icing sugar

Grind the cardamom seeds. Melt the margarine in a saucepan and add the milk. Pour into a mixing bowl. Crumble in the yeast when the milk mixture is lukewarm. Then add the sugar, salt and cardamom and mix. Add enough flour until you have a slightly smooth dough that is still soft. It is better to have a slightly loose dough that can rise and then add more flour after it has risen. Let it rise for 40–60 minutes in a slightly warm place to double in size. Knead the dough together with some more plain flour, not for long, but to make it pliable enough to create balls. Divide into 12–17 pieces of around 70–80g. Form into balls, place on a baking tray and leave to rise for 20–40 minutes until well risen. Preheat the oven to 225°C/425°F/gas 7. Brush the balls of dough with cream and bake in the centre of the oven for 9–14 minutes, depending on the size. When cool, cut the top off each bun to create a lid. Mix the grated almond paste with water in a bowl until smooth and pipe on top of the buns. Whip the cream until fluffy, add a few millilitres of lemon juice or vinegar, and whip again thoroughly for several minutes until you have a firm cream. Cover the almond paste in the buns with the whipped cream, put the tops back on and dust icing sugar over the lids. Dust with more icing sugar before serving.

ALMOND PASTE

100g	whole sweet almonds
90g	sugar
1–3 tbsp	water

If you are allergic to almonds or would prefer something different, you can use almost any nut or seed you want to create your favourite. It is important that they are not roasted. I like sunflower paste, pistachio paste and walnut paste. This recipe gives around 200g of paste.

Process the nuts or the seeds in a food processor or blender until fine. Add sugar and mix a little more to combine. Add 1 tablespoon of water to make a classic firm paste. Add a little more water if you want to spread or pipe the paste on the semlor.

SUGAR KNOTS & CUSTARD BUNS

The recipe gives 12–17 buns or knots depending on how big you make them. You can also make half the quantity of dough. In my wheat dough for custard buns and sugar knots, I use a dough where the fat is melted with a large amount of sugar because I want my buns to be really light and fluffy. This dough should barely be kneaded at all and it is important not to add too much flour. It should be soft and smooth but not be kneaded until smooth for a long time. If you want to save some for later, freeze them immediately when cool and brush with melted margarine and dip in sugar when thawed. If you do not have any cardamom seeds at home, you can use ground cardamom. I developed the custard buns with blueberry pastry cream (instead of vanilla pastry cream) in 2020 and my daughter named them moon buns. You can also use strong bread flour instead of plain flour.

DOUGH

1–2 tsp	cardamom seeds
100g	margarine
400ml	milk
50g/12g	fresh/dried yeast
135g	sugar
½ tsp	salt
600–720g plain flour	

cream, for brushing
melted margarine, for brushing
sugar

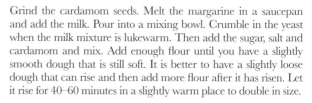

VANILLA PASTRY CREAM FOR CUSTARD BUNS (PAGE 424)

Grind the cardamom seeds. Melt the margarine in a saucepan and add the milk. Pour into a mixing bowl. Crumble in the yeast when the milk mixture is lukewarm. Then add the sugar, salt and cardamom and mix. Add enough flour until you have a slightly smooth dough that is still soft. It is better to have a slightly loose dough that can rise and then add more flour after it has risen. Let it rise for 40–60 minutes in a slightly warm place to double in size.

CUSTARD BUNS

Knead the dough together with some more plain flour, not for long, but to make it pliable enough to create balls. Divide into 12–17 pieces of around 70–80g. Form into balls and leave to rise for 20–40 minutes until well risen. Preheat the oven to 225°C/425°F/gas 7. Brush with cream and fill with vanilla cream, either by pressing the piping nozzle far down into the centre of the bun, but not right to the bottom, and fill up with a good amount of vanilla cream; or by making a hole in the top of the bun with two fingers, and then filling with vanilla cream. If you want a lot of vanilla cream in your bun, I think the second method works best. Bake in the centre of the oven at 225°C/425°F/gas 7 for 9–14 minutes, depending on the size. Brush the buns with melted margarine and roll them in sugar before serving.

SUGAR KNOTS

Knead the dough together with some more plain flour, not for long, but to make it pliable enough to create balls. Divide into 12–17 pieces of around 70–80g. Roll out long rolls of dough, form into knots and leave to rise for 20–40 minutes until well risen. Preheat the oven to 225°C/425°F/gas 7. Brush with cream and bake in the centre of the oven for 9–14 minutes, depending on the size. Brush the buns with melted margarine and roll them in sugar before serving.

BLUEBERRY PASTRY CREAM FOR MOON BUNS (SEE PAGE 424)

TWO WINNING SAFFRON BUNS

I developed the first of these recipes many years ago. In Sweden we eat saffron buns when we celebrate Lucia on december the 13:th, but they are also baked during the whole of December. It is the small details that together give an amazing result: soft margarine instead of the melted margarine means you add less plain flour; the raisins are soaked thoroughly in water to prevent them from drying out; the saffron is boiled together with the liquid and is allowed to sit overnight to develop a strong saffron flavour. When I make saffron buns, I like to use a lot of saffron, but ½g of saffron is enough to colour and flavour one batch. Makes 15–20 buns, depending on what size you like them. If you want them as shiny as those shown opposite, you need to roll them out on an unfloured surface and brush with cream before baking.

60–70g	raisins
350ml	milk
½g	saffron
50g/12g	fresh/dried yeast
135g	sugar
½ tsp	salt
100–125g	room-temperature margarine
540–720g	plain flour
cream, for brushing	

Soak the raisins in water. Heat the milk together with saffron in a pan and let it cool completely, preferably the night before baking. Mix the cold milk mixture with the yeast, sugar, salt, soft margarine and plain flour in a bowl to a slightly firm dough. Allow to rise for 1–3 hours. Knead the dough for 10–15 minutes in a stand mixer or for 15–20 minutes by hand. Add flour to keep the dough smooth. You need to add the flour a little at a time as the dough needs more plain flour the longer it is kneaded. Allow to rise for another 20 minutes. Roll and shape the saffron buns, press in the raisins and allow to rise for 20–30 minutes on the baking tray. Preheat the oven to 225°C/425°F/gas 7. Brush the buns with cream and bake in the centre of the oven for 6–10 minutes, depending on the size and the oven.

After baking saffron buns around 20 times and several taste tests in the test kitchen for Swedish supermarket ICA's magazine *Buffé*, they presented the best recipe for saffron buns. You did not need eggs, quark or yoghurt to make fluffy, moist saffron buns. Quite the opposite – they were drier. This is their recipe but veganized by me, which really makes amazing saffron buns!

½g	saffron
500ml	room-temperature milk
175g	room-temperature margarine
50g/12g	fresh/dried yeast
180g	sugar
½ tsp	salt
720–800g	plain flour
60–70g	raisins
cream, for brushing	

Heat the milk and saffron together in a pan and leave to cool to room temperature, otherwise it will melt the margarine. Dice the margarine. Crumble the yeast and mix with the saffron milk and margarine in a bowl, or the bowl for the stand mixer. Add the sugar, salt and half of the flour. Work the dough for 15 minutes in the stand mixer with a dough hook or for 20 minutes by hand. Add more flour to a make a smooth dough but be careful not to add too much. Start with a small amount and add a little at a time until the dough is smooth. You need to add it in stages as the dough needs more flour the longer it is kneaded. Allow the dough to rise for 1 hour. Let the raisins soak in water while the dough is rising; strain off the water after 30 minutes. Put the dough on a floured surface, knead and shape your saffron buns. Make sure you roll your saffron buns without flour if you want them extra shiny. Press in the raisins. Allow to rise for 30 minutes. Preheat the oven to 225°C/425°F/gas 7. Brush with cream and bake in the oven for 8–10 minutes.

DANISH PASTRY DOUGH

This is a recipe for Danish pastry dough where the eggs are replaced with aquafaba. On page 342, there is a recipe that doesn't use legumes. Previously margarine rather than butter was recommended for dough that was rolled out like this one, as it is easier to roll and make perfect slices.

When margarine is rolled into the Danish pastry dough, the first step is to incorporate the fat. The square of margarine is put on one side and then the sides are folded over. The other side is then folded over and the dough is rolled and folded many times to introduce many layers of fat into the dough. When you have learned the technique for rolling you can increase the amount of fat to 500g of margarine. Only roll in two directions and turn the dough over after each time you have chilled it. The folded dough is put horizontally (as in picture 6 but turned through 90 degrees) to be rolled out to look like picture 7. Chill or freeze the flour before starting. For this recipe, you can use strong flour that contains extra gluten. This recipe makes 15–17 pastries.

400–500g	margarine
50g/12g	fresh/dried yeast
300ml	water
100ml	aquafaba or water
45g	sugar
1 tsp	salt
around	
600g	ice-cold strong bread flour

flour, for shaping the dough
cream, for brushing

Cut the margarine into slices of 25g and let it come to room temperature on a piece of baking paper. Roll the slices of margarine into a rectangle; rolling it makes the fat softer, which is an important part of getting all the fat into the dough.

Crumble the yeast into water in a bowl, then add the aquafaba, sugar and salt. Mix everything to a smooth dough with the flour. Add a little flour at a time and work with it for a maximum of 5 minutes in a stand mixer; chill the dough in the fridge for 20 minutes.

Bring the dough out and roll out to a large rectangle of 50 × 90cm. Place the margarine on the right-hand side, fold the right-hand edges over the margarine, and then fold the left-hand side to enclose the margarine (pictures 1–3). Carefully roll to a rectangle of around 50 × 30cm on a well-floured surface (picture 4), then fold three layers together (pictures 5–6). Make a small hole in the dough with your finger so that you can see that you have folded it once. Chill for 20 minutes. Carefully roll out a square of around 50 × 30cm on a floured surface (picture 7), fold three layers together.

Make two small holes in the dough with your fingers so you can see that you have folded it twice. Chill for 20 minutes. Carefully roll out a square of around 50 × 30cm on a floured surface, fold three layers together. Make three small holes in the dough with your fingers so that you can see that you have folded it three times. Chill for 20 minutes. Carefully roll out a rectangle of around 50 × 30cm. After this stage, you can use the dough for different pastries using Danish pastry dough as the base.

Picture 8 shows the making of Danish pastry eights out of long twisted strips of Danish pastry dough. Form the strip of dough like the one at the top. Then fold the top right loop to create a figure of eight with the dough. Press down with a spoon or with your finger before adding the filling.

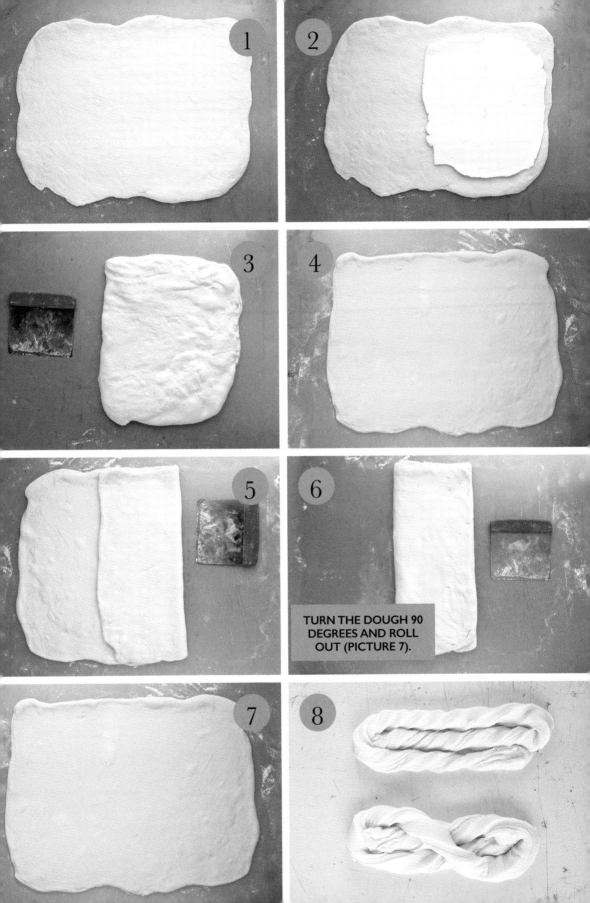

TURN THE DOUGH 90 DEGREES AND ROLL OUT (PICTURE 7).

PAIN AU CHOCOLAT

This is one of my older recipes for pain au chocolat and it was developed from studying many traditional egg-free recipes for Danish pastry dough. If you want, you can use my newer recipe on page 340, but if you want to avoid legumes, this recipe is perfect! It is preferable to use strong flour.

Do not make the pastries too big, either in length or the number of rolls in the dough. They will rise in the oven and if they are too big they will not bake properly. Chill the milk, flour and the bowl before you start. Cut the margarine in thin slices and leave out until they come up to room temperature on a piece of baking paper. This is why you will need to prepare them in advance and take some time to roll out the dough. Make sure you do not roll it out too firmly as the layers of dough between the fat will be too compressed. Unfortunately, this is a matter of practice makes perfect but I cannot think of a better technique to practice and perfect! Read more on how to get the best result for these doughs on pages 340–341. This recipe makes 12–15 pain au chocolats.

200g	room-temperature margarine
25g/6g	fresh/dried yeast
300ml	cold milk
2 tbsp	sugar
1 tsp	salt
2 tbsp	cornstarch
300–420g	ice-cold strong bread flour

100–200g chopped dark chocolate

flour, for shaping the dough
cream, for brushing

Cut the margarine into slices of 25g and let them come to room temperature on a piece of baking paper. Roll the slices of margarine into a rectangle; rolling makes the fat softer, which plays an important part in getting all the fat into the dough.

Crumble the yeast and dissolve in the milk, sugar and salt in a mixing bowl. Add the cornstarch and plain flour and quickly mix to a smooth dough; put it in the fridge for 10 minutes. Bring the dough out and roll out to a large rectangle. Place the margarine on the right-hand side, fold the right-hand edges over the margarine, and then fold the left-hand side to enclose the margarine. Carefully roll out to a rectangle, 1cm thick, on a floured surface. Fold into three layers, folding both ends of the rectangle towards the middle (see pictures 5–6 on page 341), chill for 10 minutes. Roll the dough out again and repeat the process. Chill and fold three times for 20–30 minutes. Roll the dough out to 1cm thick once more, around 30cm wide, and cut lengthways. Cut pieces of around 7 × 15cm for each pastry and roll up with chopped chocolate in the centre. Place on a baking tray. Brush the pastries with cream. Allow to rise for 40–60 minutes at room temperature. Preheat the oven to 225°C/425°F/gas 7. Brush the pastries with cream again and bake in the centre of the oven for 13–15 minutes.

DANISH PASTRIES

Danish pastries are sweet, crisp and creamy all at the same time, and they are simpler and take less time than you might think to bake yourself. It is important to roll the margarine to a rectangle for the best result and when you are used to the technique for rolling, you can increase the amount of fat to 500g of margarine. See the guide on pages 340 and 341. Strong bread flour can also be used here. This recipe makes 15–17 pastries.

400–500g margarine
50g/12g   fresh/dried yeast
300ml   water
100ml   aquafaba or water
45g   sugar
1 tsp   salt
around
600g   ice-cold plain flour

flour, for shaping the dough
cream, for brushing

**ONE LARGE BATCH OF
VANILLA PASTRY CREAM
(SEE PAGE 424)**

Preferably freeze the flour before you start. Cut the margarine into slices of 25g and let them come to room temperature on a piece of baking paper. Roll the slices of margarine into a rectangle; rolling it makes the fat softer which is an important part in getting all of the fat into the dough.

Crumble the yeast into the water, aquafaba or water, sugar and salt in a bowl. Mix everything to a smooth dough with the flour. Add a little plain flour at a time and work with it for a maximum of 5 minutes in a stand mixer; chill the dough in the fridge for 20 minutes.

Bring out the dough and roll out to a large rectangle of 50 × 90cm. Place the margarine on the right-hand side, fold the right-hand edges over the margarine, and then fold the left-hand side to enclose the margarine (pictures 1–3 on page 341). Carefully roll out to a rectangle of around 50 × 30cm on a well-floured surface (picture 4), fold three layers together (pictures 5–6). Make a small hole in the dough with your finger so that you can see that you have folded it once. Chill for 20 minutes. Carefully roll out a rectangle of around 50 × 30cm on a floured surface (picture 7); fold three layers together. Make two small holes in the dough with your fingers so that you can see that you have folded it twice. Chill for 20 minutes. Carefully roll out a rectangle of around 50 × 30cm on a floured surface; fold three layers together. Make three small holes in the dough with your fingers so that you can see that you have folded it three times. Chill for 20 minutes.

Roll the dough out to a rectangle of 50 × 30cm, cut strips 1.5cm wide and twist and fold them. See picture 8 on page 341 for tips on how to fold the Danish pastries easily. Place on a baking tray. Allow to rise for 1–1½ hours until the Danish pastries have risen thoroughly. Preheat the oven to 225°C/425°F/gas 7. Brush with cream and press holes into the dough so that you can pipe in some vanilla cream. Bake in the centre of the oven at 225°C/425°F/gas 7 for 13–15 minutes.

ICING SUGAR GLAZE
180g   icing sugar
2 tbsp   water

Mix the icing sugar and water together in a bowl to a consistency of your liking and drizzle over the cool Danish pastries. Leave to set before serving.

DOUGHNUTS

This recipe makes around 15–20 doughnuts of around 7–8cm. You can double the recipe to make more. Take care not to roll the dough out too thin – thick doughnuts are luxurious doughnuts! The doughnut pyramid on page 349 is made from around 30 doughnuts. Doughnuts should be served fresh, so deep-fry them near to serving. Coconut fat is especially good for deep-frying since it can handle high temperatures and does not add any flavour, but any frying oil will do. 1 litre or around 1kg of fat is enough for a smaller saucepan. The oil can then be reused a few times if it is kept cool. Never pour any of the used coconut oil down the sink as it hardens when cool. It is better to recycle it if possible, or cool in the saucepan and once it is hard put it into a bag in your general waste. That way it will not clog the drains. I really recommend using a thermometer for deep-frying doughnuts, otherwise it is almost impossible to get the oil to the right temperature. Always have a lid ready when deep-frying in case the oil catches fire. Never put water on burning oil, cover with a lid instead. The doughnuts in the picture have been shaken in a bag of icing sugar according to the instructions below. Doughnut glazes can be found on page 348. Instructions for vanilla cream-filled doughnuts can be found on page 425.

100g	margarine
400ml	milk
50g/12g	fresh/dried yeast
45g	sugar
¼ tsp	salt
50ml	oil
1 tsp	baking powder
30g	cornstarch
480–540g	plain flour

Melt the margarine, add the milk and let the mixture cool to lukewarm. Crumble the yeast into a mixing bowl and add the milk mixture, sugar, salt and oil. Mix the baking powder and cornstarch with 60g of the flour and add to the batter. Then add 60g of plain flour at a time and work to a loose dough. If it is too firm, it will not rise to make light doughnuts. Allow to rise for 50–60 minutes, until the dough has doubled in size. Roll the dough out to 2cm thick and cut out doughnuts. Do not make them too thin and make sure that the surface is floured to make it easy to pick up the doughnuts when frying them. Place on a tray. Allow to rise for another 30 minutes. Meanwhile, preheat the oil to 175–180°C/375°C in a heavy-based saucepan. Measure with a thermometer or test a small piece of dough that should turn golden after around 1 minute of frying. I keep the thermometer close by, or attach it to the edge of the saucepan, and always adjust the heat of the hob to make sure I am using the right temperature. Have a plate ready next to the hob with lots of folded kitchen paper. Deep-fry the doughnuts until golden on both sides. Fry the side that was facing up while rising first. Do not put too many doughnuts in the pan at the same time as this will lower the temperature. When cooked, place the doughnuts on the kitchen paper first and then let them cool on a wire rack. If you want to dip the doughnuts in caster sugar or icing sugar, do this when they are still warm. Glazed doughnuts need to be completely cool, then dipped in the glaze and then put on a wire rack to set. Read more about this on page 348.

ICING SUGAR DOUGHNUTS

1	plastic freezer bag
	icing sugar

Put some icing sugar and the warm doughnuts in a freezer bag, 3–4 at a time, and shake the bag until the doughnuts are completely covered. Set aside for a few minutes and repeat a couple of times.

GLAZING SCHOOL

If you want perfectly glazed doughnuts you need to let them cool completely before dipping them in the glaze or spreading the glaze on top. All glazes can be seen in the doughnut pyramid opposite.

THIN ICING SUGAR GLAZE

480–540g	icing sugar
1 tsp	vanilla extract
2 tbsp	glucose syrup
100ml	room-temperature milk

This glaze will give a thin layer on top of the doughnuts. To make a thin chocolate glaze, add a tablespoon or two of sifted cocoa and reduce the icing sugar by the same amount. When using a thin icing sugar glaze, dip in the whole doughnut and let the excess drip down onto a wire rack. You might need to dip it twice if the glaze is too thin.

For a thin glaze, mix all the ingredients together in a bowl until you have a smooth, creamy but runny glaze. It is better to dip the doughnuts twice to get enough glaze all over. Test dip one doughnut before dipping all of them and adjust the thickness of the glaze.

THICK CHOCOLATE GLAZE

50g	chocolate
50ml	boiling water
¼ tsp	salt
1 tsp	syrup
½–1 tsp	vanilla extract
300–360g	icing sugar
1 tbsp	cocoa

Melt the chocolate according to the instructions on page 57. Mix the hot water, salt, syrup, vanilla extract, icing sugar and sifted cocoa in a bowl. Stir in the melted chocolate and then dip in the cooled doughnuts (or spread over a layer cake). If the glaze is too thick, you can increase the amount of water or syrup by 1 teaspoon at a time. If it is too loose, add more icing sugar. Spread the glaze over the doughnuts with a knife or a spatula and let them set on a wire rack.

THICK ICING SUGAR GLAZE

540–600g	icing sugar
1 tsp	vanilla extract
2 tbsp	glucose syrup
100ml	room temperature milk

This glaze is also perfect on top of American cinnamon buns instead of nibbed sugar. For this, use 50g of melted margarine and 50ml of milk instead of just milk. Spread thinly over the cooled buns.

For a thick glaze on top of doughnuts, mix all the ingredients in a bowl to a smooth glaze. The glaze is supposed to be quite thick; you should not be able to dip in the doughnuts. Instead, spread the glaze on top and allow it to even out. If the glaze is too thick, add some more syrup or milk; if it is too thin, increase the amount of icing sugar. Spread the glaze over the doughnuts with a knife or a spatula and let it set on a wire rack.

DIAMONDS

These diamonds were made using royal icing from page 324. They were piped on a piece of baking paper that was put over patterns drawn on a piece of paper. They were then dried for at least 24 hours.

BRIOCHE

Brioche is a light, fluffy French wheat bread, which is higher in fat and softer than other bread, almost like a combination of sponge cake and bread. Work room-temperature margarine into a well-kneaded dough and you will not need too much plain flour to make it smooth. Preferably bake the brioche the night before you want to eat it for breakfast; it can easily rest (covered) in the tin overnight. Temperatures of both 175°C/350°F/gas 4 and 200°C/400°F/gas 6 work for baking brioches; the biggest difference is that at 200°C/400°F/gas 6 they will bake slightly faster and have a slightly darker colour. You can also bake the dough in small tins for brioches and cook at 200°C/400°F/gas 6 for 15–20 minutes (see page 330). Here are two recipes, an older one without aquafaba, and a newer one with aquafaba. Strong bread flour can also be used here.

25g/6g	fresh/dried yeast
50ml	room-temperature milk
150g	room-temperature yoghurt
180–300g	plain flour
½ tsp	salt
½ tsp	baking powder
2 tbsp	sugar
2 tbsp	cornstarch
125g	room-temperature margarine

fat, for greasing the tin
cream, for brushing

Grease a 1.5-litre loaf tin with margarine. Crumble the yeast into a bowl and add the milk and yoghurt, plain flour (start with the smaller amount), salt, baking powder, sugar and cornstarch. Knead the dough in a stand mixer for 5 minutes or 10 minutes by hand, adding as much more plain flour as you need to make a smooth dough. Put the dough in the fridge for 1 hour. Divide the dough into three and roll into balls, then put side by side in the greased loaf tin. You can make a little cut in the top of each ball. Brush the dough with cream and allow to rise for another 30–40 minutes in a warm place – the dough needs to rise a lot. Preheat the oven to 200°C/400°F/gas 6. Brush one more time with cream and then bake in the bottom of the oven for 25–30 minutes. Leave to cool before removing it from the tin.

200ml	milk, cold from the fridge
50ml	aquafaba
25g/6g	fresh/dried yeast
90g	sugar
½ tsp	salt
300–420g	plain flour
150g	room-temperature margarine

fat, for greasing the tin
cream, for brushing

Grease a 2-litre loaf tin with margarine. Mix the milk with the aquafaba, crumbled yeast, sugar and salt. Add the smaller amount of plain flour gradually until you have a slightly firm dough. Knead the dough for 10–15 minutes in a stand mixer or 15–20 minutes by hand, adding as much more plain flour as you need to make a smooth dough. You need to add it gradually as the dough needs more plain flour the more it is kneaded. Dice in the margarine and knead it into the dough. Allow to rise thoroughly for 1–2 hours. Divide the dough into three and roll into balls, then put side by side on the greased loaf tin. You can make a little cut in the top of each bun. Allow to rise again for 30–60 minutes. Preheat the oven to 175°C/350°F/gas 4. Brush the dough with cream and bake in the centre of the oven for 30–40 minutes. Leave to cool before removing it from the tin.

CONCHAS

Conchas is a sweet, soft Mexican bread with a beautiful surface that will crack when the bread is baked. The dough is similar to the brioche and the outside is often flavoured with both cocoa and vanilla. You can colour the dough with colouring for beautiful, luxurious bread. Without the coating, these buns are perfect for hamburgers. In that case, brush them with cream and sprinkle with sesame seeds before baking. Strong bread flour can also be used her.

DOUGH

200ml	milk, cold from the fridge
50ml	aquafaba
25g/6g	fresh/dried yeast
½ tsp	salt
300–420g	plain flour
150g	room-temperature margarine

COATING

125g	room-temperature margarine
120g	icing sugar
150g	plain flour
1 tsp	vanilla sugar or vanilla extract
1 tbsp	cocoa colouring (optional)

Mix the milk with the aquafaba, yeast, sugar and salt in a bowl, and gradually add enough plain flour to make a somewhat firm dough. Then knead the dough for 10–15 minutes in a stand mixer or 15–20 minutes by hand; add as much plain flour as you need to make a smooth dough. You need to add it gradually as the dough needs more plain flour the more it is kneaded. Dice in the margarine and knead it into the dough. Allow to rise thoroughly for 1–2 hours. Meanwhile, prepare the dough for the coating. Mix the margarine with the icing sugar in a bowl and add the flour and vanilla. Knead the dough and if you want different colours for the coating, divide the dough into several pieces. If you want cocoa in all the dough, you can use 1–2 tablespoons of sifted cocoa. Knead the cocoa or colouring into the portion(s) of dough.

Divide the concha dough into 10–12 pieces. Roll each piece into a ball, flatten it out thoroughly, knead one piece of the coating until thin and press it onto the flattened ball of dough. Cut patterns with a knife or a scraper through the coating, but not into the dough. Arrange them on baking paper on two baking trays and allow to rise again for 30–60 minutes. Preheat the oven to 175°C/350°F/gas 4. Bake in the centre of the oven for 20–25 minutes until they have a nice colour.

JAPANESE MILK BREAD

This bread, which is called Hokkaido, was developed in Japan during the 1920s. The dough is made from a thickener, tangzhong (water roux), which makes it elastic, binds the liquid and makes the bread soft. The recipe make two loaves but it is difficult to halve it as the thickener is tricky to make in a smaller batch. If you just want one loaf, you can halve the thickening after cooking it and then halve the rest of the ingredients. In this case, use 150g of thickener for the dough instead of all of it.

You can also divide the dough into six pieces and make three rolls of dough in each tin instead of four as shown opposite. You can halve the amount of sugar if you want your bread less sweet. If the dough is baked as buns of around 60g they are perfect for hamburgers. Brush with cream and sprinkle sesame seeds over them before baking. Both aquafaba and water in the dough give a good result. Strong bread flour can also be used her.

45g	plain flour
100ml	water
150ml	milk
50g/12g	fresh/dried yeast
90g	sugar
½–1 tsp	salt
250ml	milk
100ml	aquafaba or water
650g	plain flour
125g	room temperature margarine
cream, for brushing	

Boil the flour, water and milk together in a saucepan, stirring, to make a thick cream. Remove from the hob and let it cool.

Crumble the yeast into a bowl; you can use both a stand mixer with a dough hook or work it by hand. Add the sugar, salt, milk and aquafaba or water. Add the thickener and some of the flour and start to mix. Add the flour gradually until you have a smooth dough and knead for 5 minutes. Then fold in the margarine and knead for another 10–15 minutes until the fat has been incorporated in the dough. Allow to rise for 40–60 minutes, until the dough has doubled in size.

Grease two smaller loaf tins of around 1.5 litres with margarine. Knead the dough for a minute or two. Divide into four and form into balls, then set aside for another 10–15 minutes. You can also divide the dough into six and make three rolls of dough for each tin. Next, roll out each ball to an oblong oval of around 30 × 15cm. Fold the long sides towards one another so that the oval becomes a rectangle. Roll from the short end to make a thick roll and press together slightly to make it fill half a tin. Repeat with the rest of the balls, and allow the two loaves to rise substantially in the tins for 30–40 minutes. Preheat the oven to 175°C/350°F/gas 4. Brush the loaves with cream and bake for 35–40 minutes until beautifully golden. Let the loaves cool in the tins for 20 minutes before putting them on a wire rack to cool. Ideally wait for the bread to cool completely before slicing it.

BAGELS

Making bagels requires a few extra steps but the result is a nice chewy bread that improves every breakfast, brunch or lunch. Strong bread flour can also be used here.

12 BAGELS

25g/6g	fresh/dried yeast
500ml	lukewarm water
1 tbsp	golden syrup
½ tsp	salt
600–780g	plain flour

24 BAGELS

50g/12g	fresh/dried yeast
1 litre	lukewarm water
2 tbsp	golden syrup
1 tsp	salt
1.2–1.5kg	plain flour

COOKING

2–3 litres	water
2 tbsp	sugar

cream, for brushing

DECORATION

poppy seeds or sesame seeds

Crumble the yeast into a bowl. Add the water, syrup, salt and around half of the flour. Work the dough in a stand mixer or with your hands and add more flour to make a smooth, firm dough; this takes around 5–10 minutes. Cover and allow to rise for 40–60 minutes until doubled in size. Bring the dough out onto a floured surface and divide into 12 or 24 pieces the same size. You can do this in two different ways: either roll a ball and make a hole in the middle that you spread out with your fingers; or roll out each piece to around 30cm in length. Join the ends together to make a ring. Both methods work perfectly. You tend to get larger holes in the middle when rolling lengths. Put the rings on baking paper dusted with flour on baking trays, and make sure that there is enough flour underneath, as you need to be able to move them when fully risen.

Allow to rise for 20 minutes. Preheat the oven to 225°C/425°F/gas 7. Boil the water and sugar together in a wide saucepan. Add 3–4 dough rings and simmer for around 3 minutes. Flip them over a few times. Remove using a slotted spoon or a fork and place on a baking tray covered with baking paper. I usually allow them to sit for a while on kitchen paper so they are not wet underneath when put on the baking paper. Brush with cream and sprinkle seeds over each bagel. Or, if you are quick, you may be able to get the seeds to stick on the top of your bagels when still sticky from the pan. If you dip the bagels into seeds on a plate, you will get more layers of seeds and they will fall off when the bread is handled, which is why it is better to sprinkle over the bread in a single layer. Reduce the oven temperature to 175°C/350°F/gas 4. Bake in the centre of the oven for around 17–20 minutes; the bagels should be slightly golden.

CHOCOLATE BREAD

This bread tastes strongly of cocoa but is not sweet; it goes best with sweet toppings like chocolate spread, nut spread or nut butter. For savoury toppings, the taste of the bread can be too strong. If you want to prepare the bread the day before, put it in the fridge after it has been allowed to rise for 2 hours, cut it before letting it rise again. Bring the bread out of the fridge when preheating the oven in the morning and follow the instructions. I usually make a double batch and bake two loaves of bread. If you can get hold of Dutch cocoa, also called black cocoa, I think this gives the bread the best flavour, but the darkest cocoa you can find also works. You can skip putting the ice in the oven if that makes things too complicated – then you do not need to open the oven at the end. Recipes for chocolate spread and chocolate hazelnut spread can be found on page 260. You get a better result using strong bread flour, but plain flour also works. For simple chocolate rolls that are allowed to rise overnight, add 40g of cocoa and 50ml of water.

10–15g/ 2.5–4g	fresh/dried yeast
300ml	lukewarm water
½–1 tsp	salt
40g	dark cocoa
180–300g	strong bread flour

Crumble the yeast into the lukewarm water in a bowl, add the salt and sifted cocoa and gradually add enough flour to make a slightly firm dough. Knead the dough for 10–15 minutes in a stand mixer or 15–20 minutes by hand, and keep adding more flour to keep the dough smooth. You need to add it gradually as the dough needs more plain flour the more it is kneaded. Cover and allow to rise for 2 hours. When there are only a few minutes left, preheat the oven to 250°C/480°F/gas 9½. Knead the dough for a minute or two and shape into a loaf of bread. Place on a baking tray. Allow to rise for 20–30 minutes. Cut the bread and put it in the centre of the oven. Ideally also put a few pieces of ice at the bottom of the oven – the steam will give the bread a good crust. Bake for 15 minutes, lower the temperature to 150°C/300°F/gas 2 and bake for another 15–20 minutes. Open the oven slightly and let some steam out at the end of the baking time.

OVERNIGHT RAISED ROLLS

I have used this recipe more than any of the others in this book and it originally comes from Martin Johansson's book *Bröd och Pizza* ('Bread and Pizza'). If you are interested in baking bread, Martin's book is a goldmine of information and his methods for making knead-free bread are revolutionary. I have used this dough as the base for my panettone, which can be found in my Christmas book. In my recipe, I skip one rising stage as I realized that they are amazing anyway. I usually make 6–8 rolls, but you can choose to divide the dough into smaller pieces than I do. You can also easily double the recipe. In that case, make sure to use a large bowl as the dough will rise quite a bit overnight. You can dip the top of the rolls in poppy seeds before putting them on the baking tray. You do not need to brush the rolls to make the seeds stick as the dough is already quite sticky. You can use strong bread flour, but plain flour works as well. I usually use 360g of plain flour, but Martin gives the option of 360–420g depending on whether you want a fluffy bread (the smaller amount) or a firmer bread (the larger amount). For the double batch, you need 720–840g.

STANDARD DOUBLE

STANDARD	DOUBLE	
½ tsp	I tsp	fresh/dried yeast
¹/₈ tsp	¼ tsp	
300ml	600ml	cold water
360g	720g	strong bread flour
1½ tsp	2–3 tsp	salt

DECORATION
poppy seeds or sesame seeds (optional)

Dissolve the yeast in the water in a mixing bowl. Add the flour and salt. Mix the dough together, cover and allow to sit overnight at room temperature. When you wake up in the morning, the dough will have risen a lot and become loose.

In the morning, preheat the oven to 250°C 480°F/gas 9½. Remove the dough from the bowl and put it on a floured surface. Try working it with gentle hands to avoid knocking the air out of the dough as much as possible. Divide into 6–8 pieces for the standard batch and 12–16 for the double quantity. You can shape the pieces of dough into balls by pulling the sides together underneath. You can dip them in the seeds before placing them on the baking tray. When the oven has reached the correct temperature, bake the rolls for 10–15 minutes.

In Martin's recipe, the shaped rolls are allowed to rise for 30–40 minutes before baking, but if you work the dough with gentle hands they will also be fluffy with a short rising time, which is the time it takes for the oven to preheat.

Raspberry ice cream (left) and peanut ice cream with strawberry drizzle (below).

Ice cream

My recipes for ice cream are based on Sicilian ice-cream making, where you make a custard from cornstarch which is then mixed with cream, which is called an ice cream base. These recipes contain just the right amount of sugar and fat for freezing without creating ice crystals, and give the perfect balance of flavour on your tongue when it melts. Ice cream made without custard is slightly easier but is always full of ice. Imagine the difference between freezing sugared milk compared to freezing a thick and creamy custard. There are more ice crystals in the first, and if you add the right amount of starch to the cream, the flavour or texture of the starch will not be apparent. Starch is often added to ice cream recipes that include egg yolks, but if the cream is made just using starch there will not be the worry of keeping the cream under 80°C/176°F to avoid ruining it completely – the cream can boil without ruining the ice cream base, which can easily happen in custards based on egg yolks. The starch custard does not need to set to prevent the creation of ice crystals like egg-based custard. However, I think the flavour develops best when the ice cream base is allowed to sit overnight.

I think the best type of starch to use is cornstarch. Potato starch also works and you can use the same amount. Other starches do not give as good a result and I do not recommend using arrowroot in ice cream custard, which is used in some books. Custard made with arrowroot is not as good as starch-based custard and is also sensitive to temperatures just like egg whites, so you need to monitor your custard, which is not necessary when using cornstarch or potato starch.

The recipes in this book all make around 1 litre of ice cream; the fruit ice creams make a little more. If you whip the cream as described in the section about ice cream, without using an ice-cream maker, you will get more than 1 litre of ice cream.

It is important to replace the difference in the amount of fat between plant-based and dairy cream when making vegan ice cream. I have calculated the difference and added the correct amount of fat with neutral-flavoured oil in my recipes. Do not use coconut oil for making ice cream, it is too firm when cold to make a smooth ice cream to make scoops from.

ICE CREAM MAKING

Ice-cream makers

If you were to freeze the ice cream base as it is in the bowl this would not make a creamy ice cream, but a large piece of ice instead! The difference between ice and a creamy ice cream lies in stirring the base all the time and making sure that no large ice crystals are created. There are many different kinds of ice-cream makers that you can invest in if you are an ice cream lover and want to be able to make your own ice cream at home. You should also be aware that it is possible to make ice cream without an ice-cream maker, but it will take a few extra hours and it will not be as airy.

Some ice-cream makers have a bowl that is frozen before use so that it can handle the chilling of the ice cream. If you get yourself an ice-cream maker for your stand mixer you might need to make sure you have got space for it in your freezer. Do not forget to freeze your bowl well in advance of making your ice cream. If you are using a small ice cream bowl for your ice-cream maker, you can use 400ml of milk instead of the 500ml in my recipes. For really small bowls, the recipes can be halved. There are also ice-cream makers with a built-in chiller, but they are often more expensive. They usually chill more effectively, which means that they can make airier ice creams than other types of ice-cream makers. Factory-made ice cream includes a lot more whipped-in air than it is not possible to do at home. This means that home-made ice cream needs to thaw for a good while before serving in scoops. Let the ice cream stand out of the freezer for 10–30 minutes. This is why you should avoid freezing too much in each container, otherwise you will have to bring the container out of the freezer and put it back in a number of times. Thawed ice cream will contain ice crystals when it is put back in the freezer, which means it will not taste as nice once it has thawed and refrozen.

Without an ice-cream maker

You can make ice cream without an ice-cream maker in a number of ways. You need to stir it regularly while it freezes to dissolve any ice crystals – stir a few times an hour for 3–5 hours. When it has the consistency of soft ice cream, you can mix using an electric hand mixer or a hand blender to dissolve the ice crystals before leaving it to harden before serving. Leave the ice cream in the freezer for 1–2 hours after the soft ice cream stage to reach the consistency for scooping. If it is left for longer, it will need to thaw for 10–30 minutes until it is nice and soft again. You can also whip the whipped cream in the recipe, like a parfait. When the ice cream custard is cool, add it carefully and gradually to the whipped cream. Then you freeze it and you do not need to stir it while it is freezing. This will give you a larger quantity and it will be very light and airy.

Tips for easy ice cream making

Glucose is inverted sugar where the sugar molecules are longer, which prevents other sugars that it is mixed with from forming crystals and becoming granular. This characteristic also affects the way ice crystals are created in the ice cream base and gives it a smoother and creamier texture. A couple of teaspoons of alcohol in an ice cream base gives a softer ice cream with a lower freezing point. This is why the ice cream will not be as firm when frozen. Too much alcohol will stop the ice cream from freezing at all, so don't add more than 1–2 tablespoons to your ice cream base. Freeze your ice cream bowl well in advance if it needs to be frozen. Before you start, prepare everything you need so that it is close at hand. Read the recipes and instructions before you start mixing the ingredients. Prepare the ice cream base the day before churning it in the ice-cream maker and the ice cream will taste better.

MILKSHAKE

Ideally freeze the glass for at least 30 minutes before you start. Then pour 200ml of milk and 4–5 scoops of your favourite ice cream into a cup or in a mixer. Mix using a hand blender or a mixer until the milkshake is foamy and well mixed. If you do not add enough ice cream, the milkshake will easily become granular. Add either more ice cream or milk to get the right consistency, mix again and pour into a large glass.

VANILLA
ICE CREAM

Vanilla is one of the most loved ice cream flavours and this is my best recipe. Choose a milk that you like the basic taste of as it will affect your ice cream the most in this particular recipe. I use a sweet soya milk with a mild vanilla flavour. All types of vanilla can be used wherever you see vanilla in the recipe. I usually use $1/8-1/4$ tsp vanilla powder, which is made from pure vanilla seeds. These have a stronger taste, the seeds look attractive in the ice cream and they give a lot of flavour. Vanilla extract is more widely available and is made with alcohol, which makes for a softer ice cream if added in a modest amount. However, vanilla extract should be used carefully as more than a tablespoon could prohibit the ice cream from freezing properly. You can also use 1 teaspoon of vanilla paste or 2 teaspoons of vanilla sugar. Keep tasting until you have a vanilla flavour that is to your liking. The picture shows the brownies from page 272 with vanilla ice cream.

500ml	milk
30g	cornstarch
2 tbsp	glucose syrup (optional)
135g	sugar
50ml	oil (not coconut oil)
1 tsp	vanilla extract
1/8 tsp	salt
250ml	double cream, unwhipped

Heat the milk, cornstarch and glucose, if using, in a saucepan, stirring. Remove from the hob when thickened and add the sugar, oil, vanilla and salt. Let it cool completely and then mix with the unwhipped double cream. Ideally, let the ice cream base sit for 24 hours or overnight in the fridge. Put the base mixture in the ice-cream maker and churn it until the base is ready for the freezer, at the soft ice cream consistency. Then let the ice cream firm up in the freezer for 1–2 hours, until it is perfect for scooping. Bring it out 10–30 minutes before serving if it has been in the freezer for more than a couple of hours.

If you are making ice cream without an ice-cream maker, you can find the instructions on page 364.

STRACCIATELLA
1 batch	vanilla ice cream
100g	dark chocolate

Prepare the ice cream up to the point of the final freezing, then add finely chopped or grated chocolate. You can also melt the chocolate, cool it slightly and add it slowly into the ice-cream maker when the ice cream is ready for freezing.

CHOCOLATE CHIP COOKIE ICE CREAM
1 batch	vanilla ice cream
1 batch	cookie dough (see page 310)

This is a classic luxurious ice cream with chunks of cookie dough in vanilla ice cream. You can also replace the 135g of caster sugar with 150g of soft brown sugar, use vanilla extract instead of powder and add chocolate chips in the ice cream base. This gives an ice cream that tastes of cookies, rather than vanilla ice cream flavoured with cookie dough.

Prepare as for vanilla ice cream up to the point of final freezing, and add chunks of cookie dough.

MISO VANILLA ICE CREAM
1 batch	vanilla ice cream
1–3 tbsp	white miso paste

This recipe was inspired by award-winning baker Nicole Bermensolo and his miso ice cream. Use saikyo miso or shiro miso. Read more about miso paste on page 265.

Add miso paste to taste when making the custard in the instructions for vanilla ice cream above.

FRUIT ICE CREAM

I use a large proportion of fruit in my ice creams; I create a creamy, fruity ice cream that is full of flavour by making sure that the amount of fat and sugar in the ice cream is perfect. Depending on the amount of water in the fruit, you will need different quantities of sugar. The amount of water your fruit contains can vary from year to year, but as a guide, if the fruit or berries become a thick purée when mixed, use the first recipe. If the mixture is soft or watery, use the second recipe. Blueberries, raspberries, sea buckthorn, etc., can be sieved to remove the pips and stems. If you know that you will be sieving the fruit, you can increase the quantity of berries by around 100g. If you are using peaches, apricots or apples, you need to peel and stone/core the fruit.

FRUIT ICE CREAM WITH FIRM FRUIT & BERRIES

500g	prepared fruit or berries
200ml	milk
30g	cornstarch
2 tbsp	glucose syrup (optional)
180g	sugar
100ml	oil (not coconut oil)
1 tsp	vanilla extract
1/8 tsp	salt
250ml	double cream, unwhipped

FRUIT ICE CREAM WITH FRUIT & BERRIES CONTAINING MORE WATER

500g	prepared fruit or berries
200ml	milk
30g	cornstarch
2 tbsp	glucose syrup (optional)
100ml	oil (not coconut oil)
1 tsp	vanilla extract
1/8 tsp	salt
250ml	double cream, unwhipped

Rinse and top and tail or remove the pips or stones (and peel) from the fruit or berries. Blend to a smooth purée. Boil the milk, cornstarch and glucose syrup, if using (and the purée if the berries need to be boiled), in a saucepan, stirring. Remove from the hob when thickened and add the purée (if it has not already been added), sugar, oil, vanilla and salt. Let it cool completely and then mix with the unwhipped double cream. Ideally, let the ice cream base sit for 24 hours or overnight in the fridge. Put in the ice-cream maker and churn it until it is ready for freezing at the soft ice cream stage. Put in the freezer and leave for 1–2 hours, which is when it will be perfect for scooping. Bring out the ice cream 10–30 minutes before serving if it has been in the freezer for more than a couple of hours.

If you are making ice cream without an ice-cream maker, you will find instructions on page 364.

CARAMELIZED BANANA ICE CREAM

2 tbsp	margarine
300g	bananas, mashed
110g	soft brown sugar or muscovado sugar
300ml	milk
30g	cornstarch
2 tbsp	glucose syrup (optional)
50ml	oil (not coconut oil)
1/8 tsp	salt
1 tsp	vanilla extract
250ml	double cream

Heat the margarine in a frying pan on a medium heat and then fry the mashed banana and soft brown sugar for 5–7 minutes until the mixture has come together and reduced slightly. Boil the milk, cornstarch and glucose syrup, if using, in a saucepan, stirring, and remove from the hob when thickened. Add the oil, salt, vanilla and mashed banana mixture and stir to combine. Leave to cool completely and then mix with the double cream. Ideally, let the ice cream base sit for 24 hours or overnight in the fridge. Put in the ice-cream maker and churn it until it is ready for freezing at the soft ice cream stage. Put in the freezer and leave for 1–2 hours, which is when it will be perfect for scooping. Bring out the ice cream 10–30 minutes before serving if it has been in the freezer for more than a couple of hours.

CHERRY ICE CREAM

Cherry ice cream is amazing when you have the right type of cherry. Sweet cherries from grocery shops are good to eat, but don't have much taste and will not make a well-flavoured cherry ice cream. If you have a cherry tree close by, this is an amazing way to preserve the taste of cherries once the cherry season is over. Sour cherries also make fantastic ice cream. In many countries around the world, it is common to go to a fruit farm and pick your own cherries, but this is not the case in Sweden, which is a shame. Depending on how sweet the cherries are, you may need to adjust the quantity of sugar. Taste the ice cream base but remember that when warm this tends to taste sweeter than when it is frozen. Also, make sure you use clean spoons as otherwise enzymes can ruin your ice cream base.

SOUR CHERRIES

500g	sour cherries
200ml	milk
30g	cornstarch
2 tbsp	glucose syrup (optional)
225–270g	sugar, to taste
100ml	oil (not coconut oil)
1 tsp	vanilla extract
$^1/_8$ tsp	salt
250ml	double cream

There are many different sour cherries; amarelles with clear juice and morellos with a coloured juice. If you find sour cherries that are sweet enough to eat, use 225g of sugar. If you find sour cherries that are good enough for cooking, but sufficiently sour that you do not want to eat them as they are, increase the amount of sugar to 270g. If you are making ice cream without an ice-cream maker, you can find the instructions on page 364.

Rinse and remove the stones from the cherries. Blend in a blender or mix with a hand blender to a smooth purée. Boil the milk, cornstarch and glucose syrup, if using, in a saucepan, stirring. Remove from the hob when thickened and add the cherry purée, sugar, oil, vanilla and salt. Let it cool completely and then mix with the double cream. Ideally, let the ice cream base sit for 24 hours or overnight in the fridge. Put the base mixture in the ice-cream maker and churn it until it is ready for freezing at the soft ice cream stage. Put in the freezer and leave it for 1–2 hours, which is when it will be perfect for scooping. Bring out the ice cream 10–30 minutes before serving if it has been in the freezer for more than a couple of hours.

SWEET CHERRIES

500g	sweet cherries
200ml	milk
30g	cornstarch
2 tbsp	glucose syrup (optional)
135–180g	sugar, to taste
100ml	oil (not coconut oil)
1 tsp	vanilla extract
$^1/_8$ tsp	salt
250ml	double cream

Follow the instructions above to make the ice cream.

SWEET
BLACK
CHERRIES

AMARELLES

MORELLOS

CHOCOLATE ICE CREAM

Here are two versions of chocolate ice cream, one darker and one milder. You can also use the recipe for vanilla ice cream and add 20g of cocoa, hot chocolate powder or caramel hot chocolate powder to the custard for an even milder chocolate ice cream.

DARK CHOCOLATE ICE CREAM

500ml	milk
30g	cornstarch
2 tbsp	glucose syrup (optional)
40g	cocoa
50g	dark chocolate
135g	sugar
50ml	oil (not coconut oil)
1/8 tsp	salt
I tsp	vanilla extract
250ml	double cream

For this ice cream, I often use dark sugar with lots of flavour instead of caster.

Boil the milk, cornstarch, glucose, if using, and sifted cocoa, in a saucepan, stirring, and remove from the hob when thickened. Break or chop the chocolate into pieces and add them to the thickened mixture, they will melt in the heat. Add the sugar, oil, salt and vanilla. Let it cool completely and then mix with the double cream. Ideally, let the ice cream base sit for 24 hours or overnight in the fridge. Put the base mixture in the ice-cream maker and churn it until it is ready for freezing at the soft ice cream stage. Put in the freezer and leave for 1–2 hours, which is when it will be perfect for scooping. Bring out the ice cream 10–30 minutes before serving if it has been in the freezer for more than a couple of hours.

If you are making ice cream without an ice-cream maker, you can find the instructions on page 364.

LIGHT CHOCOLATE ICE CREAM

500ml	milk
30g	cornstarch
2 tbsp	glucose syrup (optional)
20g	cocoa
50g	milk/dark chocolate
50ml	oil
135g	sugar
1/8 tsp	salt
I tsp	vanilla extract
250ml	double cream

This light chocolate ice cream is shown in the picture opposite.

Follow the instructions for vanilla ice cream, but add cocoa. Add the pieces of chocolate when the custard has thickened, they will melt in the hot mixture.

CARAMEL ICE CREAM

Salted and burnt caramel makes an amazing base for ice cream. You need to be careful when working with melted caramelized sugar as it can reach over 150°C/300°F and will spit when liquid is added. Are there lumps in your caramel? If you add too much liquid at once, the caramelized sugar will cool too quickly, which will produce lumps. If this happens, you can put the saucepan back on the hob to dissolve the lumps. If there are any lumps left, you can strain them in a metal sieve when it is ready to cool. Fill the saucepan with hot water when you have finished, and the leftover caramel will dissolve. Caramel sauce and burnt caramel sauce both go well with caramel ice cream and can be found on page 236.

180g	sugar
300ml	water
30g	cornstarch
200ml	milk
50ml	oil (not coconut oil)
1 tsp	vanilla extract (optional)
¼–1 tsp	salt, to taste
250ml	double cream

Melt the sugar in a frying pan; start with 45g and keep adding the same amount gradually until all the sugar has melted. Make sure all the sugar has caramelized thoroughly in the frying pan. Carefully add the water and let all the sugar melt again, which can take up to 10 minutes. Add the cornstarch, dissolved in the milk, and boil, stirring. Remove from the hob when thickened and add the oil, vanilla and salt, if using. Let it cool completely and mix with the double cream. Ideally, let the ice cream base sit for 24 hours or overnight in the fridge. Put in the ice-cream maker and churn it until it is ready for freezing at the soft ice cream stage. Put in the freezer and leave for 1–2 hours, which is when it will be perfect for scooping. Bring out the ice cream 10–30 minutes before serving if it has been in the freezer for more than a couple of hours.

If you are making ice cream without an ice-cream maker, you can find the instructions on page 364.

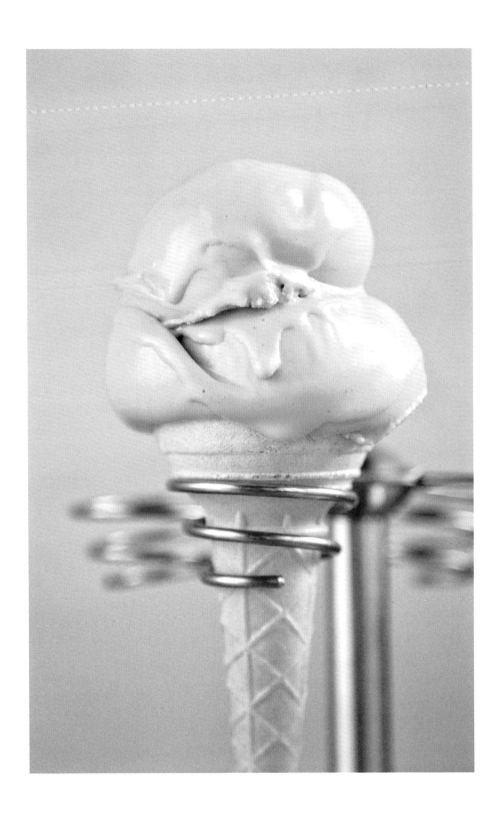

COFFEE
ICE CREAM

I love coffee and everyone who meets me probably sees me with a cup of coffee in my hand. As making a well-flavoured coffee ice cream can be complicated, I have spent extra time to make this recipe perfect. The ice cream is made with ordinary ground coffee powder for coffee makers. You can brew your coffee in a large French press/cafetière as well, if you have one of those. In that case, you will not need to strain it in a sieve before using. Heat the milk until simmering before adding the milk and coffee into your French press, and let it brew for around 10 minutes. Then press it down and pour out the milky coffee.

500ml	milk
30g	ground coffee
30g	cornstarch
2 tbsp	glucose syrup (optional)
135g	sugar
50ml	oil (not coconut oil)
1 tsp	vanilla extract
1/8 tsp	salt
250ml	double cream

Let the milk and coffee simmer in a saucepan, then remove from the hob when the edges are starting to bubble. Cover with a lid and let it brew for 10 minutes. Strain through a sieve and allow to cool. Boil the coffee milk with the cornstarch and glucose syrup, if using, in a saucepan, stirring. Remove from the hob when thickened and add the sugar, oil, vanilla and salt. Let it cool completely and then mix with double cream. Ideally let the ice cream base sit for 24 hours or overnight in the fridge. Put in the ice-cream maker and churn it until it is ready for freezing at the soft ice cream stage. Put in the freezer and leave for 1–2 hours, which is when it will be perfect for scooping. Bring out the ice cream 10–30 minutes before serving if it has been in the freezer for more than a couple of hours.

If you are making ice cream without an ice-cream maker, you can find the instructions on page 364.

RUM & RAISIN
ICE CREAM

As a child, rum and raisin, Stracciatella and pistachio ice creams were my favourites. When I am making my own rum and raisin ice cream, I prefer to use currants instead of raisins as they are smaller and will stay whole in the ice cream for longer. Also, I always add the whole mixture of dried fruit and rum to the ice cream, but you can pick up the fruits and leave any rum that is left for a more light coloured ice cream than the one in the picture. Prepare the raisins, or the currants, the day before making the ice cream.

90–105g	raisins or currants
2 tbsp	rum
500ml	milk
30g	cornstarch
2 tbsp	glucose syrup (optional)
135g	sugar
50ml	oil (not coconut oil)
1 tsp	vanilla extract
1/8 tsp	salt
250ml	double cream

Put the dried fruit and rum in a sealed jar and let them sit overnight. Boil the milk, cornstarch and glucose, if using, in a saucepan, stirring. Remove from the hob when thickened and add the sugar, oil, vanilla and salt. Let it cool completely and then mix with the double cream and the rum mixture. Ideally let the ice cream base sit for 24 hours or overnight in the fridge. Put in the ice-cream maker and churn it until it is ready for freezing at the soft ice cream stage. Put in the freezer and leave for 1–2 hours, which is when it will be perfect for scooping. Bring out the ice cream 10–30 minutes before serving if it has been in the freezer for more than a couple of hours.

If you are making ice cream without an ice-cream maker, you can find the instructions on page 364.

SAFFRON RUM & RAISIN ICE CREAM

1 batch	rum & raisin ice cream (see above)
¼–½ g	saffron

Follow the instructions for rum and raisin ice cream above, but add the saffron to the milk when you cook the custard.

NUT ICE CREAM

PEANUT ICE CREAM

500ml	milk
30g	cornstarch
2 tbsp	glucose syrup (optional)
135g	sugar
100g	peanut butter
1 tsp	vanilla extract
1/8 tsp	salt
250ml	double cream

STRAWBERRY DRIZZLE

50–100g	strawberry jam

To create the classic peanut butter and jelly flavour, drizzle strawberry jam or strawberry compôte through the peanut ice cream when freezing. This is shown on page 362.

Boil the milk, cornstarch and glucose, if using, in a saucepan, stirring. Remove from the hob when thickened and add the sugar, peanut butter, vanilla and salt. Let it cool completely and then mix with the double cream. Ideally let the ice cream base sit for 24 hours or overnight in the fridge. Put in the ice-cream maker and churn it until it is ready for freezing at the soft ice cream stage. Put in the freezer and leave for 1–2 hours, which is when it will be perfect for scooping. Bring out the ice cream 10–30 minutes before serving if it has been in the freezer for more than a couple of hours.

If you are making ice cream without an ice-cream maker, you can find the instructions on page 364.

PISTACHIO ICE CREAM

100g	unsalted pistachio nuts
500ml	milk
30g	cornstarch
2 tbsp	glucose syrup (optional)
135g	sugar
1/8 tsp	salt
250ml	double cream

Roasted pistachio nuts give a strong flavour to this ice cream. The ice cream in the picture opposite does not include any colouring, and has not been sieved, which gives a crunchy texture that I like. Sieve the ice cream base for a smooth ice cream.

Roast the nuts on a baking tray in the oven at 175°C/350°F/gas 4 for 5–6 minutes. Rub the nuts in a clean tea towel to remove as much of the skin as possible. Blitz the nuts in a food processor, or combine the nuts with the milk and mix with a hand blender. Boil the milk, nuts, cornstarch and glucose if using, in a saucepan, stirring and remove from the hob when thickened. Mix the custard until it's as smooth as possible. Add the sugar and salt. Let it cool completely and then mix with the double cream. Ideally let the ice cream base sit for 24 hours or overnight in the fridge. Sieve the ice cream base to remove the larger nut pieces, if you prefer. Put in the ice-cream maker and churn it until it is ready for freezing at the soft ice cream stage. Put in the freezer and leave for 1–2 hours, which is when it will be perfect for scooping. Bring out the ice cream 10–30 minutes before serving if it has been in the freezer for more than a couple of hours.

HAZELNUT ICE CREAM

200g	hazelnuts
500ml	milk
30g	cornstarch
2 tbsp	glucose syrup (optional)
135g	sugar
1/8 tsp	salt
250ml	double cream

When our ice cream machine was delivered from Italy, we received one recipe, and it was for hazelnut ice cream. That says something about how popular hazelnut ice cream is in Italy and this recipe is well worth making if you like hazelnuts.

Follow the instructions for pistachio ice cream above.

382

GINGER ICE CREAM

Freshly grated ginger gives the ice cream a strong ginger flavour. Ginger is an acid and can make the milk split, but the recipe has been developed so you will avoid any mishaps.

45g	fresh ginger
500ml	milk
30g	cornstarch
2 tbsp	glucose syrup (optional)
135g	sugar
50ml	oil (not coconut oil)
1/8 tsp	salt
250ml	double cream

Peel the ginger with a spoon, which will help you remove the skin easily. Then grate the ginger into the milk and heat until simmering. Remove the saucepan from the hob and let the mixture sit for 5 minutes. Strain away the ginger using a sieve and let the milk cool. Boil the ginger milk, cornstarch and glucose syrup, if using, in a saucepan, stirring. Remove from the hob when thickened and add the sugar, oil and salt. Let it cool completely and then mix with the double cream. Ideally let the ice cream base sit for 24 hours or overnight in the fridge. Put in the ice-cream maker and churn it until it is ready for freezing at the soft ice cream stage. Put in the freezer and leave for 1–2 hours, which is when it will be perfect for scooping. Bring out the ice cream 10–30 minutes before serving if it has been in the freezer for more than a couple of hours.

If you are making ice cream without an ice-cream maker, you can find the instructions on page 364.

COCONUT ICE CREAM

This ice cream does not only use coconut milk, but is also flavoured with toasted coconut. This gives a strong coconut flavour, which is well worth the extra effort.

80g	desiccated coconut
100ml	milk
400g	coconut milk (17% fat)
30g	cornstarch
2 tbsp	glucose syrup (optional)
135g	sugar
1/4 tsp	vanilla extract
1 pinch	salt
250ml	double cream

First, toast the desiccated coconut in a dry frying pan on a medium heat until golden. Then bring the milk and coconut milk to the boil in another pan together with the toasted coconut. Remove the saucepan from the hob and let the mixture sit for 5 minutes. Strain away the desiccated coconut using a sieve and let the milk cool. Boil the coconut milk, cornstarch and glucose syrup, if using, in a saucepan, stirring. Remove from the hob when thickened and add the sugar, vanilla extract and salt. Let it cool completely and then mix with the double cream. Ideally let the ice cream base sit for 24 hours or overnight in the fridge. Put in the ice-cream maker and churn it until it is ready for freezing at the soft ice cream stage. Put in the freezer and leave for 1–2 hours, which is when it will be perfect for scooping. Bring out the ice cream 10–30 minutes before serving if it has been in the freezer for more than a couple of hours.

If you are making ice cream without an ice-cream maker, you can find the instructions on page 364.

LEMON ICE CREAM

The tricky thing with making lemon ice cream is getting a nice tart flavour without the cream turning sour. I have used my recipe for lemon curd as a base for this recipe, but you can use any citrus fruit. If you don't have enough citrus juice, you can simply add water until you have 250ml. If you want to make extra curd to ripple into the ice cream, just follow the base recipe for the curd and chill in a jar until the lemon ice cream (or vanilla ice cream rather) has reached the soft ice cream stage.

LEMON CURD

250ml	lemon juice + zest (3–5 unwaxed lemons)
30g	cornstarch
135g	sugar
100g	margarine, diced

ICE CREAM BASE

250ml	milk
1 pinch	salt
250ml	double cream

Start by grating the zest from the lemons, don't include the pith. Then halve and juice the lemons. Set aside 100ml of the lemon juice. Bring the remaining 150ml lemon juice and zest to the boil in a pan. Remove the saucepan from the hob and let the mixture sit for 5 minutes. Strain away the lemon zest using a sieve. Return the strained lemon juice to the pan, add the cornstarch and the sugar and bring to the boil, while stirring, until the mixture has thickened. Remove the pan from the heat and add the diced margarine. Stir until the margarine has melted. Once the curd returns to the boil, stir in the milk and salt to taste. Let it cool completely and then mix with the double cream. Ideally let the ice cream base sit for 24 hours or overnight in the fridge. Put in the ice-cream maker and churn it until it is ready for freezing at the soft ice cream stage. Put in the freezer and leave for 1–2 hours, which is when it will be perfect for scooping. Bring out the ice cream 10–30 minutes before serving if it has been in the freezer for more than a couple of hours.

If you are making ice cream without an ice-cream maker, you can find the instructions on page 364.

TIP!

Buy organic citrus fruit.
We'll be using the zest in
the ice cream and don't
want any pesticides in
there too!

WEIGHTS

You can use rice, beans, peas, sugar or baking beans in ceramic dishes to act as pie weights. Pages 411 and 413 show two different ways to hold these in place, but baking paper, roasting bags or aluminum foil all work to keep the weights in place and make it easy to remove the weights after baking without damaging the pastry. However, be very careful when doing this. You can bake pastry cases without weights, but they stop the pastry from shrinking.

MINI PIES

If you have leftover pie dough you can make mini pies, or tarts like the ones on page 418. Brush the mini pies with cream and sprinkle sugar on top. Bake at 200°C/400°F/gas 6 until golden brown.

PUT A BAKING TRAY UNDER THE PIE DISH TO CATCH ANY FILLING THAT FLOWS OVER THE EDGES.

IF THERE IS A LOT OF LIQUID IN THE FILLING, YOU CAN REMOVE SOME OF IT BEFORE POURING THE FILLING INTO THE PASTRY CASE.

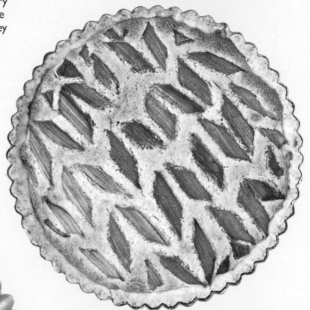

FRANGIPANE PIE WITH RHUBARB

GLUTEN

To avoid the gluten strands in the dough becoming over-developed you can add something acidic, like vinegar or vodka. In my recipes the vinegar can be replaced with vodka.

TWO DIFFERENT PASTRY BLENDERS

Pies

Always use cold margarine and cold plain flour and work the dough as little as possible when making American pies. Use a mixer or a pastry blender to quickly mix the ingredients together. It is important not to overwork pie dough.

If you are having problems rolling out the dough you can roll it between two pieces of baking paper. It might also help to leave it at room temperature for 5–10 minutes before rolling it out. If it is cold from the fridge it cracks easily. Cracked dough is easy to pinch together using your fingers, so cracks are not the end of the world.

Starch that can be used in pie fillings include cornstarch, potato starch, arrowroot or tapioca starch. Cornstarch is good to begin with, but sometimes one of the other starches is better. For apple pie, plain flour is enough. Blueberries and rhubarb work well with potato starch and arrowroot. Strawberries and cherries are extra good with tapioca starch. Test along the way to find the best starch. Always use the same quantity, so if my recipe says use 1 tablespoon of cornstarch, you can try a tablespoon of another type of starch. For fruit containing a lot of water, arrowroot should be increased by 30 per cent.

Sprinkle sugar and plain flour on the bottom of the pie dish before putting in the pie dough.

If your filling bubbles up over the edges, it will burn in the oven. This is why you need to make sure you get as much fruit filling in your pie as possible, but not all of the juice.

American-style pies are best baked in ceramic or glass dishes. Disposable tins made of aluminium foil, which can be found in many grocery shops, are good if you do not have any classic American pie dishes. Metal tins will bake the crust unevenly and the temperature needs to be around 10°C/18°F lower for metal tins. My recipes were developed in metal tins, so when using ceramic or glass dishes the cooking times may need to be increased slightly, or you may need to increase the oven temperature by around 10°C/18°F. Springform tins are needed for both baked and cooled cheesecakes or mousse cakes so that you can remove them from the tin when ready.

Are the edges burning in the oven? The outer edge of a pie tin with a detachable bottom turned upside-down can be placed over the edges of a pie the same size to protect the edges from burning. You can also use a piece of aluminium foil that is a little wider than the pie dish, fold it and cut out a circle that is a little smaller than the pie. This will give you a piece of foil with a hole in the middle that allows the pie to be baked in the middle without being burned at the edges. If you have a baking stone or baking steel (pizza stones/steel) for the oven, use them for baking American pies on, resulting in a perfectly baked pie crust.

CRUMBLES

For blueberry and rhubarb crumble, potato starch is perfect and for most other berries, cornstarch works best. For strawberries, tapioca starch also works really well. For blueberries, strawberries and rhubarb, you use the larger quantity of potato starch; for most other berries and fruits, the smaller quantity is enough. The amount of sugar needed varies depending on how sour your fruits or berries are. The crumble is enough to cover a large pie with a thin layer, but for the larger amount of fruit you can increase the crumble for a thick layer. The picture opposite shows a crumble filled with red rhubarb.

CRUMBLE
180g	plain flour
45g	sugar
½ tsp	salt
125g	margarine
1–2 tbsp	water or aquafaba (optional)

Preheat the oven to 200°C/400°F/gas 6. Mix the flour, sugar and salt in a bowl. Dice in the margarine and rub together to make a crumble. If the dough is too dry, you can add the water or aquafaba, which will make the dough come together nicely. Mix the starch and sugar with the fruit, depending on how sour your fruit is or how much water it contains. Put the fruit in the pie dish. Top with the crumble mixture. Bake in the centre of the oven for 20–25 minutes for a small crumble and for 25–35 minutes for a large crumble or a crumble made with frozen berries.

QUANTITIES FOR THE FILLING
small	large	larger	largest	
200g	500g	700g	1kg	fruit or berries, fresh or frozen
2–3 tsp	1–2 tbsp	2–3 tbsp	3 tbsp	potato starch or cornstarch
2 tbsp	4 tbsp	90g	90–135g	sugar

GLUTEN-FREE CRUMBLE
60g	jowar flour
120g	white rice flour
70g	sugar
100g	margarine
1 tbsp	syrup

OAT CRUMBLE
180g	plain flour
25g	oats
70g	sugar
100g	margarine
1 tbsp	syrup

Replace the flour with white rice flour and use gluten-free oats for a gluten-free oat crumble.

Preheat the oven to 200°C/400°F/gas 6. Mix the flours, oats, if using, and sugar in a bowl. Dice in the margarine and rub together to a form crumble with the syrup. Mix the potato starch and sugar with the berries according to the guide above and depending on how sour your fruit is or how much water it contains. Put the fruit in the pie dish. Top with the crumble mixture. Do not make lumps that are too big since they will not bake thoroughly. Bake in the centre of the oven for 20–25 minutes.

SWEDISH APPLE CAKE

This apple cake from the Skåne region of southern Sweden, can be baked in many different ways, using sweetened rye bread or breadcrumbs, ready-made apple sauce or by making your own apple filling. As a shortcut, you can use both apple sauce and fresh apples for a filling with small pieces of apple and I have included two recipes to choose from. In the picture opposite, the apple cake is served with my vanilla sauce from page 432. You can use many different apple varieties, such as Cox, Pink Lady or Granny Smith or your local variety.

CRUMBLE

500g	sweetened or regular rye bread
150g	margarine
½ tbsp	ground ginger
½ tbsp	ground cinnamon
½ tbsp	ground aniseeds
½ tbsp	ground cardamom
90g	sugar

Preheat the oven to 175°C/350°F/gas 4. Dice the bread. Blitz to small crumbs in a food processor or grate coarsely with a grater. Melt the margarine in a frying pan and fry the breadcrumbs and spices together for 5–6 minutes, until the bread is dry and toasted, stirring regularly. Add the sugar and fry for another couple of minutes.

FILLING VERSION 1

10	apples
180g	sugar
1	lemon, zest and juice
100ml	water

FILLING VERSION 2

2–3	apples
300–400g	apple sauce

Filling version 1

Remove the cores from the apples and cut into pieces. Put the pieces in a saucepan together with the sugar, lemon zest, lemon juice and water. Cover, bring to the boil and simmer on a medium heat until the apples are soft. Mash them with a fork to a coarse purée.

Filling version 2

Remove the cores from the apples and cut into pieces. Mix with the apple sauce.

Grease a pie dish with margarine, put half of the breadcrumbs at the bottom and press down slightly. Fill up with the apple mixture and then cover with the rest of the breadcrumbs. Bake at 175°C/350°F/gas 4 for 25–35 minutes. Serve with vanilla ice cream or vanilla sauce.

COBBLER

Technically a cobbler is a pie with made with scones, or biscuits as they are called in the southern states of the USA, on top of the fruit instead of crumble. For blueberries and rhubarb, potato starch is perfect and for most other berries, cornstarch works best. For strawberries, tapioca starch also works really well. Do not use too much starch in the fruit mixture. The technique of cooking the fruit first was developed by *Cooks Illustrated,* a baking bible from America, to make a perfectly baked filling and topping. If you make a larger quantity of filling in a large tin, you may need to double the quantity of cobbler dough. Choose cream, milk or yoghurt, but only one of them should be used here. The picture opposite shows a pie filling made with strawberries and rhubarb, which is an amazing fruit combination.

QUANTITY OF FILLING

small	large	larger	largest	
200g	500g	700g	1kg	fruit or berries, fresh or frozen
1–2 tsp	2–3 tsp	1–2 tbsp	2–3 tbsp	potato starch or cornstarch
2 tbsp	4 tbsp	90g	90–135g	sugar

COBBLER

75g	cold margarine
180g	plain flour
45g	sugar
1½ tsp	baking powder
1 pinch	salt
125ml/g	cream, milk or yoghurt

Preheat the oven to 200°C/400°F/gas 6. Mix the fruit with the starch and sugar, spread in the tin and bake at 200°C/400°F/gas 6 for 15 minutes.

Rub together the margarine, plain flour, sugar, baking powder and salt in a bowl, by hand, using a pastry blender or in a mixer. When the margarine is well-combined, add the cream, milk or yoghurt a little at a time (you may not need it all) and knead the dough together; do not overwork it, just let it come together as a dough. The cobbler dough should be quite soft but it should not become runny like a cake batter. (If it does become too runny, you can spread it over the fruit and bake it anyway.) Roll the dough out to 2–3cm thick and cut out the cobblers/scones using a round cookie cutter.

Carefully bring the tin of fruit out of the oven. Arrange the scones on top of the fruit, and bake for another 15–20 minutes until the dough has a nice colour. Serve with vanilla sauce or vanilla ice cream.

AMERICAN APPLE PIE

Prepare the filling first so that the apples have time to soften. Cut them thinly so they can be packed together in the tin. I use a lot of apples in my recipe, preferably 2kg, even though I used a 18–20-cm tin, but you can halve the filling. You can also add ¼ teaspoon of ginger as well for a more intense flavour. You can also replace half of the caster sugar with soft brown sugar. Some people think that tapioca starch is better than potato starch, but plain flour also works for apples that are rich in pectin. If you allow the pie to cool for a couple of hours, the slices will hold their shape when cut and look really good.

APPLE FILLING

1.5–2kg	firm, tart apples
135g	sugar
30g	plain flour or potato starch
¼ tsp	grated nutmeg
2 tsp	ground cinnamon

Prepare the filling before the crust. Peel and core the apples, then cut into thin slices. Place the apple slices in a bowl. Add the sugar, potato starch or plain flour and spices on top and mix. Leave to sit while the pastry is being prepared.

This pastry makes enough for a larger pie or two smaller ones. If you have leftover dough, you can save them in the fridge for up to three days or freeze for a few months. You can also make mini pies that are baked at 200°C/400°F/gas 6 until golden.

CLASSIC PASTRY CASE

390g	plain flour
2–3 tbsp	sugar
¼ tsp	salt
225g	cold, diced margarine
50ml	ice-cold water
50ml	apple cider vinegar

margarine, for the pie dish
cream, for brushing
raw cane sugar, for the lid

Make sure the water is ice cold. Mix the flour, sugar and salt in a bowl or mixer. Mix the margarine into the flour mixture using a mixer or a simple pastry blender; you can also work it in quickly using your hands. Mix the water and apple cider vinegar in a glass. When the margarine is the size of peas, add the cold apple cider mixture, 1 tablespoon at a time, until the dough is just mixed together. Divide the dough in half and leave to rest for at least 30 minutes in the fridge, covered in clingfilm or in a sealed container. Preheat the oven to 200°C/400°F/gas 6. Grease the pie dish. Bring out one piece of dough and roll it out thinly so it covers the pie dish; put the pastry into the pie dish. You can roll it out on clingfilm, baking paper or similar so that you can move it easily, but this is usually no problem anyway. Make sure that the pastry fits well in the pie dish. Add the apple filling to the pie dish; if there is a lot of liquid just spoon out the filling and leave some of the liquid in the bowl. Roll out the other half of the pastry and cover the pie with a pastry lid or with strips of pastry. First, cut off any excess around the outside with a knife and pinch the edges together all the way around. When covering with a pastry lid, make small cuts in it to let out the steam. Brush with cream and sprinkle a thin, even layer of sugar on top. Bake in the centre of the oven at 200°C/400°F/gas 6 for 40–70 minutes, depending on the size of the pie and your oven. The pie should be golden when baked. If the pie has a golden colour already after 30–40 minutes, lower the temperature to 150°C/300°F/gas 2 or cover the sides (see page 387) with some aluminium foil, and it will not burn during the rest of its time in the oven.

SOUR CHERRY PIE

CLASSIC PASTRY CASE

390g	plain flour
2–3 tbsp	sugar
¼ tsp	salt
225g	cold, diced margarine
50ml	ice-cold water
50ml	apple cider vinegar

The pastry is enough for a larger pie or two smaller ones. If you have leftovers, you can keep them in the fridge for up to three days or freeze for a few months. You can also make mini pies that are baked at 200°C/400°F/gas 6 until golden.

Make sure the water is ice cold. Mix the flour, sugar and salt in a bowl or mixer. Mix the margarine into the flour mixture using a mixer or a simple pastry blender; you can also work it in quickly using your hands. Mix the water and apple cider vinegar in a glass. When the margarine is the size of peas, add the cold apple cider mixture, 1 tablespoon at a time, until the dough is just mixed together. Divide the dough in half and leave to rest for at least 30 minutes in the fridge, covered in clingfilm or in a sealed container.

CHERRY FILLING

500g	cherries with the stones removed
135g	sugar
2 tbsp	cornstarch
¼ tsp	ground cinnamon
¼ tsp	salt

margarine, for the pie dish
cream, for brushing
raw cane sugar, for the lid

The quantity of filling can be doubled if you have a lot of cherries. During years with a lot of cherries, I usually cook the filling and put it in sterile glass jars so that I can make cherry pie all year round. When using the filling, I put the contents of the jar in a colander and remove any lumps of starch from the syrup. If you are using arrowroot as the starch, you will need to use 3 tablespoons instead of 2.

Grease the pie dish. Bring out one piece of the chilled dough and roll it out thinly so it covers the pie dish; put the pastry into the pie dish. You can roll it out on a piece of clingfilm, baking paper or similar so you can move it around easily, but this is usually no problem anyway. Make sure that the pastry fits well in the pie dish and put it in the fridge again. Now, prepare the cherry filling. Mix the cherries with the sugar, cornstarch or tapioca, cinnamon and salt and let it sit for 10–15 minutes. Meanwhile, preheat the oven to 200°C/400°F/gas 6. Put the filling into the pastry case, leave some of the liquid in the bowl. Roll out the other half of the dough and cover the pie with a pastry lid or with strips of pastry. First, cut off any excess around the outside with a knife and pinch the edges together all the way around. When covering with a pastry lid, make small cuts in it to let out the steam. Brush with cream and sprinkle a thin, even layer of sugar on top. Put a baking tray covered in baking paper in the bottom of the oven if there is a risk of the filling bubbling out over the sides. Bake in the centre of the oven at 200°C/400°F/gas 6 for 60–70 minutes, depending on the size of the pie and your oven. The pie will be slightly golden when baked. If the pie is already golden in colour after 20–30 minutes, you can put the pie in the lower part of the oven and cover with some foil (see page 387) and it will not burn during the rest of its time in the oven. If you allow the baked pie to cool for a couple of hours, the slices will hold their shape when cut.

This is one of my favourite recipes and I really love morello cherries. If you can get hold of dark red sour cherries, try this recipe when the cherries are ripe. Read more about different types of cherries on page 370.

This pie is baked with sour amarello cherries. Amarello juice is clear, not dark red like the morellos that have been used in the rest of the pies on this page. The flavours are not that different. Read more about cherries on page 370.

PEAR PIE

CLASSIC PASTRY CASE

390g	plain flour
2–3 tbsp	sugar
¼ tsp	salt
225g	cold, diced margarine
50ml	ice-cold water
50ml	apple cider vinegar

The pastry is enough for a larger pie or two smaller ones. If you have leftovers, you can save them in the fridge for up to three days, or freeze for a few months. You can also make mini pies that are baked at 200°C/400°F/gas 6 until golden.

Make sure the water is ice cold. Mix the flour, sugar and salt in a bowl or mixer. Mix the margarine into the flour mixture using a mixer or a simple pastry blender; you can also work it in quickly using your hands. Mix the water and apple cider vinegar in a glass. When the margarine is the size of peas, add the cold apple cider mixture, 1 tablespoon at a time, until the dough is just mixed together. Divide the dough in half and leave to rest for at least 30 minutes in the fridge, covered in clingfilm or in a sealed container. Grease the pie dish. Bring out one piece of chilled dough and roll out thinly so it covers the pie dish; put the pastry into the pie dish. You can roll it out on a piece of clingfilm, baking paper or similar so you can move it around easily, but this is usually no problem anyway. Make sure that the pastry fits well in the pie dish and put it in the fridge again.

PEAR FILLING

1kg	pears, peeled, cored and sliced
135g	sugar
40g	soft brown sugar
40g	preferred starch
1 tsp	ground ginger
¼ tsp	ground cinnamon
¼ tsp	grated nutmeg
¼ tsp	salt

margarine, for the pie dish
cream, for brushing
raw cane sugar, for the lid

To thicken the filling you can use whichever type of starch you prefer. Read more about this on page 387.

Preheat the oven to 200°C/400°F/gas 6. Peel and core the pears and slice thinly. Add the sugars, starch and spices to a bowl and add the pears. Mix together thoroughly and spoon into the pastry case. Leave any liquid in the bowl. Roll out the other half of the dough and cover the pie with a pastry lid or with strips of pastry. First, cut off any excess around the outside with a knife and pinch the edges together all the way around. When covering with a pastry lid, make a few cuts in it to let out the steam. Brush with cream and sprinkle a thin, even layer of sugar on top. Put a baking tray covered in baking paper in the bottom of the oven if there is a risk of the filling bubbling out over the sides. Bake in the centre of the oven at 200°C/400°F/gas 6 for 60–70 minutes, depending on the size of the pie and your oven. The pie will be slightly golden when baked. If the pie is already golden after 20–30 minutes, move the pie to the lower part of the oven and cover with foil.

stop

PEACH FILLING

This is another filling that can be used for the classic pastry case opposite. I usually peel peaches with a small knife. If they are really firm, you can use a potato peeler, but you can also blanch them. To do this, make a cross at the bottom of each peach with a knife and let the peaches sit in boiling water for 30–60 seconds until the peel is loose. Transfer to a bowl of ice-cold water for 1 minute. When cool the skins can be slipped off easily. To thicken the filling you can use whichever type of starch you prefer. Read more about this on page 387.

PEACH FILLING

1kg	peaches, peeled, stoned and sliced
2 tbsp	freshly squeezed lemon juice
135g	sugar
40g	soft brown sugar
40g	preferred starch
½ tsp	ground ginger
¼ tsp	ground cinnamon
¼ tsp	grated nutmeg
¼ tsp	salt

margarine, for the pie dish
cream, for brushing
raw cane sugar, for the lid

Prepare the pastry case according to the recipe opposite. Preheat the oven to 200°C/400°F/gas 6. Peel, stone and slice the peaches. Add the lemon juice, sugar, brown sugar, potato starch, spices and salt and mix thoroughly. Put the mixture into the pastry case. Leave the liquid in the bowl. Roll out the other half of the dough and cover the pie with a pastry lid or with strips of pastry. First, cut off any excess around the outside with a knife and pinch the edges together all the way around. When covering with a pastry lid, make small cuts in it to let out the steam. Brush with cream and sprinkle a thin, even layer of sugar on top. Put a baking tray covered in baking paper in the bottom of the oven if there is a risk of the filling bubbling out over the sides. Bake in the centre of the oven at 200°C/400°F/gas 6 for 60–70 minutes, depending on the size of the pie and your oven. The pie should be golden when baked. If the pie is already golden after 20–30 minutes, move the pie to the lower part of the oven, cover with foil and it will not burn during the rest of its time in the oven.

BLUEBERRY PIE

This pastry is enough for a larger pie or two smaller ones. If you have leftover dough, you can keep them in the fridge for up to three days or freeze for a few months. You can also make mini pies that are baked at 200°C/400°F/gas 6 until golden.

CLASSIC PASTRY CASE

390g	plain flour
2–3 tbsp	sugar
¼ tsp	salt
225g	cold, diced margarine
50ml	ice-cold water
50ml	apple cider vinegar

Make sure the water is ice cold. Mix the flour, sugar and salt in a bowl or mixer. Mix the margarine into the flour mixture using a mixer or a simple pastry blender; you can also work it in quickly using your hands. Mix the water and apple cider vinegar in a glass. When the margarine is the size of peas, add the cold apple cider mixture, 1 tablespoon at a time, until the dough is just mixed together. Divide the dough in half and leave to rest for at least 30 minutes in the fridge, covered in clingfilm or in a sealed container.

BLUEBERRY FILLING

850g	blueberries
135g	sugar
2 tbsp	lemon juice
4–5 tbsp	preferred starch
¼ tsp	salt

margarine, for the pie dish
cream, for brushing
raw cane sugar, for the lid

Blueberry pie is best when baked with a lid, with a few small holes for the steam to escape. To thicken the filling, potato starch, arrowroot or tapioca starch are the best options (4–5 tablespoons for each), which is different from most other pies. For a runnier filling, use 2–3 tablespoons of potato starch instead. You can also grate a tart eating apple into the filling and the pectin in the apple will give the filling a firmer consistency.

Preheat the oven to 200°C/400°F/gas 6. Grease the pie dish. Bring out one piece of dough and roll it out thinly to make it cover the pie dish, put the dough into the pie dish. You can roll it out on a piece of clingfilm, baking paper or the like so that you can move it easily but this is usually no problem anyway. Make sure that the pastry fits well in the pie dish and put it back in the fridge. For the filling, mix the blueberries with sugar, lemon juice, cinnamon and potato starch or arrowroot and let sit for 10–15 minutes. Fill, cover and bake as for the peach pie opposite.

FRANGIPANE PIE

Frangipane is a French almond cream, which is the base for many recipes, such as mazarins. In similar recipes for fillings, like this almond filling, the egg is there to act as a stabilizer; here, I have replaced the egg with a mixture of cornstarch and plain flour. If you spread a thin layer of frangipane at the bottom of your pie dish, it will rise in the oven. The pie dish in the picture opposite is around 20cm in diameter and is baked with a small batch of frangipane no. 1. Pie tins measuring 25cm in diameter may need the larger amount of frangipane when using the first recipe. Recipe no. 2 is enough for a larger tin. Recipe no. 1 can be baked with almond paste that has a lower percentage of almonds. When using recipe no. 2 with almond flour, you can change the type of nut and make a pie that has a pistachio or pecan nut filling, for instance. It is important that the margarine for the pie dough is cold, and you can dice the margarine and put it in the freezer to give a better result. A frangipane pie with rhubarb is shown on page 386.

CLASSIC PASTRY CASE

125g	cold margarine
150g	plain flour
1½ tbsp	sugar

Keep the margarine in the freezer for a while before starting. Mix the flour and sugar in a bowl or mixer. Dice in the cold margarine and rub together to make a dough. If you use a mixer or a pastry blender, the dough will not have as much time to warm up, but you can also use your hands. Place the dough in a sealed container and chill in the fridge for at least 30 minutes. Preheat the oven to 200°C/400°F/gas 6. Roll the dough out thinly and put into your pie dish measuring 20–25cm in diameter. Cut off any excess dough. Prick the dough with a fork and blind bake for 10–15 minutes depending, on how thin it is; the crust should have slightly golden edges. Leave to cool.

FRANGIPANE NO. 1

SMALL	LARGE	
150g	200g	almond paste
75g	100g	margarine
1½ tbsp	2 tbsp	sugar
1½ tbsp	2 tbsp	cornstarch
1½ tbsp	2 tbsp	cream
1½ tbsp	2 tbsp	plain flour
1–4	1–4	pieces of fruit

Grate the almond paste and mix with the margarine, sugar, cornstarch, cream and plain flour in a bowl. Make sure that everything is well mixed. Spread out the almond mixture in the cooled pastry case with slightly wet hands. Peel, core/stone and cut the fruit into thin slices (leave berries whole). Spread out sliced fruit like a fan, keeping each fruit together, and put on top of the almond cream. Bake in the centre of the oven at 200°C/400°F/gas 6 for 20–30 minutes, depending on your oven and the size and depth of your pie dish. The pie should be golden when it is ready.

FRANGIPANE NO. 2

50g	margarine
120g	icing sugar
75ml	aquafaba
45g	plain flour
100g	almond flour
1 pinch	salt
1–4	pieces of fruit

Melt the margarine and let it cool slightly. Mix the icing sugar and aquafaba until frothy in a bowl. Carefully fold in the flour, then the almond flour and salt, and finally the melted margarine. Spread the mixture into the cooled pastry case. Peel, core/stone and cut the fruit into thin slices (leave berries whole). Spread out sliced fruit like a fan, keeping each fruit together, and put on top of the almond cream. Bake in the centre of the oven at 200°C/400°F/gas 6 for 20–30 minutes, depending on your oven and the size and depth of your pie dish. The pie should be golden when it is ready.

APPLE BUTTER PIE

Apple butter is a seasoned apple sauce that has been cooked on a low heat for a long time and is creamy and spreadable like butter. Apple butter is good for fillings in layer cakes or served with scones and toast. With its caramel-like flavour, it also makes an amazing filling for pies together with condensed milk. For a darker apple butter, you can use soft brown sugar instead of caster sugar. The pie goes well with both a crushed biscuit base and a pastry case. This type of pie is traditionally baked with eggs in the filling and is thickened for a short time in the oven; this is my veganized method of achieving the same creamy result. The cornstarch is cooked for a short time to a creamy custard, which is then put in the fridge to rest. This method gives the same smooth texture and beautiful surface as a traditionally baked cream pie, which otherwise is difficult to achieve when using cornstarch to thicken. Oven-baked fillings using cornstarch can have slightly transparent edges and an unpleasant taste. In this recipe, you get the best of both taste and texture, while the cornstarch recreates the function of egg in the custard in a slightly different way to produce the same creamy end result. I also use this method in the lime pie on page 408.

APPLE BUTTER

1kg	cooking apples
75ml	apple cider vinegar
300ml	water
270g	sugar
1 tsp	ground cinnamon

Dice the apples, but keep the core and the peel, as they contain pectin that helps to thicken the apple butter. Put in a heavy-based saucepan with the apple cider vinegar and water and simmer on a low heat for 20–40 minutes until the apples are soft. Pass the mixture through a strainer attachment on a stand mixer or press through a sieve to make a smooth apple sauce. When using the strainer, swipe a spatula or a spoon around the inside of the strainer to push through as much apple sauce as possible. Put the sauce back into the heavy-based saucepan. Stir in the sugar and cinnamon and leave to simmer on a low heat for 1–1½ hours without a lid so that the apple butter thickens. Cool a plate in the fridge and drip a teaspoon of apple sauce onto the plate. If the apple butter is thick enough and stays in a blob instead of spreading out into a thin layer, it is ready. Pour into sterilized jars, seal and keep cool.

For this pie use a fully baked pie case, either made with crushed biscuits as on page 408, or with a classic pastry case as on page 406.

APPLE FILLING

200g	apple butter
150ml	cream
250g	sweetened condensed coconut milk
2 tbsp	oil
3 tbsp	cornstarch
1 tbsp	plain flour
½ tsp	ground cinnamon

Bring the apple butter, cream, condensed milk, oil, cornstarch, plain flour and cinnamon to the boil in a saucepan on a medium heat while stirring and then let it simmer for a few minutes, stirring constantly, to make the custard really thick. This may take some time. Pour over the biscuit base or into the pastry case and let it cool before carefully putting it in the fridge for a couple of hours to set. Serve with cream or vanilla ice cream.

LEMON MERINGUE PIE

PASTRY

180g	plain flour
½ tsp	salt
1 tbsp	sugar
150g	cold, diced margarine
2–4 tbsp	ice-cold water

Mix together the flour, salt and sugar in a bowl or mixer. Add the diced margarine and lightly rub in until the margarine is the size of peas; do not mix for too long. Then add 1 tablespoon of ice-cold water at a time until you have a smooth dough. Chill in a sealed container for at least an hour, or for up to 2 days in the fridge. Roll out the dough on a lightly floured surface and lay in the pie dish. Make sure it fits the pie tin and cut off the excess dough. Make a few holes with a fork.

Freeze the pastry-lined pie dish until it is really cold, for at least 20 minutes. Preheat the oven to 175°C/350°F/gas 4. Then line and fill with either aluminium foil or baking paper and baking beans and bake in the centre of the oven for 15 minutes. You can do this without baking beans but the pastry will shrink slightly more. Carefully remove the beans. The easiest way to do this is to wrap the beans up in the foil or paper before lifting them out of the pastry case. Bake for a further 15–20 minutes until the pastry has a nice golden colour.

LEMON FILLING

150ml	lemon juice + zest (3–5 unwaxed lemons)
225g	sugar
150ml	cream
30g	cornstarch
30g	plain flour
175g	margarine, diced
1 pinch	salt

First, grate the zest from the lemons; do not include the pith. Slice the lemons in half and squeeze out the juice. Boil the lemon juice, zest and sugar; strain off the zest from the lemon juice mixture and put the juice back in the saucepan. Mix the cream with the cornstarch and plain flour and add to the citrus syrup. Boil, while stirring, until the mixture thickens. It will take some time before all of the cornstarch and plain flour has properly thickened, but keep stirring until you have a thick cream. The cream will split at first due to the acid citrus syrup but will come together while mixing with the custard. Remove the saucepan from the hob and add the diced margarine and the salt. Stir, or preferably mix using a hand blender, without lifting out the head, so you do not mix air into the lemon cream, until the margarine has completely melted and been incorporated. Then pour into the pastry case.

MERINGUE

135g	sugar
125ml	aquafaba
⅛ tsp	cream of tartar

You will need a sugar thermometer for this. Boil the sugar and 50ml of aquafaba in a saucepan while stirring carefully to stop it from burning at the edges, and allow it to reach 130°C/266°F. Meanwhile, mix the remaining 75ml of aquafaba and the cream of tartar to a firm foam in a bowl. Add this to the hot mixture, a little at a time, and mix until the meringue cools slightly and is very firm. Pipe or spoon the meringue over the pie. Brown with a chef's blowtorch to get a nice colour or bake at in a preheated oven at 250°C/480°F/gas 9½ for 3–5 minutes until the meringue has a nice colour.

TARTE
AU CITRON

If you want a simple lemon pie, you can skip the meringue and serve the pie with whipped cream.

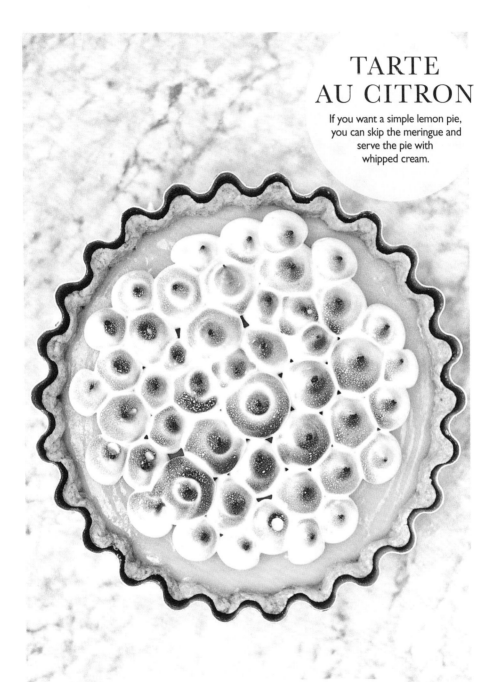

If you do not have a hand blender or a blender, it might be better to reduce the amount of fat in the lemon curd because it is more difficult to get a perfect emulsion using a hand whisk; 150g of margarine is enough. The pie will be slightly softer.

LIME PIE

I love baking with citrus fruit, and when you mix lime juice with condensed milk, something amazing happens to the flavour and the texture, which I suppose is why this pie is so popular. In most traditional recipes from the southern states of America this pie is baked, but I have not managed to make that method work for a vegan version. Here, the thickening function of the egg is hard to replicate as the pie is supposed to be in the oven for a very short time for the custard to firm up. Read more about my technique for recreating cream pies on page 404. The pie is affected by the type of condensed milk you use and how caramelized and condensed it is, but all the versions I have tried make good pies. Some produce a pie that is darker in colour but they are just as good. If you cannot find condensed milk you can make lime pie from the lemon meringue pie filling on page 406 and replace the lemon zest and juice with lime. The pie needs to chill for a couple of hours in the fridge, preferably overnight, to set. Prepare your pie well in advance.

BISCUIT BASE

| 150g | digestive biscuits |
| 50g | margarine |

Preheat the oven to 175°C/350°F/gas 4. Crumble or crush the biscuits for the base and mix with margarine. Press the crumbs evenly over the base and sides of a springform tin and bake in the centre of the oven for 10–15 minutes. Leave to cool.

LIME FILLING

150ml	lime juice + zest (4–6 limes)
150ml	cream
250g	sweetened condensed coconut milk
2 tbsp	oil
4 tbsp	cornstarch
1 tbsp	plain flour

First, grate the zest from the limes, but do not include pith. Squeeze the juice from the limes and measure out 150ml of juice. Let the zest soak in the lime juice for at least 30 minutes. Bring the cream, condensed milk, oil, 3 tablespoons of cornstarch and the flour to the boil in a saucepan on a medium heat, while stirring. Then let the mixture simmer for a few minutes on a low heat, while stirring constantly, so that it can thicken properly. This will take a little while but keep stirring until the mixture has thickened, and then remove from the hob.

Strain the lime juice through a sieve into a container to remove the zest; add the remaining tablespoon of cornstarch before putting the juice into the saucepan. Combine the two mixtures well while stirring carefully on a low heat. At first, the reaction between the condensed milk and the lime juice will create a lot of foam. Let it simmer again while stirring for a short while after adding the liquid until it thickens again. Then pour it over the biscuit base and let it cool before carefully putting it in the fridge for at least 8 hours to firm up. Serve with whipped cream.

WHIPPED CREAM

To make a firm whipping cream for serving with pies and chocolate recipes, or for using in layer cakes and semlor, you need to whip the double cream slightly. When it is starting to increase in size, add a few drops of something acid, like lemon juice or a light, mild vinegar, such as white wine vinegar or apple cider vinegar. You can add up to a teaspoon if it tastes okay, so just add to taste. After adding the acid, whip thoroughly for several minutes. If you add the acid right at the start, the cream might go hard and not whip properly. Some whipping creams can get too stiff when using this method, so keep an eye on the cream while you whip it to make sure you get the result you want.

PASSION FRUIT PIE

PASTRY CASE
180g — plain flour
¼–½ tsp — salt
1 tbsp — sugar
150g — margarine, diced
2–4 tbsp — ice-cold water

Mix together the flour, salt and sugar in a bowl. Add the diced margarine and lightly rub in until the margarine is the size of peas; do not mix for too long. Then add 1 tablespoon of ice-cold water at a time until you have a smooth dough. Chill in a sealed container for at least an hour, or for up to 2 days in the fridge (1). Roll out the dough on a lightly floured surface and lay in the pie dish. Make sure it fits the pie tin and cut of the excess dough. Make a few holes with a fork (2).

Freeze the pastry-lined pie dish until it is really cold, for at least 20 minutes. Preheat the oven to 175°C/350°F/gas 4. Then line and fill with either aluminium foil or baking paper and pie weights (3) and bake in the centre of the oven for 15 minutes (4). You can do this without baking beans but the pastry will shrink slightly more. Carefully remove the weights. The easiest way to do this is to wrap the weights up in the foil or paper before lifting them out of the pastry case. Bake for a further 15–20 minutes until the pastry has a nice golden colour (5).

PASSION FRUIT FILLING
250g — passion fruit pulp (with seeds)
180g — sugar
100ml — cream
30g — cornstarch
30g — plain flour
1 pinch — salt,
150g — margarine

Strain the seeds out of the passion fruit pulp and keep them in the fridge if you want to stir them in once the filling has been made. If the seeds remain, you cannot mix it properly and it is difficult to get it really smooth. Heat the passion fruit pulp, sugar, cream, cornstarch, flour and salt in a saucepan. The cream may split but will come together again while the filling thickens. Bring to the boil, while stirring, until the mixture has thickened. It will take some time before all the cornstarch and plain flour has thickened properly, but keep stirring until you have a thick filling. Stir, or preferably mix using a hand blender, without lifting out the head, so you do not mix air into the filling, until the margarine has completely melted and been incorporated. Stir in some of the seeds if you like. Then pour into the pastry and leave to set in the fridge for at least 6–8 hours (6).

Decorate with whipped cream or meringue (see page 406). In the picture opposite I have used a St Honoré nozzle (7) and Italian meringue (8). I browned the meringue with a chef's blowtorch to give it a nice colour (9).

NO HAND BLENDER?
If you do not have a hand blender or a blender, it might be better to reduce the amount of fat in the lemon curd because it is more difficult to get a perfect emulsion using a hand whisk; 125g of margarine is enough. The pie will be slightly softer.

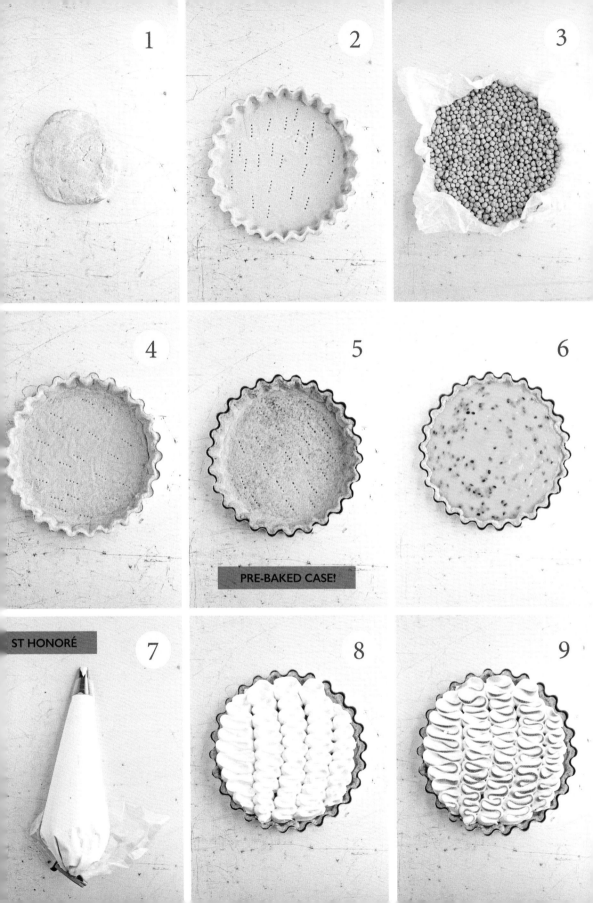

1

2

3

4

5

PRE-BAKED CASE!

ST HONORÉ

7

8

9

STRAWBERRY PIE

The wonderful baker Erin McDowell was my inspiration for this strawberry pie. Despite using 1.5kg of strawberries, you end up with a fairly small amount of filling, so don't use a pie tin that is too big. The tin in the pictures opposite is around 20cm in diameter. Erin roasts the strawberries at 135°C/275°F, so if you can set your oven digitally you can use this temperature instead. Citrus zest added to the strawberries is optional, but I usually go for lime zest. The filling is very sweet, so a slightly sour cream goes perfectly with the roasted strawberry filling. If your strawberries become very firm after they have been roasted, you don't have to bake the pie; in that case, prepare a ready-baked pie crust according to the instructions on page 410. For frozen strawberries you may need to increase the roasting time to around 3 hours.

CLASSIC PASTRY CASE

210g	plain flour
1–2 tbsp	sugar
¼–½ tsp	salt
100g	margarine, diced
25ml	ice-cold water
25ml	cider vinegar
	soft fat, for greasing

Make sure you have your ice-cold water handy. Mix the flour, sugar and salt in a bowl. Dice the margarine into the flour mixture using a food processor or a pastry blender; you can also work quickly using your hands. Make sure the margarine is well distributed. Mix together the water and cider vinegar in a glass. When the margarine is the size of peas, add the cold cider vinegar mixture, 1 tablespoon at a time, until the dough just comes together. Divide the dough in half and leave to rest for at least 30 minutes in the fridge, wrapped in clingfilm or in an airtight container. Preheat the oven to 225°C/425°F/gas 7. Grease the pie tin. Take out your dough and roll it out until it is thin enough to cover the pie tin; transfer the dough to the greased pie tin. Make sure that the dough sits flush with the pie dish and prick the base with a fork. Place the tin back in the fridge (1). Place baking paper, aluminium foil or a roasting bag into the tin (2) and fill with ceramic baking beans, dry beans, dry peas or dry rice (3). Bake the crust with baking beans for 15–20 minutes at 225°C/425°F/gas 7, then remove them carefully (4). Return the pastry to the oven for a further 5–10 minutes or until the base is no longer moist or transparent (5).

STRAWBERRY FILLING

1.5kg	fresh strawberries, hulled
90g	sugar
1 lime	zest
1 tsp	vanilla extract
¼–½ tsp	salt

Preheat the oven to 150°C/300°F/gas 2. Cut the strawberries into chunks: cut the large ones into quarters, smaller ones in half and leave the smallest ones whole. Mix together the sugar, lime zest, vanilla and salt in a bowl and then mix together with the fruit. Spread out the fruit on a large, clean baking tray and bake in the centre of the oven at 150°C/300°F/gas 2 for 2–3 hours. I set a timer for 1 hour and stir every time the timer sounds for the first two hours. Keep an eye on them after that: you don't want them to become too dark and dry. My strawberries usually take 2½ hours, but if your oven is hotter they could be done more quickly, so set an alarm for 20 minutes after they have been in the oven for 2 hours, and repeat if they're not done. In pictures 6 and 7 you can see an example of what they should look like – there should still be some juice. When you are ready to bake your pie, preheat the oven to 200°C/400°F/gas 6. Fill the cooled pastry case with strawberry filling (7) and bake for 20–25 minutes (8). The pie shown was decorated with whipping cream piped using a St Honoré nozzle (see page 225) (9).

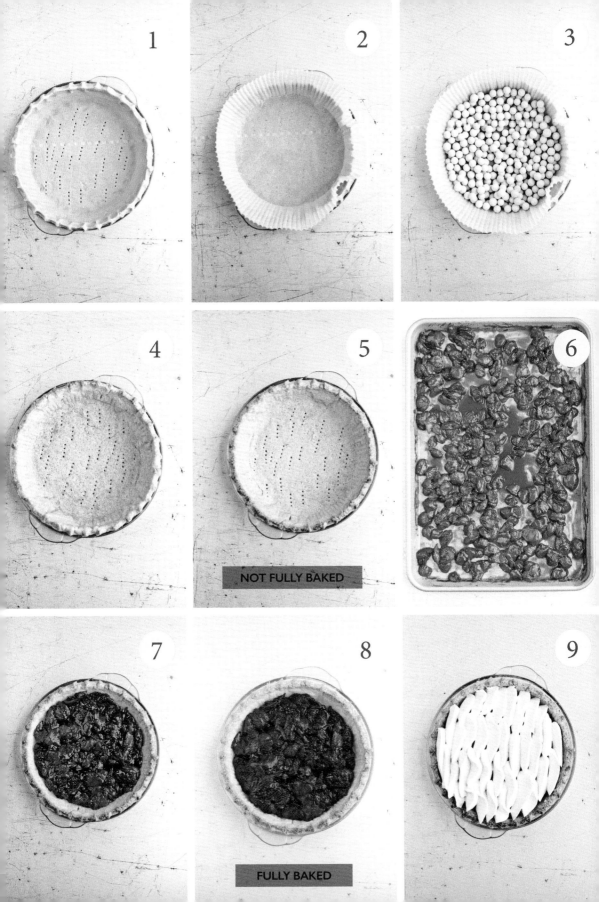

NOT FULLY BAKED

FULLY BAKED

MOUSSE CAKES

In Sweden, chilled mousse cakes are often called cheesecakes even when they have been made without cream cheese. My chilled mousse cakes include plant-based cream cheese, but if you cannot find cream cheese or want to make classic mousse cakes, the fruit mousses on page 234 can be used for this. Use room temperature ingredients, otherwise the agar jelly will set when the fruit purée is added. Chilled cheesecakes need to set overnight, but after they have been kept in the fridge for more than 1–2 days the acid starts to dissolve the gelling agent. Do not prepare them too far in advance before serving. The recipes are designed for springform tins of 20–25cm in diameter. You can easily substitute gluten-free digestive biscuits to make the cake gluten free.

MOUSSE CAKE

BISCUIT BASE
200g	digestive biscuits
100g	margarine

FILLING
300g	unsweetened fruit purée
200g	room-temperature cream cheese
90g	sugar
200ml	cream
2 tsp	agar powder

Preheat the oven to 175°C/350°F/gas 4. Crumble or crush the biscuits for the base and mix with margarine. Press the crumbs evenly over the base and sides of a springform tin and bake in the centre of the oven for 10–15 minutes. Leave to cool.

For the filling, mix the fruit purée (sieved if you would like a completely smooth mousse cake) with the cream cheese in a bowl and let the mixture come up to room temperature if any of the ingredients have been cold. Mix the sugar, cream and agar powder in a saucepan, bring to the boil and then remove from the hob. Add one ladleful of the fruit mixture at a time, until everything is combined and then pour the mixture over the base straight away. You can easily make patterns in the cake before the mousse sets. Chill in the fridge for at least 3–4 hours, and preferably overnight. For cutting perfect slices, rinse your knife in hot water between slices.

COLD BANANA CHEESECAKE

BISCUIT BASE
200g	digestive biscuits
100g	margarine

FILLING
100g	mashed bananas
200g	room-temperature cream cheese
90g	sugar
300ml	cream
1½ tsp	agar powder

This recipe comes from a book I wrote back in 2011 and is inspired by the Hummingbird Bakery's banana cheesecake.

Crumble or crush the biscuits for the base and mix with margarine. Press the crumbs into a springform tin. Press the crumbs evenly over the base and sides of a springform tin. Set aside.

For the banana mousse filling, mix the mashed banana with the cream cheese in a bowl; it is important that the mixture is room temperature. Mix the sugar, cream and agar powder in a saucepan, bring to the boil, stirring, and then simmer for a minute or two on a low heat while stirring, then remove the saucepan from the hob. Add one ladleful of banana mixture at a time, stirring, until everything is combined and then pour the mixture over the biscuit base. Put in the fridge for at least 3–4 hours, and preferably overnight.

HEART PATTERNS
You can easily create heart-shaped patterns in mousse cakes with a runny batter. Use several drops of a liquid of another colour, for instance, fruit purée or ganache, and swipe a thin tool (like a shewer) through the drops to create hearts.

CHEESECAKE

A really good cheesecake requires several things: a good cream cheese and waiting at least 8 hours for the pie to firm up and for the flavour to develop. While we are all waiting for more good vegan cream cheeses to become available, I have included ths recipe as it is an amazing base to work with when you have one. When I developed my cheesecake recipes, I devoted a whole summer to test baking and reading everything I could find on the subject. For a firmer cheesecake or when baking with a soft cream cheese, the smaller quantity of cream or yoghurt is enough. I like a really creamy cheesecake and often use the larger amount.

SMALLER BISCUIT BASE

| 150g | digestive biscuits |
| 50g | margarine |

CREAM CHEESE FILLING

400g	cream cheese
120g	icing sugar
1 tbsp	lemon juice
150–200g/ml	yoghurt or cream
2 tbsp	plain flour
2 tbsp	cornstarch
1 tsp	vanilla extract
1 pinch	salt

LARGER BISCUIT BASE

| 200g | digestive biscuits |
| 75g | margarine |

CREAM CHEESE FILLING

600g	cream cheese
120g	icing sugar
2 tbsp	lemon juice
200–300g/mg	yoghurt or cream
30g	plain flour
30g	cornstarch
2 tsp	vanilla extract
1 pinch	salt

Preheat the oven to 175°C/350°F/gas 4. Crumble or crush the biscuits for the base and mix with margarine. Press the crumbs evenly over the base and sides of a springform tin and bake in the centre of the oven for 10–15 minutes.

Lower the temperature of the oven to 150°C/300°F/gas 2. For the filling, mix the cream cheese, icing sugar and lemon juice in a bowl. Add the yoghurt or cream, plain flour, cornstarch, vanilla extract and salt and mix until smooth. Pour the filling over the biscuit base and bake in the lower part of the oven at 150°C/300°F/gas 2 (see below for baking times). Leave to cool and then allow to set in the fridge for at least a couple of hours, or preferably overnight. For cutting perfect slices, rinse your knife in hot water between slices.

For a gluten-free cheesecake, use gluten-free digestive biscuits and replace the flour with the same quantity of cornstarch.

TINS & BAKING TIMES
Below, suitable tins for different quantities of batter are given, together with the relevant baking times.

20cm: smaller amount = 70–80 minutes
22–25cm: smaller amount = 50–60 minutes
22–25cm: larger amount = 70–80 minutes

The picture just above shows a cheesecake with the smaller amount of filling, baked in a tin 22cm in diameter. In the cheesecake top right, thinly sliced peaches have been pushed into the batter. You can also add 50–60g of blueberries on top of the batter before baking, or mix them into the batter for a blueberry cheesecake.

PUFF PASTRY TARTS

Tarts are the perfect dessert as you can make them quickly and easily using ready-made puff pastry. Puff pastry is usually vegan – read the contents to make sure it does not contain butter. I think chilled ready-rolled pastry is the easiest to work with as you do not have to thaw them or roll them out, but you can also find them frozen.

You can just use fruit but you can also add almond paste (see page 402) or apple sauce at the bottom to make the pie a little more elaborate. In the picture below, blueberry tarts are served with the strawberry ice cream from page 368. You can mix your fruit and berries with a few teaspoons of sugar and a tablespoon or two of melted margarine before putting them on the puff pastry. Do not make it too much like a sauce – the berries are just supposed to be covered by a little sugar that sticks to the fruit. When using apples, pears, peaches and bananas, make sure you slice them thinly so the fruit has time to bake through.

Opposite, I have shown simple instructions for making beautiful mini pies from puff pastry. You can see how to cut, fold, press, brush with cream and sugar the pies. In the pictures below, the edges are simply folded. in around the filling. In the text below there are instructions for a third version where you cut two layers for each pie, one for the bottom and one for the sides.

ready-made puff pastry
prepared raw fruit or berries
a little sugar and cooking fat
almond filling or apple sauce
(optional)
cream
sugar, for sprinkling

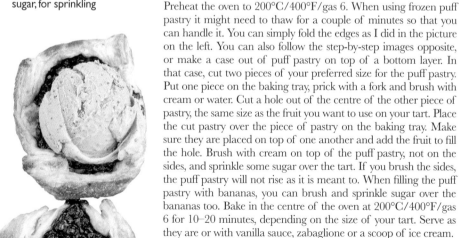

The recipe does not include quantities as these will vary depending on what kind of puff pastry, fruit and method you are using. For the blueberry tarts left, I did not use any filling, apart from the blueberries, and I folded the edges instead of using two layers of puff pastry.

Preheat the oven to 200°C/400°F/gas 6. When using frozen puff pastry it might need to thaw for a couple of minutes so that you can handle it. You can simply fold the edges as I did in the picture on the left. You can also follow the step-by-step images opposite, or make a case out of puff pastry on top of a bottom layer. In that case, cut two pieces of your preferred size for the puff pastry. Put one piece on the baking tray, prick with a fork and brush with cream or water. Cut a hole out of the centre of the other piece of pastry, the same size as the fruit you want to use on your tart. Place the cut pastry over the piece of pastry on the baking tray. Make sure they are placed on top of one another and add the fruit to fill the hole. Brush with cream on top of the puff pastry, not on the sides, and sprinkle some sugar over the tart. If you brush the sides, the puff pastry will not rise as it is meant to. When filling the puff pastry with bananas, you can brush and sprinkle sugar over the bananas too. Bake in the centre of the oven at 200°C/400°F/gas 6 for 10–20 minutes, depending on the size of your tart. Serve as they are or with vanilla sauce, zabaglione or a scoop of ice cream.

TARTE TATIN

Tart tatin is the perfect dessert as you can make them quickly and easily using ready-made puff pastry. Puff pastry is usually vegan – read the contents to make sure it does not contain butter. I think chilled ready-rolled pastry is the easiest to work with as you do not have to thaw them or roll them out, but you can also find them frozen. In the picture opposite, the puff pastry tarte has been turned upside-down, but it is baked with the puff pastry lid on top of the caramelized fruits and is then turned out like this for serving.

TARTE TATIN WITH APPLES

5	eating apples
2 tbsp	sugar
75g	margarine
1 pinch	salt
250–400g	puff pastry

Use a metal frying pan that can be baked in the oven. Preheat the oven to 175°C/350°F/gas 4. Peel the apples and remove the cores. Cut the apples in half if they are small, or into thicker pieces for larger apples. Heat the sugar in the frying pan until all the sugar has melted and caramelized slightly, being careful not to let it burn. Remove from the hob and carefully add the margarine, salt and the pieces of apple and let it cook for 10–15 minutes. Remove from the heat. Cover with the puff pastry and fold the edges in towards the apples in the frying pan. Cut a small cross or make a few holes in the puff pastry with a fork or skewer. Bake for 25–30 minutes until the puff pastry has risen and looks well baked. Bring the tarte out of the oven and carefully invert it onto a plate.

TARTE TATIN WITH BANANA

TARTE TATIN WITH BANANA

90g	sugar
50g	margarine
1 pinch	salt
4–5	firm bananas
1 tsp	vanilla extract
250–400g	puff pastry

Use a metal frying pan that can be baked in the oven. Preheat the oven to 175°C/350°F/gas 4. Heat the sugar in the frying pan until all the sugar has melted and caramelized slightly, being careful not to let it burn. Remove from the hob and carefully add the margarine and salt. When everything is melted, peel and slice the bananas into 2cm rounds or lengthways, and place them in the frying pan. Sprinkle vanilla on top. Remove from the heat. Cover with the puff pastry and tuck the edges in towards the bananas in the frying pan. Cut a small cross or make a few holes in the puff pastry with a fork or skewer. Bake as above.

BUN
Filled with vanilla pastry cream coloured using yellow colouring powder.

DOUGH-NUT
Filled with vanilla pastry cream without yellow colouring.

Creams & sauces

Here are my best recipes for pastry creams, custards and sauces. Many creams use cream as a base. Usually, I use cream made from soya because I think it tastes the best. Unfortunately, some plant-based creams are not as good for cooking or sauces, such as some oat creams. Test different versions and find one that you like as there are many good brands available today made from different products, such as soya, oats, coconut and almonds.

Sprinkle some sugar over the surface of a pastry cream if you want it to cool without forming a skin; you can also cover it with clingfilm.

PASTRY CREAMS

As opposed to classic recipes for sauces and pastry creams that include egg yolk as the stabilizer, you do not need to worry about the sauces boiling and coagulating. When using starch, the mixture can boil and you know that it is ready when it is properly thickened, the bubbles created while stirring have gone and the custard is thick and smooth. You can add a pinch of yellow colouring powder to give the same colour as custards made with egg yolks. Cornstarch, as used here, needs to boil for a minute or two to thicken and should be removed from the hob after that. I use starch to make a creamy custard for my vanilla pastry cream and vanilla sauce, but I also replace the fat that is missing from the egg yolk and the cream, which has a lower percentage of fat than dairy cream, with oil. This makes my recipes just as creamy as when using dairy cream. Usually, I use cream made from soya because I think it tastes the best. Unfortunately, some plant-based creams are not as good for cooking or sauces, such as some oat creams. Test different versions and find one that you like as there are many good brands available today.

VANILLA (SMALL)

200ml	cream
2 tbsp	oil
2 tbsp	sugar
2 tbsp	cornstarch
2 tbsp	water
½ tsp	vanilla extract
I pinch	salt
I pinch	yellow colouring

VANILLA (LARGE)

300ml	cream
50ml	oil
45g	sugar
30g	cornstarch
50ml	water
½ tsp	vanilla extract
I pinch	salt
I pinch	yellow colouring

The small quantity of cream is enough for layer cakes and fillings for biskvis, while the large quantity is enough for Danish pastries and cream buns.

Bring the cream, oil and sugar to the boil in a saucepan, add the cornstarch dissolved in the water and simmer the mixture, stirring, until thickened. Remove the saucepan from the hob and add the vanilla, salt and yellow colouring if using. Leave to cool before use. Cover the surface with clingfilm or sprinkle over some sugar if the cream is chilled.

TONKA BEAN PASTRY CREAM

For the tonka bean pastry cream, follow the instructions for vanilla cream, but add 2–3 grated tonka beans with the other ingredients before heating the cream. Tonka bean cream goes well in biskvis, cream cakes, marzipan cakes and in cream buns.

BLUEBERRY PASTRY CREAM

200ml	cream
100g	blueberries
50ml	oil
45g	sugar
30g	cornstarch
50ml	water
½ tsp	vanilla extract
I pinch	salt

Both fresh and frozen blueberries can be used here and the pastry cream goes well with both cream buns and biskvis, and for filling layer cakes.

Bring the cream, oil and sugar to the boil in a saucepan, add the cornstarch dissolved in the water and simmer the mixture, stirring, until thickened. Remove the saucepan from the hob and add the vanilla and salt. Leave to cool before use; the flavour is better if left overnight. Cover the surface with clingfilm or sprinkle over some sugar if the cream is chilled.

DOUGHNUTS

These round doughnuts were deep fried and allowed to cool before being rolled in sugar and filled with vanilla pastry cream. You can use a nozzle to reach the centre, but you can also insert a little knife into the bun, wriggle it around a little and then use a normal round nozzle.

PETITS POTS DE CRÈME

This classic cream dessert has, as the name reveals, a French origin. Petits pots de crème, or petit pots au chocolat, are small, single servings made with cream and baked in a water bath. In this recipe, I have replaced the thickening function of the egg yolk with starch that has the same baking characteristics. I have also added some oil to replace the fat from the egg yolks. Use good quality cream and chocolate that you like the basic taste of as both will add flavour to your dessert. The quantity of sugar is adjusted to your taste and will depend on the sweetness of your cream and chocolate. The recipe below gives around 400ml of mixture, and if you want a larger quantity, the batch can be doubled. I usually make them in small glass jars, and as a guide the mixture here is usually enough for three small baby food jars, or two slightly bigger baby food jars. The water that the jars are baked in needs to come up as far as possible around the sides of the jars. The water will not boil, which means you can fill it a lot. The taller the tin, the more even the top of the chocolate cream will be; I always try to fill the water level to almost as high as the top of the jars.

250ml	cream
100g	dark chocolate
50ml	oil
1 tbsp	cornstarch
1 tsp	vanilla extract
1–3 tbsp	sugar

Preheat the oven to 125°C/250°F/gas ½. Boil the cream and remove from the hob. Break in the chocolate and stir until melted. Mix the oil, cornstarch and vanilla extract together and add to the mixture. Stir in the sugar and taste the mixture. The amount of sugar will depend on the chocolate and how sweet you want your chocolate cream. Pour the chocolate cream into oven-safe jars/pots and place in a roasting tin or shallow baking tray. Add water until it reaches at least halfway up the jars/pots. Bake in the centre of the oven at 125°C/250°F/gas ½ for 1 hour. Cool, then chill for at least 3 hours before serving.

CRÈME BRÛLÉE

In this recipe, you do not just need to replace the difference in the quantity of fat between vegan cream and dairy double cream, but also the fat from the 5–7 egg yolks that are usually added to the cream. Crème brûlée is often baked in a water bath in the oven, but you can also make a custard on the hob. Here, I have given both options. In a water bath the crème brûlée is smoother in texture. The crème brûlée can be baked in any oven-proof dish, but I like large, low dishes as they give you a thinner layer of crème brûlée and more caramelized topping. The recipe is enough for around 8 individual dishes; for 4 dishes, you can halve the recipe. I have worked with 90g, of sugar but you can test to find a cream with the sweetness you prefer, up to 135g of sugar works well. For this recipe, it is helpful to have a small chef's blowtorch. You can caramelize the sugar under the grill, but it is a lot trickier.

OVEN METHOD

1	vanilla pod or
	2 tsp vanilla extract
500ml	cream
150ml	oil
90g	sugar
2 tsp	cornstarch
1 pinch	salt
55g	cornstarch
100ml	milk
¼ tsp	yellow colouring (optional)

raw cane sugar, for sprinkling

Preheat the oven to 125°C/250°F/gas ½. When using a vanilla pod, cut it lengthways, scrape out the seeds, and heat the pod and the seeds together with the cream, oil, sugar, 2 teaspoons of cornstarch and the salt in a saucepan, stirring. When the mixture comes to the boil and has thickened slightly, remove the saucepan from the hob. Let the vanilla pod sit in the saucepan for 10 minutes before removing it. If you are not using a vanilla pod, boil the vanilla extract with the cream, etc., and then let it cool. Add the remaining 55g of cornstarch dissolved in the milk and some yellow colouring, if using, to the cream mixture. Pour it into ceramic dishes and place in a high-sided roasting tin. Fill the tin with water so it reaches at least halfway up the sides of the ceramic dishes. Bake at 125°C/250°F/gas ½ for 50–60 minutes until the cream is set. If you shake the tin slightly, the cream is supposed to wobble slightly. Remove from the water bath. Let them cool completely, then chill, preferably for a couple of hours in the fridge or overnight. Just before serving, sprinkle raw cane sugar over the cream and caramelize with a chef's blowtorch or for a short time under the grill on the highest heat setting. The sugar burns easily, so do not leave the dishes unattended; they only take a minute or two to caramelize. For extra caramelization, repeat this process once more when using a chef's blowtorch.

HOB METHOD

1	vanilla pod or
	2 tsp vanilla extract
500ml	cream
150ml	oil
90g	sugar
1 pinch	salt
55g	cornstarch
100ml	milk
¼ tsp	yellow colouring

raw cane sugar, for sprinkling

When using a vanilla pod, cut it lengthways, scrape out the seeds, and heat the pod and the seeds together with the cream, oil, sugar and salt in a saucepan. When the mixture comes to the boil, remove the saucepan from the hob. Let the vanilla pod sit in the saucepan for 10 minutes before removing it. If you are not using a vanilla pod, boil the vanilla extract with the cream, etc., and then let it cool. Stir in the cornstarch dissolved in the milk. Let it simmer until the cream has thickened, stirring. When thickened, remove from the hob and add ¼ teaspoon of yellow colouring, if using, before pouring the mixture into ceramic dishes. Leave to cool completely, then chill in the fridge. Just before serving, caramelize as above.

PANNA COTTA
& JELLY

Panna cotta is an Italian cream dessert, which consists of cooked cream, a little sugar, flavouring and gelling agent. The fat in the cream and the caster sugar included in a panna cotta makes the amount of gelling agent used slightly different to pure jelly recipes. A panna cotta is not supposed to be a firm jelly, but it should have a soft, mousse-like consistency which is partly supported by the high-fat cream. Use a cream with the taste you prefer of all the brands available. Soya, oat, almond, rice and coconut are cream alternatives that all work well for panna cotta. I think that Carrageenan IOTA gives a smoother panna cotta. Carrageenan KAPPA also works; it is slightly firmer and more bubbly. You can find these in speciality stores online.

250ml of cream is the base for my panna cotta. It is enough for 2–4 portions depending on the glasses you use. Choose one of the gelling agents and follow the instructions after the quantities.

PANNA COTTA
+	gelling agent below
45g	sugar
I tsp	vanilla extract
250ml	cream

CHOOSE ONE OF THE FOLLOWING GELLING AGENTS FOR PANNA COTTA
½ tsp   Vegeset: the sugar mixture is added to the cream and then boiled.
I sachet   Vegegel: the sugar mixture is added to the cream and then boiled.
½ tsp   Agar powder: boil and simmer for a few minutes until dissolved in the liquid.
½ tsp   Carrageenan IOTA: heat the cream to 70°C/158°F and add the sugar mixture.
½ tsp   Carrageenan KAPPA: the sugar mixture is added to the cream and then boiled.
½ tsp   Low Acyl Gellan Gum: the sugar mixture is added to the cream and then boiled.

Mix the gelling agent with the sugar and vanilla, and follow the instructions for your chosen gelling agent. Fill a small glass for each person and leave to set.

JELLY
400ml   liquid
90g   sugar
see gelling agent below

CHOOSE ONE OF THE FOLLOWING:
I tsp   agar powder
I sachet   Vegegel
I tsp   Vegeset

In the recipe for jelly, you can use fruit juice or water and add sugar and flavouring to your taste. For a sweet jelly, 90g of sugar for 400ml of liquid is a good starting point. Depending on the amount of sugar you include in the recipe, your jelly will either be soft or firm; find your preferred consistency and sweetness. Several gelling agents used for the panna cotta above are not as easy to use when making a clear jelly, which is why they are not included here.

Mix the liquid, gelling agent and sugar in a saucepan. For agar powder, wait until all the agar is dissolved in the liquid and then simmer for around 5 minutes for maximum strength, then pour into a serving dish/dishes and leave to set. For Vegegel and Vegeset, the liquid is brought to the boil and is then ready. Vegeset sets quickly after boiling and should be poured into the serving dish/dishes immediately.

FLAVOURS

Vanilla is a classic flavour for panna cotta. $^1/_8$ teaspoon of vanilla powder or 1–2 teaspoons of vanilla sugar/ extract is enough for 250ml of cream. A few teaspoons of rose water is a classic flavour. $^1/_4$–$^1/_2$g of saffron is another favourite.

SAUCES

In contrast to classic recipes for sauces and creams that include egg yolk as the stabilizer, for these sauces you do not need to worry about the mixture boiling and destroying the proteins from the eggs. When using starch, the mixture can boil and you know that it is ready when it is properly thickened, the bubbles created while stirring have gone and the sauce is thick and smooth. You can add a pinch of yellow colouring to create the same colour as creams made with egg yolks. Cornstarch, as used here, needs to boil for a minute or two to thicken and should be removed from the hob after that. I use starch to make a creamy vanilla pastry cream and vanilla sauce, but I also replace the fat that is missing from the egg yolk and the cream, which has a lower percentage of fat than dairy cream, with oil. This makes my recipes just as creamy as using dairy cream. Usually, I use cream made from soya because I think it tastes the best. Test different versions and find one that you like as there are many good brands available today.

VANILLA SAUCE

200ml	milk
250ml	cream
50g	margarine
45g	sugar
2 tbsp	cornstarch
1 pinch	salt
¼ tsp	vanilla
¼ tsp	yellow colouring

Bring the milk, cream, margarine, sugar, cornstarch and salt to the boil in a saucepan, while stirring, until the custard thickens. Remove the saucepan from the hob and add the vanilla and yellow colouring, if using. Serve hot or cold. Cover the surface with clingfilm if the sauce is chilled.

Sabayon, zabaglione or zabaione is usually made from sweet wines like Marsala, but Chablis, Prosecco or Champagne are also common depending on which country it is made in. Versions made with whisky and beer can also be found. The sweet white wine in the recipe can be replaced with the drink of your choice if you want to try out your own favourite. The egg yolks have many functions in this recipe, as they create a foam, thicken the mixture and add fat. This is why this recipe was hard to veganize. Here, the egg yolks are replaced with a starch to thicken the sauce and aquafaba is added to make the mixture light, and oil makes it creamy and full of flavour. Sabayon is usually made with equal quantities of egg yolks, sugar and wine. The fat from the egg yolks is important for the character of the sabayon and needs to be replaced to make a perfect vegan recipe. The oil is not added until the cornstarch has thickened, which stops the foam from the aquafaba from collapsing due to the fat. Sabayon works well as a luxurious accompaniment for pies and sponge cakes, but also for ice cream and fruit. This version, even with a small quantity of ingredients, makes quite a large amount of whipped zabaglione, but if you are serving lots of guests, you can double the quantities.

SABAYON

100ml	sweet white wine
2 tbsp	sugar
50ml	aquafaba
1 tbsp	cornstarch
1 tbsp	oil

Prepare a saucepan of simmering water that can fit a round, heatproof bowl suitable for whipping sitting on top of it. Add the wine, sugar, aquafaba and cornstarch to the bowl and place it over the water bath. Whip to a thick, fluffy cream using a hand-help mixer. Add the oil. If the cream is too hot, too thick and starts to shrink before the oil is added, just add the oil. This will make it fluffy and creamy again. Remove from the heat, and then whisk with an electric mixer or in a stand mixer until the sauce has cooled and turned very airy. Serve immediately or as soon as possible with warmed sponge cake, pies or with fruit and berries.

COOKING CARAMEL

It is impossible to find exactly the right temperature for caramel using the cold-water test, but when boiling it carefully at the end of the boiling time, on a low temperature while stirring, you can get a good result. To make perfect sweets, however, you will need a sugar thermometer. When using a thermometer, you can use the intervals below, but you need to stir the mixture to make sure it has all reached the right temperature. When the thermometer reaches the right temperature, I usually stir the whole saucepan and wait for it to reach that temperature again. Then you know for certain that all the mixture is warm enough. How long your sweets take to cook depends on the temperature and the saucepan that is used and it does vary a great deal. This is why no timings are given, not even approximate ones, for cooking sweets. However, you can see that the mixture is almost ready when it starts to thicken.

128°C/262°F = my favourite consistency of caramel
125–126°C/257–259°C = soft caramel or fudge
126–129°C/259–264°F = slightly firmer caramel or fudge
140–145°C/284–293°F = hard caramel, chewy in the middle
160°C/320°F = solid toffee

COLD-WATER TEST

The cold-water test means that the hot mixture, using a teaspoon, is dripped into a glass of cold water. If the mixture can be formed into a ball using your fingers after staying in the cold water for a while, it passes the cold-water test. Test the mixture with a few minutes in between. Depending on how you want your caramel, let it cook until the mixture makes a soft or a hard ball using the cold-water test. The cold-water test for hard-crack stage mixture means that when some of the mixture is dripped into a cup of cold water, it will be hard enough that you can break it. If using a sugar thermometer, the temperature is around 150–160°C/302–320°F.

CARAMEL KNOW-HOW FROM ICA'S TESTING LAB

Swedish supermarket ICA's testing lab says this about why we are able to make soft caramel from sugar, cream and butter:

'The reason is that the sugar browns when it is melted in the saucepan, and at the same time proteins and sugars in the cream and the butter also take on a darker colour. The chewy consistency adds to the flavour experience as the chewing action squeezes out drops of fat from the butter in the caramel. To make it chewy, the cooking must be stopped at the right time, when the mixture reaches 125°C/257°F. When cooking to a higher temperature, your caramel will be hard instead of chewy. When comparing different basic recipes, the best ones contain both salt and vinegar, which is fairly surprising. The vinegar gives the caramel a slightly sour flavour, but most importantly, more elasticity, and the salt balances the sweetness. We are trying to replace vinegar with white wine vinegar, which gives the caramel a better colour, and that is why we want to use it. For our basic recipe, we use ½ tsp vinegar (12 per cent) or 1 tsp of white wine vinegar. When we add 70ml of glucose syrup, we get a caramel with a firmer consistency that is slightly less sweet. Glucose syrup, as well as regular syrup, prevents crystals forming in the sugar when it cools. A perfect caramel should be soft and smooth, with no crackle when you take a bite.'

Both the Testing Lab and I found that at least 125°C/257°F. gives the best caramel, and my favourite temperature for perfect hard vegan caramel is 128°C/262°F.

Sweets

This is what I have come up with after working to create toffee, caramel and fudge with the same flavour as those made with butter and dairy cream. I developed a method of varying the sugar to get a buttery caramel taste during Christmas 2018, which resulted in a whole new standard of toffee, caramel and fudge.

The flavours that are created when cooking with high-fat cow's milk are sometimes missing in vegan caramel when using cream, syrup and sugar, but you can easily replace it with a little salt and use a sugar with a deeper flavour to get a richer caramel taste. Both raw cane sugar and demerara sugar work as the basic sweetener.

Usually, I use single cream, but double cream works too.

Some books say that it is important to cook toffee and fudge without stirring the saucepan to prevent sugar crystals forming, but I usually stir it carefully every now and then to stop it burning at the bottom. In any case, it is important to use a heavy-based saucepan that distributes the heat evenly to reduce the risk of burning. By the end of the cooking time, when the mixture goes over 110°C/230°F, you need to stir right down to the bottom every now and then to prevent a burned layer forming. A slight burn is okay, you can mix this into the rest of the mixture, but if it burns and turns black, the whole mixture is ruined. Many sugars or syrups burn easily when cooking caramel; these recipes have been developed to give wonderfully tasty toffee, caramel and fudge that do not burn easily.

Glucose syrup can be added to soft caramel but should never be used for fudge as it prevents the crystallization that is supposed to happen when the fudge is beaten or whipped until thick.

SOFT CARAMEL

Here, the caramel with caramelized sugar contains glucose syrup – the sugar is heated to a high temperature, so the recipe doesn't follow the guide on page 434. The caramelized caramel will reach a good consistency at around 124°C/255°F. This way of making the caramel allows the sugar to achieve a greater degree of caramelization, but it is also more complicated. The simple caramel also gives a good result. Adding 1–2 teaspoons of miso paste gives a nice saltiness and echoes the umami flavours that develop when dairy butter and milk are heated and caramelized. It's best to use a light or white miso paste. The vinegar reduces the risk of the sugar crystallising.

SIMPLE CARAMEL

100g	margarine
200ml	cream
270g	raw cane sugar
140g/100ml	golden syrup
1 pinch	salt
¼ tsp	vanilla extract
1–2 tsp	white miso paste
½–1 tsp	white wine vinegar

Fold and staple a tin using baking paper, 15 × 15–20 × 20cm (see pages 62 and 63), depending on how thick you want your caramel to be. Mix the margarine, cream, sugar, syrup, salt, vanilla, miso paste, and vinegar, if using, in a saucepan and heat while stirring. Boil over a medium heat until the caramel reaches around 125°C/257°F or becomes a hard ball in the cold-water test. Remove from the hob and pour into the paper tin. Leave to cool for a while and then cut the caramel into good-sized pieces. Wrap or fold the caramel pieces in baking paper. Keep at room temperature, or in the fridge in a sealed jar. However, they do easily become sticky in the fridge. If kept sealed at room temperature, the surface will dry and not become sticky.

CARAMELIZED CARAMEL

100g	margarine
200ml	cream
½ tsp	salt
1–2 tsp	white miso paste
¼ tsp	vanilla extract
250g	raw cane sugar
170g	glucose syrup

Fold and staple a tin using baking paper, 15 × 15–20 × 20cm (see pages 62 and 63), depending on how thick you want your caramel to be. In a small pan, bring the margarine, cream, salt, miso paste and vanilla extract to the boil and remove from the heat. Now it's time to caramelize the sugar and the glucose. Add both to a heavy-based saucepan and place over a fairly high heat. When the sugar has started to melt you can stir the mixture slightly. As it is nearing 170°C/338°F you must watch carefully as the temperature will rise quickly. At 170°C/338°F, remove the pan from the heat immediately. Add the cream mixture to the caramelized sugar in three batches (be careful, it will spit), and stir right down to the bottom to ensure that all the sugar has dissolved. Return the pan to the heat and cook over a medium heat, stirring occasionally, until the caramel has reached 124°C/255°F or becomes a hard ball in the cold-water test. Remove from the heat and pour the caramel into the paper case. Leave to cool at room temperature for at least 4–6 hours and then cut the caramel into good-sized pieces. Wrap or fold the caramel pieces in baking paper. Store in an airtight container in a cool, dry place, not in the fridge.

CHOCOLATE CARAMEL

20g	cocoa

Add 20g of sifted cocoa powder together with the cream to either of the recipes above. Follow the instructions for each recipe.

FUDGE

Cooking fudge can be a little trickier than cooking caramel, as there are more steps to follow after it comes to the boil. Most recipes for fudge give 117°C/243°F as the optimal boiling point, but while conducting lots of tests, I don't think this makes the fudge firm enough. That is why I have increased the temperature, and I think that for making perfect fudge, you need to use a sugar thermometer. It should be attached to the side of the saucepan and not touch the bottom. Make sure you can see the temperature at all times. I also stir my mixture quite often, especially towards the end. You need to be aware that when you are doing this, you will decrease the temperature as you are adding air to the mixture. When it is close to 125°C/257°F and if you are worried it will burn, you can mix thoroughly using the whisk, but the temperature will decrease as a result, so be careful of this near the end of the cooking time. You cannot add glucose syrup when making fudge as it affects the crystallization, and often creates caramel instead of fudge.

If your fudge is firm immediately after cooling, it does not need to set before serving, but if it is soft, you can let it set in a cool place for a few days, cut into pieces, or as a whole piece to help it dry and become a little firmer. Put in a cool and dry place, even at room temperature, if it is not too warm. Fudge made with chocolate in the mixture will become firm more easily than other ingredients, and should not be allowed to set in the pan after reaching the right temperature and adding the margarine and the chocolate. Adding the chocolate makes the mixture harden quickly, so when mixing the fudge you need to be ready to pour it into the tin quickly to get a nice smooth surface. When using cooking chocolate, the fudge will harden even more quickly as this type of chocolate uses a different fat to cocoa butter. This is why you need to work a little faster with this kind of fudge to get it even when pouring into the tin before hardening. This fudge will also be a little firmer than the fudge made with chocolate that just contains cocoa butter.

WHITE CHOCOLATE FUDGE

140g/100ml	golden syrup
270g	raw cane sugar
300ml	cream
1 pinch	salt
50g	margarine
100–150g	white, dairy-free chocolate
¼ tsp	vanilla extract

White chocolate makes a fantastic vanilla fudge. How firm your fudge will be depends, among other things, on the temperature you cook your caramel to and which kind of white chocolate you use. If you use white cooking chocolate, the result is usually firmer as cooking chocolate contains a different type of fat. White chocolate that comes in thin slabs also work well. 100g chocolate will give a softer fudge and 150g chocolate will give a firmer fudge. Soft fudge can also be made firmer by leaving it to set in a cool, dry place for 4–5 days.

Line a tin of the size of your choosing with baking paper, or fold and staple together a tin made of baking paper, 15 × 15–20 × 20cm, depending on how thick you want your fudge (see the instructions on pages 62 and 63). Use a heavy-based saucepan and cook the golden syrup, raw cane sugar, cream and salt, while stirring, on a medium heat. You do not need to stir it constantly but stir it right down to the bottom from time to time so that it doesn't burn, especially towards the end of the cooking time when the mixture reaches 105°C/221°F. Bring the temperature up to 125–129°C/257–264°F. Remove from the hob, break the chocolate into chunks and add the margarine, chocolate and vanilla to the hot caramel and mix until melted. Mix thoroughly for a few minutes using a wooden spoon or a spatula until it is no longer shiny. Spread out in the tin to your preferred thickness. Keep in the fridge overnight or at least for a few hours before cutting. Let the pieces dry slightly at room temperature after cutting. Keep in a sealed jar.

DARK CHOCOLATE FUDGE

140g/ 100ml   golden syrup
270g   raw cane sugar
300ml   cream
1 pinch   salt
50g   margarine
¼ tsp   vanilla extract
100g   dark chocolate or cooking chocolate

Line a tin of the size of your choosing with baking paper, or fold and staple together a tin made of baking paper, 15 × 15–20 × 20cm, depending on how thick you want your fudge; see the instructions on pages 62 and 63. Use a heavy-based saucepan and cook the syrup or treacle, raw cane sugar, cream and salt while stirring on a medium heat. You do not need to stir constantly but stir it right down to the bottom from time to time so that it doesn't burn, especially towards the end of the cooking time when the mixture reaches 105°C/221°F. Bring the temperature up to 125–129°C/257–264°F. Remove from the hob immediately, break the chocolate into pieces and add the margarine, vanilla and chocolate to the hot fudge mixture and mix until melted. Mix using a wooden spoon or a spatula until the mixture has become lighter in colour, has thickened and is no longer shiny. Spread out in the tin to your preferred thickness. Cut the fudge into pieces when completely cool and set. Keep in a sealed jar.

LUXURY FUDGE

If you can get hold of sweetened condensed milk made from coconut milk or soya milk you can simplify the process of making fudge considerably. Equal quantities of each usually gives a good result, and if your tin contains more or less condensed milk, use the same amount of chocolate (e.g. if you have 100g condensed milk, use 100g chocolate). If the sweetened milk is very runny, you can instead use 150g chocolate for 100g sweetened condensed milk instead (50 per cent more chocolate).

200– 300g   dark chocolate or cooking chocolate
200g   sweetened condensed milk

Line a tin of the size of your choosing with baking paper, or fold and staple together a tin made of baking paper, 15 × 15–20 × 20cm, depending on how thick you want your fudge; see the instructions on pages 62 and 63. Melt the chocolate according to the instructions on page 57. Warm the sweetened condensed milk in another bowl over water bath. Stir the hot condensed milk and chocolate together and spread out immediately in the prepared baking tray and leave to cool. Cut into pieces once completely cooled and set. Keep in a sealed jar.

FUDGE!

Read more about cooking caramel on pages 434–435, and what to think about when making chocolate fudge on page 438.

THANK YOU!

If no one had bought my first books, my recipes would never have improved and this book would never have existed. For each book project, I am given an opportunity to learn new things about ingredients, decoration and photography and I also get to connect with more people from all over the world who are passionate about the same things! You, who have bought the books and made this possible, are the best! My interest in baking began when I was little. I was unstoppable and was already making tier cakes at the age of ten. This must have meant huge piles of dirty dishes and I want to thank my parents for never banning me from baking despite the mess.

I want to thank my husband who has supported me during my recipe development journey. He even started a publishing firm in 2010 when no publishing company believed it was possible to make phenomenal vegan baking recipes. A huge thank you for all the pep talks during this crazy project.

Over all these years our volunteer proofreaders have given their time so that these books can be read and used. Without you, no one would be able to use these books! Thank you Rasmus Klockljung, Staffan Fredelius, Camilla Dunér, Josefin Landerberg, Erik Anderberg, Anna Velander Gisslén, Johan Lundgren, Malin Axzell, Agnes Fogelberg, Felicia Hamberg, Elize Wästanfors, Kristina Lindgren, Helena Ferry, Åsa Melander, Helen Ridger, Anna Grahn, Linda Levay, Nina Färdig and her parents, who helped with the language in the text, the design and the recipes. You have helped us to publish a total of 16 books and together you have eliminated thousands of silly mistakes on more than 2000 pages so far! Rasmus Klockljung and Staffan Fredelius put in extra time for this particular book – I do not know what the manuscript would have been like without your help! Also, thank you to all of my followers on social media who picked up the mistakes in the recipes, it has helped me when working on this book, perhaps more than you think! Aware Mustafa, who took the time to teach me the basics of photo editing deserves a huge thank you! My Swedish publisher, Mia Steen, deserves one too for all the time she has put into our book project!

Thank you Goose Wohlt who told all of us vegan bakers about Joël Roessel in France using aquafaba for making light sponge in his www.revolutionvegetale.com. Thank you Goose for all of our funny discussions on the correct ratio of aquafaba for meringues and other nerdy things. Thank you Rebecca August, who started the Facebook group Vegan Meringue – Hits and Misses (now called Aquafaba Vegan Meringue – Hits and Misses!). With its open source ethos and members from all over the world, the group has created a community where everyone is able to share their findings. Thanks to this Facebook group, I now have a large network of vegan bakers from Hawaii, Canada, England, Australia, Tasmania, Malaysia, Denmark and America to philosophize with. I want to give a special thank you to a few people who have contributed to this particular book: Linda Julien in Massachusetts who worked methodically with meringue buttercream when I had given up on my tests. We discussed meringue buttercreams and other recipes from all angles and it is her findings that I have worked with to develop all versions in this book. Somer McGowan was the first person who realized that aquafaba could be use unwhipped with fat and was able to bind both fat and sugar in batters and doughs. I will use this when baking for the rest of my life – thank you!! Charis Mitchell from England devoted all her spare time to trying to make perfect macarons using aquafaba, while I was working on my cake layers. She managed it and even let me use the recipe in this book. Thank you so much!!

I also want to say thank you to Isa Chandra Moskowitz, Terry Hope Romero, Fran Costigan, Chloe Costarello, Nina Andersson and Daniel Rolke, who published books on vegan baking before, or at the same time I started. They worked hard to develop recipes which helped me a lot when I was learning everything about vegan baking. You have been amazing role models for many people and cleared the way for me!

I am incredibly happy that Sophie Allen and Pavilion Books saw a value in my work and took over so that I do not have to do everything myself anymore – now I can sneak back to the kitchen!

INDEX

A

Almond biskvis	294
Almond cookies	298
Almond paste	334
Almond tuiles	306
Amaretti	308
Ambrosia cake	116
American apple pie	394
American banana bread	146
American bundt cake	98
American layer cake	198
American chocolate layer	202
American custard frosting	226
American ginger cake	152
Apple butter	404
Apple butter pie	404
Apple cakes	132
Apple cake, Swedish	390
Apple crumble	138
Apple pie	394
Apple sponge cake	130
Apple squares	188
Aquafaba	22
Aquafaba pancakes	242
Australian chocolate layer	202
Autumn squares	176

B

Bagels	356
Baking powder	48
Bicarbonate of soda	47
Banana breads	142, 146
Banana carrot cake	162
Banana cheesecake	414
Banana crumble	138
Banana muffins	76
Banana pancakes	246
Banana sponge cake	148
Banana squares	182
Basic sponge cakes	92
Belgian waffles	252
Berry squares	172
Biscotti	309
Biskvis	294
Blueberry cheesecake	417
Blueberry cream	424
Blueberry pie	401
Bolo de fubá	106
Brioche	350
Brownie cookies	314
Brownies	272
Bundt cake	98
Burnt caramel sauce	236
Butter biscuits	283

Buttercream	
Meringue	232
White chocolate	228

C

Cake layers	192
Cake pops	328
Candy fluff	228
Caramel	436
Caramel banana bread	144
Caramel cookies	304
Caramel frosting	236
Caramel ice cream	374
Caramel sauce	236
Carrot cakes	156, 158, 160
Carrot layer cake	206
Carrot muffins	78
Carrot squares	184
Cheesecake	414
Cherry cake	141
Cherry ice cream	370
Chocolate balls	326
Chocolate cake	114
Chocolate caramel	436
Chocolate chip cookie ice cream	366
Chocolate chip cookies	310
Chocolate courgette cake	186
Chocolate cream	426
Chocolate frosting	230
Chocolate fudge	440
Chocolate glaze	230
Chocolate hazelnut spread	260
Chocolate ice cream	372
Chocolate layer cake	200, 202, 204
Chocolate mousse	234
Chocolate muffins	74
Chocolate soufflé	276
Chocolate sponge cake	112
Chocolate spreads	260
Chocolate squares	180
Chocolate Swiss roll	88
Cinnamon buns	332
Citrus cake	128
Classic apple cakes	130
Classic banana breads	142
Classic carrot cake	156
Classic frosting	226
Classic muffins	68
Classic sponge cake	94
Clementine cake	126
Cobbler	392
Coconut caramel balls	326
Coconut frosting	228
Coconut macaroons	300

Coffee ice cream 376
Colouring 54
Conchas 352
Corn muffins 82
Corn scones 258
Covering a layer cake
  Frosting 216
  Marzipan 194
  Sugar paste 218
Cream cheese frosting 226
Crème brûlèe 428
Crispy waffles 248
Crumble 388
Crumble cake 170
Crumble squares 174
Curd 262
Custard buns 336
Custard frosting 226

D
Danish pastry 344
Danish pastry dough 340
Dark chocolate layer cake 200
Dark chocolate muffins 72
Double chocolate chip cookies 311
Doughnuts 346

E
Egg replacement 18
Eton mess 286

F
Fat 37
Filled layer cakes
  Frosting 216
  Mousse & curd 214
Finnish sticks 283
Firm whipping cream 409
Flat-topped cupcakes 70
Flour 38
Fortune cookies 302
Frangipane pie 402
French apple cake 132
French toast 254
Frosting 223
Fruit crumble 138
Fruit curd 262
Fruit ice cream 368
Fruit kladdkaka 268
Fruit mousse 234
Fruit squares 172
Fudge 438, 440
Fudge brownies 272
Fudge layers 204

G
Ganache 238
Ganache drip 238
Gelling agent 16, 50, 430
Genoise 96
Ginger cake 152
Ginger ice cream 382
Gingerbread 320
Gingerbread cake 164
Gingerbread house 322
Glaze 348
Gluten-free baking 52
Gluten-free flour mixtures 53
Grandmother's lingonberry cake 164

H
Hamburger bread 352, 354
Hazelnut cake 122
Helena pastry 290
Hokkaido 354
Honeycomb 236
Hummingbird cake 208

I
Ice cream 363
Icing 324
Italian almond cookies 298
Italian meringues 286

J
Japanese milk bread 354
Jelly 430

K
Kladdkaka 266, 268

L
Leavening agent 44
Lemon & poppy cake 102
Lemon & yoghurt cake 100
Lemon cake layer 210
Lemon curd 262
Lemon meringue pie 406
Lemon mousse 234
Liège waffles 252
Light coloured apple cake 136
Light coloured kladdkaka 268
Light sponge cakes 28
Lime pie 408
Liquid in baking 35
Love treats 178

M

Macarons	288
Madeleines	84
Marängsviss	287
Marble cake	110
Mazarin cake	120
Mazarins	292
Melting chocolate	57, 220
Meringue buttercream	232
Meringues	286
Milk bread	354
Milkshake	365
Mini cakes	196
Moist sponge cakes	30
Mousse	234
Mousse cakes	414
Muffins	67

N

Nut ice cream	380
Nut sponge cake	122

O

Oat crumble	388
Olive oil cake	108
Ovenlys chocolate chip cookies	312
Overnight raised rolls	360

P

Pain au chocolat	342
Pancakes	244
Panna cotta	430
Peach pie	400
Peanut frosting	228
Peanut ice cream	380
Petit pots de crème	426
Pies	387
Pignoli	298
Piped cookies	284
Piping	224
Pistachio ice cream	380
Pistachio paste	334
Polyné	290
Poppy cake	102
Princess cake	194
Princess cake length	193
Puff pastry tarts	418
Pumpkin cake	212
Pumpkin muffins	80
Punsch rolls	327

R

Reduced meringue buttercream	232
Reverse creaming	32

Reverse cupcakes	71
Rhubarb curd	262
Rhubarb squares	174
Rolls	360
Royal icing	324
Rum raisin ice cream	378
Rye & whisky chocolate chip cookies	311

S

Saffron apple cake	132
Saffron buns	338
Saffron cakes	166
Saffron kladdkaka	268
Salt caramel frosting	236
Scones	258
Semla	334
Shortbread	282
Shortcrust pastry	282
Silvia cake	116
Silvia squares	176
Simple muffins	68
Snickerdoodles	316
Snoddas	178
Soft chocolate frosting	230
Soft waffles	248
Soufflé	276
Sour cherry pie	396
Spicy apple cake	136
Spiced banana bread	142
Sponge cakes	92
Stracciatella	366
Strasbourger	284
Strawberry cake	140
Sugar	40
Sugar cookies	318
Sugar knots	336
Sunflower paste	334
Sunken apple cake	134
Swedish pancakes	242
Swiss roll	86

T

Tahini chocolate chip cookies	313
Tarte au citron	407
Tarte tatin	420
Tarts	418
Tins	60
Toffee	436
Tonka bean pastry cream	424
Tonka beans	50
Torta di mandorle	122
Tosca cake	118

U
Upside-down cake 150

V
Vanilla 50
Vanilla cream 424
Vanilla cupcakes 70
Vanilla frosting 226
Vanilla fudge 438
Vanilla ice cream 366
Vanilla sauce 432

W
Waffles with yeast 250
Waffles 248, 250, 252
Wheat bread 331
Whipped margarine 258
Whipping cream, firm 409
White chocolate balls 326
White chocolate buttercream 228
White chocolate mousse 234
White kladdkaka 268

X
Xanthan gum 50

Z
Zabaglione 432
Zabaione 432

GLUTEN-FREE RECIPES
Amaretti 308
Banana cheesecake 414
Banana pancakes 246
Biskvis 294
Cheesecake 414
Chocolate balls 326
Chocolate spreads 260
Coconut caramel balls 326
Coconut macaroons 300
Corn scones 258
Crumble 388
Gluten-free flour mixes 53
Ice cream 363
Macarons 288
Meringues 286
Mousse cakes 414
Nut cookies 308
Oat crumble 388
Pignoli 298
Scones 258
Swedish pancakes 242
Waffles 248

This picture was taken in about 1990 by the old barn with Karolina's little sister sitting next to their mum. Karolina is holding her dad's hand. Her little brother was born a few years later. The dog is a Swedish sheepdog and the beautiful tractor is a red Massey Ferguson.

Dr Karolina Tegelaar, daughter of two dairy farmers, grew up on a small farm in central Sweden. Baking and photography were an early favourite pastime and when she became a vegan in 2006 she started to develop excellent egg-free and dairy-free bakes. The standard of recipes and baking available were not of a quality she found acceptable. With painstaking effort and scientific methods, she has published 16 baking books since 2010. By thinking about chemical reactions, discarding old baking norms and focusing on the challenge of baking without eggs and milk, revolutionary new techniques have been discovered and developed. Karolina is also a biologist, has a PhD in ethology and is a science teacher. By ignoring old baking traditions and focusing on the challenge of baking vegan, several new indispensable methods have been discovered and developed. Swedish national radio featured a programme on her work with aquafaba in 2021. Her book *Vegan Baking* won the prestigious prize 'Sweet pastry of the year' by the Måltidsakademien (The Swedish Meal Academy) 2020.